T0210956

Communications in Computer and Information Science 1132

Commenced Publication in 2007
Founding and Former Series Editors:
Phoebe Chen, Alfredo Cuzzocrea, Xiaoyong Du, Orhun Kara, Ting Liu,
Krishna M. Sivalingam, Dominik Ślęzak, Takashi Washio, Xiaokang Yang,
and Junsong Yuan

More information about this series at http://www.springer.com/series/7899

Mohammed Anbar · Nibras Abdullah ·
Selvakumar Manickam (Eds.)

Advances in Cyber Security

First International Conference, ACeS 2019
Penang, Malaysia, July 30 – August 1, 2019
Revised Selected Papers

 Springer

Editors
Mohammed Anbar 🆔
Universiti Sains Malaysia
Penang, Malaysia

Nibras Abdullah 🆔
Universiti Sains Malaysia
Penang, Malaysia

Selvakumar Manickam 🆔
Universiti Sains Malaysia
Penang, Malaysia

ISSN 1865-0929   ISSN 1865-0937 (electronic)
Communications in Computer and Information Science
ISBN 978-981-15-2692-3   ISBN 978-981-15-2693-0 (eBook)
https://doi.org/10.1007/978-981-15-2693-0

This Springer imprint is published by the registered company Springer Nature Singapore Pte Ltd.
The registered company address is: 152 Beach Road, #21-01/04 Gateway East, Singapore 189721, Singapore

Preface

This volume contains the papers from the First International Conference on Advances in Cybersecurity (ACeS 2019). The event was organized by the National Advanced IPv6 Centre, a research department at Universiti Sains Malaysia, Penang, Malaysia, specializing in areas such as Cybersecurity, the Internet of Things (IoT), Wireless Communication, and other network technologies.

ACeS 2019 focused on advances in Cybersecurity including security and safety trends, solutions, and issues, which could be examined, shared, and learned from, taking into account several perspectives from academics, professionals, and researchers around the globe. Currently, there is no other similar conference held by any other university in Malaysia.

AceS 2019 was supported by the Malaysian Communications and Multimedia Commission (MCMC), Cisco Systems (M) Sdn Bhd, Malaysia Digital Economy Corporation Sdn Bhd (MDEC), CyberSecurity Malaysia, The Institution of Engineer, Malaysia (IEM), Japan Malaysia Technical Institute (JMTI), Nehru Group of Institutions, India, and Malaysia Crime Prevention Foundation (MCPF). ACeS 2019 was organized as a conference, forum, seminar, exhibition, and hands-on workshops involving renowned speakers, presenters, and participants from around the world. Eminent speakers participated in the event from various organizations including Cybersecurity Working Group of ERAB; Ministry of Economy, Trade and Industry, Japan; Cisco Systems, South Africa; and Favoriot Sdn Bhd–to name a few.

ACeS 2019 focused on both existing and emerging areas in Cybersecurity associated with the advances of the systems and infrastructures, lifestyle, policy, and governance. The conference encouraged interaction between researchers, practitioners, and academics to present and discuss work on Cybersecurity, especially in the newly emerging domains such as IoT, Industry 4.0, Blockchain, Cloud and Edge Computing.

The conference attracted a total of 80 submissions from countries including Bangladesh, Brazil, China, Croatia, India, Indonesia, Iraq, Jordan, Saudi Arabia, Nigeria, Malaysia, Oman, Pakistan, Russia, Singapore, Yemen, and the UK. All submissions underwent a strict peer review and paper selection process which resulted in the acceptance of 29 submissions (40%) of the total submissions. The accepted submissions were presented at the conference. All the accepted papers were peer reviewed by three qualified reviewers chosen from our Scientific Committee based on their qualifications and experience.

The proceedings editors wish to thank the dedicated Scientific Committee members and all the other reviewers for their contributions. We also thank Springer for their trust and for publishing the proceedings of ACeS 2019.

July 2019

Mohammed Anbar
Nibras Abdullah
Selvakumar Manickam

Organization

Organizing Committee

Honorary Chairs

Rosni Abullah   Universiti Sains Malaysia, Malaysia
Sundramoorthy Pathman   Universiti Sains Malaysia, Malaysia

General Chair

Selvakumar Manickam   Universiti Sains Malaysia, Malaysia

Program Chairs

Mohammed Anbar   Universiti Sains Malaysia, Malaysia
Nibras Abdullah Ahmed Faqera   Universiti Sains Malaysia, Malaysia

Publication Chairs

Mohammed Anbar   Universiti Sains Malaysia, Malaysia
Nibras Abdullah Ahmed Faqera   Universiti Sains Malaysia, Malaysia

Finance and Treasurer

Lim Say Khiam   Universiti Sains Malaysia, Malaysia

Sponsorship and Exhibition

Wan Tat Chee   Universiti Sains Malaysia, Malaysia

Technical

Iznan Husainy Hasbullah   Universiti Sains Malaysia, Malaysia
Ashish Jaisan   Universiti Sains Malaysia, Malaysia
Alwan Abdullah   Universiti Sains Malaysia, Malaysia

Publicity and Public Relations

Zaitul Iradah Mahid	Universiti Sains Malaysia, Malaysia
Nathan Balasubramanian	Universiti Sains Malaysia, Malaysia
Manmeet Mahinderjit Singh	Universiti Sains Malaysia, Malaysia

Local Arrangements

Malar Devi Kanagasabai	Universiti Sains Malaysia, Malaysia

Registration Secretaries

Siti Asma Osman	Universiti Sains Malaysia, Malaysia
Erum Ashraf	Universiti Sains Malaysia, Malaysia

Web Master

Asamoah Kwaku Acheampong	Universiti Sains Malaysia, Malaysia

Supporting Members

Sabri Mohammed Abdhood Hanshi	Universiti Sains Malaysia, Malaysia
Shankar Karuppayah	Universiti Sains Malaysia, Malaysia
Zakaria Noor Aldeen Mahmood Alqattan	Universiti Sains Malaysia, Malaysia
Ahmed Khallel Ibrahim Al-Ani	Universiti Sains Malaysia, Malaysia
Arkan Hammoodi Hasan Kabla	Universiti Sains Malaysia, Malaysia
Asyraf Mustaqim Bin Abd Manaf	Universiti Sains Malaysia, Malaysia
Ayman Khallel Ibrahim Al-Ani	Universiti Sains Malaysia, Malaysia
Haider Dhia Alzubaydi	Universiti Sains Malaysia, Malaysia
Iznan Husainy Hasbullah	Universiti Sains Malaysia, Malaysia
Mohammad Adnan Ahmad Aladaileh	Universiti Sains Malaysia, Malaysia
Saif Almashhadi	Universiti Sains Malaysia, Malaysia
Shams ul Arfeen Laghari	Universiti Sains Malaysia, Malaysia
Taief Alaa Hamdi Al Amiedy	Universiti Sains Malaysia, Malaysia
Yousef Khader Khattar Sanjalawe	Universiti Sains Malaysia, Malaysia

International Advisory Committee

Ahmed Al-Dubai	Edinburgh Napier University, UK
Rajni Goel	Howard University, USA
Ahmed Manasrah	Yarmouk University, Jordan
Masaki Umejima	Keio University, Japan
Achmad Basuki	Universitas Brawijaya, Indonesia
Hosam Al-Samarraie	Coventry University, UK

Review Committee

Abdelmageed Algamdi	University of Bisha, Saudi Arabia
Abdulqader Mohsen	University of Science and Technology, Yemen
Adel Saleh	Gaist Solutions Limited, UK
Ahmed Hintaw	AlSafwa University College, Iraq
Ahmed Manasrah	Higher Colleges of Technology, UAE
Akashdeep Bhardwaj	University of Petroleum and Energy Studies, India
Anang Hudaya Muhamad Amin	Higher Colleges of Technology, UAE
Andrea Visconti	Università degli Studi di Milano, Italy
Badiea Abdulkarem M. Alshaibani	Hodeidah University, Yemen
Bandar M. Alshammari	Jouf University, Saudi Arabia
Basim Ahmad Alabsi	Najran University, Saudi Arabia
Boon Yaik Ooi	Universiti Tunku Abdul Rahman, Malaysia
D. P. Sharma	AMUIT MOEFDRE under UNDP, India
Emmanouil Vasilomanolakis	Aalborg University, Denmark
Esraa Alomari	Wasit University, Iraq
Fathey Mohammed	Universiti Utara Malaysia, Malaysia
Febin Prakash	CT University, India
Ghassan Ali	Najran University, Saudi Arabia
Hamid Al-Raimi	Hodiedah University, Yemen
Hani Almimi	Al-Zaytoonah University of Jordan, Jordan
Hossen Mustafa	BUET, Bangladesh
Issa Atoum	The World Islamic Sciences and Education University, Jordan
Jamil Saif	University of Bisha, Saudi Arabia
Karim H. Al-Saedi	Mustansiriyah University, Iraq
Karthikeyan Eswaramurthy	Government Arts College, Udumalpet, India
Kavitha Manickam	Universiti Tunku Abdul Rahman, Malaysia
Konstantin Kogos	NRNU MEPhI, Russia
Mahmoud Baklizi	The World Islamic Sciences and Education University, Jordan
Midhunchakkaravarthy Janarthanan	Lincoln University College, Malaysia
Mie Mie Su Thwin	University of Computer Studies, Yangon, Myanmar
Mohammed Abomaali	Alsafwa University College, Iraq
Mohammed Allayla	University of Arkansas at Little Rock, USA
Mohammed Al-Mashraee	Free University Berlin, Germany
Mosleh Abualhaj	Al-Ahliyya Amman University, Jordan
Muna Al-Hawawreh	The University of New South Wales, Australia
Munadil Al-Sammarraie	Universiti Utara Malaysia, Malaysia
Ola A. Al-Wesabi	Hodeidah University, Yemen
Omar Elejla	Islamic University of Gaza, Palestine
Redhwan Saad	Ibb University, Yemen

Sadik Al-Taweel	University of Science and Technology, Yemen
Saif Almashhadi	Communication and Media Commission, Iraq
Salam Al-E'mari	Umm Al-Qura University, Saudi Arabia
Sami Salih	Sudan University of Science and Technology, Sudan
Seng Poh Lim	Universiti Tunku Abdul Rahman, Malaysia
Shady Hamouda	Emirates College of Technology, UAE
Supriyanto Praptodiyono	Universitas Sultan Ageng Tirtayasa, Indonesia
Vivekanandam Balasubramaniam	Lincoln University College, Malaysia
Wai Kong Lee	Universiti Tunku Abdul Rahman, Malaysia
Waled Almakhawi	University of Siegen, Germany
Yagasena Appannah	Quest International University, Malaysia
Yousef Hamouda	Al-Aqsa University, Palestine
Yousef Sanjalawe	Northern Border University, Saudi Arabia
Yu Beng Leau	Universiti Malaysia Sabah, Malaysia
Yung Wey Chong	Universiti Sains Malaysia, Malaysia
Ziad Saraireh	Emirates College of Technology, UAE

Contents

Social Media, Mobile and Web, Data Policy, and Privacy and Fake News

Internet of Things, Industry and Blockchain, and Cryptology

A Survey on Privacy Concerns in Blockchain Applications and Current Blockchain Solutions to Preserve Data Privacy

Hasventhran Baskaran[1]([⊠]), Salman Yussof[2]([⊠]),
and Fiza Abdul Rahim[1]([⊠])

[1] College of Computing and Informatics, Universiti Tenaga Nasional,
Kajang, Malaysia
hasventhran@gmail.com, Fiza@uniten.edu.my
[2] Institute of Informatics and Computing in Energy, Universiti Tenaga Nasional,
Kajang, Malaysia
salman@uniten.edu.my

Abstract. Due to the offering of many benefits, blockchain is a useful environment to build many applications in multiple fields such as cryptocurrency, Internet of Things (IoT), mobile applications and healthcare industry. However, it has a problem in ensuring the privacy of user data due to its public nature. Data on a blockchain is public and can reveal someone's personal data or transactions. Many applications that venture in blockchain such as financial applications, Internet of Things (IoT) and healthcare applications can fall victim to revelation of personal data and linking attack. Many solutions such as automated access-control protocol that does not require a third party, a local miner operating in a local private blockchain that enforces users' access control policy, a cryptographic protocol that lets contractual parties interact by using zero-knowledge proof, and computation of data query in a distributed way by using secure multi-party computation have been proposed to tackle this privacy issue in using blockchain. Hence, this paper provides a review on the current solutions that addresses the privacy issues of blockchain in different platforms. However, these solutions have some limitations that cannot be overlooked and proper measures must be taken to make blockchain to be able to better protect the privacy of its users. This paper also discusses the limitations of the solutions and looks into the aspects that need to be addressed.

Keywords: Blockchain · Smart contracts · Decentralization · Immutable · Data privacy

1 Introduction

Protecting personal data has been a major issue recently due to the Facebook-Cambridge Analytica scandal. Revelation of personal data is a major privacy concern among blockchain users. Blockchain comes as a handy solution to address tampering issue due to its immutability. Since the ingenious invention of Satoshi Nakamoto and the revelation of Bitcoin, blockchain had evolved into something greater and it is ever

© Springer Nature Singapore Pte Ltd. 2020
M. Anbar et al. (Eds.): ACeS 2019, CCIS 1132, pp. 3–17, 2020.
https://doi.org/10.1007/978-981-15-2693-0_1

improving [2]. It is about to revolutionize the way we are using the Internet. The current network infrastructure that we are using now might evolve into something entirely new, like how modern Internet had its breakthrough in 1983. Initially, blockchain gained its popularity through the cryptocurrency platforms because it is a non-destructive way to detect data changes over time.

Blockchain utilize different types of consensus algorithms among the nodes to help them to transact securely with each other, instead of relying on a central authority. These consensus algorithms is useful in validating transactions and recording data to prevent them from being corrupted. They help to achieve agreement among nodes for getting reward for their work and to promote reliability in a network involving multiple unreliable nodes.

Blockchain goes one step higher than centralized authorities, by providing digital trust by enforcing ownership and authentication to users through its smart contracts. It might revolutionize the way we trust people to transact safely. The authentication and permissions are granted by the possession of cryptographic private keys.

Users do not have to share more personal information than required to do any transaction through blockchain. Verification of transaction is done by comparing the provided private keys and this eliminates the need of a central authority to do the verification process. It has certain properties that makes it ideal to build many applications that requires to preserve data integrity.

1.1 Transparency

Blockchain is a chain of blocks that contains information or transactions. It acts as a distributed ledger that is open to anyone in the particular blockchain network. The contents in blockchain can be viewed by anyone and the nodes can choose to connect to the network to receive a copy of the blockchain that is updated automatically whenever a new block is added.

1.2 No Single Point of Failure

Centralized database usually stores large amount of data and users will have little or no control over their data [15]. Unlike, centralized database, a blockchain database is not stored in any single location, meaning the records it keeps are truly public and easily verifiable [2]. Each node in the network will have a copy of the blockchain, which means that there could be millions of copies of the same blockchain.

1.3 Immutability

A blockchain network is immutable because once a data is recorded inside a blockchain, it becomes very hard to modify. Basically, blockchain is a list of data that is verified cryptographically [12]. Each block stores a unique code called a "hash" that allows us to differentiate from other blocks. And the consequent blocks are chained to the previous blocks by referring to the previous block's hash.

When a significant change occurs to a cipher text due to any slight modification on the plaintext, it is called as Avalanche effect. If there is any modification done on the content of a block, the particular block's hash will change due to Avalanche effect.

However, the next block will still have the old hash, and the hacker need to update that block to cover his footprints. This will lead to the change of hash in the second block. The hacker has to repeat the same steps for consequent blocks.

1.4 Decentralization

By having a peer-to peer network architecture, a blockchain network becomes decentralized and distributed. Since the information or the copy of the blockchain is spreaded across millions of nodes in the network, no centralized version of this information exists for a hacker to corrupt. If the hacker intends to modify any information in a block, the hacker has to do the same modifications on all nodes in the networks. This attack will be limited by the need for huge amount of computing resources.

1.5 Smart Contracts

One of the important features of blockchain is Smart Contracts. These digital contracts let users to define their own data policy to allow the blockchain application to access selected data only. Moreover, the users can opt to not reveal their identity and get their data identified or verified by the Smart Contract's ID.

However, blockchain has its fair share of disadvantages too. Being technically complex, blockchain will consume time to be a mainstream architecture for many real life applications [6]. Blockchain involves an entirely new vocabulary and common people will have a difficult time in trying to comprehend the use of a blockchain based application. Blockchain's strength grows with the number of nodes as it becomes more immutable. However, if the blockchain network size is small, the network can be an easy target for 51% attack, where malicious nodes will wait to get majority and trust, to sabotage the network.

Blockchain's advantage of being a public ledger and transparent can also be a disadvantage. If someone intends to save confidential data in a particular chain, the security goal of confidentiality will not be achieved since it is publicly viewable. Moreover, monetizing user's data had been a major concern to data owners since the details are on a public ledger. Hence, a privacy preserving technique to overcome this issue had to be implemented on the current blockchain architectures.

In this paper, we have reviewed various privacy issues that can occur in blockchain applications and various solutions for privacy preserving methods for blockchain. Our contribution also includes a comparison of various privacy preserving methods for blockchain that assists in protecting data privacy. This paper also discusses the limitations of the solutions and looks into the aspects that need to be addressed.

2 Methodology

The IEEE and ScienceDirect electronic database from 2015 to 2019 were searched. These were chosen because of the technical focus that encompasses literature in engineering and technology. Search terms were 'privacy', 'blockchain', and 'smart contracts'. The IEEE produced 184 results from the search criteria, while ScienceDirect produced 340 results. Inclusion criteria for the articles was to have publications which was a study that examined the blockchain based architectures or proposed algorithms that preserves data privacy. Articles were rejected if it was determined from the title and the abstract that the study failed to meet the inclusion criteria. Any ambiguities regarding the application of the selection criteria were resolved through discussions between all the researchers involved.

3   Privacy Concerns in Blockchain Applications

As the Web 3.0 revolution keeps on expanding, blockchain is becoming a viable platform for many applications to thrive [1]. Due to its key features, developers find blockchain as a suitable environment to build applications in various fields. Since blockchain has an append-only data structure, it is easier for them to protect valuable data from being tampered. Apart from being a perfect foil for cryptocurrency platforms to thrive, blockchain also plied its trade in intelligent manufacturing, supply chain management, Internet of Things (IoT), digital asset transactions, and other fields [13].

3.1   Financial Applications

Blockchain has almost become a synonym for Bitcoin among common people. Such has been the impact of blockchain on Bitcoin which has seen the cryptocurrency platform's value to soar high. However, apart from cryptocurrency platforms, blockchain can be used for other financial purposes too. Blockchain offers a cheaper and faster transactions compared to traditional systems. Once the pre-programmed rules in a Smart Contract is fulfilled, the bondholder gets paid immediately and the record of the transaction is stored on a public ledger.

However, blockchain's fundamental design of being public can be very useful for any exploiters. The immutable record is open to public's view even though the data cannot be tampered. This gets even worse due to the use of public ledger where all the transaction records are chained together and allows opportunities for identification.

As mentioned in an article on bitcoin investigations on Journal of Forensic Research, by monitoring the communication between nodes on the blockchain, the transaction and the corresponding internet protocol address can be associated [9]. A cryptocurrency wallet software can be cracked without the need of passwords by performing a forensic analysis.

Such incident happened in, 'Silk Road' website's owner, Ross Ulbricht's arrest in the United States of America [9]. He was operating a dark web site as an illegal online market. His bitcoin transactions were tracked down by an Internal Revenue Service special agent, whom managed to find one of the source address for a transaction leading to Ulbricht's computer.

```
txdata: date, timestamp, tx-hash, value
txdata: 2013-07-05 1373072281
7d28d38f3d7ae53a76d490667b005eea368b89629a13a84615a0f8052333caf5 3.6
txdata: 2013-07-05 1373072824
586689a0286809c27ad38e4cf4e8751bbd6ebff7a5ac4c8410ed48006fc270ca  0.7
txdata: 2013-07-05 1373072829
1f4a23b2bdfe1e80549261bb4ce7158d3aefdc199e5611cdb4b611492e5f087e 7.0547
txdata: 2013-07-05 1373073499
9e8c950db2946570dc2fe695ced19fe35f26f8c7e226e246b471ef3fedc111e8  2.61
txdata: 2013-07-05 1373073500
87834b8521209d5a8e5c4bfbb8d4acdec9c9139bed688a233f0c4d14da6c0048 8.0999
txdata: 2013-07-05 1373073500
cafc1af1daf56be5f89dc502a2020b7f957fab800989ce8ae38a14abc5d1b9df   4.0808
txdata: 2013-07-05 1373073711
2e9d28417c4017699da18a51f5d992ed55b2c0b77abd143efe6cc609aa664bd3 4.68
txdata: 2013-07-05 1373073957
0d30b5b2f4433b342bbd04f7aaa518154f77be68e0b200c3d2973c5f6288b4fe  6.8792
```

The dataset above shows a portion of the Bitcoin transactions of Ulbricht, which were tracked down by FBI [9]. A program was written to isolate every transactions and one of the source addresses was seized by the FBI from the Silk Road server, and the destination was seized from Ulbricht's computer. Each entry consists of the date, the timestamp, the Bitcoin transaction hash, and the value transferred from Silk Road to Ulbricht. This shows how privacy is not being preserved properly on blockchain and could expose someone's lifetime financial records to the public.

3.2 Healthcare Industry

Healthcare organizations are looking are looking to adopt blockchain in health record management to improve their quality, transparency, and efficiency of the data storage system [18]. This will provide a lifelong record of a patient's data which can protect patient data privacy and contribute to medical researches [17]. According to a study conducted by IBM, 56% of healthcare executives are expected to adopt blockchain by 2020 and 16% were planning to implement blockchain solution in their works in 2018 [14]. Instead of having different medical history of a patient in different healthcare facilities, blockchain has the potential to improve the system because of having patient's data on a blockchain's ledger. The doctors could update the patient's medical history and store it on the public ledger for future references.

However, converting physically documented patient data to digitized data on blockchain will come with its own disadvantages. Since the patient data is updated by the doctor, the patient has less control over their data. Usually the identities in blockchain are pseudonymous after being obscured by a public key. However, due to the public nature of blockchain, an individual's public key can be matched to their identity and the individual also can be identified by basic demographic information [10].

Blockchain might aid in information blocking that could create a patient information sharing marketplace for commercial purposes. These patient data can be sold to pharmaceutical companies without user consent [19]. If any malicious person gets access to this data on the blockchain, the attacker could take advantage to sabotage the patient based on their health problems. Putting a patient's record on a public ledger might be damaging to his/her self-respect if they have any embarrassing or chronic disease.

3.3   Internet of Things

In the near future, our current communication infrastructure might extend beyond just smartphones or mass media. From, a smart whiteboard to any random farm in the other corner of the world, we will be more connected through IoT than ever before. Such connections need strong security measures to protect the data flowing through them. However, IoT is not immune to attacks and can be an easy target for DDoS attacks. So far, hackers managed to get control of smart cars, cardiac devices and also launched the biggest DDoS attack, Dyn Attack.

Being just at the beginning of the adoption curve, blockchain and IoT can be a revolutionary technology. Blockchain can help the data transmitted from IoT devices to be encrypted and tamper-proof [20]. Smart Contracts can be a game-changer by providing the user defined data policy and rules to the IoT device. Any actions of the IoT will be authorized by the rules in the Smart Contract. The transactions and its corresponding cryptographic puzzles will be processed by a miner, since IoT devices are low-powered. All the connections of user to the smart devices will be transparent and untampered.

Generally, IoT devices has the tendency to aggregate personal data and store it. This can invite potential threat of privacy breach. IoT devices like Smart Meter has the highest risk of falling victim to this attack. The load profile from smart meters will aid the inference of personal data from a smart meter [5]. Blockchain might prevent the data from being untampered but, blockchain is a public ledger and storing usage data of an IoT device such as Smart Meter might reveal an individual's activities to others. This can be done by analyzing the statistical data of the IoT device stored in the blockchain [21]. This high-profile measurement will definitely cause a major threat to users' privacy [7].

IoT devices deal with personal and sensitive data in real time. Blockchain seems to be strong and safe option from any compromises. It is also able to avoid accessing user data without their consent [3]. Hence, it has a weak point in the form of the owners of each node. If the owner makes any mistake, the mistake could compromise the chain. A linking of transactions belonging to an owner can be done if the owner of a key is revealed [6]. The transaction can reveal information like the time of transaction, transacted amount, or the type of data transferred.

4   Current Blockchain Solutions for Data Privacy Issues

Blockchain is revolutionary and it protects our data integrity by being tamper proof. Many fields and applications are either using blockchain in their system or planning to adopt it. However it has a fundamental privacy issue by the virtue of its design. Blockchain's public nature is a big issue in preserving data privacy. Hence, many developer and researchers are working towards making blockchain to be able to better protect data privacy. This section provides a review on existing privacy preservation techniques that have been proposed for various applications of blockchain.

4.1 Blockchain Based Mobile Application Architecture

Smartphones have become an integral part of our lives now. These small yet powerful devices are capable of doing many tasks concurrently. However, good things comes with a cost. Smart phone and its mobile applications are always vulnerable to security threats. From Hollywood celebrities' iCloud pictures leaks to Facebook-Cambridge Analytica scandal, many private data were exposed and used for commercial and personal purposes. Due to centralized architecture of mobile applications, exposure of private data is a serious issue when the applications' security measures are breached.

To prevent the problem mentioned above, a wide range of enterprise mobile apps can take advantage of blockchain's distributed and cryptographically secure nature. To protect data against leaks and cyberattacks, blockchain uses cryptographic technologies, including private key encryption, which provides users with unique digital signatures. Since some mobile applications might deal with sensitive information such as user credentials or their current location, blockchain can protect them from being tampered or revealed. Users have less control over their data as the user can grant a set of permission upon sign-up only.

A blockchain architecture for mobile applications was proposed by Zyskind et al. in [22] to tackle this problem. The authors have mentioned that third party apps can collect and control massive amounts of personal data. This increases the possibility of security breaches and compromises users' privacy. This paper suggests the use of blockchain for a mobile application that allows the users to have control over which services can have access to their mobile application data. A protocol turns this blockchain into an automated access-control manager that allows it not to require trust in a third party.

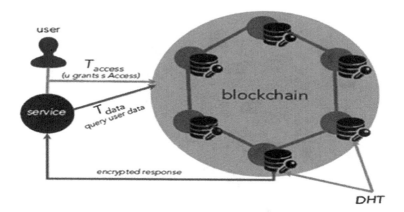

Fig. 1. Blockchain architecture for mobile application [22]

Figure 1 shows the blockchain architecture for mobile application as discussed in the. In this architecture, the blockchain accepts 2 new types of transactions. The first transaction is Taccess, which is used for access control management. This transaction allows users to change the set of permissions granted to a service by sending a policy set or revoke the all access-rights by sending an empty set. The second transaction is Tdata, which is used for data storage and retrieval. Tdata governs read/write operations. The users are always allowed to access the data, whereas the service can access the data when it has the permission to it.

Usually mobile applications require users' permission upon sign-up only. This results in a one-time permission granting and if user needs to revoke the permissions, they have to uninstall and install back the applications to grant a new set of permissions. This architecture provides fine-grained access control by enabling the user to alter the set of permissions and revoke access to previously collected data at any time. The access-control policy will be stored on the blockchain and only the user is allowed to change them.

4.2 Blockchain Based Smart Home Architecture

More and more smart home devices are being released to the market nowadays. These devices are making a lot of daily task to be performed in a much easier and efficient way. However, IoT devices are connected in a centralized architecture and have the risk of data collection by the manufacturing company.

Fortunately, with a blockchain-powered smart home system, other parties can be given permission to access specific areas and devices without giving them access to everything. This can be done through the implementation of Smart Contract. However, due to lightweight nature of IoT devices, most of the available energy is devoted to perform the core tasks and preserving privacy becomes a challenging task due to the limited energy. Since blockchain requires more resource to perform its core functionalities, IoT and blockchain has a huge gap to fill in.

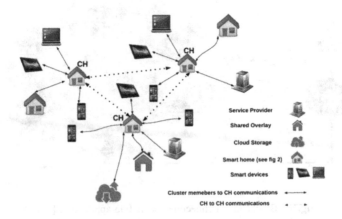

Fig. 2. Smart home based blockchain architecture [4]

Figure 2 shows a proposed design of a smart home architecture based on a light-weight instantiation of blockchain proposed by Ali Dorri et al. in [4]. This architecture consists of three tier to be fully functional. The resource consuming Proof of Work and the concept of coins are eliminated in this architecture. The 3 tiers are Smart Home, Cloud Storage and Overlay. A miner will centrally manage the smart devices located inside the smart home tier. Nodes in the overlay are grouped into clusters and each cluster elects a Cluster Head (CH) to decrease network overload and delay. Transactions, local blockchain, home miner and local storage are core components in this design.

This design includes a local private blockchain that can keep track of transactions and enforce users' access control policy for incoming and outgoing transactions. The access control policy is defined by user. This design also can prevent linking attack. Each device's data is shared and stored by a unique key. Then, the miner creates unique ledger of data in the cloud storage for each device by generating a different public key. From the overlay point of view, the miner should use a unique key for each transaction.

The device that processes incoming and outgoing transactions to and from the smart home is the home miner. The local storage in the smart home can be integrated with the miner. It implements a First-In-First-Out (FIFO) method to store the data and stores each devices' data as a ledger to the devices' starting point. It authenticates, authorizes and audits transactions. So, no transaction can be known to others without going through the home miner which has the user defined permissions.

4.3 Hawk Protocol

Generally, Smart Contracts are utilized for cryptocurrency platforms. This feature allows two parties to handle the transaction with little trust and without a third party. If the contract is breached or aborted, the blockchain can ensure that the honest party gets proper compensation. However, existing systems lacks transactional privacy due to the fact that transactions, flow of money between pseudonyms and amount transacted are exposed on the blockchain. Ross Ulbricht's case is a perfect example for this issue.

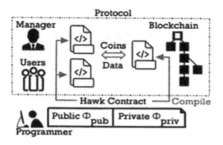

Fig. 3. Execution flow of Hawk protocol breach [16]

As suggested by Kosba et al. in [16], these smart contracts do not have to store any transactions explicitly on the blockchain to retain the privacy of the transaction from public view. As shown in Fig. 3, the authors had proposed the use of Hawk protocol in compiling program to a cryptographic protocol between the blockchain and the users.

Private smart contracts can be written without having to implement cryptography. The protocol's compiler will generate a cryptographic protocol where the contractual parties interact with the blockchain using cryptographic primitives such as zero-knowledge proof. This cryptographic primitive enables a sender node to prove to a verifier that it knows information *abc*, without having to reveal any other information except for the fact that the sender node knows *abc*. The protocol will compile the program into certain pieces which jointly define a cryptographic protocol between users, the manager, and the blockchain.

The pieces are the blockchain's program which will be executed by all consensus nodes, a program to be executed by the users, a program to be executed by a special facilitating party called the manager. The manager is able to see the users' inputs and is trusted to not disclose users' personal information. However, the manager should not be compared with a trusted third party. In the event that a manager aborts the protocol, it is financially punished, and users get compensation consequently. This architecture guarantees on-chain privacy and contractual security.

4.4   Project Enigma

Blockchain cannot handle private data whether it's a private or public blockchain due to its current architecture. Most of the modern applications require heavy processing of private data to perform its sensitive parts. Since blockchain is a public ledger, storing sensitive data on it is impossible. Blockchain's public nature lets private data to flow through every full node on the blockchain and gets fully exposed [23]. This restricts the growth of applications that relies on blockchain.

Project Enigma by MIT had produced a better protocol that helps decentralized applications to preserve data privacy with multi-party computation. Enigma promises "secret contracts", as opposed to existing "smart contracts", with nodes on the blockchain able to compute data without ever "seeing" it. Blockchain is a revolutionary technology, but it is still held back by fundamental limitations.

The MIT researchers claim that, Project Enigma will allow users to maintain control over personal data, particularly through preventing its monetization or analysis by platforms. They also claim that it could unlock a new system of lending, in which prospective borrowers can establish their trustworthiness without having to give individual lenders access to their specific personal data [11].

Table 1. Comparison between blockchain based solutions.

Papers	Techniques	Problem	Proposed solution
Decentralizing Privacy: Using Blockchain to Protect Personal Data [22]	Access-control moderator and off-blockchain storage solution	Third party apps can collect and control massive amounts of personal advantage. This increases the possibility of security breaches and compromises users' privacy.	Implementation of a protocol that turns a blockchain into an automated access-control manager that does not require trust in a third party
Blockchain for IoT security and privacy: The case study of a smart home [4]	Lightweight instantiation of private blockchain	IoT devices are connected in a centralized architecture and have the risk of data collection by the manufacturing company	A local private blockchain is created to keep track of transactions and enforce users' access control policy for incoming and outgoing transactions. A local miner authenticates and authorizes all the incoming and outgoing transactions
Hawk: The Blockchain Model of Cryptography and Privacy-Preserving Smart Contracts breach [16]	Compilation of a program to a cryptographic protocol between a blockchain and users	Smart Contract system lacks transactional privacy. All transactions, flow of money, and amount transacted are exposed on the blockchain	Private smart contracts can be written without having to implement cryptography. The compiler will generate a cryptographic protocol where the contractual parties interact with the blockchain using cryptographic primitives such as zero-knowledge proofs
Enigma: Decentralized Computatiion with Guarenteed Privacy [23]	Multi-party computation	The two major issues in blockchain are privacy and scalability. Due to blockchain's implementation of consensus algorithms, computing on the blockchain is too slow and expensive. Storing and computing over large amount of data on a blockchain is almost impossible	Data can be computed without having access to all the raw data. Data queries are computed in a distributed way by using secure multi-party computation without leaking information to other nodes. A compromised node will not be able to get an explicit overview of the data because the computations and data storage are not replicated by every node

Without the need of a trusted third party, data queries are computed in a distributed way by using secure multi-party computation. The data will be split to different nodes. These nodes will then compute the functions together without leaking their pieces of data to other nodes. Data redundancy is avoided by eliminating the replication of computations and storage. Only a small subset perform each computation over different parts of the data. The decreased redundancy in storage and computations enables more demanding computations.

Since, the data is split into multiple pieces before reaching the recipient, it is ensured that no single node has access to the entire data and. Every single node will only have a meaningless piece of data. Attackers will not be able to get an explicit overview of the data sent through the blockchain even if they managed to control any nodes in the network. The need for a trusted third party is eliminated and the users are granted autonomous control of personal data.

Table 1 summarizes the current work on privacy preservation methods on blockchain from various researchers. The problems found for different contexts and its corresponding solutions are presented briefly in the table.

5 Discussion

The growing use of blockchain in many aspects of our everyday life is forcing specialists to think more and more about security and privacy issues of the applications of this technology. Usually, privacy preserving methods for blockchain are implemented by having a certain trade-offs. For example, users have to trust the manager node in the Hawk protocol to perform any transaction breach [16]. The user will be secured by the contracts defined by them. Trade-offs can be dangerous because it might invite new attacks or problems.

Public blockchain allows everyone on the network to read the data in the nodes. Some architectures like Smart Home architecture in [4] are using private blockchain to have a better privacy preserving measures compared to public blockchain. However it has its own disadvantage too. In January 2016, Ethereum co-founder, Vitalik Buterin stated that private blockchain that is private by default, can leak information to the outside world when there is a dispute [8].

Another disadvantage of blockchain is identity theft. Identity theft is something that blockchain tries to solve. One of blockchain's core capabilities, is to protect the user identities with a unique set of private keys that can control each digital identity. However, it is not immune to phishing attacks, where attackers could get the user's identity to get full control on the data. Considering the huge damage that can occur, as in the case of bitcoin, if there is a double digit fraud and loss rate of the keys used to secure the identities, the system might not be fully workable.

Trusted nodes in a blockchain can gain more weight in the network to compute blocks more efficiently [22]. However, this method can attract attacks such as nodes increasing their reputation to act maliciously in the future. Finally, even after generating a new compound identity for each user-service pair, a small fraction of the data can be compromised in the event of an attacker obtaining both the signing and encryption keys.

Blockchain based Smart Home architecture in [4] is made up of several local private blockchain. Private blockchain shares common traits of a public blockchain. However, these private blockchain works like a centralized database system by having access controls that restricts the nodes that can join the network. If a node that has the authority in the blockchain is compromised, it will be easier to take down the network since it is easier to perform 51% attack in a smaller network.

Hawk protocol proposes the idea of a manager node to execute the defined contracts. The authors claims that this manager node is not equal to a trusted third party. However, users must put minimal trust in this manager node which can see the users' input and trusted to not disclose the private data. The manager node cannot affect the correct execution of the contract even if the node tries to abort or collide with other parties. The users will be compensated in the event of a contract breach [16]. However, the manager node has seen the data and can still publicize the data in a different medium.

These gaps are still in the process of being solved. Many researchers around the world are coming up with new solutions to solve these issues but they are held back by some trade-offs or limitations of this blockchain technology. Blockchain are complex networks and building a privacy preserving solution can make it far more complex than the blockchain itself.

6 Conclusion

In this paper, we have reviewed various privacy issues that can occur in blockchain applications and various solutions for privacy preserving methods for blockchain. Granting of user defined access control policies through Smart Contracts is the most widely used method in preserving privacy due to its capability of enabling the user to have total control over their data. The outcomes of this study provides an insight into current solutions for the privacy issues in blockchain.

Our contribution also includes a comparison of various privacy preserving methods for blockchain that assists in protecting data privacy. This paper also discusses the limitations of the solutions and looks into the aspects that need to be addressed. This will contribute to the betterment of the blockchain adoption in multiple fields and encourage the use of proper privacy preserving method for blockchain technology in preserving data privacy.

Our future work will consist in evaluating existing secure and scalable blockchain platforms and also designing a blockchain architecture to address the privacy and anonymity issues. Moreover, we will investigate mixing private and public blockchain architectures to achieve anonymity and further protect user data privacy.

Acknowledgment. The authors would like to thank the Ministry of Higher Education Malaysia (MoHE) and Universiti Tenaga Nasional (UNITEN) for funding this study under the Fundamental Research Grant Scheme (FRGS) of Grant No. FRGS/1/2017/ICT03/UNITEN/03/1.

References

1. Alabdulwahhab, F.: Web 3.0: the decentralized web blockchain networks and protocol innovation. In: 2018 1st International Conference on Computer Applications & Information Security (ICCAIS), p. 2 (2018)
2. Blockgeeks. https://blockgeeks.com/guides/what-is-blockchain-technology/. Accessed 11 Sept 2018
3. Cha, S., Tsai, T., Peng, W., Huang, T., Hsu, T., Privacy-aware and blockchain connected gateways for users to access legacy IoT devices. In: 2017 IEEE 6th Global Conference on Consumer Electronics (GCCE) (2017)
4. Dorri, A., Kanhere, S., Jurdak, R., Gauravaram, P.: Blockchain for IoT security and privacy: the case study of a smart home. In: 2017 IEEE International Conference on Pervasive Computing and Communications Workshops (Percom Workshops), pp. 1–6, (2017)
5. Eibl, G., Engel, D.: Influence of data granularity on smart meter privacy. IEEE Trans. Smart Grid 6(2), 930–939 (2015)
6. Fabiano, N.: The Internet of Things ecosystem: the blockchain and privacy issues, the challenge for a global privacy standard. In: 2017 International Conference on Internet of Things for The Global Community (Iotgc) (2017)
7. Finster, S., Baumgart, I.: Privacy-aware smart metering: a survey. IEEE Commun. Surv. Tutor. 17(2), 1088–1101 (2015)
8. Foundation. https://blog.ethereum.org/2016/01/15/privacy-on-the-blockchain/. Accessed 11 Sept 2018
9. Garcia, J.: The Evidentiary Trail Down Silk Road. ResearchGate, pp. 2–9 (2017)
10. Gordon, W., Catalini, C.: Blockchain technology for healthcare: facilitating the transition to patient-driven interoperability. Comput. Struct. Biotechnol. J. 16, 224–230 (2018)
11. The Guardian. https://www.theguardian.com/commentisfree/2018/mar/21/blockchain-privacy-data-protection-cambridge-analytica. Accessed 13 Sept 2018
12. Halpin, H., Piekarska, M.: Introduction to security and privacy on the blockchain. In: 2017 IEEE European Symposium on Security and Privacy Workshops (Euros&PW) (2017)
13. Hou, H.: The application of blockchain technology in e-government in China. In: 2017 26th International Conference on Computer Communication and Networks (ICCCN) (2017)
14. IBM: Healthcare rallies for blockchains – Keeping patients at the center (2017)
15. Kaaniche, N., Laurent, M.: A blockchain-based data usage auditing architecture with enhanced privacy and availability. In: 2017 IEEE 16th International Symposium on Network Computing and Applications (NCA) (2017)
16. Kosba, A., Miller, A., Shi, E., Wen, Z., Papamanthou, C., Hawk: the blockchain model of cryptography and privacy-preserving smart contracts. In: 2016 IEEE Symposium on Security and Privacy (SP), pp. 1–3 (2016)
17. Magyar, G., Blockchain: solving the privacy and research availability tradeoff for EHR data: a new disruptive technology in health data management. In: 2017 IEEE 30th Neumann Colloquium (NC) (2017)
18. Mertz, L.: (Block) chain reaction: a blockchain revolution sweeps into health care, offering the possibility for a much-needed data solution. IEEE Pulse 9(3), 4–7 (2018)
19. WhatIs.com. https://searchhealthit.techtarget.com/definition/information-blocking. Accessed 10 Oct 2018

20. Shrobe, H., Shrier, D., Pentland, A.: New Solutions for Cybersecurity, pp. 425–454. MIT Press (2018)
21. Singh, M., Singh, A., Kim, S.: Blockchain: a game changer for securing IoT data. In: 2018 IEEE 4th World Forum on Internet of Things (WF-IoT) (2018)
22. Weaver, K.: How Smart Meters Invade Individual Privacy. https://smartgridawareness.org/privacy-and-data-security/how-smart-meters-invade-individual-privacy/. Accessed 17 Sept 2018
23. Zyskind, G., Nathan, O., Pentland, A.: Decentralizing privacy: using blockchain to protect personal data. In: 2015 IEEE Security And Privacy Workshops, pp. 2–4 (2015)

A Study on Secured Authentication and Authorization in Internet of Things: Potential of Blockchain Technology

Syeda Mariam Muzammal⬤ and Raja Kumar Murugesan^(✉)

Taylor's University, Subang Jaya, Malaysia
syedamariammuzammal@sd.taylors.edu.my,
rajakumar.murugesan@taylors.edu.my

Abstract. With the proliferation of Internet of Things (IoT) and its influence in various use case scenarios, it can be expected that IoT services will create a global reach. Smart cities, smart grids, smart industries, smart wearables etc. are some examples of IoT services today. Besides all the benefits that IoT provide, security issues of these services and data generated by IoT are of major concern. Traditional security practices of authentication and authorization have been initially designed for security needs of centralized client/server models which are good to deal with human-machine interaction over the Internet. In centralized systems, normally devices and users are trusted for being in the same application domain. Moreover, such systems can become a bottleneck for a number of queries at the same time; or may become a single point of failure causing unavailability of connected devices that are totally relying on a single trusted party. This paper explores the IoT security issues and concerns. Moreover, it provides a review of centralized and decentralized IoT security solutions in terms of authentication and authorization. Additionally, it discusses how Blockchain technology can be leveraged to provide IoT security.

Keywords: IoT security · Authentication · Authorization · Blockchain

1 Introduction

Smart devices are ubiquitous in today's world. The emergence of IoT paradigm has given rise to the rapid escalation in use of smart heterogeneous interconnected devices and applications [1]. IoT is a network of swiftly growing complexity, whereas Blockchain has been activated for a substantial impact on IoT by its decentralized nature and other features of security enhancement and empowerment for accommodating a number of devices in the IoT paradigm [2]. Both have the antagonistic capabilities to transform concepts into realities and providing innovative opportunities to develop advanced and secured smart applications.

With its wide adoption in different industries, like supply chain management, agriculture, farming, transportation, insurance, health, etc., IoT has a number of well-known security defects that have given intensification to recent attacks [3, 4]. The enhanced and autonomous functionalities lead to exposure of sensitive data, in Device-to-Device (D2D) communications, to malicious activities. For example, personal data

© Springer Nature Singapore Pte Ltd. 2020
M. Anbar et al. (Eds.): ACeS 2019, CCIS 1132, pp. 18–32, 2020.
https://doi.org/10.1007/978-981-15-2693-0_2

communicated through wearable smart devices can be leaked to unwanted sniffing nodes, and may cause intense privacy breach for an individual [5, 6]. According to reports by Gartner, Cisco and various other companies, over 20 to 50 billion IoT devices will be connected to the Internet by year 2020 [7, 8]. The increase in number of IoT devices and applications will also give rise to security and privacy concerns.

IoT has spread from our homes to industries and cities, operating through the collection, exchange and dissemination of information via various sensors and devices. For this most commonly implemented infrastructure, efficient and reliable techniques for security and privacy have become an obligatory issue for the wide adoption of the IoT technology. According to Open Web Application Security Project (OWASP) [9], vulnerabilities in IoT varies from smart device's very limited power and memory to operating systems and firmware. Moreover, incompetent web and physical interfaces as well as insecure network access also form up the IoT security loopholes. Inadequate authentication and authorization along with lack of transport encryption play a major role in security breaches and attacks. Consequently, the security needs of IoT devices and networks have become significant. On the other hand, Blockchain, based on decentralized and distributed ledger technology is influencing IoT applications for faster adoption by enterprises towards digitized and secure smart world. Blockchain, that mainly emerged as back-end technology for cryptocurrencies, characterize a promising approach to encounter unique security needs of IoT paradigm [10]. Considerable research work is going on for the exploitation of Blockchain for IoT in different industries and many big companies, like IBM [11], have already taken on the challenges.

This paper presents a review on IoT security and privacy concerns, specifically in terms of authentication and authorization. There are various studies on IoT security issues and integration of Blockchain [12–14]. Most of previous studies discuss IoT security as a whole and give basic understanding of Blockchain technology. This paper analyzes IoT security attacks and vulnerabilities. In addition, it contributes to further exploration of smart contracts and consensus algorithms for providing security in terms of authentication and authorization in IoT. Moreover, it also describes the proposed Blockchain-based solutions in IoT and its challenges. Rest of the paper is organized into four sections. Section 2 presents background of security and privacy in IoT along with attacks and vulnerabilities in IoT systems. An overview of existing IoT security solutions, according to centralized and decentralized approaches has been presented in Sect. 3. Section 4 discusses the research challenges and opportunities. Section 5 concludes the paper.

2 Security and Privacy in IoT

Internet of Things is defined in simple terms as network of 'things'. These 'things' can be sensors, actuators, computers, smartphones, people, animals or any 'thing' that is connected to the Internet and used for information collection, generate alerts, or data exchange. The acceptance and wide adoption of IoT is based on assurance of security and privacy, since smart devices are connected in various critical paradigms with collection and processing of large amounts of sensitive data. The collected data may be disseminated to other parties for numerous reasons of decision making and analytics. Moreover, IoT software and hardware are not built with security as a priority. Additionally, once the devices are connected or setup, there is hardly any management, patching or updating.

A number of factors are considered under IoT security paradigm. Authorization, authentication, access control management, trust management, confidentiality, messages or data integrity, and availability, are just a few. The reason for this explosion of IoT security concerns being the increase in the number of devices and advanced services provided by interconnected devices across the globe. Among various security and privacy concerns in IoT, authentication and authorization form the foundation of resiliency to attacks, particularly in case of resource constrained smart devices. Lack of robust mechanisms leads to exploitation of various vulnerabilities and loopholes causing attacks.

2.1 IoT Security Attacks: Causes and Analysis

In recent years, there have been a number of cyberattacks based on smart devices, which have caused serious disruptions over the Internet and technological paradigm.

Security Attacks Using IoT Devices. One of the prominent security incident was Mirai botnet attack launched by hackers in October 2016 [15]. This was a massive Distributed Denial of Service (DDoS) attack on Dyn, an Internet Domain Name Server (DNS) provider. This brought down a couple of websites, including Twitter, Paypal and Spotify. Most importantly, this attack was launched by infiltrating interconnected smart devices, like DVRs and CCTV cameras, for flooding traffic to Dyn servers. In June 2017, a similar cyberattack was reported in North Korea causing Internet disruption [16].

Additionally, in 2018, an attack was launched for consumers' edge IoT devices to snoop data [17]. This malware called VPNFilter targeted at least 500k networking IoT devices across the globe, and the threat is still under investigation. Hence, these small interconnected smart devices, and their proliferation have the power to cause major security breach and Internet to stand still.

Information Disclosure. Personal and private data of IoT users can be exposed when it is not protected by passwords or firewalls. For example, in the case of CloudPets [18], customer's data was held for ransom and was exposed in a publicly available database for two weeks.

According to Kaspersky report [19], in only first half of 2018, number of malware variations, listed by researchers, intended at IoT devices, has exceeded three times the number registered in 2017. With this explosion of cyberattacks it is evident that the number of security risks and threats will only increase in future with increase in number of smart devices. Traditionally, security solutions are applied as an afterthought. IoT threats and attacks demonstrate that patching against even known attacks is currently insufficient [20]. Indeed, security is a major IoT challenge, that require new visions of security-by-design in IoT.

Since in IoT, a variety of computing systems are interconnected including sensors, actuators, mobile devices, control systems, cloud servers and computers. Moreover,

IoT systems and devices closely interact with human beings and environments. For example, the wearable medical devices, smart vehicles and smart energy grids. Other than providing benefits to human lives, it brings more serious and devastating security challenges. For example, medical devices and implants, such as, cardiac pacemakers and infusion pumps, if tampered by hackers may impose severe effects on health conditions. For instance, an incident of cyberattack on Ukrainian power grid happened in December 2015, causing blackout in Ivano-Frankivsk region for several hours, affecting 1.4 million residents [21]. This shows that the consequences of the cyberattacks using IoT can be more devastating and life-threatening as compared to the attacks in past causing financial or data loss. Table 1 summarize some of the security incidents in recent years and their causes due to direct or indirect vulnerabilities in IoT systems.

Table 1. IoT security incidents and causes

Attacks	Description & Cause(s)
Impersonation	Commands can be sent remotely to control vehicle functions [22] as well as access to servers [23] for malicious activities, over public cellular networks
Data/Privacy breach	Exposure of personal data and credentials [18], due to lack of strong passwords, firewall protection and proper encryption
Botnet/DDoS	Compromising users' data by snooping on traffic passing through affected routers [17], unavailability of cloud-related services [15, 24], because of default factory settings [25], usernames and passwords [26]
Malware	Disruption in routine activities [27] due to server outage and attempt to destroy whole system infrastructure through malware
Ransomware	Cracking smart key lock system, for example, shutting down hotel rooms [28] because of lack of security in smart systems
Brute-force	Targeting IoT devices, for connection and sending commands and data. Reasons include: exploiting hard-coded passwords, exposed SSH, and telnet ports; lack of strong credentials [29]; lack of standard security features and pairing encryption [24, 30]

There are two major causes to the occurrences and strengths of aforementioned security incidents. Firstly, the commonly used devices that previously do not used to be always connected to the Internet are now interconnected and the number of such devices is increasing day-by-day. This interconnectivity and heterogeneity may cause a serious security issue by providing illegal access to resources like data, services, storage and computing units from adversaries [31]. Secondly, the connected devices are not robust and have limited capabilities to stay protected from being exposed and compromised. This is mainly due to incompatible authentication and authorization techniques. Additionally, the existing solutions for providing authentication and authorization are not suitable enough to secure IoT devices and data. Thus, resulting in increased number of attacks. Therefore, preventing illegal access to resources by unauthorized entities is regarded as a progressively vigorous research problem in IoT [32].

2.2 Vulnerabilities in IoT Systems

There are certain vulnerabilities in IoT ecosystem causing security threats and risks to smart devices. One of the key reasons is that IoT devices are resource constrained in nature, hence traditional security practices are not easily and efficiently adapted. As a result, IoT suffers from a number of vulnerabilities.

Table 2. Authentication and authorization challenges in IoT

Issues	Attacks, risks & vulnerabilities	Challenges in IoT
Authentication & Authorization	- Identity theft [33] - Data leaks and target data breach [33] - Impersonation attack [23, 34] - Brute-force attack -multiple login attempts and credentials abuse [35] - Digital key system breach [36] - Cryptographic attacks [37] - Rainbow Tables - Keylogging - Third party involvement - Risks at cloud-related services [24] - Desynchronization - Insider attacks - Public Verifiability - Confidentiality - No check on multiple login attempts [35] - Lack of identity verification [38] - Privilege escalation - Inherited vulnerabilities due to integration of WSNs in IoT [39] - Presence of battery-powered sensors - Ciphertext authenticity	- Centralization - High computational cost - Energy and power efficiency - Scalability - Security attacks consideration - Limitations due to any intermediary and trusted third party involvement - Unsatisfactory security analysis - Assumptions on hub nodes - Difficult real-time adaptation - Lack revocation mechanism for access control - Lack of performance analysis - Lack of experimental and implementation results - Time and resource constraints - Heterogeneity

Reliance on Centralized Server. In current centralized client/server based IoT models, authentication and authorization are provided through a third party or specific server. More devices connected and more requests coming to one centralized server can form up a bottleneck. For example, in the Industrial Wireless Sensor Networks

(IWSNs) where sensor nodes have to be connected to the Internet in terms of Industrial IoT. In this scenario, a base station acts as an intermediary for parsing the incoming and outgoing information between IWSNs and the Internet. This base station may become a bottleneck or single point of failure [39]. This massive server overload can destroy centralized structure. Moreover, centralization also carry the risk of intentional data tampering and cyber-attacks by malicious third parties or dissemination of data to non-trusted authorities. Additionally, security services, such as authentication and authorization, provided by cloud servers and other centralized authorities are dependent on the availability and efficiency of these servers. Moreover, the maintenance of such servers incurs high costs. Also, the model fails when the centralized entity is compromised by any means. Additionally, the Trusted Third Party (TTP) can tamper records without accountability.

Privilege Escalation. Attackers are always looking for bugs in a system to gain elevated access to resources that are protected from unidentified access. Due to lack of proper fine-grained access control mechanism in IoT, an unauthorized entity may illegally access a resource, causing security breach.

Lack of Security Considerations. IoT devices are not manufactured with security in mind and lack fundamental security requirements. Moreover, there is no standardization in IoT protocols that leads to security loopholes. For data leaks and privacy breach, there is no clarity on who is responsible for security violations. Additionally, IoT applications are being deployed in heterogeneous environments, without considering security aspects. A number of attacks, risks, vulnerabilities and challenges for authentication and authorization in IoT are summarized in Table 2.

3   IoT Security Solutions – Authentication and Authorization

Before connecting and exchanging data, an IoT device needs to be identified and authenticated that it is legitimately eligible to be connected to the IoT system or other IoT devices. Authentication is based on the process of identifying or verifying an entity, that someone or something is actually the same who it claims to be. Authorization is the process to determine whether the already authenticated entity has the privilege to access particular resources including read/write data, execute transactions/instructions or control the sensors/actuators. Hence, authentication is the pre-requisite of authorization in mostly cases [40]. Additionally, authorization involves the granting as well as revoking access privileges to devices or resources.

One of the major foundations of security breaches in heterogeneous scenarios is the lack of strong authentication mechanism. The increasing attack vectors in IoT ecosystem indicate the need for a solution that can operate in resource constrained smart devices and achieve significant security [41]. Generically, IoT security solutions for authentication and authorization can be divided into centralized or decentralized approaches in alliance with the requirements of the IoT applications.

3.1 Centralized Solutions

Centralized solutions mainly rely on a central authority, that can be a third-party or a cloud server. Centralized approaches face different types of challenges like, the assumption of TTP to be always authentic, trusted and available. More devices and number of requests from IoT devices can form a bottleneck around the TTP causing unavailability. Also, the system gets disrupted when the centralized entity is compromised. Moreover, TTP can tamper records without accountability.

OAuth 2.0 (IETF standard) and OpenID Connect 1.0 (OIDF standard) are two authentication and authorization standardized frameworks that promise to serve as important tools for the IoT's requirements [42]. In OAuth2, client/server model has an advantage of saving effort and time since user has to authenticate to a single entity only and can access multiple entities. However, in an OAuth2 deployment, user has to authenticate to a trusted OAuth2 provider in order to access the device [43]. OpenID Connect 1.0 is an extension of OAuth 2.0 to identity layer. In addition, User Managed Access (UMA) extends OAuth 2.0 to support a centralized authorized manager in order to manage user consent and decisions in a scalable manner.

A centralized solution primarily based on Elliptic Curve Digital Signature Algorithm (ECDSA) [44] has been proposed recently for authentication in federated IoT-enabled Vehicle-to-Grid (V2G) networks. The scheme is based on a lightweight protocol for capacity-based security access authentication and admission control at Network layer. However, it is limited to the application of federated IoT-enabled V2G environment and, more importantly, based on trusted entities called Certification Authority (CA). Smart and electronic vehicles are becoming an important part of smart cities. For Vehicle-to-Vehicle (V2V) and Vehicle-to-Road-Side-Unit (V2R), existing schemes based on anonymous certificates and signatures by trusted CA are not computationally efficient enough [45]. For reducing the authentication time of vehicle and message authentication, a mutual batch authentication scheme is proposed [45] for Vehicular ad-hoc networks (VANETs). This works by reducing the verification cost on receiver end and verify the authenticity of OBU's (On-board Units) without revealing their original identities to the RSUs (Road-side Units). The scheme enables verification of a batch of vehicles in V2V communications, rather than authenticating one by one, and same for RSUs to vehicles communication. The integrity of messages is verified by anonymous signatures adhered to the received message. Moreover, efficiency is achieved by batch authentication, that is, authenticating multiple vehicles or messages concurrently and anonymously, as well as by decreasing pairing operations. However, it adopts weaknesses of a centralized approach.

Similarly, Sicari et al. [46] proposes a policy enforcement framework based on centralized scheme. The access roles are described using XML in a format inspired by Attribute-based Access Control (ABAC). However, it demonstrates only a preliminary performance analysis for storage, software, hardware and bandwidth requirements along with generic theories for security consideration of framework. A framework for safer access to cloud services has been proposed by Le et al. [47], specifically evaluated for medical wearable devices. It employs OpenID Connect for authentication and, OAuth protocol and third-party tokens release for authorization. There has not been any security consideration for framework. Moreover, OpenID is more demanding in computation and network resources.

In centralized systems, a common attack vector is the phishing attack which has a high success rate and intensifying rapidly. According to Symantec Latest Intelligence Report for June 2017, 76% of organizations suffered from phishing attacks in 2016 [48]. Additionally, current access control standards cannot be directly implemented on the resource constrained smart objects [49]. Furthermore, the introduction of powerful TTP or CA for handling access control logic can lead to security and privacy breaches. In short, existing centralized approaches have drawbacks that possibly affect scalability, performance, trust and availability, and thus may not be suitable for IoT scenarios.

3.2   Decentralized Solutions and Blockchain Innovation

Blockchain, a Distributed Ledger Technology (DLT) is believed to be emerging as a technology with intrinsic features to support secure authentication, access control management and authorization to IoT devices and data, in decentralized way [14]. Moreover, it has inborn advantages of high trust, scalability, integrity, and resiliency. For example, IoT devices can connect and communicate with each other through distributed ledgers. Smart Contracts use data from these devices to update and validate the transaction log and sequentially disseminate it to every node, active participants or devices in the blockchain network. This mechanism will eventually cut the requirement for human administration, monitoring, decisions and activities by promoting trust among devices.

A major weakness in existing access control systems is the centralized authorization server, that can possibly become a performance limitation or single point of failure. Moreover, scalability issues may arise as the number of IoT devices will increase in the network. Centralization also incurs high cost for maintenance. A summarized comparison of traditional and centralized systems with Blockchain technology is highlighted in Table 3 below.

Table 3. Comparison of traditional and blockchain-based solutions

Problems with traditional schemes	Blockchain-based **solutions**
- Centralized - Trusted Third Party (TTP) involvement - High Cost - Single point of failure - Easy hacking and privacy evasion	- Decentralized - No third party or intermediary - Distributed Ledger Technology (DLT) - Resiliency with smart contract and consensus mechanism of blockchain

3.3   Ethereum and Smart Contracts

Ethereum is a popular open source, Blockchain-based decentralized platform that run applications without any possibility of fraud, downtime or middleman interference [50]. It is a distributed public Blockchain network that unlike Bitcoin has different purpose and capability. Along with the electronic cash system, Ethereum is also a platform for decentralized applications (dApps), and execute programs known as Smart Contracts [51]. Furthermore, Ethereum enables development of different applications on one Blockchain platform. In Ethereum, Ethereum Virtual Machine (EVM) [52] is used to execute Smart Contracts by participating nodes. The block size in Ethereum is smaller than in Bitcoin. Additionally, time for validation of block or transaction in Ethereum takes only 14 s in comparison to 10 min in Bitcoin. However, 14 s processing time is still not acceptable for some IoT scenarios. Hence this can be further investigated to reduce the transaction processing and validation time to make it suitable for IoT.

A privacy-preserving authorization management framework has been proposed as FairAccess [49], by leveraging Blockchain technology. Novo [53] has also proposed a similar framework for scalable access management. The difference between Novo's approach [53] and FairAccess [49] is that in the later IoT devices are part of Blockchain network. Moreover, for every resource-requester pair, different Smart Contracts are created for the access control policy. The Capability-based Access Control (CapBAC) model can be implemented directly on IoT devices within a fully distributed approach but that is coarse-grained, not particularly user-driven and does not take context into consideration.

Correspondingly, another authentication and trust mechanism has been proposed by Hammi et al. [54]. It used Ethereum based public Blockchain, to create secure virtual zones allowing things to identify and trust each other. The approach is limited in aspect that there is no mechanism defined for communication of things belonging to different bubbles or zones, for example, different IoT domains. Moreover, a simple Smart Contract implementation has been done to define communication rules for objects belonging to particular group can only communicate within the group. However, the approach is flexible in the sense that it uses public Blockchain to add new nodes, which ensures scalability. In Hammi et. al's scheme [54], the involvement of cryptocurrency cost and 14 s transaction time hinders its adaptation to common users.

Most of the proposed solutions include a TTP as an authorization server to regulate access control logic. Whereas, in a bitcoin Blockchain system, whenever there is a transaction, user has to determine the proof of ownership for the money he wants to spend. Output of each transaction consists of a script that locks the money linked with the unspent transaction output (UTXO). A script is a component of every input and output of a transaction. A Smart Contract system is the generalization of scripting language computation to arbitrary Turing complete logic. In FairAccess [49], the integrity of the transaction is checked by hashing the transaction using SHA256 and comparing it with the index of current transaction to ensure that the transaction has not been changed while its dissemination in the network. However, FairAccess framework does not include the authentication as separate concern, rather it seems like a preliminary for the authorization and access control framework.

Likewise, Dorri et al. [55] considers the authorization problem in IoT network including cloud storage and Service Providers (SPs) for a smart home scenario with multiple IoT devices. It uses a private Blockchain including a policy header to store access control policies for controlling all incoming and outgoing access requests. This access control scheme is untrustworthy because it totally eliminates the consensus algorithm, resulting in waste of computing capability of Blockchain. However, the proof-of-work is skipped purposefully to make the solution lightweight and suitable for resource-constrained IoT devices. This notion of only storing access control policies has also been adopted by Di and Maesa [56]. Ramachandran and Kantarcioglu [57] have also adopted blockchain for managing data records and access control using smart contracts. Since, along with providing decentralized security, Blockchain solutions involve significant energy, delay, and computational overhead. To address the limitations and effective use of Blockchain, Zhang et al. [58] has recently proposed smart contracts based access control framework for IoT. The framework composed of multiple access control smart contracts for each pair of peers in the network. It means that when the size of the network increases, the number of smart contracts will also increase exponentially. However, the framework provides both the static as well as dynamic access rights validation. Although, there is no security consideration, but it demonstrates that smart contracts can achieve a distributed and trustworthy access control in IoT system.

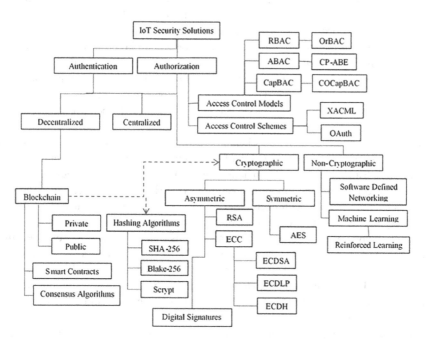

Fig. 1. Existing IoT security solutions for authentication and authorization

There have been a lot of consensus algorithms introduced according to the needs and requirements of the systems they are applied to. For example, after Proof-of-Work, Proof-of-Stake, Proof-of-Activity, Proof-of-Capacity, Proof-of-Importance and several others have been proposed with relevance to considered domains and applications. However, due to the computational cost, consensus algorithms have not been explored to be applied efficiently for IoT. A summary of existing IoT security solutions for authentication and authorization is depicted in Fig. 1.

4 Research Challenges and Opportunities

The underlying security issues related to IoT systems, devices and networks are very much likely to be increased with the rise in number and use of smart devices. IoT devices are not designed keeping security in mind. Moreover, traditional solutions are good enough for client/server models but are not easily adaptable according to the needs of IoT. Major challenges in IoT security solutions include centralization, single point of failure and trusted third-party involvement, privilege escalation and lack of security consideration.

Additionally, there is a need to provide scalable security solution for IoT since the prediction of billions of devices in coming years. The network and device size in IoT ecosystem is also an issue, since current security protocols and technologies have not been planned for billions of interconnected smart devices [20]. Furthermore, a number of budget and resource-constrained IoT devices have limited memory, computational and energy power [59]. For power concern, battery replacement in IoT devices, deployed at critical places like on top of a pole or human body, is very expensive or impossible. Similarly, IoT sensing devices are not capable enough, also in terms of memory, to perform heavy computational tasks of security solutions. Neither they have the margin of execution time to pass through time-consuming security check. Hence, the resources consumption optimization become critical for IoT operations as well as its security.

Currently, the idea of using Blockchain technology to enhance IoT security is in a preliminary stage. With the structure of Blockchain and its in-born features, it is evident that Blockchain has the potential to provide robust and efficient security solutions especially for the emerging paradigm of IoT. Using Blockchain, untrusted parties can safely interact with each other in a trustful manner. Elimination of trusted third party seems to make the transactions between parties faster and secure [60]. Moreover, heavy use of cryptography in consensus algorithms and self-executing scripts of smart contract are key characteristics of Blockchain networks and its security power. These features of Blockchain for distributed and automated workflows make its application in IoT domain enticing. However, the question lies in how computationally exhaustive Blockchain technology can be applied to resource constrained IoT devices, domains and networks.

Consensus algorithms and smart contracts are the crucial elements of Blockchain technology. Proof-of-Work (PoW) is the first consensus algorithm that has been basically introduced for robustness of Bitcoin cryptocurrency blockchain. However, it involves strong cryptography and computationally intensive tasks, that are not directly applicable to IoT. Similarly, smart contracts are automated and digitally signed contracts among communicating parties that can provide tamper-proof authorization and access control management. Along with storing and managing access control policies, smart contracts as part of distributed ledger as well as Blockchain, can be leveraged to enforce secure access control to IoT. For Blockchain technology adaptation and integration to provide IoT security solution, consensus algorithms and smart contracts needs further exploration.

5   Conclusion

With rapid increase in the number of IoT devices, the number of security threats, attacks, risks and concerns have also increased. Moreover, IoT devices and networks operate more closely to human and environment. This makes the consequences of security breaches and attacks more serious and devastating. Several solutions have been proposed to enhance IoT security with respect to different layers and perspectives of IoT systems and applications. The potential features of Blockchain represent that it is a true game changer technology in providing IoT security solutions. However, it is still uncertain that how its specialties can be adapted effectively for resource constrained IoT devices. For the properties of consensus algorithms, it needs to be explored that how it can be optimized for adaptation to secure authentication in IoT. There is current research on the use of smart contracts in IoT applications. However, the use of smart contracts to provide secure authorization in IoT needs further research. Hence, it can be concluded that IoT security concerns will keep on increasing with increase in number of IoT applications and devices. Traditional or centralized solutions are not enough to provide adequate authentication and authorization in IoT. On the other hand, promising features of Blockchain, such as, consensus algorithms and smart contracts, require further investigation to enhance IoT security.

References

1. Muzammal, S.M., Shah, M.A., Zhang, S.-J., Yang, H.-J.: Conceivable security risks and authentication techniques for smart devices: a comparative evaluation of security practices. Int. J. Autom. Comput. **13**, (2016). https://doi.org/10.1007/s11633-016-1011-5
2. Fernández-Caramés, T.M., Fraga-Lamas, P., Fernandez-Carames, T.M., Fraga-Lamas, P.: A review on the use of blockchain for the internet of things. IEEE Access **6**, 32979–33001 (2018). https://doi.org/10.1109/ACCESS.2018.2842685
3. Fremantle, P., Aziz, B., Kirkham, T.: Enhancing IoT security and privacy with distributed ledgers - a position paper. In: Proceedings of 2nd International Conference on Internet Things, Big Data Security, pp. 344–349 (2017). https://doi.org/10.5220/0006353903440349
4. Muzammal, S.M., et al.: Counter measuring conceivable security threats on smart healthcare devices. IEEE Access (2018). https://doi.org/10.1109/access.2018.2826225
5. Lomotey, R.K.: Enhancing privacy in wearable IoT through a provenance architecture (2018). https://doi.org/10.3390/mti2020018

6. Muzammal, S.M., Shah, M.A.: ScreenStealer: addressing screenshot attacks on Android devices. In: 2016 22nd International Conference on Automation and Computing, ICAC 2016: Tackling the New Challenges in Automation and Computing (2016)

7. Gartner Says 6.4 Billion Connected "Things" Will Be in Use in 2016, Up 30 Percent From 2015. https://www.gartner.com/en/newsroom/press-releases/2017-02-07-gartner-says-8-billi on-connected-things-will-be-in-use-in-2017-up-31-percent-from-2016

8. Afshar, V.: Cisco: Enterprises Are Leading the Internet of Things Innovation. https://www. huffingtonpost.com/entry/cisco-enterprises-are-leading-the-internet-of-things_us_59a41fcee 4b0a62d0987b0c6

9. OWASP Internet of Things Project – OWASP. https://www.owasp.org/index.php/OWASP_ Internet_of_Things_Project

10. Panarello, A., Tapas, N., Merlino, G., Longo, F., Puliafito, A.: Blockchain and IoT integration: a systematic survey (2018)

11. IBM: IoT for Blockchain - IBM Watson IoT. https://www.ibm.com/internet-of-things/ trending/blockchain

12. Noor, M.B.M., Hassan, W.H.: Current research on Internet of Things (IoT) security: a survey. Comput. Netw. (2018). https://doi.org/10.1016/j.comnet.2018.11.025

13. Trnka, M., Cerny, T., Stickney, N.: Survey of authentication and authorization for the internet of things. Secur. Commun. Netw. **2018** (2018). https://doi.org/10.1155/2018/ 4351603

14. Jesus, E.F., Chicarino, V.R.L., De Albuquerque, C.V.N., Rocha, A.A.D.A.: A survey of how to use blockchain to secure internet of things and the stalker attack. Secur. Commun. Netw. **2018** (2018). https://doi.org/10.1155/2018/9675050

15. Hilton, S.: Dyn Analysis Summary of Friday October 21 Attack—Dyn Blog (2016). https:// dyn.com/blog/dyn-analysis-summary-of-friday-october-21-attack/

16. Ferrante, A.J.: Battening down for the rising tide of IoT risks. ISSA J. **15**, 20–24 (2017)

17. CISCO: Cisco's Talos Intelligence Group Blog: New VPNFilter malware targets at least 500K networking devices worldwide. https://blog.talosintelligence.com/2018/05/VPNFilter. html

18. Khandelwal, S.: Internet-Connected Teddy Bear Leaks Millions of Voice Messages and Password. https://thehackernews.com/2017/02/iot-teddy-bear.html

19. New IoT-malware grew three-fold in H1 2018—Kaspersky Lab. https://www.kaspersky. com/about/press-releases/2018_new-iot-malware-grew-three-fold-in-h1-2018

20. Restuccia, F., D'Oro, S., Melodia, T.: Securing the internet of things in the age of machine learning and software-defined networking. IEEE Internet Things J. **5**, 4829–4842 (2018). https://doi.org/10.1109/JIOT.2018.2846040

21. Electricity Information Sharing and Analysis Center(E-ISAC): Analysis of the Cyber Attack on the Ukrainian Power Grid Table of Contents (2016)

22. Greenberg, A.: Hackers Remotely Kill a Jeep on the Highway—With Me in It—WIRED. https://www.wired.com/2015/07/hackers-remotely-kill-jeep-highway/

23. Osborne, C.: Over a dozen vulnerabilities uncovered in BMW vehicles—ZDNet. https:// www.zdnet.com/article/over-a-dozen-vulnerabilities-uncovered-in-bmw-vehicles/

24. Kruse-brandao, J., Garcia, J.L., Edwards, M.: Baseline Security Recommendations for IoT (2017)

25. Krebs, B.: Study: Attack on KrebsOnSecurity Cost IoT Device Owners $323K—Krebs on Security. https://krebsonsecurity.com/2018/05/study-attack-on-krebsonsecurity-cost-iot-devi ce-owners-323k/

26. Grange, W.: Hajime worm battles Mirai for control of the Internet of Things. https://www. symantec.com/connect/blogs/hajime-worm-battles-mirai-control-internet-things

27. Tony, B., Meg, J., Reyes, E.A.: Malware attack disrupts delivery of L.A. Times and Tribune papers across the U.S. (2018). https://www.latimes.com/local/lanow/la-me-ln-times-delivery-disruption-20181229-story.html
28. Bilefsky, D.: Hackers Use New Tactic at Austrian Hotel: Locking the Doors. https://www.nytimes.com/2017/01/30/world/europe/hotel-austria-bitcoin-ransom.html
29. Goodin, D.: BrickerBot, the permanent denial-of-service botnet, is back with a vengeance—Ars Technica. https://arstechnica.com/information-technology/2017/04/brickerbot-the-perm anent-denial-of-service-botnet-is-back-with-a-vengeance/
30. Bundesnetzagentur - News - Bundesnetzagentur withdraws dummy "Cayla" from circulation (2017). https://www.bundesnetzagentur.de/SharedDocs/Pressemitteilungen/DE/2017/14012 017_cayla.html
31. D'Orazio, C.J., Choo, K.K.R., Yang, L.T.: Data exfiltration from internet of things devices: IOS devices as case studies. IEEE Internet Things J. **4**, 524–535 (2017). https://doi.org/10. 1109/JIOT.2016.2569094
32. Ouaddah, A., Mousannif, H., Abou Elkalam, A., Ait Ouahman, A.: Access control in the Internet of Things: big challenges and new opportunities. Comput. Netw. **112**, 237–262 (2017). https://doi.org/10.1016/j.comnet.2016.11.007
33. Sharma, A.: Blockchain for Authentication—Benefits, and Challenges. https://hackernoon. com/blockchain-for-authentication-benefits-and-challenges-94a93f034f40
34. Gope, P., Hwang, T.: BSN-Care: a secure IoT-based modern healthcare system using body sensor network. IEEE Sens. J. **16**, 1368–1376 (2016). https://doi.org/10.1109/JSEN.2015. 2502401
35. Chan, A.: Proactive security strategies to stave off growing cyber-attacks in IoT and credential abuse – CSO—The Resource for Data Security Executives. https://www.cso.com. au/article/648557/proactive-security-strategies-stave-off-growing-cyber-attacks-iot-credentia l-abuse/
36. Burgess, M.: Austrian hotel Romantik Seehotel Jaegerwirt was hit by a cyberattack—WIRED UK. https://www.wired.co.uk/article/austria-hotel-ransomware-true-doors-lock-hackers
37. Farash, M.S., Turkanović, M., Kumari, S., Hölbl, M.: An efficient user authentication and key agreement scheme for heterogeneous wireless sensor network tailored for the Internet of Things environment. Ad Hoc Netw. **36**, 152–176 (2016). https://doi.org/10.1016/J.ADHOC. 2015.05.014
38. Peris-Lopez, P., González-Manzano, L., Camara, C., de Fuentes, J.M.: Effect of attacker characterization in ECG-based continuous authentication mechanisms for Internet of Things. Future Gener. Comput. Syst. **81**, 67–77 (2018). https://doi.org/10.1016/j.future.2017.11.037
39. Li, F., Hong, J., Omala, A.A.: Efficient certificateless access control for industrial Internet of Things. Future Gener. Comput. Syst. **76**, 285–292 (2017). https://doi.org/10.1016/j.future. 2016.12.036
40. Kim, H., Lee, E.A.: Authentication and authorization for the internet of things. IT Prof. **19**, 27–33 (2017). https://doi.org/10.1039/b904090k
41. Ngu, A.H.H., Gutierrez, M., Metsis, V., Nepal, S., Sheng, M.Z.: IoT middleware: a survey on issues and enabling technologies. IEEE Internet Things J. (2016). https://doi.org/10.1109/ jiot.2016.2615180
42. Madsen, P.: Standardized Identity Protocols and the Internet of Things (2015)
43. Ourad, A.Z., Belgacem, B., Salah, K.: Using blockchain for IOT access control and authentication management. In: Georgakopoulos, D., Zhang, L.-J. (eds.) ICIOT 2018. LNCS, vol. 10972, pp. 150–164. Springer, Cham (2018). https://doi.org/10.1007/978-3-319-94370-1_11

44. Tao, M., Ota, K., Dong, M., Qian, Z.: AccessAuth: capacity-aware security access authentication in federated-IoT-enabled V2G networks. J. Parallel Distrib. Comput. **118**, 107–117 (2018). https://doi.org/10.1016/j.jpdc.2017.09.004

45. Vijayakumar, P., Chang, V., Jegatha Deborah, L., Balusamy, B., Shynu, P.G.: Computationally efficient privacy preserving anonymous mutual and batch authentication schemes for vehicular ad hoc networks. Future Gener. Comput. Syst. **78**, 943–955 (2018). https://doi.org/10.1016/j.future.2016.11.024

46. Sicari, S., Rizzardi, A., Grieco, L.A., Piro, G., Coen-Porisini, A.: A policy enforcement framework for Internet of Things applications in the smart health. Smart Health **3–4**, 39–74 (2017). https://doi.org/10.1016/J.SMHL.2017.06.001

47. Lee, S.-H., Huang, K.-W., Yang, C.-S.: TBAS: token-based authorization service architecture in Internet of things scenarios. Int. J. Distrib. Sens. Netw. **13** (2017). https://doi.org/10.1177/1550147717718496

48. Symantec Security Response: Latest Intelligence for September 2017—Symantec Connect Community. https://www.symantec.com/connect/blogs/latest-intelligence-june-2017

49. Ouaddah, A., Elkalam, A.A., Ouahman, A.A.: Towards a novel privacy-preserving access control model based on blockchain technology in IoT. In: Rocha, Á., Serrhini, M., Felgueiras, C. (eds.) Europe and MENA Cooperation Advances in Information and Communication Technologies. Advances in Intelligent Systems and Computing, vol. 520, pp. 523–533. Springer, Cham (2017). https://doi.org/10.1007/978-3-319-46568-5_53

50. Ethereum.org: Ethereum Project. https://www.ethereum.org/

51. Hammi, M.T., Bellot, P., Serhrouchni, A.: BCTrust: a decentralized authentication blockchain-based mechanism. In: IEEE Wireless Communications and Networking Conference WCNC, 1–6 April 2018 (2018). https://doi.org/10.1109/wcnc.2018.8376948

52. ethdocs: Ethereum Homestead Documentation—Ethereum Homestead 0.1 documentation. http://www.ethdocs.org/en/latest/index.html

53. Novo, O.: Blockchain meets IoT: an architecture for scalable access management in IoT. IEEE Internet Things J. **5**, 1184–1195 (2018). https://doi.org/10.1109/JIOT.2018.2812239

54. Hammi, M.T., Hammi, B., Bellot, P., Serhrouchni, A., Tahar Hammi, M.: Bubbles of trust: a decentralized blockchain-based authentication system for IoT. Comput. Secur. (2018). https://doi.org/10.1016/j.cose.2018.06.004

55. Dorri, A., Kanhere, S.S., Jurdak, R., Gauravaram, P.: Blockchain for IoT security and privacy: the case study of a smart home. In: 2017 IEEE International Conference on Pervasive Computing and Communications Workshops (PerCom Workshops), pp. 618–623 (2017). https://doi.org/10.1109/percomw.2017.7917634

56. Di, D., Maesa, F.: Blockchain based access control services. In: IEEE International Symposium on Recent Advances on Blockchain and Its Applications (BlockchainApp), 2018 IEEE International Conference on Blockchain (2018)

57. Ramachandran, A., Kantarcioglu, D.M.: Using Blockchain and smart contracts for secure data provenance management (2017)

58. Zhang, Y., Kasahara, S., Shen, Y., Jiang, X., Wan, J.: Smart contract-based access control for the internet of things, 1–11 (2018). https://doi.org/10.1109/jiot.2018.2847705

59. Singh, K.J., Kapoor, D.S.: Create your own internet of things: a survey of IoT platforms. IEEE Consum. Electron. Mag. **6**, 57–68 (2017). https://doi.org/10.1109/MCE.2016.2640718

60. Christidis, K., Devetsikiotis, M.: Blockchains and smart contracts for the internet of things. IEEE Access **4**, 2292–2303 (2016). https://doi.org/10.1109/ACCESS.2016.2566339

Patterns and Colors: A Simple yet Innovative Way to Solve Pattern Tracking

Abigail Achiamma Joshua, Samanza Kishwar Parvez, Weng Ken Lee, and Ee Xion Tan[✉]

Taylor's University, Subang Jaya, Malaysia
`Abigail.Joshua32@gmail.com`, `Samanza.Kp@gmail.com`, {`WengKen.Lee,EeXion.Tan`}`@taylors.edu.my`

Abstract. Authentication is one of the essential defense mechanisms to prevent unauthorized access to our personal gadgets. Several authentication schemes have been proposed over the years, such as passwords, PIN and biometrics. Although there are many types of authentication methods equipped in our devices, they still have their limitations. This study compares the different types of commonly used knowledge-based authentication systems and identifies the shortcomings of these authentication methods by thoroughly exploring their vulnerabilities. In this study, we propose an innovative idea that modifies the existing pattern-lock authentication method by using a combination of patterns, colors and randomization to authenticate users to their mobile device. This proposed method can prevent unauthorized users from shoulder-surfing and analyzing the static repeated patterns drawn by users on their mobile devices.

Keywords: Pattern lock · Authentication · Salt and Hash cryptography

1 Introduction

The security of authentication is on the rise with attackers finding ways to break into the databases of different organizations and the gadgets of individuals, such as the smartphone, laptop, tablet, and other such devices. Nowadays, with each user having one or more than one device, cyber-attacks on smartphone are becoming more frequent. The main reason is that these mobile devices store private information of their users such as name, email, session cookies, and financial information when users carry out online payment and transactions. Attackers target these devices to gain this user information for their benefits.

Today, mobile devices use authentication as a tool of protection against non-technological intruders. There are different types of authentication used in mobile devices. iOS gadgets such as iPhones and iPads use an advanced face recognition which adapts to the changes of the user's appearance [1]. Mobile device authentication also uses Personal Identification Number (PIN), passwords, patterns and fingerprint recognition. For example, PIN authenticates the user by typing in a series of numbers that is initially registered by the user. Password authentication methods are similar to PINs except that they require the use of alphanumeric and symbolic keyboard characters. Biometric authentication such as fingerprints, are recognized when the user

© Springer Nature Singapore Pte Ltd. 2020
M. Anbar et al. (Eds.): ACeS 2019, CCIS 1132, pp. 33–45, 2020.
https://doi.org/10.1007/978-981-15-2693-0_3

places their fingerprint onto the sensor, and it will authenticate based on the user's biometric profile. Pattern-based recognition, which is commonly used by Android users, is where users draw out a registered pattern to gain access to their devices.

However, despite having many different types of authentication methods in the devices, each of them has certain flaws. For example, PIN codes and patterns can be broken into or hacked with the use of snooping, sniffing and even with a simple technique such as shoulder surfing [2]. Therefore, this study proposes a colored-pattern authentication to improve authentication in the mobile devices to better the existing PIN, passwords and pattern recognition method. Section 2 of this article reviews the existing types of authentication methods in mobile devices and their vulnerabilities. Section 3 explains the details about the proposed Colored-Pattern authentication, and Sect. 4 highlight the proposed impacts of the suggested solution, and finally, Sect. 5 presents the conclusion and future work.

2 Existing Mobile Authentication Methods

This section compares the various methods of authentication that are commonly used in smartphones today. The two methods that will be discussed are knowledge-based authentication and biometric authentication. The knowledge-based authentication that this study focuses on are Personal Identification Number (PIN) and pattern lock. Interesting existing mobile biometric authentication methods such as fingerprint scanning and facial recognition will also be discussed.

2.1 Knowledge-Based Authentication

Knowledge-based authentication relies on a piece of information that has been set by the user. PIN and pattern lock are the two most commonly employed authentication method for smartphones in this digital age.

Personal Identification Number (PIN)
One of the most widespread methods of authentication is the PIN, a password that is usually composed of 4 to 16 digits [3, 4]. In this authentication method, the user must enter their PIN in the very sequence that they set it, in order to gain access to their device. The PIN method of authentication had been introduced in the 1960s and was largely used to ease public administration and the banking experience [5]. However, its relative simplicity in authentication made it ideal for various other media that required protection. It is very much common for smartphones to have this feature to prevent access to one's phone or even certain applications stored in the phone. PIN authentication in certain devices may even be alphanumeric (more accurately referred to as a 'passcode') and up to 6-digits instead of 4-digits.

Pattern Lock
Pattern lock is used more commonly in Android devices. The pattern lock has become more prevalent in recent years as another form of user authentication. This method usually includes a 3×3 grid of dots where the user sets the password by connecting the dots and creating a memorable formation [6]. However, certain requirements need

to be fulfilled in order to use this pattern lock method. For example, the pattern must at least connect four dots (and not greater than nine dots) to unlock the device. The limitation is that a user cannot use the same node more than once, and it does not allow jumps across unused nodes.

A survey conducted in [7] has shown that out of 31 participants, only 29 of them were able to enter the correct PIN 18 times out of 20. On the other hand, no more than 23 participants thought that they could enter the right pattern 18 times out of 20 [7].

A brief comparison of the two is described in Table 1 [7]. While both have their share of advantages, studies show that PIN is considered more reliable by most users.

Table 1. Comparison between PIN and pattern lock

Method	PIN	Pattern Lock
Technology used	Private numerical value	Formation of the pattern on a 3 × 3 grid of dots
Login success rate	88%	83%
Memorability	81%	56%

2.2   Biometric Authentication

Biometric authentication is reliant on the unique physiological attributes of the user. Examples of biometric authentication include fingerprint scanning and facial recognition. These are the most prevalent forms of biometric authentication in smartphones nowadays.

Fingerprint Scanning

Fingerprint authentication relies on the recognition of unique traits called 'minutiae' in an individual's fingerprint. There are certain phases in fingerprint verification. First, the image of the fingerprint is obtained. Then, the image is processed. The distinct characteristics of the fingerprint are located during the processes. A template is created and matched the fingerprint characteristics [8]. A fingerprint template is a file containing information about an individual's fingerprint. It is the template, not the image of the fingerprint, that is stored in the fingerprint scanning system. According to Asha and Chellappan [8], the advantage of storing the template is that the template size is smaller than the image, which results in faster processing time. In other words, during the authentication process, the user's fingerprint will be compared to those stored in the database. When there is a match, the user will be granted access to the device.

Fingerprint scanning authentication has certain advantages. It's quite easy and straightforward to use. Fingerprints are unique to each person and the arrangement remains permanent during one's lifetime given that no distinct scarring or injury occurs in the area [9]. Hence, fingerprint scanners are now widely available in all sorts of smartphones, not just those that are top-tier.

There are three latest fingerprint scanners (e.g. optical scanners, capacitive scanners, and ultrasonic scanners) available in the market for portal devices which includes tablets and smartphones [10]. Optical scanners capture an optical image and use certain algorithms to find specific patterns of the fingertips by studying the lightest and darkest parts of the image. The higher the resolution of the sensor, the better it can analyze the characteristics of the fingerprints. However, optical scanners are not very secure as they may be fooled by prosthetics or images of very good quality. The use of optical scanners for smartphone authentication is now slowly decreasing [10].

Capacitive scanners are commonly used in most smartphones nowadays [10]. This type of scanners use tiny capacitor circuits to collect information from a specific fingerprint. The capacitors store electrical charges and once connected to conductive plates on the scanner's surface, they can trace the features of a person's fingerprints.

The Ultrasonic scanner is the latest technology in fingerprint scanning in the market [10]. It uses ultrasonic transmitter and a receiver to track the details of a fingerprint. When the fingertip is placed on the surface of the scanner, an ultrasonic pulse is transmitted against it. Some of it is absorbed and some rebound back to the sensor depending on certain details of the fingerprint. A sensor calculates the force of the returning pulses at different points on the scanner. The longer the scanning process, the better the data collection, and the fingerprint may be stored as a 3D model. This would make it an even more secure form of authentication than the capacitive scanner. However, it has certain shortcomings, e.g. it may not work well with all screen protectors for the devices. Thus, it is still not very widely used.

Facial Recognition

Facial recognition authentication, as the name suggests, uses cameras to analyze the characteristics of a person's face in order to recognize a user. This method of authentication has two major phases, detection and isolation. In the first phase, a human face is detected in an image. In the second phase, that face is isolated from other elements in the image so that it may be compared to those faces that are stored in the system's database. If the recognition is successful, the user may gain access to their device. Facial recognition uses techniques such as facial geometry, skin pattern recognition, smile, and facial thermogram. There are many advantages to this kind of user authentication. It is simple to implement as most phones possess the required cameras. It is also quite straightforward as user need only be still in front of their camera for a few seconds.

Fingerprint and facial recognition biometric authentication methods are distinct in terms of ease of use, error incidence, accuracy and user acceptance. Asha and Chellappan [8] have compared these two biometrics authentication methods and found that fingerprint scanning is very easy to use compared to facial recognition. However, there a few drawbacks highlighted by the researchers. For example, dry fingertips, dirt and ageing may cause errors in fingerprint scanning. Facial recognition may encounter errors when there are lighting concerns, or subtle changes in the user's appearance which may cause the system to be unable to recognize the user (e.g. when they are wearing glasses or due to ageing). Despite all this, accuracy and user acceptance results are promising for both biometric authentication methods.

Both types of authentication have their share of advantages and disadvantages, it is up to users to determine their personal preference. Knowledge based authentication is usually offered as a backup if biometric authentication should fail to recognize users.

2.3 Security Challenges and Vulnerabilities Faced by Existing Mobile Authentication Methods

Mobile authentication methods were developed to curb and mitigate threats and security challenges. Although unique, they themselves face several threats and vulnerabilities.

In recent times, authentication plays a significant role in the lives of most people. Moving towards a digitalized society, people are becoming heavily reliant on electronic devices. It is not rare for individuals to own more than one, or rather more than one type of devices. From smartphones to tablets to personal computers, people may now find themselves in possession of a great number of electronics. As convenient as they are, personal gadgets may also prove to be a double-edged sword. A point after people find themselves relying on devices; they may find that they are becoming rather dependent on them.

As people begin to stockpile more of their lives onto them, each valuable and precious article stored further increase the importance of the devices themselves. For example, users store their memories in the form of pictures or writing with loved ones, personal images, important conversation matter, or even applications linking to bank accounts – all such crucial content can be found in today people's smartphones and laptops. With the ever-increasing wealth stored, it becomes ever more important to ensure that these devices are secure. Hence, it must be ensured that the devices are accessible only by the users, and perhaps, a few trusted people. That is where authentication, such as knowledge-based and biometrics authentications (as discussed in Sects. 2.1 and 2.2) is needed.

Vulnerabilities of Knowledge-Based Authentication

Authentication for gadgets can be of various kinds. However, as people gear up and take steps to protect their devices, attackers also take steps to bypass their security. While using authentication methods like PIN and patterns are better than not using any at all, it may still be countered by persistent attackers.

A user's password consists of any order of characters – be it letters, numbers, or symbols, that must be entered when requested, to gain access to a private system resource. However, characters while plenty, are still of a finite amount. Also, users generally tend to choose simple passwords that they would be able to remember. Such passwords may fall victim to Dictionary attacks. Attackers use password dictionaries (e.g. word lists) which contain a collection of familiar words and variations of those words that may be the user's actual password. The sheer number and variety of characters is not enough to fend off such attacks especially for simple passwords.

Certain attackers may attain a user's password simply by watching the user tap it in. This trick is termed as shoulder surfing and is a simple and basic way to get someone's passcode. It is effective on all graphical schemes, not just text-based passwords [11]. Hence, neither PIN or password, nor pattern lock will be immune to this kind of attack.

Relatively smaller passwords may fall prey to Brute Force attacks. Text-based passwords are said to have limited password space [11]. Attackers will try every possible combination available for the password until they can reach the correct one.

The attacker might have difficulty to carry out such a scheme for longer passwords, but it is much easier and possible for a relatively shorter password.

Pattern locks have certain vulnerabilities as well. Oil residues or smudges are a side effect of touchscreen devices [12]. Attackers can trace the pattern from oil residues on the touch screen from the user's fingertips. Besides tracing the oil residues on the touch screen device, pattern lock method is also vulnerable to video-attack. In [13], a simulation of a video-attack was conducted on Android devices. The filming could be done as far as two meters away from the victim, which may help the attacker to remain unnoticed. Once the attacker takes hold of the device, they may trace and track the user's fingertip locations with the captured video. The tracked locations are then transformed from the camera's angle to that of the users. After that, the attacker's software defines the tracked movement direction to several possible patterns. Those patterns are narrowed down after certain calculations. The last and final step is for the attacker to try the patterns on the victim's device. This kind of attack will most likely be successful if: (i) the attacker has information regarding the device's pattern grid, (ii) the video is of tolerable quality so that victim's finger movement can be tracked, and (iii) the attacker is able to properly analyze the video where the authentication process takes place. Ye et al. [13] have shown that the success rate is 95% with not more than five attempts. Hence, pattern lock can be deemed unsafe and quite vulnerable.

It is also possible for attackers to determine the graphical pattern lock of the user's device with a certain system called 'WiPass'. Most smart devices contain numerous sensors and functions that boost sensing capabilities. These may rather aid in leakage of user privacy as it is possible to recognize user passwords. WiPass is able to determine the passwords or patterns "through the impacts of finder motions on wireless signals even in Nonline of Sight scenarios" [14]. There a chance for attacker to exploit the smart device using WiPass.

Quite similar to the issue of smudge attacks, attackers have also employed the use of thermal cameras in order to regenerate a user's password. When the user unlocks their smartphone by sliding their fingers across the touchscreen, heat traces are left on the device from their bare fingers. The thermal camera can pick up these traces and thereby recreate the pattern for attackers to see. As thermal cameras become more accessible and affordable, the dangers of thermal attacks increase. The thermal camera could also be integrated to an attacker's smartphone. In [15], a simulation of thermal-attack is conducted and the results are analyzed. The attacker will wait for a chance to find a victim's device unattended soon after the victim has unlocked his/her device. While the concept is similar to smudge attacks, it should be noted that unlike smudge attacks, the order of entry of the code can be leaked as well. Also, unlike with smudge attacks, thermal attacks do not require an ideal angle for seeing the heat traces. The light conditions of the environment do not affect the attack as well. Thermal attacks take place after authentication which makes it less evident to victims. It was also noted that the difference in temperature between the hand and the device's screen had an impact on the success of the attack. Passcodes containing overlaps are also key to increasing resistance against these types of attacks. Abdelrahman et al. [15] have reported that

100% of the conducted experiments were successful for passcodes without overlaps. However, if the passcode has one overlap then the success rates decreased significantly. The main reason is that the overlaps affect the direction detection and order of the patterns.

Vulnerabilities of Biometric Authentication

Biometric locks cannot be bypassed by shoulder surfers and the like. However, that does not make it without faults. There are several issues surrounding the use of biometrics as well. The problems mention in [16] associated with biometrics are identified as follows:

- Some users may find the use of biometrics to be quite intrusive. They may not want to share their biometric data with the developers.
- Biometric recognition is expensive to implement.
- Failure of biometric recognition may be blamed on the technology of the device, rather than users. If a user forgets their password it is without a doubt their fault. However, should the device fail to recognize the user's face or iris or voice, it may be blamed on faulty technology or poor development.
- Biometric recognition may have false readings; false positive or false negatives. In other words, the device might accept readings when it should not be accepted and vice versa.
- Forgeries are still possible even in the case of biometric data (e.g. Mat02).
- The accuracy of biometric recognition is weakened by the required speed for authentication. Users may complain if the authentication process takes too long, so it is made as fast as possible, resulting in decreased efficiency.

3 Password Management: A Survey

Before we proposed an authentication method on the smartphone, a preliminary survey was conducted online on 155 participants in a higher learning institution, to understand how an individual manages their online platforms, as well as their devices' password setup in general. The survey focuses on three password management areas: (1) password selection processes, (2) processes of remembering or recalling a password, and (3) how an individual is securing their password.

First part of the questions pertain to the password selection processes. They are related to the ways an individual uses combination of different characters such as alphanumeric or symbols or special characters to form a password for login purposes, and the use of personal information such as interests, part of the birth date and pet names. Importance of the factors to consider when selecting a new password were also captured. The results have shown that 79.35% of the participants selected a password with different character combinations and 60.65% include their personal information in the password selection process. Participants are keen to create a password that is 'short' and 'easy to remember' (with 52.90%) followed by the password strength 30.97% and 'fun' or 'interesting' stand a 16.13%.

The second part of the survey pertains to the process of remembering or recalling their password, either by memorizing the password, writing it down in a notepad/diary or saving it into a portable device such as their smartphone. As predicted, the majority remember their password via memory (67.10%). A notable percentage (13.55%) has been reported to write their passwords on a notepad or diary, and 17.42% saved their passwords on their smart devices. About three participants (1.94%) reported they have their own way of remembering the passwords. The question of "Do you use the 'remember me' feature on websites to save your passwords?" had arisen and the majority disclosed that they indeed agreed to use the feature (59.35%).

The final part of the survey relates to how an individual is securing their password. Interestingly, 45.16% of the participants create and alternate their password between their online accounts. Among the 155 participants, 35.48% have same password across different platforms (either online or offline). The minority have reported that they have a few duplicated passwords, but most are unique. Only 7.10% (which is eleven participants) clearly mentioned that they have different passwords for each account they own.

4   Colored-Pattern Authentication with Cryptography – Salt and Hash Method

A study was conducted to show that, the input speed and error rates of the PIN is better than that of the pattern lock. Nevertheless, users tend to favor pattern lock more than PIN due to its ease of use [17]. However, according to Sect. 2.3, most of the vulnerabilities of Android pattern locks are related to the analysis of the patterns drawn. Whether it is gathering information through reconnaissance and predictions [13], or determining the password using thermal sensors [15], both techniques require the analysis of the repeated, everyday pattern the user inputs each time they login to their devices.

In this paper, we have proposed a colored-pattern authentication which uses the Salt and Hash cryptography method. We believe the proposed authentication may effortlessly reduce the vulnerabilities, and improve the traditional Android PIN and Pattern design to unlock smartphones. The proposed solution designed involves the use of colors, patterns, and randomization methods.

As shown in Fig. 1, the proposed pattern-lock authentication consists of nine colored nodes forming a 3 × 3 grid, and three icons situated below them in parallel. The chosen colors for the nodes are green, navy blue, red, yellow, pink, purple, brown, orange, and sky blue. The colors were chosen in hues that are distinct and easy to differentiate. Even after the order is randomized, it should be easier for the elderly, or other people with eyesight problems to discern between them. The colors are vibrant and striking and it is hoped that they could leave a lasting impression on the user.

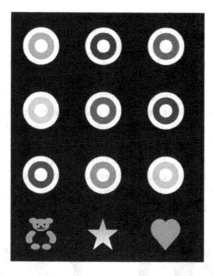

Fig. 1. Pattern-colored authentication (Color figure online)

Additionally, to further secure the proposed colored-pattern authentication, cryptographic Salt and Hash is included. The user login pattern will be encrypted before it is stored, so that man-in-the-middle attacks may be prevented.

The colored-pattern authentication in this study is defined in three steps: First, to set the colored-pattern authentication, the user needs to select a minimum of four colored nodes and one icon in a pattern of their choice. The selection sequence of the pattern is important and must be the same when unlocking the smartphone. For example, the user sets their pattern combination to 'Star - Red - Green - Yellow - Pink'. During the next login attempt, the same sequence and combination must be entered in the same order. Then, the randomization algorithm is used to shuffle the nine colored nodes, as well as the icons. This is to prevent shoulder surfing. Randomization will take place when the user has unlocked the pattern during their first login attempt. The colored nodes will automatically shuffle into a new arrangement for the second login attempt and so on. The random colored nodes are arranged differently within the same 3×3 grids pane, while the three icons will be shuffled in a 3×1 row, as shown in Fig. 2.

Finally, Salt and Hash cryptography takes place in order to secure the colored-pattern authentication. Salting the pattern includes appending a secure random generated string to a string-based password. This is to ensure the passwords are difficult to break, and to maintain the integrity of the data [18]. When the user selects a colored node, a method is triggered to generate a fixed string for each node and icon. For example, the star icon will generate the string "Sta", and the navy-blue node will generate the string "Nav". For example, if the user sets their pattern combination to 'Star - Red - Green - Yellow - Pink', the patterned string will be set to "StaRedGreYelPin". This string will then be concatenated with a salt value, which will be produced "StaRedGreYelPin + salt value" as the new string to represent the pattern. The salt value is randomly produced using the SecureRandom class which supports

SHA1 pseudo random number generator algorithm [18]. The encrypted string will then be stored in the database to be retrieved and to authenticate the user to access the device.

Another feature this study has included in the proposed solution is that the user will receive a number of attempts (e.g. with five tries each) to enter the correct code. If the pattern is drawn wrongly the first five times, the phone will be inaccessible for a minute. This is a grace period for the user in case they unintentionally drew the wrong pattern. For the second attempt, the user will receive another five tries to unlock the device. If the user fails to draw the correct pattern again, they will have to wait for five minutes before the next attempt. Failing the third attempt will cause the user to wait for ten minutes before they can try again. The period of inaccessibility will then double for each failed attempt, e.g. fourth, fifth and sixth attempts will cause the device to be inaccessible for 20, 40 and 80 min respectively.

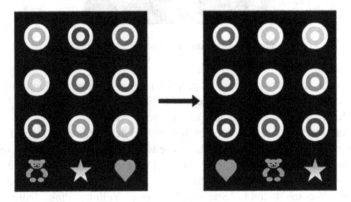

Fig. 2. Pattern changes color after login in the second time (Color figure online)

5 Impacts of the Solution

The Android colored-pattern authentication method has a number of 389,112 possibilities of creating a pattern. Similar to [19, 20]. However, this study includes the random positioning of the colored nodes and icons each time the user attempts to login (shown in Fig. 2). Randomizing the position of the colored nodes consists of $2.18 * 10^6$ possibilities of combinations while the icons can be arranged in six different possibilities. These possibilities can ensure that the attacker is not able to brute force the password. It also assures that attackers are not able to copy and analyze the pattern drawn as shown by Ye et al. [13]. Users have a choice to register almost $2.96 * 10^6$ combinations of patterns as their password from a minimum of five nodes per pattern. If a shoulder surfing or brute force attack were to happen, the attacker would probably need to go through a maximum of $4.42 * 10^{11}$ possibilities of patterns to break the pattern of the users. Table 2 shows the maximum number of possibilities for the attackers to commit a traditional brute force attack by only knowing the numbers of nodes the user has registered.

Table 2. Number of possibilities to brute force patterns

Number of nodes registered to user	Max. number of possibilities to break the pattern
5	217,728
6	5,443,200
7	130,636,800
8	2,743,372,800
9	43,893,964,800
10	395,045,683,200

Despite the advantages, this proposed authentication method is not suitable for users who are diagnosed with severe color blindness. Alternative authentication methods should be included for colorblind users, such as the classic PIN code and biometric scanners. To ensure that the user remembers their color pattern in a random format, authentication process might be longer than classic PIN code as it the colors changed position each time the user logs in. This authentication process is only suitable for device authentication that require a regular accessibility such as smart devices and applications that are used almost every day by users. This is because the user needs to authenticate themselves every time they login or unlock the devices. Other than that, there is a chance of a high error rate, where users may input the wrong pattern by accident. This will cause users to input the pattern more than once, and perhaps even trigger the inaccessibility countdown to input the password again if the user has forgotten the patterns.

6 Conclusion

The usage and demand of mobile devices have increased in the past few years, and cyber-attacks on these devices have sadly become quite commonplace. This is mainly because many users have their private information (e.g. financial information, contact details, payment transactions, email account and personal details) stored in these devices, causing them to attract malicious people who wish to abuse such information. In addition, the statistical preliminary results have shown that people that are having more than one passwords might choose to have their passwords saved in their devices for reference. The 'Remember me' feature available in many Web 2.0 has gained its popularity and users use it to ease the process of remembering the passwords to login into websites. Same or duplicate passwords across different platforms are noted in the result.

Hence, strong authentication methods have become extremely crucial in safeguarding all such sensitive data. Researchers have explored many different authentication methods to mitigate the chances of attacks, whether it should occur against large companies or individual users alike. Unlike the classic PIN and pattern authentication methods, this study proposes a colored-pattern authentication (i.e. combination of a minimum of four-color nodes and one icon as the login pattern) which can prevent attackers from tracking and analyzing static patterns via shoulder surfing. This study also includes Salt and Hash cryptography to secure the colored-pattern in the mobile device. With this cryptography in place, it will ensure the passwords are difficult to break, and to maintain the data integrity and protect the user from authorized access.

Future studies may test the usefulness of this colored-pattern authentication with advanced experimentation such as ease of use and vulnerability test of the authentication method. If proven to be an acceptable method of authentication and with increasing popularity, customizable features may be introduced so that users can select between color schemes and icons. It is also hoped that certain color schemes may be introduced in colorblind-friendly palettes.

Acknowledgment. This project has received funding from the Taylor's University under the Taylor's Internal Research Grant Scheme - Emerging Research Funding Scheme agreement no. TRGS/ERFS/1/2018/SOCIT/008.

References

1. About Face ID Advanced Technology. https://support.apple.com/en-my/HT208108. Accessed 01 May 2019
2. Aloul, F., Zahidi, S., El-Hajj, W.: Two factor authentication using mobile phones. In: IEEE/ACS International Conference on Computer Systems and Applications, pp. 641–644. IEEE (2009)
3. Soni, P., Sahoo, M.: Multi-factor authentication security framework in cloud computing. Int. J. Adv. Res Comput. Sci. Softw. Eng. **5**, 1065–1071 (2015)
4. Srilekha, R., Jayakumar, D.: A secure screen lock system for android smart phones using accelerometer sensor. Int. J. Sci. Technol. Eng. **1**(10), 96–100 (2015)
5. Years with Personal Identification Number in Norway. https://www.ssb.no/en/omssb/samarbeid/internasjonalt-utviklingssamarbeid/personal-identification-numbers-50-years-old-and-ripe-for-upgrading. Accessed 01 May 2019
6. Adarsh, S.: Implementation of color based Android shuffling pattern lock. Int. J. Comput. Sci. and Mob Comput. **5**, 357–362 (2016)
7. Anwar, M., Imran, A.: A comparative study of graphical and alphanumeric passwords for mobile device authentication. In: Modern AI and Cognitive Science Conference, pp. 13–18 (2015)
8. Asha, S., Chellappan, C.: Biometrics: an overview of the technology, issues and applications. Int. J. Comput. Appl. **39**, 35–52 (2012)
9. What is a Fingerprint Template? Webopedia Definition. https://www.webopedia.com/TERM/F/fingerprint_template.html. Accessed 01 May 2019
10. How Fingerprint Scanners Work: Optical, Capacitive, and Ultrasonic Variants Explained. https://www.androidauthority.com/how-fingerprint-scanners-work-670934/. Accessed 02 May 2019
11. Padma, B., Kumar, G.R.: A review on Android authentication system vulnerabilities. Int. J. Mod. Trends Eng. Res. **3**, 118–123 (2016)
12. Aviv, A.J., Gibson, K.L., Mossop, E., Blaze, M., Smith, J.M.: Smudge attacks on smartphone touch screens. In: USENIX 4th Workshop on Offensive Technology, pp. 1–7 (2010)
13. Ye, G., et al.: Cracking Android pattern lock in five attempts. In: Proceeding of ISOC NDSS (2017)

14. Zhang, J., et al.: Privacy leakage in mobile sensing: your unlock passwords can be leaked through wireless hotspot functionality. J. Mob. Inf. Sys. **2016**, 1–14 (2016)
15. Abdelrahman, Y., Khamis, M., Schneegass, S., Alt, F.: Stay cool! Understanding thermal attacks on mobile-based user authentication. In: CHI Conference on Human Factors in Computing Systems, pp. 3751–3763. ACM (2017)
16. Pfleeger, C.P., Pfleeger, S.L., Margulies, J.: Security in Computing. Prentice Hall Professional Technical Reference, 5th edn. Prentice Hall, Upper Saddle River (2006)
17. Von Zezschwitz, E., Dunphy, P., De Luca, A.: Patterns in the wild: a field study of the usability of pattern and pin-based authentication on mobile devices. In: Proceedings of the 15th International Conference on Human-Computer Interaction with Mobile Devices and Services, pp. 261–270. ACM (2013)
18. Mayoral, F.: Instant Java Password and Authentication Security. Packt Publishing Ltd., Birmingham (2013)
19. How Many Combinations of Locking Pattern are Possible for a Samsung 3 * 3 Locking Grid. https://www.quora.com/How-many-combinations-of-locking-pattern-are-possible-for-a-Samsung-3*3-locking-grid. Accessed 02 May 2019
20. Andriotis, P., Tryfonas, T., Oikonomou, G., Yildiz, C.: A pilot study on the security of pattern screen-lock methods and soft side channel attacks. In: Proceedings of the 6th ACM Conference on Security and Privacy in Wireless and Mobile Networks, pp. 1–6. ACM (2013)

Blockchain-Based Image Sharing Application

Zhen-Kai Wong and Swee-Huay Heng$^{(\boxtimes)}$ (iD)

Faculty of Information Science and Technology, Multimedia University,
Melaka, Malaysia
zk.wong96@gmail.com, shheng@mmu.edu.my

Abstract. The major drawback of a centralised system is using a shared database among the network users. If a server failed to operate, then the whole system will be affected. Leakage of sensitive data such as name of user, home address and contact number is a big issue faced by most networking sites. In this research, a blockchain-based image sharing web application will be developed which makes the process of exchanging image more secure and reliable. Upon launching the application, users are strongly encouraged to publish their original image. Users can view all the published images on news feed. Besides, users are allowed to update their profile by changing the avatar and description of user profile. Since all images are stored by using InterPlanetary File System (IPFS), hence a little capacity is needed to save the related Uniform Resource Locator (URL) for retrieval purpose.

Keywords: Blockchain · Image sharing · Interplanetary File System · Ethereum

1 Introduction

1.1 Background

Are you curious about how the leading social media platforms such as Facebook and YouTube earn profit from their services provided? The main revenue stream of both sites are in fact coming from the advertisements. According to an article of CNBC [3], Facebook and Google have been recorded to make $106 billion from advertising in 2017, almost half of the world's digital advertisements spent. However, how many percent of the total advertising revenue had been allocated to the content creators? The answer is not even half of the total profit. We are able to watch various types of videos on YouTube where most of these videos were published by the users worldwide. The respective users have their channel to upload and share video with others and different advertisements will appear on the embedded videos. This eventually forms a crucial part of YouTube but somehow these users are not rewarded well enough for their efforts as this third party platform tends to take some cuts of the profit made from sharing the content on their site.

Through the introduction of blockchain technology, this situation can be improved by building networks that are decentralised without the involvement of any third party. There is no control between the content owner and user which means they can interact directly with each other. In a decentralised application, specifically for content sharing

© Springer Nature Singapore Pte Ltd. 2020
M. Anbar et al. (Eds.): ACeS 2019, CCIS 1132, pp. 46–59, 2020.
https://doi.org/10.1007/978-981-15-2693-0_4

platform, content creators are highly encouraged to publish their creative and innovative ideas. For those who are interested after reading the description of the content, they are welcomed to pay in order to gain full access to the selected content. In order to make a successful transaction, users have to transfer a specific amount of token to the corresponding creator's address.

We also note that blockchain is a budding technology which may resolve dispute especially in fraud cases. For instance, in the event of industrial espionage that an employee stole the company sensitive data and transmit it through an instant messaging app, upon conducting initial investigation, the company declared the employee as main suspect. However, the employee tried to deny even though some evidence has been found that could lead him to be prosecuted. In fact, the employee can question about the accuracy and credibility of those evidences in court. By adopting blockchain technology, nobody can escape from the lawsuit as data is stored in block which cannot be modified. Moreover, transaction hash can be used to prove the identity of sender and receiver.

Nevertheless, there are some factors that influence the wide adoption and evolution of blockchain technology. Firstly, traditional social media companies have dominated the content sharing market currently. Some centralised sites such as YouTube and Facebook have large amount of existing users as compared to decentralised sites. The former is getting popular since the term Web 2.0 was invented by DiNucci in 2004 [4]. The latter became well-known after Bitcoin was initially released to the market in the early 2009. Secondly, there is lack of understanding on cryptocurrency. Most people mistaken cryptocurrency or Bitcoin as a medium to perform illegal transactions. Some people criticised cryptocurrency as an economic bubble as its price strongly exceeds its intrinsic value. Thus, Bitcoin is still not recognised or has restricted usage in some countries. Thirdly, there is improper usage of cryptocurrency by some people who has misused the convenience brought by cryptocurrency. For instance, the WannaCry ransomware attack [16] encrypted data of the targeted computers and Bitcoin was used as ransom payment in order to decrypt and recover the data of the affected computers.

1.2 Motivation

There are several data breaches occurred in the past few years. For instance, Uber has confirmed existence of a hack that affected 57 million customers and drivers worldwide as reported by Techworld in 2018 [12]. Personal details of customer such as name, email address and mobile phone number were exposed and drivers had their name and licence details compromised. In order to prevent data breach, a centralised database should be avoided as much as possible. Blockchain network treats every node as a shared database and nobody can have extreme power to control the network or attempt to compromise the database. Have you ever read the whole terms and conditions before signing up an online account such as YouTube? By agreeing upon the terms and conditions, a video author grants permission to YouTube for embedding advertisement. There is also unfair profit distribution between the video sharing platform and the content owner. A decentralised application allows the creator to obtain revenue that is worth their effort by averting any intermediate cost or profit cut. In a centralised network, users can easily create a fake account within few minutes. For instance, a person with malicious intention may write some negative comments about another person in social networking sites, such as Facebook, Twitter and Instagram. The victims of social abuse will then feel depressed and may even commit suicide. A decentralised network helps to reduce the probability of occurrence of social abuse and unauthorised transaction. This is because activities performed in blockchain network are immutable, non-repudiable and transparent with the distributed ledger technology. Everything is recorded and everybody knows.

1.3 Our Contributions

We first review the state-of-the-art of blockchain technology, in particular, the advantages of decentralisation over centralisation in the existing content sharing platforms. We then proceed with the design and implementation of a blockchain-based image sharing application. This decentralisation application assures the benefits of all users and avoids the intermediate cost charged by the third party. In addition, the application provides an openness image sharing to let users express their thoughts and state of mind to other users. Users are allowed to update their user profile by changing avatar and self-description. This application will run on localhost and all data will be stored in InterPlanetary File System (IPFS) protocol. In a mobile platform, users have to sign in to the application through Coinbase Wallet. For a web platform, users can login to the application via MetaMask. By connecting to web3, there is a proof of identity from Ethereum public address. Users are allowed to browse the published images on news feed. In order to upload an image, users must have sufficient amount of Ether. Besides, Ganache will provide you with 10 accounts preloaded with 100 fake Ether. Ether acts as medium of exchange and runs the smart contract that has been deployed to process the transactions requested by users. Furthermore, users are allowed to delete images which they posted earlier. Improvement in terms of user experience can be done by allowing users to upload an avatar image and write description about themselves.

2 Review of Existing Content Sharing Platforms

2.1 Centralised Content Sharing Platform

(1) **YouTube** (https://www.youtube.com/)

YouTube was founded in 2005 and owned by Google. It is the largest search engine and the most prevalent video sites. Millions of videos have been uploaded and shared through the YouTube channels. It is available in nearly every country and in many different languages.

Some limitations of YouTube:

High Requirements for Entering YouTube Partner Programme
Your channel has to reach 4000 watch hours in the previous 12 months and 1000 subscribers in order to be enrolled into the particular programme. The monetisation feature will only be enabled when you successfully joined the programme [19].

Limitation on YouTube Monetised Markets
There are some countries where YouTube has launched a monetised site. However, a small number of countries including China is not allowed to earn money from the particular site [18].

Hidden Costs of YouTube's Controversial Revenue Split
YouTube will pay 55% of the total net revenues to the video owners as reported by The Daily Dot [13]. On the other hand, it means that the other 45% of the total net revenues will be absorbed by YouTube.

(2) **Facebook** (https://www.facebook.com/)

Facebook is a social networking site launched in 2003 as FaceMash. It was changed to Facebook in 2004. The founders are Mark Zuckerberg and his three college roommates and fellow Harvard University student Eduardo Saverin [17]. Facebook has offered many attractive features to retain their large volume of users such as creating post, playing games, buying or selling products in marketplace and holding a live video, etc. It is available in most countries except China and instead China offered Sina Weibo which was launched by Sina Corporation in 2009 [15].

Some limitations of Facebook:

Retaining Users' Deleted Videos
Basically we assume that a deleted video will be disappeared not only from our sight, it should also be removed from the database server. However, Facebook still keeps the videos after users deleted them from their account. Users are not being informed about the data retention.

Facebook is Misused to Spread Hate Speech
Facebook is a social media platform which provides freedom to users to express anything they would like to share. This is helpful for users to connect and build a closer relationship with friends and family if all users respect each other. This is not always the case unfortunately. For instance, more than 1000 anti-Rohingya posts featuring calls for their murder among other hate speeches were live on Facebook, according to Reuters [10].

2.2 Decentralised Content Sharing Platform

(1) **AC3** (https://ac3.io/)

AC3 is the leading blockchain powered digital content marketplace [1]. This decentralised application encourages user to purchase digital content and e-learning courses from the content creators and educators. Its main focus is raising the content creator's revenue while protecting their content. AC3 has its own digital wallet which allows user to discover, pay and consume content directly.

Some advantages of using the AC3 digital wallet and owned its coins [1]:

Have a Reliable Decentralised Payment System
Users may transfer the specific amount of money to a creator with corresponding AC3 address. In other words, a creator may also receive money from users by giving them a different AC3 address to easily keep track of the transaction.

Purchase Original Content from the Owner
Users can visit the content creators and purchase contents by making payment to the relevant AC3 address. All transactions are made in AC3 coins. Through implementation of AC3 blockchain, there is no intermediary and external fee needed.

Exchange AC3 Coins with Other Cryptocurrencies
AC3 coins are exchangeable with other cryptocurrencies such as Bitcoin.

(2) **Viuly** (https://viuly.com/)

Viuly is a decentralised video sharing platform that uses the blockchain technology to pay and reward video consumers and creators. They trade in VIU tokens. Besides, users are rewarded for watching free videos. This application is based on the Ethereum blockchain smart contract. All data from Viuly users is stored on the blockchain network. IPFS hash of each content is used for retrieval purpose.

Some distinctive features of this application:

Support and Donate to Content Creators
Viuly users may donate their VIU tokens to content creators that they like.

Be Rewarded for Watching Free Videos
Users will be rewarded with VIU tokens once they have watched free videos uploaded by other users.

Sell Access to Your Premium Content
Users can choose to have either a payable or free channel. In a payable channel, users can set the day, week, month and year price as subscription fee for accessing or watching videos from their channels.

(3) **Decent Go** (https://www.decentgo.com/)

Decent Go is a new blockchain-based content distribution platform launched by DECENT in 2017. This sharing platform was released in beta version to collect feedback from users for further development. As estimated by DECENT, writers lose over 30-75% of their profits when publishing with Amazon. Similarly, a musician loses around 30% when they sell a track on iTunes. Matej Michalko, the founder and CEO at DECENT explicitly said that majority of the power is concentrated in the hands of a few players controlling the industry. Current industry giant for video sharing platform is YouTube which has a total number of 30 million daily active users around the world. DECENT has promised that the content distribution platform will also provide content producers more freedom and control over ownership and distribution. Authors can upload their own content, assign into a category, write description of the content, choose its lifetime duration, set its price and IP rights themselves. The fees gained from other user accounts will be transferred fairly and instantly to the content owner's account immediately upon successful transactions.. Every transaction from this particular platform will trade in an electronic form of money, the so called Digital Content Token (DCT) which will be stored in user wallet.

2.3 Comparison Between Specified Centralised and Decentralised Platforms

(1) Business-Focused Social Networking Sites: *LinkedIn vs. Indorse*

(a) Accessibility

There are some different plans offered by LinkedIn in order to have unique features when using the site. For example, a job seeker may choose the career plan to obtain some features such as direct messaging to recruiters, to be able to know who viewed the profile, getting instant access to salary insights, etc. These functionalities will cost you a specific amount of money before getting to secure a job from LinkedIn. Normal or free account will not bring these benefits to you.

There is no additional plan available on Indorse. Every user will have the same accessibility level while using the social networking site. At Indorse, similar outcome could be gained or achieved just like in LinkedIn, without spending a penny.

(b) Privacy Issues

Most people would agree that the top drawbacks to centralised social media are the loss of personal privacy [20], data protection and ownership of information. If we want to apply for a job position through LinkedIn, then we need to fill up the relevant information and submit our curriculum vitae to the potential employers. However, who can assure that the information submitted will be received at employer's hands in a safe condition and it is not being misused by the employer. Selling of user data is one way to make money by the traditional social media companies.

By introducing Indorse, a reward-based decentralised professional network on Ethereum blockchain, the privacy issues faced by most Internet users could be resolved. This is because members can handle their own information. At the same time, they also can earn money from sharing their professional skills to other members.

(2) Music Sharing Platforms: *Spotify vs. VOISE*

(a) Percentage of Revenue Gained

According to ArtistCore [19], music artists will gain $0.00014213 per stream for music with supported advertisement. Meanwhile they receive $0.00066481 per stream from Spotify when a premium account user is listening to their music. There is high percentage of profit cut that was taken by Spotify and it is not beneficial to music owner.

Artists can earn nearly 100% of revenue on VOISE. Furthermore, the successful payment will be transferred instantly into the music owner's account without any intermediaries or fees. Hence, the music artists will be rewarded fairly for their efforts to create a song.

(b) Additional Features for Different Account Level

A user has to make extra payment to upgrade from basic account to a premium account on Spotify. Examples of additional features are allowed to download music, listening music without ads, play any song you liked and skip the current song by just hitting next button.

On VOISE, everyone will have the same app features. Listen to a music, users have to pay for it by using VOISE tokens. These tokens, built around Ethereum smart contract technology is safe to use within the users and it can be exchanged to another cryptocurrencies.

2.4 Differences Between Centralised and Decentralised Network

(1) **Centralised Network:**

- A central database is used and shared among the network users.
- If one site or server fails, then the entire network will stop running.
- Loss of control over data.
- Misuse of personal data took by third party.

(2) **Decentralised Network:**

- No data storage, all the nodes contain information.
- The system will keep running although some of the sites have failed.
- Retention of data ownership.
- Data misuse can be avoided because all pieces of data are stored separately in different nodes.

3 Proposed Image Sharing Application

An image sharing application is developed in Ethereum blockchain which allows users to publish their images and other users can view it on their news feed. In order to launch a decentralised application in blockchain network, the owner must choose a network such as Ethereum blockchain network with smart contract that is written in Solidity [11].

3.1 Why Use Ethereum Rather Than Bitcoin [2]

Smart contract is widely used in decentralised blockchain network because it allows trusted transactions and agreements to be carried out among distinct, anonymous parties without the need for a central authority. Ethereum has the biggest capitalisation among the smart contract networks due to its ledger technology. There exist two factors on why Bitcoin should not be used in writing a programme. First, Bitcoin does not support loop functions while Ethereum does support loop functions. If a programme needs to be run as much as hundred times, then the programmer may need to create a loop, set condition and a counter. Loop enables a lot of application features such as the number of attempts when someone keeps entering wrong password and the number of withdrawal requests for each user in an online banking system. Bitcoin has another limitation on its complicated calculation while Ethereum basically resolves the calculation problem for every transaction. Algorithms used by Ethereum network are quite similar to how we transfer money to other bank account through Internet banking. In order to execute an application feature which is already deployed on blockchain network, the user has to pay a small amount of Ether. The charges vary according to the file size. Ether is used within the Ethereum blockchain to pay for the execution of contracts on the Ethereum Virtual Machine (EVM).

3.2 Why Use React Instead of HTML and CSS

According to freeCodeCamp [5], there are a few reasons why React has become so popular. The main reason why we adopt React instead of HTML and CSS is that Apps built in React are more secure than those built in HTML and CSS. In React, HTML and CSS programming code can be included in the render() properties. The source code in React is complicated while the source code of HTML and CSS is human-readable. React is a new open-source JavaScript library to build front-end application which was initially released in 2013. Furthermore, React has been nominated as the top JavaScript trends to look for in 2019 as reported by Hackernoon [7].

3.3 Functional Design

(1) **Use Case Diagramme**

The functions that users can perform on this DApp are as follows: connect to web3, browse published image, publish and delete image, change avatar image, update description. In order to authenticate a user, web3 is used to establish a connection between MetaMask and the application. Once connection is successful, users may browse all the published images on news feed. Another feature such as delete posted image is also provided by the DApp. Moreover, users can view and update their profile, description and avatar image can be changed anytime.

(2) **Flowchart**

Based on Fig. 1, users first start the connection to web3, this enables MetaMask to interact with the DApp. If the connection is established, users will be redirected to the homepage of application. Otherwise, users will be disabled from browsing the DApp. In order to post an image to the DApp, users need to pay an amount of Ether according to the file size. Users are allowed to post as many images as they like as long as the particular MetaMask account contains sufficient Ether. Besides, users can update their profile by changing avatar and description about themselves. Both actions will require Ether to process in order to store new records in Ethereum blockchain.

3.4 Development Tools and Techniques

There are many tools and techniques used to develop, test and evaluate this decentralised application:

(1) *Ganache:* Ganache [6] is a personal blockchain for Ethereum development you may use to develop applications, deploy contracts and run tests. 10 accounts will be automatically generated with each consists of 100 ETH and a unique private key.

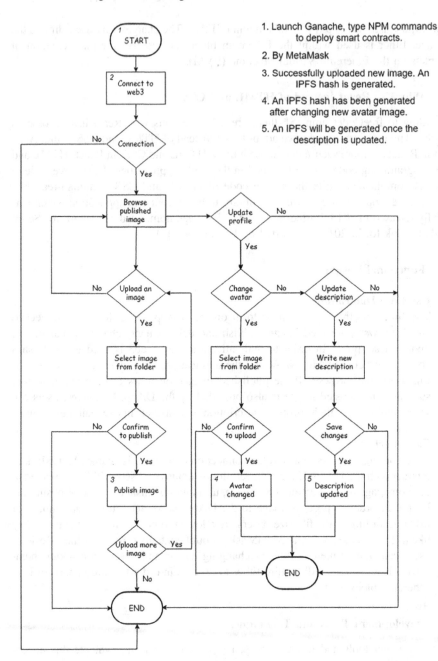

1. Launch Ganache, type NPM commands to deploy smart contracts.

2. By MetaMask

3. Successfully uploaded new image. An IPFS hash is generated.

4. An IPFS hash has been generated after changing new avatar image.

5. An IPFS will be generated once the description is updated.

Fig. 1. Flowchart

(2) *MetaMask:* MetaMask [9] is a bridge that allows you to visit the distributed web in your browser. Besides, decentralised application can be executed in your Chrome browser without the need of any Ethereum node. It can be considered as a digital wallet.

(3) *Atom:* Atom is a free source code editor for many operating systems which include macOS, Microsoft Windows and Linux. A lot of packages can be installed to provide better user experiences.

(4) *Node.js:* Node.js is an open-source, cross-platform JavaScript run-time environment that executes JavaScript code outside of a browser. NPM, a command line client, will be used frequently to create this application.

(5) *Truffle:* Truffle [14] is a development framework which provides you some Truffle boxes to choose during initial development phase. You can type certain commands to unbox and get modules in a folder.

(6) *InterPlanetary File System (IPFS):* IPFS [8] is a protocol and network designed to generate an address which can be used to retrieve and view the uploaded content. Once the IPFS hash is generated, it will not be able to be removed in any method.

(7) *React:* React is a collection of JavaScript library for designing user interfaces. It is widely used to develop a single-page or mobile apps. Facebook and some companies or developers are responsible to maintain it. This is to ensure React can be used more frequently and has more library to be used in development.

(8) *Git:* Git is a distributed version control system for detecting changes in source code during software development. Git provides some advantages such as data integrity and shorten the time to successfully develop an application.

3.5 Truffle Unbox

Truffle Boxes are helpful tools to software programmers in early development phase. In addition to Truffle, Truffle Boxes consist of many modules, smart contracts and open-source libraries, user views and more, in order to build a working decentralised application. We use React box in this research. 5 folders will be created when unbox process is completed:

(a) **contract directory:** where all smart contracts are stored. Migration contract will be automatically generated to handle the migrations to blockchain.

(b) **migration directory:** where all of the migration files are stored. These files are needed when we deploy smart contracts to update the state of the blockchain.

(c) **node_module directory:** contain the Node dependencies.

(d) **src directory:** where we develop our front end application.

(e) **test directory:** where smart contracts can be tested prior to deploying into blockchain.

(f) **truffle-config.js:** a configuration file for our Truffle project. You will get the filename of configuration file as truffle.js.

4 The Implementation Steps

4.1 Steps to Create a New Network

(1) Open Ganache, remember the Network ID and RPC Server.

(2) Open MetaMask, go to Networks and choose Custom RPC.

(3) To add New Network, copy the RPC URL from Ganache and paste it to textbox. Ex. HTTP://127.0.0.1:7545, you can rename HTTP to localhost.
(4) Once new network is added to MetaMask, you may see the RPC URL in Step 3 under Networks list.

4.2   Steps to Import Account from Ganache to MetaMask

(1) There are 10 accounts preloaded with balance of 100 ETH in Ganache.
(2) In Ganache, choose any account you wish to import and press the key icon to show its private key.
(3) Open MetaMask, click Import Account.
(4) Make sure the Select Type is Private Key, then copy and paste the private key as into the textbox.
(5) Once account has been successfully imported, you will have 100 ETH to use in contract deployment for making transaction.

4.3   Steps to Deploy Smart Contracts

(1) Open command prompt, locate your project directory, and then run the commands below:

$ truffle migrate when it is the first time you want to deploy smart contracts.
$ truffle migrate – reset when you have restarted the Ganache.

(2) Go to Ganache, under BLOCKS, you should see a total of 4 blocks. Please note that block 0 is the genesis block, where the blockchain starts to run.
(3) Switch to TRANSACTIONS, you will see a total of 4 transactions made. Please note that every deployed contract will produce two transactions, which have the contract creation and contract call function. Besides, sender address and contract address are listed in each transaction as well.

4.4   Steps to Use Git Bash

(1) After installing Git on your computer, open Git Bash application.
(2) Locate your project directory.
(3) There are three commands you shall use regularly, which include:
    (a) **$ git status** to track any changes from all the source files.
    (b) **$ git add.** to list all the modified source files and get ready to be overwritten.
    (c) **$ git commit -m "Your comment"** Add comment to the file changes.
(4) For instance, both App.js and App.css files have been modified due to several changes on front end application.

5   Testing/Evaluation

5.1   Step by Step Guide to Launch the Application

Steps to Run Application
(1) Open command prompt, locate project directory, and run the command:
    $ npm run start
(2) A localhost server will be triggered to run. A browser will pop out and display the homepage of front end application.
(3) The current time is shown at the top right corner of the page.

Steps to Upload an Image to News Feed
(1) Click the Choose File button, then select an image file from the device folder.
(2) After the image file is selected, press the Submit button.
(3) A MetaMask notification is prompted. Choose CONFIRM to proceed.
(4) In Ganache, a new block is added to the blockchain.
(5) Once image is posted, you may see it on news feed. The newest image will always be placed at the top of the page. Besides, you may also see the IPFS hash of the posted image at the bottom of post.

Steps to Get and Display Image from IPFS Hash through CMD
(1) Open command prompt on the computer and locate the project directory.
(2) In order to gain access to the DApp, type the command: **$ truffle console**
(3) To create an instance, please type command below:
    $ SimpleStorage.deployed().then(function(i)
    {app = i;})
(4) To get IPFS hash of the uploaded image, you should type the commands:
    $ app.get().then(function(value) {ipfsHash = value}); $ ipfsHash
    Open Chrome browser, type the URL together with your IPFS hash below:
    https://ipfs.io/ipfs/[IPFShash]
(5) The uploaded image has been stored on blockchain.

Steps to Delete Image
(1) To delete an image, just click on the close button which is located at the top right corner of a post.
(2) A MetaMask notification is prompted. Choose CONFIRM to proceed.
(3) There is no post on news feed once you have successfully deleted the image.

Steps to Change Avatar Image
(1) The default avatar has been assigned to every new user.
(2) To upload a new avatar image, just move the cursor to the default avatar and click on it.
(3) You will be asked to select an image from the device folder as new avatar image.
(4) A MetaMask notification is prompted. Choose CONFIRM to proceed.
(5) Your avatar has been updated with the chosen image.

Steps to Update Description
(1) The default description for every new user is "New user on MyCS".
(2) To update description, type the new description in the input textbox.
(3) After typing the new description for the profile, click the Save changes button.
(4) A MetaMask notification is prompted. Choose CONFIRM to proceed.
(5) Your description has been updated.

5.2 Comparison Between Proposed Image Sharing Application (MyCS) and Existing Applications

A comparison has been made as per Table 1 with some existing content sharing applications, namely, Pheme (https://aloha.pheme.app/), Viuly (https://viuly.io/), and Mysay (http://www.mysay.xyz/). We observe that each of the applications has their own distinctive features and suitable application should be adopted based on the user requirements.

Table 1. Comparison between MyCS and existing applications

	MyCS	Pheme	Viuly	Mysay
Content to be shared	Image file from user's device folder	Article which may consist of text and image	Original video made by authors	Text message
User identity	Ethereum public address is used	Able to create alias or username	Email account	Ethereum public address is used
Network	Run on localhost	Run on Ropsten Test Network	Run on Mainnet Network	Run on Rinkeby Test Network
IPFS protocol	IPFS daemon is used	IPFS infura is used	IPFS infura is used	Go-IPFS is used
Cryptocurrency	Ether (ETH)	Ether (ETH)	VIU token	Ether (ETH)
Reward-based	No	No	Yes, get reward after watching videos	No
User profile	Yes, avatar image and description	Yes, username, avatar image and description	Yes, username and avatar image	No
Service provided	Image sharing	Article sharing	Video sharing	Text message sharing

Acknowledgement. The authors would like to acknowledge the Malaysia government's Fundamental Research Grant Scheme (FRGS/1/2018/ICT04/MMU/01/01) for supporting this work.

References

1. AC3 Digital Wallet: Application (2018)
2. Bashir, I.: The block validation mechanism. In: Mastering Blockchain. Packt (2017)
3. CNBC: Facebook and Google predicted to make $106 billion from advertising in 2017, almost half of world's digital ad spend. CNBC (2017). https://www.cnbc.com/2017/03/21/facebook-and-google-ad-youtubemake-advertising-in-2017.html
4. DiNucci, D.: Web 2.0. Wikipedia (2004). https://en.wikipedia.org/wiki/Web_2.0
5. freeCodeCamp: Yes, React is taking over front-end development. The question is why (2017)
6. Ganache: Truffle Suite. truffleframework.com (n.d.). https://truffleframework.com/docs/ganache/overview
7. Hackernoon: Top JavaScript trends to look for in 2019 (2018)
8. IPFS: InterPlanetary File System. Wikipedia (n.d.). https://en.wikipedia.org/wiki/InterPlanetary_File_System
9. MetaMask: MetaMask (n.d.). https://metamask.io/
10. Reuters: Why Facebook is losing the war on hate speech in Myanmar (2018)
11. Solidity: Layout of a Solidity source file. solidity.readthedocs.io (n.d.). https://solidity.readthedocs.io/en/v0.4.24/layout-ofsource-files.html
12. Techworld, S.: The most infamous data breaches (2018)
13. The Daily Dot: The hidden costs of YouTube's controversial revenue split (2015)
14. Truffle: Truffle Suite (n.d.). https://truffleframework.com/truffle
15. Weibo, S.: An Introduction to Sina Weibo. What's On Weibo (2015). https://www.whatsonweibo.com/sinaweibo/
16. Wikipedia: WannaCry Ransomware attack. Wikipedia (2017). https://en.wikipedia.org/wiki/WannaCry_ransomware_attack
17. Wikipedia: History of Facebook. Wikipedia (n.d.). https://en.wikipedia.org/wiki/History_of_Facebook
18. YouTube: YouTube monetized markets. YouTube Help (n.d.). https://support.google.com/youtube/answer/1342206?hl=en
19. ArtistCore: U.S. Spotify per stream mechanical royalty rate (2017)
20. SocialMediaHQ: Social media and the death of personal privacy (2018)

Proof of Bid as Alternative to Proof of Work

Wai Kok Chan[1]([✉]), Ji-Jian Chin[2], and Vik Tor Goh[2]

[1] Faculty of Informatics and Computing, Multimedia University,
63000 Cyberjaya, Malaysia
wkchan@mmu.edu.my
[2] Faculty of Engineering, Multimedia University, 63000 Cyberjaya, Malaysia

Abstract. Proof of Work (PoW) protocol for cryptocurrency uses an excessive amount of electricity to secure the network. Many PoW coins do not have sufficient hashing power to secure itself. There are many alternatives to PoW, such as Proof of Stake (PoS), merge-mining etcetera, which uses much less electricity. However, these alternatives have some drawbacks either in terms of security, complexity, and scalability. In this paper, an alternative to Proof of Work (PoW) called "Proof of BID" (PoB) protocol introduced. PoB makes use of existing bitcoin PoW to secure all transactions, thus consuming virtually no electricity. PoB also addresses most of the drawbacks faced by PoW alternatives. We have disclosed a systematic method on how to effectively re-used bitcoin PoW to secure a blockchain with the same level of bitcoin security. A few designs issue to improve the blockchain scalability is given. We have explored various attack scenarios and suggested some remedies.

Keywords: Blockchain · Proof of Work · Proof of Bid · Consensus

1 Introduction

In bitcoin, each miner will merge the "unconfirmed transaction output" (UTXO) into a block. All included transactions are hashed to obtain a Merkle root to form a bitcoin block header. Then, a miner performs sha256 hashes multiple times by changing the 32bit nonce, timestamp and other possible fields on the bitcoin header. The miner would repeat this process until the hash output of the bitcoin header matches the bitcoin current difficulty level. If it failed to do so, the miner would have to change the Merkle root value and repeat the process. Changing the Merkle root value, it may involve adding, removing or changing some of the transactions in the current mine bitcoin block.

As of 8th Sept 2018, the current bitcoin mining difficulty level is 7,019,199,231,177 (https://bitcoinwisdom.com/bitcoin/difficulty) and current hash rate is 49,290,360,795 GH/s. A difficulty level of 1 is equivalent to performing a 2^{32} SHA256 hash computation. Throughout 2009, the bitcoin difficulty level is 1. The first bitcoin miner which produces a block with the nonce value that matches the current level of difficulty will be rewarded with 12.5 bitcoin as of 2018. A block is deemed to match the current difficulty level when the hash output of the bitcoin block is lower than the current difficulty target. The mining difficulty will be readjusted every 2016 blocks so that on average, one block

M. Anbar et al. (Eds.): ACeS 2019, CCIS 1132, pp. 60–73, 2020.
https://doi.org/10.1007/978-981-15-2693-0_5

is produced every 10 min. All this computation is useless and consumed an excessive amount of electricity. According to de Vries [1], in 2018 bitcoin network is using 2.55 GW of power which is comparable to countries like Ireland 3.1 GW.

There are many alternatives to "Proof of Work" (PoW) such as Hybrid Proof of Work/Stake (*DASH* coin), Delegated Proof of Stake (*EOS* coin), Delegated Byzantine Fault Tolerance Proof of Stake (*NEO* coin), Proof of Authority (*VeChain* Coin), Proof of Burnt (*XCP* and *SlimCoin*), Proof of Importance (*NEM* Coin), Proof of Devotion (*Nebulas* Coin), Proof of Space (*FileCoin*), Delayed Proof of Work (*Komodo* Coin), Hash Graph (*Hedera* Coin), Directed Acyclic Graph (DAG: *IOTA* Coin), Distributed Hash Table (*HOLOCHAIN* Coin) and Block Lattice (*NANO* Coin). Most of these non-100% PoW alternatives use an alternative consensus protocol that consumes very little electricity. However, these alternatives come with one or multiple disadvantages in terms of security, scalability, complexity and most importantly, an extremely high learning curve for a user to understand. Section 3 will discuss some of the key consensus protocols.

In this paper, we proposed PoB, which uses bitcoin block as an external source of randomness. Thus, virtually no electricity is used. Whenever, the latest found bitcoin block arrived, the whole Bitcoin block is hashed to obtain a 256-bit hash value. The general idea is to have miners bid for the hash value for every BTC block interval. Miner with the closest bid will get the mining reward and will consolidate the block into PoB blockchain. This idea sounds simple, but there are many security, network and consensus issues that need to be addressed before PoB can operate safely. Some of the security issues are Denial of Service Attack, Scalability, Bitcoin Block Orphaning, Fork and Costless Simulation. Some of the consensus issues include bid cost revision, consensus on bids submissions and which chain is valid in the event of a fork.

In Sect. 2, the related work on alternatives to PoW is described. Section 3 describes some of the preliminaries. The detail description of the PoB protocol is described in Sect. 4. The non-bidding transaction is not described here because these transactions can be modeled similar to bitcoin or other alt-coin transactions. Security issues are discussed, in Sect. 5, followed by the conclusion in Sect. 6.

2   Related Work

In Proof of stake system [2], some signing keys can determine the future blocks. This key may belong to original users who later lost their coin or sold their coin to someone else. These keys can fork another chain which new users cannot distinguish from true ones. At the same time, it is costless to recreate any alternative history which favors the majority of the randomly selected key owner. In addition to that, an adversary may bribe other stakeholders to extend an invalid block which favors them instead of extending a valid block. In Proof of stake [3, 4], periodic check-point in the blockchain is proposed to prevent an attack that attempts to change the history beyond a certain point. However, it is argued in [2], that this is not a distributed consensus.

In Proof of Activity [5], a miner generates an empty block with a certain level of difficulty and then it broadcast the block to N stakeholder. The network selects these N stakeholders. The first N-1 stakeholders check the validity of the entire block, signs it and broadcast it. The Nth (last) stakeholder wraps the blocks with all the transactions and broadcasts it to the network. The mining reward is divided between the N stakeholders and the miner. An attacker who has x-fraction of stakeholders will have a probability of x^N to mining a block under attacker control. The probability to mine a block under an honest network is $(1 - x)^N$. Thus, the attacker must be fast enough to generate with a p fraction of the honest stake is online. An attacker with y fraction of the total stake needs more than $\left(\left(\frac{1}{y} - 1\right) . p\right)^N$ times the hash power of the honest miners to gain an advantage over the network. Thus, the hash power required to performed any attacker is amplified by power N times, making it much better than traditional PoW.

In Proof of Luck [6], a Trusted Execution Environment (TEE) in the Intel SGX platform is used to compute the luck via POLMINE and POLROUND function. In TEE, system time cannot be fake (Proof of time) and the owner can verify that a specific device has done a particular computation (Proof of Ownership). The POLROUND function ensures each device waits for the start of each round before mining the block. The POLMINE function takes the current block header and the previous block to generate a random nonce execute. The largest nonce value will be the winner and the block will be added into a blockchain. However, there is a need to trust the hardware vendor.

Cryptocurrency such as NANO [7], DAGCoin and IOTA are based on Directed Acyclic Graph (DAG). These DAG-based coins have improved performance and security because most of the transaction verification is distributed. In NANO, each account managed its' own transaction and balance via its' blockchain. Few representatives are selected to monitor the network. These representatives will prevent conflicting transactions (double spending) via a voting process. Only blocks with the majority vote are included in the blockchain. In IOTA, each new transaction must choose two previous transactions to verify. In this way, the transaction can be feeless.

PHANTOM [8] proposed a scalable BlockDAG protocol as an improvement over Spectre [9, 10]. Phantom can support faster block generation. In PHANTOM, the user decides the kind of throughput required and set the relevant "k" value. A k-cluster is a subset of blocks in a DAG that is connected to every block but not connected to at most k blocks. A greedy algorithm is used to distinguish honest blocks from a dishonest one. The author suggested that PHANTOM and Spectre should be run together. This ensures faster confirmation time for non-conflicting transactions and also able to detect conflicting transactions such as double-spending. However, the detection time is very slow.

In Proof of Burnt [11], a user can send a trance of bitcoins to a burn address which is un-spendable in exchange for another token coin. A burn address is an address with an unknown private key. However, there is a need to prove that the burner does not know the private key. Thus in bitcoin, any addresses with the hashes of any script that evaluate to false such as 2 + 2 = 5 can be used as a burnt address. This script proves that a user had burnt their bitcoin.

Proof of Burnt can be used to boot scrap another coin such as Counterparty XCP. This process ensures a particular coin having some intrinsic value, the initial XCP token ex-changed at around 1000 XCP token per one bitcoin (BTC). Thus, the XCP token has some intrinsic value because it is created by burning bitcoin. This burning process has created some criticism from the community because the actual bitcoin is lost forever. There are alternatives to Proof of Burn which does not destroy any bitcoin. The bitcoin can be locked in the main bitcoin blockchain when it is converted to an alternative coin running in a side-chain [12]. Users can convert back their alternative coin back to bitcoin by destroying/burning their alternative coin in the side-chain. Once these alternative coins are destroyed, an equivalent value of bitcoin is un-locked in the main bitcoin blockchain. However, theses alternative coins in the side chain still need to run a consensus protocol and some of them might use merge-mining.

In SlimCoin [13] Proof of burnt, miner will use real money to buy the SlimCoin. Miner will burn SlimCoins in its mining process to produce a transaction hash. The burn hash is calculated by multiplying a decay multiplier with the internal hash (presumably it is the transaction hash however it is not mentioned in the white paper). Miner with the best hash will get the block reward. Burning existing coin is for min-ing is almost similar to buying a mining rig in PoW. There are many missing details in the whitepaper. A more detail review may require source code investigation however the Github last commit was done on 7th Nov 2014. https://github.com/kryptoslab/slimcoin.

In PoW coin such as NameCoin, Ixcoin, DevCoin, IOCoin and GroupCoin [14, 15] uses the same PoW algorithm as bitcoin. Merge mining is used to secure these coins. In merge-mining, one or more PoW alt-coin is mined together with bitcoin by inserted a scriptSig 44 bytes long containing the block hash of the alt-coin into the bitcoin block. Merge-mining enables PoW alt-coin to improve their hash rate by leveraging on bitcoin mining power. However, a bitcoin miner must first know which alt-coin to merge-mine. Bitcoin miner must find it is profitability and lastly agreed to merge mining it in its mining pool. Thus, not every bitcoin miner performed merged-mining and not every PoW alt-coin will be selected to be merge-mined in a merged mining pool. Generally, bitcoin miners are already preoccupied with many other issues. Since bitcoin miner can merge-mining any child blockchains almost at zero additional cost, it can attack any child blockchain. In 2012, bitcoin mining pool Eligius performed a 51% attack on Coiled-Coin by mining empty blocks [15]. This event had annihilated Coiled-Coin.

3   Preliminaries

Table 1 below shows the variable definition. In our PoB protocol, users can transfer funds to any Coinbase addresses for bidding purposes.

Table 1. Variable definition

Variable	Description
a_i	bidder with a Coinbase address a_i
b_i	the bid value submitted by bidder a_i
$t1_i$	timestamp when the bid is submitted
$t2_i$	timestamp when the blinded bid is revealed
F	Fix parameter values for current block such as current block height, previous Block Hash, bidding cost, timestamp etcetera
$h1_i$	$h1_i = \text{blake256}(a_i, b_i, t_i, F)$ This hash value calculated and sent by a_i, it is used to prevents a_i from changing its bid value. Note: b_i is never sent during the bidding process
sk_i	Secret key for bidder with address a_i
pk_i	Public key for bidder with address a_i
B_i	Bid message by sent by a_i $B_i = \{a_i, 0, t_i, h1_i, F\}$; sign (B_i, sk_i); Receiving full node will accept B_i if verify $(B_i, pk_i) = true$;
R_i	Bid Reveal Message sent by a_i; $R_i = \{sign(B_i, b_i, sk_i), B_i, b_i, F\}$; Receiving full node will accept R_i is valid if $h1_i = \text{blake256}(a_i, b_i, t_i, F) \wedge \text{verify } (R_i, pk_i) = true$;
BidHash	$\text{blake256}(\text{sort}(B_1, B_2, ..., B_n))$
BidHash'	BidHash value of previous PoB Block
τ_i	TraceBid Message sent by a_i; $\tau_i = \{sign(BidHash', sk_i), F\}$; Receiving full node will accept τ_i is valid if verify $(\tau_i, pk_i) = true$;

The hash function used must have the property of collision resistance, preimage resistance and second preimage resistance.

4 PoB Protocol

4.1 General Overview

PoB uses the latest bitcoin block as an external source of randomness which nobody can predict. A miner must maintain a bitcoin full-node status and a full copy of the PoB blockchain for PoB mining operation. PoB Block time is the same as Bitcoin. When a new bitcoin block is discovered, the miner will hash the whole Bitcoin block with blake256 [16] hash function to obtain a 256-bit BTCHash.

```
BTCHash = Blake256(FutureBTCBlock);
```

A few blocks before the calculation of BTCHash, each bidder/miner submits a bid to a few random "Peer-to-Peer" (P2P) full nodes. These bids propagate to the whole network via GOSSIP [17] protocol. A bid will consist of the predicted BLAKE2 hash value (256 bits) of a future full bitcoin block. In order to simplify the protocol, each Coinbase address can submit only one bid per block interval. The winning miner is chosen by this self-explanatory tie-breaking pseudocode function.

```
Winner = CoinBaseAddress(LowerBidValue(Nearest(AllBids,BTCHash)));
```

If there are multiple miners submitted the same bid then the miner with the lowest Coinbase address will win. There is only one winner per PoB Block. Thus, the blockchain will not be bloated. In this PoB protocol, we make four assumptions

(i)   Every node is synchronized to the "Network Time Protocol" (NTP) server right to seconds.
(ii) The broadcast message delivery via gossiping is reliable where all miners will receive the sent message within 15 s.
(iii) More than 50% of the participating miner is honest. However, dishonest miners can collude together by adding or deleting certain bidding information to their advantage.
(iv) The (Time Stamp Authority) TSA server service [18, 19] is reliable and the expired keys are still available for historical verification.

4.2 Bidding Transaction Control

Bid Filtering and Fair Bidding. PoB protocol will accept a maximum of 100 bid submission per block interval so that only a small fraction of the blockchain belongs to bid transaction. Adversaries can acquire many coin base addresses to submit as many bids as possible. Thus, a bid filtering algorithm is required to prevent excessive bid flooding. For each block, each bid transaction will go through these two functions, as shown in the pseudocode below.

```
BidderString = XOR(BidderAddress, Blake256(LastBTCBlock),LastBTCHeight);
AcceptBid = mod(BidderString,1000) + (PastStatistic(BidderAddress)x100);
```

The first 100 bids with the lowest AcceptBid value will be accepted. If the Accept-Bid value is the same, then the lowest coin base address is considered. Thus, a miner with the most fund can monopolize the mining process. In order to prevent that each miner will retrieve every bid transaction Coinbase address from confirmed block PoB (1000L +1) to PoB(1000L + 1000) where L ε {0, 1, 2,..}. The retrieved Coinbase address will be hashed into a counting BLOOM filter. The function prototype PastStatistic (BidderAddress) will return the number of times each address had bided for every 1000 PoB blocks. Thus, the value of AcceptBid increased tremendously for repeated bidders. Thus, Coinbase addresses which bided in the past have a lesser chance to bid. Every 1000 blocks, the BLOOM filter is reset.

Bidding Reward Carried Forward. The winning bidder takes all the transaction fees ($TX, excluding the bids reward) within a single block. The total Bid ($TotB) reward consists of the total bid ($Bid) by all bidders in the current block and carried forward bid ($C/F) from the previous block. If all reward is paid within a single block, a miner may place as many bids as possible using different Coinbase addresses.

If the $TotB is more than $10, then half of the bidding capital will be carried forward as a reward for the next block. This method will prevent a monopolistic miner from grabbing all the reward. The miner is indirectly forced to bid for a more extended period to minimize loss. Due to the high $C/F value, other miners may be incentified to place their bid. Figure 1 show the pseudocode for mining reward ($Reward) paid to the miner in each block.

```
$TotB = $Cur + $C/F;
If $TotB < $10
    $Reward = $TotB + $TX;
Else
    $Reward = $TX +   ($TotB)/2;
    $C/F = $TotB/2;
```

Fig. 1. Mining Reward Pseudocode

Bidding Cost Adjustion. For each block interval that received more than 100 bids, the bidding and deposit cost will be increased by $x1\%$ to reduce the number of eligible bidders. The initial bidding cost per miner is $1 plus $19 deposit. The bidding and deposit cost will be reduced by $x2\%$ if there are not more than 100 bids per block received for $x3$ consecutive blocks. The optimal value for $x1$, $x2$ and $x3$ is still under investigation. The cost adjustment pseudocode is shown in Fig. 2.

```
If NoOfBid > 100
{ BidCost = BidCost x (1 + x1%);
  DepositCost = DepositCost x (1 + x1%);
  Count = 0;
}
Else
{ Count++;
  If (Count ==x3)
  { BidCost = max(MinBidCost, BidCost x (1 - x2%));
    DepositCost = max(MinDepositCost, DepositCost x (1 - x2%));
    Count = 0;
  }
}
```

Fig. 2. Bidding Cost Revision Pseudocode

Aggressive cost adjustment algorithm can result in zero eligible bidders for the next block interval. There may be a possibility that PoB protocol is used for alt-coins or coin running in a side-chain. Initially, there may be no activity for months or years. Thus the side-chain or alt-coin operator must be the miner of last resort. In each block interval, if there is no bid, no block can be generated even though there are some transactions not related to bidding. Thus, one free mandatory bid must be made available to side-chain or alt-coin operators so that mining can continue. When the number of transactions grows, new miners will join.

4.3 Bidding Details

Block Numbering: Bitcoin Block G and PoB Block G are defined as BTC(G) and PoB (G) respectively. PoB genesis block PoB(G) is created at BTC(G) where G ε {1, 2, ..}, K ε {4, 5, 6, ..} and (K-3) > G. PoB and Bitcoin have the same block height. When BTC(K) is found, PoB(K) is created with one block delay. The Bid data in PoB(K-3), BidRevelation data in PoB(K-2) and TraceBid data in PoB(K-1) determines the winning miner for BTC(K). The winning miner will then construct PoB(K) consists of Bids for BTC(K+3), BidRevelation for BTC(K+2) and TraceBid for BTC(K+1).

Bitcoin Block Orphaning: Bitcoin has an orphaning rate of 0.5%. Miner will bid three blocks in advance to prevent PoB from bidding on an orphan block. Most of the orphaning process already resolved by then. However, this enables adversaries to create three future blocks in advance. In order to prevent this, the latest PoB block PoB(K) must include the hash of the latest BTC block BTC(K). In case BTC(K) is orphaned by BTC(K'), there is a side pointer in PoB(K) that points to the whole orphaned BTC(K) block and the hash of BTC(K'). Thus in PoB, there is no blockchain reorganization. Figure 3 shows the block diagram.

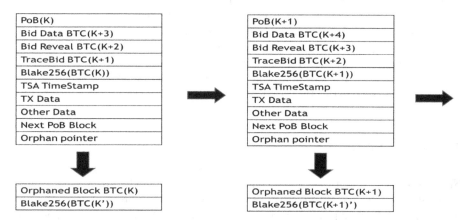

Fig. 3. Block Diagram for PoB Block.

Bidding Process: There are three separate phases in each bidding process for one BTC block. The three phases are the bidding phase in BTC(K), the Bid Revelation Phase in

BTC(K+1) and the TraceBid phase in BTC(K+2). All bidding transactions must be confirmed in the blockchain before bids revelation. All bid revelations must be confirmed before the TraceBid process. The TraceBid process prevents adversaries from forking the PoB chain and also used to resolve other consensus issues. Upon completion of the TraceBid process, when BTC(K+3) is found, the winning miner is determined and reserved the right to create PoB(K+3). Upon discovery of BTC(K+4), PoB(K+3) is created when BTC(K+4). Table 2 shows the bidding process for one bidding cycle. In the actual bidding process, the bidding process overlaps with bid revelation and the TraceBid process.

Table 2. One bidding cycle time line

Second	Event	Timing
0 s	BTC(K) is found	T1
0–200 s	Miners submit their bids for BTC(K+3) directly	
0–300 s	Submitted bids are relayed to all miner	
300–400 s	Miner sort all bids from the smallest Coinbase address and calculate the BidHash Send the BidHash to all Miner	T2
400–BTC(K+1)	All miner reach consensus on all bids	
600 s (estimate)	BTC(K+1) is found	T3
600–800 s	Miner reveals bid for BTC(K+3) directly	
600–1000 s	Reveal Bid are relayed to all miner	
1000 s–BTC(K+2)	All miner reach consensus on Reveal bids	T4
1200 s (estimate)	BTC(K+2) is found	T5
1200 s–1300 s	Miner sign the TraceBid for BTC(K+3) based on BidHash received in BTC(K+4) stored in PoB(K+1)	
1200 s–1400 s	Signed TraceBid is relayed to all miner	
1400 s–BTC(K+3)	Miner reach consensus on which blockchain to follow	T6
1800 s (estimate)	BTC(K+3) is found. Winning Miner is determined. Winning Miner will create PoB(K+3) when BTC(K+4) is found. The cycle repeats	T7

4.4   Bidding Consensus

Network Issues: A miner can cause consensus problem by sending B_i, R_i, τ_i messages during the last few seconds. In consequence of that, GOSSIP's protocol does not have sufficient time to disseminate the info to all full nodes. A full node is a node that maintains the full copy of the blockchain and may optionally participate in mining. Thus, miners have 200 s to send their B_i or R_i messages directly and 100 s to send τ_i messages. Full nodes that relay miners' messages to other nodes will have an additional

100 s. There is a mechanism to distinguish direct messages from miners and relay messages from full nodes.

According to data [20] available from 1st January 2017 until 5th April 2017, the average time to propagate a block and transaction to 50% and 90% of the node is shown in Table 3 below. Therefore, 200 s for message and block propagation should be sufficient.

Table 3. Block and transaction propagation speed

50% of block	90% of block	50% of transaction	90% of transaction
2.398874 s	11.77294 s	3.447737 s	14.26984 s

Consensus on Submitted Bid: Miner receive bid transactions $\{B_1, B_2, ..., B_n\}$ from other miners. All miners must reach a consensus on all the submitted bid. Each miner sort all bid transaction from the lowest Coinbase address and perform a Blake256 hash on the sorted message as shown in the preliminaries section.

Each miner signs the BidHash value, the number of bids received from a unique Coinbase address (NoOfBidder) and time stamp it before relaying it to other full nodes. The majority of the miners should have only one BidHash value from other peers if the message delivery is reliable and most miners are honest. The purpose of the BidHash value is to prevent illegal modification to the bid list by any miner. This BidHash value is also used to reach a consensus on the bidding list so that the correct winner can be determined later. In each block interval, each miner will monitor the number of unique Coinbase addresses received (NoOfBidderPerBidHashValue) for each BidHash value. If more than 50% of the miner received the same BidHash value, then consensus is achieved. It is achievable because more than 50% of the miner is honest and the network is reliable. Miner which calculated a different BidHash value should stop mining immediately and resynchronize it is PoB blockchain on the next block before it can mine again.

5   Security Issue

5.1   Costless Simulation

An adversary can reconstruct the blockchain with a closer or exact bid starting from a known block or genesis block to their advantage since all the past bitcoin blockchain information is available. These problems are called "Costless Simulation" or "Nothing At Stake Problem" which happened mainly in PoS protocol.

Miners must send every PoB block to a TSA server for timestamping to prevent these problems. Hash responds from the TSA server must be included in PoB blockchain. Thus, whatever data created inside the PoB cannot be changed and proven to be created at the specified time. Most TSA server certificate provided by VeriSign, Thawte and other vendors has a validity of one year upon subscription. In every 25,000 PoB block (approximately six months), all previous hashes and TSA timestamp will be rehashed together and signed with a new TSA certificate. This form a chain of timestamp signatures. In every 25,000th PoB block, PoB will include this new hash. Thus, the TSA services can prevent any adversaries from creating an alternative history base on existing available data.

Adversaries can hijack a PoB blockchain project by mining the genesis block first before everyone else. Thus, before launching a PoB blockchain, the first ten blocks must be secretly mined with zero incentives to the initial operator. The public announcements should come later. After the 10th block, the public can view the blockchain information to decide whether it is fair to mine or secure to use the blockchain. The initial operator may need to mine with zero incentives for an extended period because miners need some time to come in.

The preliminaries section shows that in each bidding message B_i, the current PoB Block includes the hash of the previous PoB block as an input. Even though an adversary can reconstruct their blockchain starting from a known block, the adversary cannot produce the correct signature for transactions not owned by them. Thus, an adversary cannot recreate the history that includes transactions that do not belong to them.

5.2 Denial of Service Prevention

Bid Transaction Filtering and Bid Cost Revision: As mentioned in Sect. 4.2, there is a bid transaction filtering mechanism to filter out excessive bid submission sent by miners. In case, the miners continue to send an excessive number of bids, the cost per bid is revised upward to reduce the number of eligible miners. Miners who monopolized the current bidding process will have their bid capital tied down as 50% of the bid reward is carried forward as the next block reward. These miners may need mine for an extended period to recover their investment. Thus further securing the PoB blockchain. In order for a miner to continuously monopolize the bidding process, there must exist a lot of funds movement transaction between Coinbase address. Chain Analysis can easily detect these activities and an early alarm can be triggered. All Coin-base addresses that are related to these activities can also be directly identified for possible blacklisting in the future.

Deposit for Bidding: Initially, before any bidding cost revision, when one miner places a bid, $20 will be charged. If the bid value is revealed correctly, $9 will be refunded. This indirectly forces miners to reveal their bids and ensure bids consistency. The final $10 is refunded after miners signed the TraceBid process. The refund will be forfeited if the miner is found to have double-sign their PoB transaction. The refund process is locked for 20 blocks to ensure sufficient time to check for fork and double-signing. This deposit locking mechanism ensures honest miners' actions.

5.3 Fork Prevention

As shown in Fig. 4, an adversary can fork the PoB blockchain at PoB(K-3) by submitting a Bid(K') instead of Bid(K). The adversary then forcibly makes a fork at PoB (K-3) which includes Bid(K'). In this case, the TraceBid process comes into the picture.

BTC/PoB BLK		K-3	K-2	K-1
NORMAL	TRACEBID	K-2	K-1 (HONEST MINER SIGN HERE)	K
	REVEAL	K-1	K	K+1
	BID	K	K+1	K+2
ADVERSARIES	TRACEBID	K-2	K-1 (ADVERSARIES MINER SIGN HERE)	K'
	REVEAL	K-1	K'	K'+1
	BID	K' (FORK)	K'+1	K'+2

Fig. 4. PoB fork prevention scenario.

An adversary miner that submitted a different set of bids will have a different BidHash value. Honest miners check the BidHash value they received in Bid(K) stored at PoB(K-3). It is found to be Bid(K) instead of Bid(K'). Thus, at PoB(K-2), honest miners will sign their TraceBid(K-1) with BidReveal(K). Miners who sign on multiple chains will have their deposit forfeited. Since adversaries cannot control more than 50% of the miner from the previous block, it cannot fork the PoB chain beyond PoB(K-3). The fork chain at PoB(K-3) will be orphaned after PoB(K-2) is created. In bitcoin, the longest chain is considered as a valid chain in case of any blockchain fork. In PoB, if a fork happened, the chain with the most number of TraceBid signature is considered as a valid chain.

If the number of TraceBid signatures is precisely 50% for both chain, then each miner must remove all the duplicate transactions from Bid(K) and Bid(K'). In the remaining unique bid list, the bid list with the lowest AcceptBid value is considered as a valid chain. If the AcceptBid value is the same, then the lowest Coinbase address is considered. If there are more than two forks at PoB(K-3), then there exists a dangerous prolong network partition among all miners. This problem is a hard problem even for bitcoin itself. Miners can indirectly detect network partitioning especially when its' discovered that a significant portion of RevealBid or TraceBid is missing in their PoB Block.

6 Conclusion

In this paper, we have described a PoB protocol that can secure the transaction by leveraging on bitcoin PoW. PoB can replace bitcoin PoW if there exists a random source of information that is publicly available, cheap to verify, with sufficient entropy and periodic. In addition to that, the randomness source must be expensive to reproduce and can output a precise value. So far, we only found bitcoin as the source of randomness.

Using PoB may have some side-effect such as mining on an orphan BTC block. Some remedies are described to remove these side-effects. Many attack scenarios similar to PoS are explored and remedies are suggested. Our PoB protocol does not need any specialized hardware such as Proof of Luck method. PoB protocol does not have any problem with Long-Range Attack and "Nothing At Stake Attack" as compared to Proof of Stake. Thus, we believe that many blockchain applications can use PoB protocol and it is a strong contender to many Proof of Stake and PoW coin. At the same time, PoB is indirectly leveraging on the security provided bitcoin PoW. Thus, it is far more secure than most of the consensus protocol. PoB does not need to coordinate with bitcoin miner to per-form any merge-mining. The information given in this paper should be sufficient for a prototype implementation and further exploratory work.

References

1. de Vries, A.: Bitcoin's growing energy problem. Joule **2**(5), 801–805 (2018)
2. Poelstra, A.: On Stake and Consensus (2016). https://download.wpsoftware.net/bitcoin/pos. pdf
3. Bentov, I., Gabizon, A., Mizrahi, A.: Cryptocurrencies without proof of work. In: Clark, J., Meiklejohn, S., Ryan, P.Y.A., Wallach, D., Brenner, M., Rohloff, K. (eds.) FC 2016. LNCS, vol. 9604, pp. 142–157. Springer, Heidelberg (2016). https://doi.org/10.1007/978-3-662-53357-4_10
4. Snider, M., Samani, K., Jain, T.: Delegated proof of stake: features & tradeoff. Multicoin Capital (2018)
5. Bentov, I., Lee, C., Mizrahi, A., Rosenfeld, M.: Proof of activity: extending Bitcoin's proof of work via proof of stake. IACR Cryptology ePrint Archive 2014, p. 452 (2014)
6. Milutinovic, M., He, W., Wu, H., Kanwal, M.: Proof of luck: an efficient blockchain consensus protocol. In: Proceedings of the 1st Workshop System Software Trusted Execution (SysTEX), pp. 1–6 (2016)
7. Colin, L.M.: Nano: a feeless distributed cryptocurrency. Network. https://nano.org/en/whitepaper
8. Sompolinsky, Y., Zohar, A.: PHANTOM: a scalable BlockDAG protocol. IACR Cryptology ePrint Archive 2018, p. 104 (2018)
9. Sompolinsky, Y., Lewenberg, Y., Zohar, A.: Spectre: a fast and scalable cryptocurrency protocol. IACR Cryptology ePrint Archive 2016, p. 1159 (2016)
10. Sompolinsky, Y., Zohar, A.: Secure high-rate transaction processing in Bitcoin. In: Böhme, R., Okamoto, T. (eds.) FC 2015. LNCS, vol. 8975, pp. 507–527. Springer, Heidelberg (2015). https://doi.org/10.1007/978-3-662-47854-7_32
11. https://en.bitcoin.it/wiki/Proof_of_burn. Accessed 11 May 2019
12. Sidechains, Drivechains, and RSK 2-Way peg Design. https://www.rsk.co/noticia/sidechains-drivechains-and-rsk-2-way-peg-design. Accessed 11 May 2019
13. P4Titan. SlimCoin.: A Peer-to-peer Crypto-Currency with Proof-of-Burn. Mining without powerful hardware, 17 May (2014)
14. https://en.bitcoin.it/wiki/Merged_mining_specification. Accessed 11 May 2019

15. Judmayer, A., Zamyatin, A., Stifter, N., Voyiatzis, A.G., Weippl, E.: Merged mining: curse or cure? In: Garcia-Alfaro, J., Navarro-Arribas, G., Hartenstein, H., Herrera-Joancomartí, J. (eds.) ESORICS/DPM/CBT -2017. LNCS, vol. 10436, pp. 316–333. Springer, Cham (2017). https://doi.org/10.1007/978-3-319-67816-0_18
16. https://en.wikipedia.org/wiki/BLAKE_(hash_function). Accessed 11 May 2019
17. https://en.wikipedia.org/wiki/Gossip_protocol. Accessed 11 May 2019
18. Adams, C., Cain, P., Pinkas, D., Zuccherato, R.: Internet X.509 Public Key Infrastructure Time-Stamp Protocol (TSP). RFC 3161, August 2001
19. Pinkas, D., Pope, N., Ross, J.: Policy Requirements for Time-Stamping Authorities (TSAs), RFC 3628, November 2003
20. http://bitcoinstats.com/network/propagation. Accessed 11 May 2019

Context-Based Blockchain Platform Definition and Analysis Methodology

Sérgio Luís Ribeiro$^{(\boxtimes)}$ and Emilio Tissato Nakamura$^{(\boxtimes)}$

CPQD, Campinas, Brazil
{sribeiro,nakamura}@cpqd.com.br

Abstract. This paper presents a Context-Based Blockchain Platform Definition and Analysis Methodology (MetaBlockX) to analyse and identify the best blockchain platform to specific context. Nowadays the number of existing platforms is enormous, in this way, assessing and identifying which best suits to context and service needs is a great challenge. In addition, each use case has its specifics, which can vary from prophecy in a certain programming language or need to keep data private, or even response time and delay to process the data. In this way a holistic and well-documented analysis is required to identify such a blockchain development platform that is proposed at this paper.

Keywords: Blockchain · Security · Privacy · Security · Digital identity · IoT

1 Introduction

It is believed that blockchain technology has the potential to be the driving force that will democratize the world economy, and it will certainly be considered one of the most important technologies in the history of the century. By the developed model, no central authority is necessary, creating the paradigm break in which we need to become accustomed and understood. In addition, the trust architecture employed in the technology is also decentralized, which makes it more efficient because it brings the end customer and the seller without intermediaries.

This paper presents a methodology and application in the BlockIoT Project[1], which indicates the platform for the development of blockchain applications that has more adherences to the specific context of a service focused on digital identity.

A brief introduction related to blockchain concepts can be seen in Sect. 2, followed by the relationship of the blockchain and information security in the Sect. 3. Section 4 present the main layers of security that should be addressed during the development of a blockchain application and Sect. 5 presents blockchain applications for IoT technology. Section 6 presents the Context-Based Blockchain Platform Definition and Analysis Methodology, together with the results of the application in the BlockIoT Project and Sect. 7 shows the future works, and finally Sect. 8 presents the conclusions of this paper followed by the bibliographic reference.

---

[1] The project BlockIoT "Blockchain Platform for Developing Secure Applications in IoT" has the objective to develop technologies for a computational platform and blockchain-based secure applications to provide digital services in IoT.

© Springer Nature Singapore Pte Ltd. 2020
M. Anbar et al. (Eds.): ACeS 2019, CCIS 1132, pp. 74–88, 2020.
https://doi.org/10.1007/978-981-15-2693-0_6

2   Blockchain Concepts

Blockchain technology can be understood in many ways. In general terms, it can be said that it is a distributed, logically distributed and distributed database system (through a peer-to-peer network - P2P), in which all participants are responsible for storing and maintaining the database [1].

The blockchain technology was built having four main architectural features in mind: (i) security of operations, (ii) decentralization of storage and computing, (iii) data integrity, and (iv) transaction immutability [2]. In other words, blockchain is a "ledger of facts" replicated on computers that participate in a peer-to-peer network where:

  i. The ledger is a digital record book, in which once a record has been validated, it can never be deleted;
 ii. A fact can mean several things, from a monetary transaction, to a certain document content, or even a computer program and even in some platforms, a small database;
iii. Participating members of the network can be anonymous and are called peers or "nodes";
 iv. Any transaction within the ledger is protected by cryptographic digital signature technologies, including to identify the issuer and receiver nodes of the transactions;
  v. When a node wants to add a new fact to the ledger, a consensus is needed between all or some previously determined nodes in the network to decide whether a fact can be recorded in the ledger;
 vi. If there is a consensus, the fact will be written and a process can never be erased.

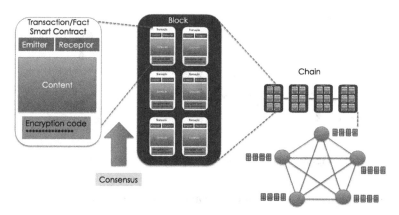

Fig. 1. Fact, block and chain. Adapted from [1].

As shown in Fig. 1, a blockchain network has the following essential elements:

  i. *Transaction/Fact/Smart Contract*: it can be a transaction, a digital content or a computer program, the latter is also called a smart contract;
 ii. *Block*: is a set of facts, usually in a predefined fixed number;
iii. *Chain*: a set of chained blocks (connected one by one) following a mathematical logic, they are not independent.

3   Blockchain and Security

Despite the security problems using blockchain technology, whether in the operation of cryptocurrency or in initiatives like DAO [3, 4], until now, the attacks were directed to the applications that use the blockchain, and not specifically the technology or the algorithm used. In addition, it has been observed that successful attacks, reported so far, on blockchain-based platforms such as Bitcoin [5], have occurred because of vulnerabilities in applications and not in the core of the blockchain technology itself [6].

Thus, with regard to the security aspect, to the present moment, there are no known vulnerabilities against the construction employed and algorithms used natively in the blockchain. Its way is possible to say that security is still one of the strengths of the blockchain solution. The algorithm in the process of inserting new blocks, that are composed of a set of transactions, they are cryptographically connected to the previous blocks, this process is called validation. In specific cases of cryptocurrency, Bitcoin for instance, is known as mining. The process is computationally intensive and this is way is unlikely that an attacker can make malicious modifications.

4   Security Layers in a Blockchain Platform

Blockchain and applications developers must adopt layered security. There are six layers of security to be considered. These layers are the result of the compilation of Information security best practices. Figure 2 shows the Security layers that will be describe below [7].

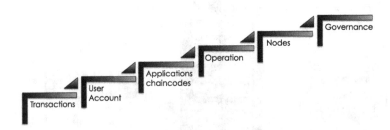

Fig. 2. Security layers for a blockchain development.

4.1   The Fundamental Layer Is the Security of the Transaction

The minimum requirements, without this, the blockchain does not make sense, this is the first layer. The blockchain should validate transactions with confidence and predictability at the end of the consensus. The consensus will confirm the purpose and the immutability of the transaction.

These are syntactic and structural protections for the transactions and the blocks that contain them. However, these protections do not prevent semantic fraud associated with the logic of the application.

4.2   The Second Layer Provides User Account Security

The user account is usually managed by the users using applications like eWallets [8]. Frequently, user account protection is confused with client software security.

This layer of security is influenced by two factors: (i) the awareness of users in the safe use of technology, and (ii) the correct implementation of security mechanisms for mobile devices and web systems.

4.3   The Third Layer Provides Security for the Application, Chaincodes or Smart Contracts

Included at this layer are: (i) good practices for secure software development, (ii) secure encryption of smart contracts and (iii) definition of security requirements, architecture assessment, and application security testing.

4.4   The Fourth Layer Addresses the Security of Deployment and Operation of the Application

This layer includes the acceptance and homologation tests of the application and chaincodes before implantation in production. Once in the production environment, the application must be monitored for malfunction and bad behaviour.

4.5   The Fifth Layer Covers the Security of the P2P Network and the Nodes

In this layer, traditional protection mechanisms of computer networks (such as firewall systems, IDS, IPS, etc.) can be applied to protect the P2P network nodes of the blockchain. In addition, specific safeguards should be applied for communication protocol and consensus security. Beside that, the minimum amount of available nodes needed to ensure consensus must be observed.

4.6   The Sixth Layer of Security Refers to the Governance of the Application and the Blockchain

This layer houses those decisions about the structure and design of the blockchain, which affect safe operation, including antifraud controls, auditing, privacy, and even compliance with industry-specific standards.

5   Blockchain and IoT

At IoT, regardless of economy sector, blockchain technology can provide a way to track the unique history of each device, recording the exchange of data between it and other devices, web services and human users. It can also allow intelligent devices to become independent agents that autonomously conduct a variety of transactions [9]. Various application examples can be identified, such as:

i. Remote monitoring of high value assets to verify, for example, whether they are being used correctly;
ii. Monitoring, control and authorization of request of certain equipment to replace some part or inputs material (washing machine requesting soap, for example); and
iii. Identity control of IoT devices for registration and control of logical access to different applications.

Other examples [10] of blockchain technology that can be applied to structuring projects that involves different actors in a value chain, such as:

i. Monitoring and tracking of a production chain (e.g. automobile manufacturing, wine production, production of computer equipment, among others);
ii. Reverse logistics management system for different products (e.g. production of medicines, electronic products and their waste); and
iii. Management and control systems for the distribution of sales of products under a strong regulatory regime (e.g. controlled-use medicines, meat origin and organic foods).

In short, IoT applications have the potential to take advantage of the benefits that blockchain technology brings that are summarized in Table 1.

Table 1. Potential benefits of blockchain in IoT.

Benefit	Description
Trusted transactions, fast and without middleman	It reduces or even eliminates the risk of mistrust between the parties and transaction costs
Empowered Users	User controls all your transactions and information
High quality data	The blockchain data is intrinsically complete, consistent, accurate, and widely available at the time it is needed
Durable, reliable and widely available	No single point of failure
Processes integrity	Trust that everything will run according to pre-defined rules without intermediaries
Transparency and immutability	All transactions may be publicly available and may not be changed or deleted from the records
Simplification of the ecosystem	A single "ledger" is created, reducing clutter and complications

As the number of connected devices grows from millions to billions, and governments and corporations run to better control devices and data, a new technology strategy will be needed to build low-cost solutions that take privacy and autonomy into account.

New business models will guide these solutions toward efficient digital economies and value creation in a collaborative way, while creating user experiences, security and improved products.

At the most abstract level, the networks themselves can become autonomous by supplanting current established systems that now depend on a centralizing authority, such as the exchange of sensitive information and services of self-installation and software auto-update on devices [11]. In this sense, any decentralized IoT solution should support: (i) reliable P2P messages, (ii) intrinsically reliable communication and (iii) decentralized autonomy.

In line with this evolutionary perspective of IoT, a Smart City is a good example of how to combine IoT and blockchain. Blockchain-based sharing services can contribute to Smart Cities.

Shared economy, in this case, is an economic-social model which various sectors of the population can use to make shared use of underutilized assets [12]. Citizens, objects and utilities would transparently connect to share the status and exchange of these assets. In this paradigm, people seek trust, access rather than ownership, reliability of shared services, including security and privacy.

Institutions need a smart community with smart governance, partnerships, transparent networking and governance, dynamic interconnection with stakeholders, and being protected from disqualified frauds, liabilities, and service providers.

Computing needs to ensure accessibility and availability of systems, intelligent database resources, control system, interface, computing, network, real-time science and advanced analytics.

There are six elements that blockchain would help in relationships between people, technology and organizations [13]: (i) not rely on trust between actors, (ii) transparency and privacy, (iii) democratization, (iv) automation, (v) distribution, and (vi) security.

6   Context-Based Blockchain Platform Definition and Analysis Methodology

This section presents a description and results of the 7 phases of the Context-Based Blockchain Platform Definition and Analysis Methodology (MetaBlockX):

- Phase 1 - Identification of blockchain platforms;
- Phase 2 - Identification and definition of aspects to be evaluated for the blockchain platform;
- Phase 3 - Definition of the levels of each identified aspect;
- Phase 4 - Definition of weights for each identified aspect;
- Phase 5 - Definition of the context of application of the service/product;
- Phase 6 - Analysis of the platforms using the aspects and context definition;
- Phase 7 - Mapping and definition of the blockchain platform based on context.

Based on the qualitative analysis of the main aspects that exert a direct influence on the platform and mainly taking into account the context of the application or service that will be made available by the platform.

The objectives of the methodology will be achieved with the execution of the 7 defined phases, in which the identifications, definitions, analyses and mappings will be documented according to criteria established in the methodology. A diagram of the phases with the identification of their dependencies can be seen in Fig. 3.

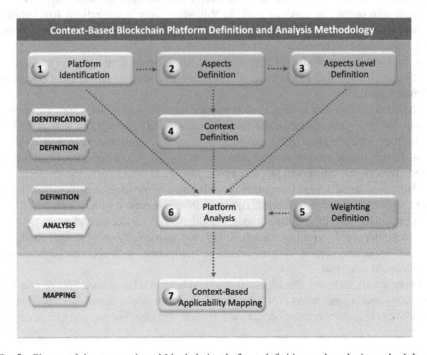

Fig. 3. Phases of the context-based blockchain platform definition and analysis methodology.

6.1   Phase 1 – Blockchain Platforms Identification

The first phase of the methodology is responsible for identifying the blockchain platforms that will be the results of the evaluation analysis. The established criteria for such identification should take into account the most relevant platforms that are in use and available for use.

Currently, it is possible to develop blockchain applications using open source or proprietary platforms, but the development trend on open source platforms predominates. Such platforms can be classified, in public or private ledger: (i) Public (public blockchain): some examples are: Bitcoin [14], Ethereum [15], Coinbase, among others; and (ii) private blockchain: Hyperledger [16], Ripple, Chain, DAH, Quorum, and others.

Phase 1 Documentation
As example er can consider the subset of the identified platforms and a summary of the key points are listed in Table 2.

Table 2. MetaBlockX - Phase 1 blockchain platforms identification.

Blockchain platform	Summary key points
Bitcoin	Blockchain public, not permissioned, PoW
Ethereum	Blockchain public (or private), not permissioned, PoW
Corda	Private/federated blockchain, permissioned, Consensus via RAFT, Smart contract
BigChainDB	Blockchain public, not permissioned, PBFT
Burrow	Private blockchain, permissioned, PoS, Smart Contract
Fabric	Private blockchain, permissioned, PoS, multiple mechanisms, Smart Contract

6.2 Phase 2 – Aspects Definition

A blockchain platform can be evaluated from different perspectives, such as number of commits, number of contributors and date of the last commit, that are important information to identify the liveliness, engagement and growth of the platform.

Other aspects include cost, use cases (context compatible or not), type of network (permissioned or not), chain type (public, private or hybrid), performance, scalability, implementation complexity, security aspects (certificate creation, user management and channel creation), tamper resistance, and tamper evidence.

At this stage the definition of the aspects to be evaluated for each blockchain platform identified and defined in Phase 1 of the methodology.

These aspects are raised from those considered more important to the blockchain platform qualification, according to the differences perspectives considered.

Phase 2 Documentation

As example a subset of the selected aspects defined, as evaluation criteria of blockchain platforms are detailed bellow:

a. Number of commits (AS01)
   This aspect should consider the number of commits executed in the project, so it is possible to estimate the community engagement and consequent level of maturity of the platform being analysed.
b. Last commit (AS02)
   The date of the last interaction of the community with the code can show if the project is still active and if improvements are being contemplated.
c. Number of contributors (AS03)
   This takes into account the size of the community that supports the platform in question.
d. Chain (AS04)
   The objective of this aspect is to categorize the platform being analysed in public, private or even hybrid, in some contexts, this may be a decisive factor, but in others, it may have no influence, and should be disregarded during the analysis (Phase 6).

e. Performance (AS05)

Currently the vast majority of platforms provide some number or even research on the performance of blockchain platforms.

f. Scalability (AS06)

The scalability of blockchain platforms and systems usually consists of two factors: (i) node scalability - refers to the extent to which the network can add more participants without loss of performance, and (ii) performance scalability - refers to the number of transactions processed per second affected by latency between transactions and each block size.

A blockchain platform is considered scalable if it can add thousands of globally distributed nodes while still processing thousands of transactions per second. Currently, just a few of the existing and in-use blockchain platform are actually self-declared scalable, using this concept. This kind of comparisons and research related to the scalability of blockchain platforms is easily finding this kind of information.

g. Complexity (AS07)

This is a key factor that must take into account other aspects that are not mapped directly by the methodology, but that should be taken into account.

The programming language used, participant management, infrastructure, among others, are some examples that should be considered at this aspect. Thus, complexity must be evaluated in order to understand the complexity to build and support from the platform infrastructure to the support of the product, application or service execution codes that will be using the blockchain platform in question.

h. Consensus (AS08)

This aspect is directly linked to the consensus model, whether it is centralized or decentralized and the correspondent algorithm that will be used.

Depending on the development context, one type may be more indicated than another.

6.3   Phase 3 – Aspects Level Definition

This phase aims to define levels of qualitative criteria to be established for each aspect defined in Phase 2. Examples of levels are High, Medium and Low or even yes or no when applicable.

The criteria for the definition of levels should take into account an overall analysis of the aspects defined in Phase 2, as well as a specific analysis of each aspect, since the representation of levels varies according to the aspect to be analysed.

In this way, each aspect should be analysed and its level should be defined according to what is established in this phase of the methodology.

Phase 3 Documentation

The levels of the aspects defined in this phase should be included in a table, with the respective explanations and justifications according to Table 3.

Table 3. MetaBlockX - Phase 3 aspects level definition.

Aspect	Level	Criteria
AS1	High (3)	≥ 3000
	Med (2)	$<3000 \geq 500$
	Low (1)	>500
AS2	High (3)	≥ 1 month
	Med (2)	≤ 1 year > 1 month
	Low (1)	>1 year
AS3	High (3)	≥ 150
	Med (2)	$<150 \geq 50$
	Low (1)	>50
AS4	High (3)	Hybrid
	Med (2)	Public
	Low (1)	Private
AS5	High (3)	≥ 100 TPS
	Med (2)	<100 TPS ≥ 10
	Low (1)	>10 TPS
AS6	High (3)	Yes
	Med (2)	N/A
	Low (1)	No
AS7	High (3)	Low implementation and maintenance complexity
	Med (2)	Medium complexity of implementation and maintenance
	Low (1)	High complexity of implementation and maintenance
AS8	High (3)	Centralized
	Med (2)	N/A
	Low (1)	Decentralized

6.4   Phase 4 – Context Definition

In order to define and identify which blockchain platform will be the most appropriate, or even the one that most "applies" to the service/product being developed, it is necessary to clearly and principally understand what the main characteristics and peculiarities of the context. Especially what are the motivators for using blockchain technology.

For example, the service to be developed needs a aspects that guarantee the trust of the application, however, the actors do not know each other, or the service to be developed has as strong characteristic the need to be scalable, the actors are all same business group and consequently the trust relationship is already a strong aspect, technology does not need to guarantee such aspect, are examples.

As seen and expected, the result of this phase will be the great driver for the next phases, in which aspects will be analysed and, mainly, the weight that will be attributed in the aspects according to the identified context.

Phase 4 Documentation

The context must be defined and should be consulted during the next phases, bellow the context with the main points (that should gain weight) are marked just for reference.

> In the case of this application to be developed, the main motivator for the choice the blockchain technology is to support mechanisms that encourage and facilitate the development of a product, application of the digital identity service. As this is an identity system, security and privacy aspects are paramount as well as user management and cryptographic keys.
>
> Preferably, the platform must have mechanisms that allow its applicability in private or public environments, and that includes aspects of performance and scalability, which, in the first instance, should be comprehensive and meet a region of a city or state. In addition, and not least, it should allow audits by all members of the network. The rules of consensus meet principles of fairness and equality of members.

6.5   Phase 5 – Weights Definition for Each Aspect

The assignment of the weights for each aspect defined in Phase 2 is fundamental for the qualification of the platform. The weights must be defined for evidences and needs, taking into account the context defined in Phase 4 of the methodology.

Phase 5 Documentation

The context identified in Phase 4 must be a direct connection with the weights, because the context lists the main characteristics desired in the application, service that will be developed. In this way these aspects should receive more weight than others: (i) easy to implement, (ii) security and privacy, (iii) user management, (iv) key management, (v) hybrid environment, (vi) performance, (vii) audit and (viii) consensus.

6.6   Phase 6 – Platform Analysis

This phase aims to analyse the level of each platform, considering each specific aspect. The analysis must be done with the qualification of the already defined levels for each blockchain platform, according to each defined aspects.

Thus, for each blockchain platform (Phase 1), its level (Phase 3) should be analysed for each aspects defined (Phase 2).

Phase 6 Documentation

The analysis is done in an objective way, validating the information collected previously, aiming that the people involved in the analysis can directly and clearly identify the level of the criterion of the aspect in focus. Table 4 presents the results of the analysis. The results should be based on the levels defined in Phase 3.

Table 4. MetaBlockX - Phase 6 platform analysis.

Platform	AS1	AS2	AS3	AS4	AS5	AS6	AS7	AS8
Weight	1	1	1	1	1	2	2	2
Bitcoin	High	High	Med	Med	Low	Low	Med	Low
Ethereum	High	Med	Med	High	Low	Med	Med	Low
Corda	Low	Med	Low	Med	Med	Med	Low	Med
BigChainDB	Low	Low	Low	Med	High	Low	Low	Low
Burrow	Med	Med	Low	Med	Med	Med	Med	Low
Fabric	High	High	High	Med	High	Med	Low	Med
Indy	Med	Low	High	Med	High	High	High	High
Iroha	Low	High	Low	Med	High	Med	Low	Low
Sawtooth	Low	High	Low	Med	Med	Med	Med	Med

6.7   Phase 7 – Context-Based Applicability Mapping

This phase aims to prioritize, among the blockchain platforms raised in Phase 1, the one that should be considered as focus for the development of the product, application or service, based on the context defined in Phase 4.

To do so, it is necessary that the qualitative values defined in Phase 3 be mapped into numbers, so that the application of the weight defined in Phase 5 can be performed.

In this phase the results of the analyses identified in Phase 6 will be applied to the realization of the blockchain platform mappings. This work results from the consolidation of the analysis and weights assigned using Eq. (1) to calculate the final grade of each blockchain platform, which will represent the level of applicability of that blockchain platform in the specific context.

$$P_{pb} = \frac{\sum_{i=1}^{A} (P_i \times N_i)}{\sum_{i=1}^{A} P_i} \qquad (1)$$

Where:

P_{pb} = Final score of the blockchain platform evaluated,
A = Number of aspects,
P_i = Weight attributed to aspect i,
N_i = Note attributed to aspect level i.

Phase 7 Documentation

A subset of the mapping and the result of the blockchain platforms based on the context are shown in a table, as seen in Table 5. The criteria used for this mapping and prioritizations were defined in the previous phases.

Table 5. MetaBlockX - Phase 7 Context-based applicability mapping.

Platform	AS1	AS2	AS3	AS4	AS5	AS6	AS7	AS8
Weight	1	1	1	1	1	2	2	2
Bitcoin	3	3	2	2	1	1	2	1
Ethereum	3	2	2	3	1	2	2	1
Corda	1	2	1	2	2	2	1	2
BigChainDB	1	1	1	2	3	1	1	1
Burrow	2	2	1	2	2	2	2	1
Fabric	3	3	3	2	3	2	1	2
Indy	2	1	3	2	3	3	3	3
Iroha	1	3	1	2	3	2	1	1
Sawtooth	1	3	1	2	2	2	2	2

With the results of the applicability mapping achieved in Phase 7, it is also possible to obtain a graph and a chart indicating the applicability of the blockchain platforms as shown in Fig. 4.

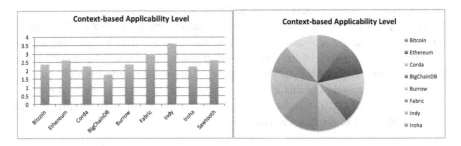

Fig. 4. Context-based applicability of blockchain platforms (Chart and Graph).

7 Future work

In recent years, it is possible to notice a witnessed and exuberant wave of application possibilities for blockchain technology, since ensuring food safety and global self-sovereign digital identities, until decentralized virtual government management. However, we also see numerous frauds in the initial ICO offerings, millions of dollars stolen from the cryptocurrency exchanges, and the lack of widespread adoption of almost anything based on blockchain, except by Bitcoin. At times, our hope of applying blockchain technology seems to have been noisy.

It is a fact that nobody else believes that blockchain can solve all the personal, social and business challenges that exist and are yet to come. However, we all know that blockchain technology will still be a tremendous opportunity to contribute advances to the next generation of the Internet and to society as a whole.

But for this, is need to understand that technology is still evolving and maturing, so is necessary to have clarity in the definition and choice of the best blockchain platform to be used and that is why the methodology described at this paper is proposed.

A tool to support and automate the methodology presented in this paper is a future work. Another work is the implementation and integration of database with broad knowledge about the existing platforms where it will be possible to simulate contexts and automated choices. In this way, choosing the best platform to the specific context will be possible to extract all the benefit that blockchain technology can offer us.

8 Conclusion

This paper presented a contextualization on blockchain technology (Sect. 2) that in its design took into account the following characteristics: (i) transparency, (ii) decentralization, (iii) security, (iv) trust and (v) automation. And an introduction about security and blockchain was presented (Sect. 3). It also presented the security layers (Sect. 4) for the development in blockchain which are: (i) security of the transaction, (ii) security of the user account, (iii) security of the application and chaincodes, (iv) security of implementation and operation of the application, (v) P2P network security of its nodes, and (vi) application and blockchain governance.

A section was dedicated to blockchain in IoT (Sect. 5), which introduced that blockchain technology is capable of providing a unique way of tracking the history of each device and also that in the near future, allowing intelligent devices to become independent agents that lead autonomously a variety of transactions.

To support the BlockIoT Project in the process of choosing the platform that will support the development of blockchain applications that have the most adherences to the context of an application with a focus on digital identity, the Context-Based Blockchain Platform Definition and Analysis Methodology (MetaBlockX) was developed and the application and results are presented (Sect. 6).

As a result of the application of MetaBlockX we have that with the target platforms chosen (Sect. 6-A), the relevant aspects and their respective levels of criticality (Sect. 6-B and C), context definition (Sect. 6-D) that took into account that the platform chosen should preferably have mechanisms that allow their applicability in private or public environments, and that includes aspects of performance and scalability which at first should be comprehensive and meet a region of a city or state. In addition, and not least, it should allow audits by all members of the network to be created and that the consensus rules comply with principles of fairness and equality of members, with the weights defined (Sect. 6-E) and after analysis and calculation for the due to mapping (Sect. 6-F and G).

Acknowledgment. The authors acknowledge the financial support given to this work, with the support of Funttel, Brazil's telecommunication technology development fund and Finep, Brazilian Innovation Agency. Agreement No. 0469/18. This paper reflects only the author's views and the Agencies are not responsible for any use that may be made of the information contained therein.

References

1. BlockchainHub. Blockchains & Distributed Ledger Technologies. https://blockchainhub.net/blockchains-and-distributed-ledger-technologies-in-general/. Accessed Mar 2019
2. Blockchain. Blockchain Whitepapers. https://www.cpqd.com.br/en/blockchain/. Accessed June 2019
3. Ethereum. How to Build a Democracy on the Blockchain. https://www.ethereum.org/dao. Accessed Mar 2019
4. Coindesk. Understand the DAO Attack. http://www.coindesk.com/understanding-dao-hack-journalists/. Accessed Mar 2019
5. Nakamoto, S.: A Peer-to-Peer Electronic Cash System. www.bitcoin.org/bitcoin.pdf. Accessed Mar 2019
6. Guegan, D.: The Digital World: I – Bitcoin: from history to real live. Centre d'Economie de la Sorbonne. https://halshs.archives-ouvertes.fr/halshs-01822962/document. Accessed June 2019
7. Blockchain. Whitepaper: Blockchain Fundamentals. https://www.cpqd.com.br/wpcontent/uploads/2017/09/whitepaper_blockchain_fundamentos_tecnologias_de_seguranca_e_desenvolvimento_de_softwar_FINAL.pdf. Accessed April 2019
8. eWallets. eWallets definition. Economic Times. https://economictimes.indiatimes.com/definition/e-wallets. Accessed May 2019
9. Dorri, A., Kanhere, S.S., Jurdak, R., Gauravaram, P.: Blockchain for IoT Security and Privacy: The Case Study of a Smart Home. https://allquantor.at/blockchainbib/pdf/dorri2017blockchain.pdf. Accessed May 2019
10. Cai, W., et al.: Decentralized Applications: The Blockchain Empowered Software System. https://www.researchgate.net/publication/327711685_Decentralized_Applications_The_Blockchain-Empowered_Software_System. Accessed Mar 2019
11. McKinsey. Blockchain beyond the hype: What is the strategic business value? https://www.mckinsey.com/business-functions/digital-mckinsey/our-insights/blockchain-beyond-the-hype-what-is-the-strategic-business-value. Accessed Mar 2019
12. Jianjun, S., Jiaqi, Y., Kem, Z.K.: Blockchain-based sharing services: what blockchain technology can contribute to smart cities. Financ. Innov. **2**, 26 (2016). https://doi.org/10.1186/s40854-016-0040-y
13. McKinsey. Using blockchain to improve data management in the public sector. https://www.mckinsey.com/business-functions/digital-mckinsey/our-insights/using-blockchain-to-improve-data-management-in-the-public-sector. Accessed Mar 2019
14. Bitcoin. Bitcoin Core. https://bitcoin.org/en/bitcoin-core/. Accessed Mar 2019
15. Ethereum. A Next-Generation Smart Contract and Decentralized Application Platform. https://github.com/ethereum/wiki/wiki/White-Paper. Accessed Mar 2019
16. Hyperledger. https://www.hyperledger.org. Accessed Mar 2019

Performance Evaluation of Wavelet SVD-Based Watermarking Schemes for Color Images

Taha H. Rassem[1]([✉]) [ID], Nasrin M. Makbol[2] [ID], and Bee Ee Khoo[2] [ID]

[1] Faculty of Computing, College of Computing and Applied Sciences,
Universiti Malaysia Pahang, Kuantan, Malaysia
tahahussein@ump.edu.my
[2] School of Electrical and Electronic Engineering, Universiti Sains Malaysia,
Nibong Tebal, Penang, Malaysia
{nasrin_makbol,beeKhoo}@usm.my

Abstract. Digital image watermarking techniques have enabled imperceptible information in images to be hidden to ensure the information can be extracted later from those images. For any watermarking scheme, there are four main requirements which are imperceptibility, Robustness, capacity and security. Recently, hybrid Singular Value Decomposition (SVD) based watermarking schemes in the transform domain have significantly gained a lot of attention. This is due to the characteristics of SVD and the wavelet. Most of these schemes were tested under different conditions using grey images only. However, due to the growth of digital technology and the huge use of the colour images, it is important to consider the colour images in the watermarking area. Three different SVD-based image watermarking schemes with different wavelet transforms are selected in this paper to be tested and evaluated for colour images. Two colour models are used to represent the colour images to perform the embedding and the extraction watermarking process to study these colour models' performances and effectiveness in the watermarking area. These colour models are RGB and YCbCr. All these colour models' channels are used as an embedding channel and then are evaluated under different attacks types. The experimental results of the selected Wavelet SVD-based watermarking schemes proved that the embedding in the RGB and YCbCr colour channels are achieved high imperceptibility. These colour channels also showed good robustness against different attacks such as cropping, cutting, rotation and JPEG compression.

Keywords: Image watermarking · Wavelet transform · Singular value decomposition · Colour models

1 Introduction

Image watermarking is the most researched and published over the last few years. The reason may be due to the large demand on image watermarking products due to the availability of so many images at no cost on the World Wide

© Springer Nature Singapore Pte Ltd. 2020
M. Anbar et al. (Eds.): ACeS 2019, CCIS 1132, pp. 89–103, 2020.
https://doi.org/10.1007/978-981-15-2693-0_7

Web that should be protected [9]. Digital watermarking protects the contents of the image by embedding a signal (i.e., image, audio, video or owner information) into the original host image without degrading visual quality of it. In the watermarking area, a watermarked image will be public and can be sent to the end-users. While the extracted or detected watermarks from the watermarked image will be used for protection and authentication purposes [23]. The watermarking researchers are suffering to handle several challenges for proposing new embedding and extracting algorithms with maintaining the required properties (requirements) to serve different intended applications. In the watermarking, the robustness, imperceptibility, security, and capacity are the main properties for any watermarking scheme.

A trade-off always exists among the watermarking properties [4,6]. In fcat, enhancing the watermark robustness may reduce the cover image imperceptibility. This is because of the higher watermark energy placed on the cover image after the embedding [3]. Furthemore, more capacity would affect the cover image imperceptibility too. This is because more modifications the cover image are needed to embed the watermark. Hence, to develop any watermarking scheme, it is important to balance among these conflicting properties [23,24]. The last property which is security, indicates to resistance of the watermark scheme against any hostile attacks. Use invisible watermarks can increase the security property and avoid any illegal access by the attackers or any attempt to remove as well as change the watermark.

The current challenge is achieving the trade-off among the most important watermarking requirements (i.e., robustness, capacity, and imperceptibility). High robustness against attacks and maintenance of good visual quality for the watermarked image, which is the core motivation for most existing watermarking schemes. The robustness and imperceptibility are the major requirements in watermarking technologies. These two requirements differentiate different data protection technologies from the watermarking [4,6]. Various image watermarking techniques have been established to address related problems. These techniques are classified into two types according to the embedding domain into spatial and transform domain techniques. The wavelet technique under the transform domain has gained popularity because of its properties. The wavelet transform has accurate model aspects HVS because of multi-resolution analysis [5,16].

Recently, the researchers are trying to enhance the new watermarking schemes by combine two or more transforms, which are considered as hybrid schemes. The idea emerged based on the assumption that combining different transforms can make up for the defects of an individual transform and result in an effective scheme [2,7,12,14]. The incentive for the idea of hybrid schemes is to use the properties of each transform to achieve the required properties. The success of hybrid schemes for achieving the watermarking requirements depends on the successful selection of the involved transforms. The transforms are selected according to each transform properties, and these properties are used to achieve a compromise between watermarking requirements. In the literature, a lot of image watermarking schemes are proposed by combined singular value decomposition (SVD) transform and different types of wavelet transform [7,10–13,15]. SVD is a mathematical tool used widely in many fields in the computer field. SVD is a matrix and this matrix can be decomposed into main three matrices with same size of the original matrix. These main matrices called U, S and V. The S matrix represents the singular values of the original image while the U and V are the left and right singular vectors of the image. Due to the powerful properties of the SVD, it is used in many applications. Most of the proposed SVD-based watermarking schemes used the S matrix for embedding. Embedding in the S matrix helps effectively in keeping minor changes in the values of the SVD matrix Because of that, the watermarking schemes based on the SVD transform successfully achieved the watermarking requirements. The SVD watermarking schemes achieved high robustness in terms of image processing as well as geometrical attacks. Furthermore, the good quality of the host image still maintained after embedding.

The study of watermarking for colour images is growing rapidly, due to the importance of the watermarking topic as well as the spread of the colour images. A huge amount of colour images are distributed every second on the Internet through the social media or webs. Due to the nature of the colour images compared with the gray images, many colour image watermarking embedding and extracting schemes were proposed recently [1,8].

In this paper, the applicability of different proposed SVD-based wavelet image watermarking schemes is evaluated for colour images. All the proposed schemes are applied on colour images instead of greyscale images due to its importance. These Hybrid SVD-based wavelet image watermarking schemes are proposed in [17–20,22]. Two colour models are used to represent the colour images to perform the embedding and the extraction watermarking process in order to study these colour models' performances and effectiveness. These colour models are RGB, and YCbCr. All these colour models' channels are used as an embedding channel, and then are evaluated against different types of attacks.

This paper is organised as follows. First, the selected hybrid SVD-based image watermarking schemes are explained in Sect. 2. Then, Sect. 3 explores the selected watermarking schemes robustness and the imperceptibility results. Finally, Sect. 4 concludes this paper.

2   Hybrid SVD-Based Image Watermarking Schemes

In this section, three related SVD-based image watermarking schemes proposed using the different wavelet transforms are explained [17–19]. These schemes successfully achieved high robustness against different types of image processing attacks (JPEG compression, salt and pepper noise, filtering, histogram equalization and gaussian noise). Also, these schemes showed resistance against several geometrical attacks (rotation, scaling, zooming, translation, cropping and cutting). In addition to the robustness, these schemes still maintain good and acceptable imperceptibility after the embedding. These schemes are used different wavelet transforms which are redundant Wavelet Transform (RDWT), Integer Wavelet Transform (IWT) and Discrete Wavelet Transform (DWT). The schemes are briefly explained in the following sub-sections.

2.1 RDWT-SVD Image Watermarking Scheme [18]

1. Embedding process
   The following are the embedding process steps of the RDWT-SVD scheme:
   - 1-level RDWT should be performed onto the host image. The image will be decomposed into four sub-bands (LL, LH, HL and HH).
   - The SVD is applied onto each sub-band as follows:

$$A^i = U^i S^i V^{iT} \tag{1}$$

   i refers to each sub-band.
   - The watermark is embedded directly into the S^i of each sub-band. Then, the result of the embedding is subject to SVD transform again as follows:

$$S^i + \alpha W = U_W^i S_W^i V_W^{iT} \tag{2}$$

   i refers to each sub-band, α is the scaling factor while W refers to the watermark. U_W^i, S_W^i and V_W^{iT} are the matrices of SVD.
   - The new coefficients of the RDWT are then calculated for all sub-bands as follows.

$$A^{inew} = U^i S_W^i V^{iT} \tag{3}$$

   i indicates to (LL, LH, HL, HH).
   - Finally, the inverse RDWT is applied using the modified RDWT coefficients to get the final watermarked image A_W.

$$A_W = RDWT^{-1} \tag{4}$$

2. RDWT-SVD Extracting Process

   The following are the extraction process steps of the RDWT-SVD scheme:
   - One-level RDWT is applied on the watermarked image A_W^* to decompose the image into LL, LH, HL, and HH sub-bands.
   - The SVD is applied onto LL, LH, HL and HH sub-band, as follows:

$$A_W^* = U^{*i} S^{*i} V^{*iT} \tag{5}$$

   i refers to LL, LH, HL and HH sub-bands.
   - Compute

$$D^{*i} = U_W^i S^{*i} V_W^{iT} \tag{6}$$

   i refers to LL, LH, HL and HH sub-bands.
   - Compute

$$W^{*i} = (D^{*i} - S^i)/\alpha \tag{7}$$

   W^{*i} refers to the extracted watermark from LL, LH, HL and HH sub-bands.

2.2 IWT-SVD-AT Image Watermarking Scheme [17]

1. Embedding process

The following are the steps of the embedding process of IWT-SVD-AT scheme:
- Perform same as RDWT-SVD in the first and second steps with replacing the RDWT by IWT.
- The watermark image is then scrambling using the Arnold Transform (AT).
- The scrambled watermark is embedded into each S^i similar to RDWT-SVD scheme as shown in Eq. 2.
- Calculate the new modified IWT coefficients for LL, LH, HL and HH sub-band using the following equation.

$$A^{inew} = U^i S_W^i V^{iT} \qquad (8)$$

- Apply the inverse IWT using the modified IWT coefficients to get the watermarked image as follows:

$$A_W = IWT^{-1} \qquad (9)$$

2. Extracting Process

The following are the steps of the extraction process of IWT-SVD-AT scheme:
- The watermarked image A_W^* is decomposed into LL, LH, HL and HH sub-bands using one-level IWT.
- SVD transform is applied onto each sub-band.

$$A_W^* = U^{*i} S^{*i} V^{*iT} \qquad (10)$$

- Calculate

$$D^{*i} = U_W^i S^{*i} V_W^{iT} \qquad (11)$$

- The extracted scrambled watermarks (W^{*i}) can be obtained as follows:

$$W^{*i} = (D^{*i} - S^i)/\alpha \qquad (12)$$

W^{*i} refers to each sub-band scrambled watermark.
- Finally, inverse AT is applied in order to get the watermarks in original form.

2.3 IWT-SVD Image Watermarking Scheme [19]

In this schemes, there are several stages:

1. Digital signature generation (DS)

   Unique digits in a binary form will be generated before embedding the hidden information into the host image. The signature should be a random to be more secure and hard to be predicted by any attacker. A random secret key is needed to generate the DS. The steps of the DS generation can be shown as the following [19]:
   - Convert the U and V orthogonal matrices from 2-D form to 1-D form.
   - Perform Hash function onto U and V using SHA-1.

   $$Digest_U = Hashing_{(SHA-1)}(U_W) \qquad (13)$$

   $$Digest_V = Hashing_{(SHA-1)}(V_W) \qquad (14)$$

   - The $Digest_U$ and $Digest_V$ should be converted into their binary digits. Then, a XORing operation should be fone between them; the result is called $R1$.
   - The selected secret key is then convert into binary digits; it refers as $R2$.
   - XORing $R1$ with $R2$ as follows:

   $$Result = R1 \oplus R2 \qquad (15)$$

   - Finally, the first 8-bits of above equation ($Result$) is used for authentication purposes, it named as Sig.
2. Signature embedding process

   - One-level DWT transform is applied onto the watermarked image.
   - The LL sub-band is divided into 8×8 blocks.
   - Eight blocks is randomly selected using the secret key.
   - Perform SVD onto each selected block.
   - In each block, each element $U_{2,1}$ is rounded to the nearest integer after multiplying it by 10, as shown below:

   $$U_{2,1}^{modified} = \lfloor U_{2,1} \times 10 \rfloor \qquad (16)$$

   - The $U_{2,1}^{modified}$ is tested as follows:
     (a) When the signature bit is 1 and $U_{2,1}^{modified}$ is even, or the signature bit equals 0 and $U_{2,1}^{modified}$ is odd, do increase $U_{2,1}^{modified}$ by 1, and the results is divided by 10.
     (b) If the above sentence is false, the $U_{2,1}^{modified}$ keep unchanged.
     (c) According on the above steps, the results is saved in $U_{2,1}$.
   - Do inverse SVD for all 8×8 selected blocks.
   - Do inverse DWT for whole.
3. Signature extraction stage
   - One-level DWT is performed on the watermarked image (possibly distorted).
   - The LL is divided into 8×8 blocks.

- The blocks is selected based on the secret key.
- Do SVD transform for all the selected blocks.
- Test $U_{2,1}$ according the following condition:

$$Sig(i) = \begin{cases} 1 & if \ mod(\lfloor U_{2,1} \div 10 \rfloor, 2) = 0 \\ 0 & if \ \text{otherwise} \end{cases} \tag{17}$$

where i indicates the length digital signature.

4. Embedding process

The following are the steps of embedding process of IWT-SVD scheme [19]:
- Perform same as IWT-SVD-AT in the first and second embedding steps
- Generate the signature using the four corresponding sets U_W^i and V_W^{iT}. Four 8-bit digital signatures will be generated. These signatures are called Sig_{LL}, Sig_{HL}, Sig_{LH} and Sig_{HH}.
- A final 8-bit DS will be established as follows:

$$Sig_{Final} = Sig_{LL} \oplus Sig_{HL} \oplus Sig_{LH} \oplus Sig_{HH} \tag{18}$$

The Sig_{Final} is the final signature and will be used in the final embedding process of IWT-SVD scheme as DS.
- Perform same as IWT-SVD-AT in the fourth and fifth embedding steps.
- Finally, the signature embedding procedure Sig_{Final} is applied into the watermarked image (A_W).

5. Extraction process

In this scheme, a safety test should be performed before extracting the watermarking. This is to check the fidelity and ensure that the proposed scheme is robust against the false positive problem (FPP) by checking the received sets of U_W^i and V_W^{iT} [21]. To do the authentication, the generated DS of the received sets of U_W^i and V_W^{iT} is compared with extracted DS from the watermarked image using the secret key. The extracting process can be continued If matching is positive, otherwise, the process should be stopped where a FPP is detected. The extraction process is same as the IWT-SVD-AT extracting process [19].

3 Colour Image Watermarking Application

In the colour image watermarking schemes, the host image which is a colour image is decomposed into its corresponding channels. They are Red (R), Green (G) and Blue (B) if the RGB colour model is used and the luminance component (Y), the blue-difference (Cb), the red-difference (Cr) if the YCbCr colour model is used. Then, the watermarking embedding procedure of the current used proposed scheme is applied to embed the greyscale watermark images into each one of these channels. For each proposed scheme in this work (RDWT-SVD, IWT-SVD-AT, and IWT-SVD), the watermarks are embedded and tested for all the channels of the colour model. For instance, if the proposed RDWT-SVD watermarking scheme is tested, the watermark images will be embedded and extracted six times. This is due to that, each time the watermark will be embedded into R/G/B channel if the RGB colour model is used and into Y/Cb/Cr channel if the YCbCr model is used. Thus, the extraction procedure is applied to extract the watermark images from the channel where they were embedded. Figures 1(a) and (b) represent the flowcharts to show how the processes embedding and extraction of the watermarks are applied for the colour images.

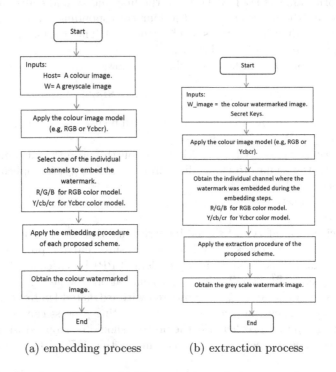

(a) embedding process   (b) extraction process

Fig. 1. The flowchart of the embedding process and the extraction process of the proposed colour image watermarking scheme.

In the following experiments, the colour Lena image with size 512×512, the colour Peppers with size 512×512, and the colour Baboon image with size 512×512 are used as host colour images. The Lena, Baboon, and Peppers colour images are shown in Fig. 2. While, the watermark was the greyscale cameraman image (Fig. 3) with size 512×512 in all schemes.

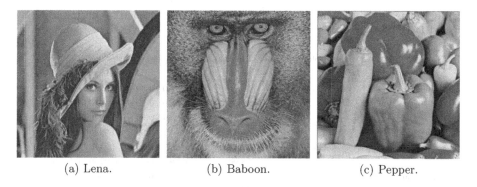

(a) Lena.   (b) Baboon.   (c) Pepper.

Fig. 2. 512 × 512 colour test images.

Fig. 3. Cameraman watermark image.

The imperceptibility performance of the proposed watermarking schemes is evaluated busing ($PSNR$) while (NC) is used to evaluate the robustness. The imperceptibility is a measurement can help to check the visual quality of the host image after embedding process and measure the similarity between the original image and the watermarked image. While robustness is a term to evaluate the similarity between the original watermark and the extracted watermark with or without subjected to attacks.

3.1 Colour Image Watermarking Experimental Results

All the proposed schemes are adopted to deal with the colour images. They have been applied successfully with colour images as well as the greyscale images.

Tables 1, 2, and 3 show the imperceptibility evaluation ($PSNR$) and robustness (NC) after applying RDWT-SVD, IWT-SVD-AT, and IWT-SVD proposed schemes on the colour models (RGB and YCbCr) for all tested colour images (Lena, Baboon, and Peppers). The $PSNR$ and NC values demonstrated that

Table 1. The imperceptibility $PSNR$ and the extracted watermark robustness (NC) of the RDWT-SVD colour image watermarking scheme.

	Colour space	Colour channel	PSNR (dB)	Extracted watermark (NC)			
				LL	LH	HL	HH
Lena	RGB	R	58.75	0.9980	0.9933	0.9936	0.8850
		G	59.46	0.9980	0.9937	0.9947	0.9481
		B	57.90	0.9984	0.9941	0.9946	0.9652
	YCbCr	Y	56.72	0.9987	0.9921	0.9935	0.9035
		Cb	57.01	0.9821	0.9565	0.9173	0.8347
		Cr	53.06	0.9988	0.9811	0.9750	0.9059
Baboon	RGB	R	60.40	0.9982	0.9965	0.9963	0.9974
		G	61.12	0.9979	0.9969	0.9970	0.9979
		B	61.74	0.9978	0.9970	0.9974	0.9978
	YCbCr	Y	57.55	0.9989	0.9953	0.9949	0.9957
		Cb	58.16	0.9703	0.9865	0.9544	0.9536
		Cr	56.53	0.9782	0.9289	0.9469	0.9374
Peppers	RGB	R	58.85	0.9984	0.9939	0.9934	0.9859
		G	61.28	0.9977	0.9947	0.9948	0.9900
		B	59.12	0.9979	0.9943	0.9942	0.9930
	YCbCr	Y	57.00	0.9988	0.9929	0.9932	0.9917
		Cb	66.45	0.9350	0.9893	0.9340	0.9676
		Cr	57.36	0.9921	0.9675	0.9888	0.9734

Table 2. The imperceptibility $PSNR$ and the extracted watermark robustness (NC) of the IWT-SVD-AT colour image watermarking scheme.

	Colour space	Colour channel	PSNR (dB)	Extracted Watermark (NC)			
				LL	LH	HL	HH
Lena	RGB	R	48.81	0.9999	0.9842	0.9908	0.9849
		G	49.10	0.9999	0.9833	0.9909	0.9858
		B	48.39	0.9999	0.9844	0.9904	0.9851
	YCbCr	Y	41.72	0.9995	0.9857	0.9855	0.9870
		Cb	38.07	0.9758	0.9867	0.9664	0.9954
		Cr	37.38	0.9883	0.9893	0.9898	0.9947
Baboon	RGB	R	47.51	0.9999	0.9863	0.9887	0.9870
		G	48.50	0.9999	0.9862	0.9901	0.9877
		B	49.34	0.9999	0.9860	0.9896	0.9867
	YCbCr	Y	41.34	0.9995	0.9846	0.9844	0.9885
		Cb	38.12	0.9673	0.9854	0.9824	0.9878
		Cr	39.07	0.9647	0.9864	0.9927	0.9868
Pepper	RGB	R	49.01	0.9999	0.9854	0.9904	0.9852
		G	50.34	0.9990	0.9841	0.9905	0.9863
		B	49.52	0.9991	0.9858	0.9907	0.9856
	YCbCr	Y	42.58	0.9989	0.9852	0.9867	0.9902
		Cb	38.81	0.9889	0.9899	0.9885	0.9785
		Cr	41.22	0.9843	0.9894	0.9895	0.9899

Table 3. The imperceptibility ($PSNR$) and the extracted watermark robustness (NC) of the IWT-SVD colour image watermarking scheme.

	Colour space	Colour channel	PSNR (dB)	Extracted Watermark (NC)			
				LL	LH	HL	HH
Lena	RGB	R	47.90	0.9998	0.9865	0.9895	0.9822
		G	49.01	0.9999	0.9858	0.9898	0.9838
		B	48.35	0.9999	0.9869	0.9881	0.9840
	YCbCr	Y	41.48	0.9992	0.9860	0.9864	0.9823
		Cb	38.22	0.9719	0.9781	0.9720	0.9921
		Cr	37.10	0.9827	0.9873	0.9876	0.9897
Baboon	RGB	R	46.73	0.9998	0.9858	0.9888	0.9853
		G	47.70	0.9998	0.9874	0.9894	0.9858
		B	48.85	0.9998	0.9877	0.9896	0.9859
	YCbCr	Y	40.91	0.9992	0.9864	0.9854	0.9906
		Cb	37.98	0.9645	0.9860	0.9844	0.9897
		Cr	38.47	0.9238	0.9872	0.9932	0.9887
Peppers	RGB	R	48.15	0.9997	0.9862	0.9900	0.9839
		G	50.71	0.9987	0.9844	0.9884	0.9853
		B	49.80	0.9990	0.9864	0.9893	0.9828
	YCbCr	Y	42.38	0.9984	0.9855	0.9864	0.9887
		Cb	38.56	0.9840	0.9879	0.9865	0.9773
		Cr	41.01	0.9776	0.9893	0.9902	0.9877

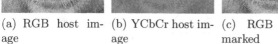

(a) RGB host image

(b) YCbCr host image

(c) RGB watermarked (embedding in R channel)

(d) YCbCr watermarked image (embedding in Y channel)

Fig. 4. IWT-SVD colour image watermarking. (YCbCr colour, embedding in Y channel).

all proposed schemes can be used for colour images as well as grey images where high imperceptibility and robustness are achieved. Figures 4, 5, 6, 7 and 8 show examples of some proposed colour image watermarking schemes in RGB and YCbCr colour models.

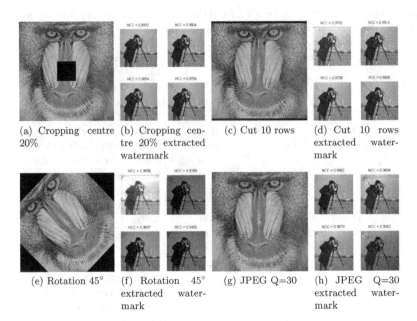

(a) Cropping centre 20% (b) Cropping centre 20% extracted watermark (c) Cut 10 rows (d) Cut 10 rows extracted watermark

(e) Rotation 45° (f) Rotation 45° extracted watermark (g) JPEG Q=30 (h) JPEG Q=30 extracted watermark

Fig. 5. IWT-SVD colour image Baboon watermarking under different attacks (YCbCr colour, embedding in Y channel).

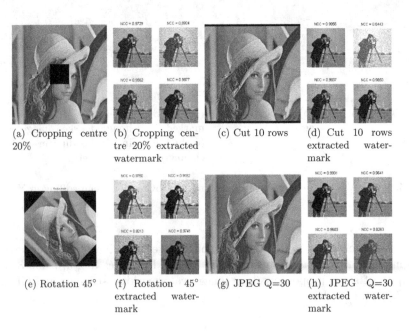

(a) Cropping centre 20% (b) Cropping centre 20% extracted watermark (c) Cut 10 rows (d) Cut 10 rows extracted watermark

(e) Rotation 45° (f) Rotation 45° extracted watermark (g) JPEG Q=30 (h) JPEG Q=30 extracted watermark

Fig. 6. IWT-SVD-AT colour Lena image watermarking under different attacks (RGB colour, embedding in R channel).

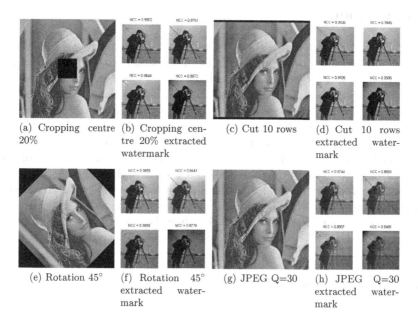

(a) Cropping centre 20% (b) Cropping centre 20% extracted watermark (c) Cut 10 rows (d) Cut 10 rows extracted watermark

(e) Rotation 45° (f) Rotation 45° extracted watermark (g) JPEG Q=30 (h) JPEG Q=30 extracted watermark

Fig. 7. RDWT-SVD colour Lena image watermarking under different attacks (RGB colour, embedding in G channel).

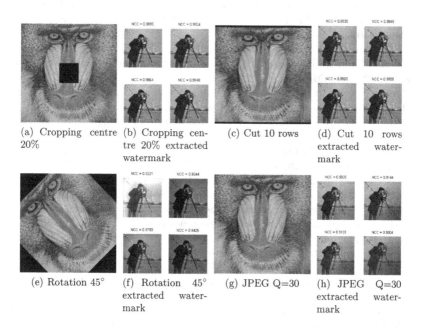

(a) Cropping centre 20% (b) Cropping centre 20% extracted watermark (c) Cut 10 rows (d) Cut 10 rows extracted watermark

(e) Rotation 45° (f) Rotation 45° extracted watermark (g) JPEG Q=30 (h) JPEG Q=30 extracted watermark

Fig. 8. RDWT-SVD colour Baboon image watermarking under different attacks (RGB colour, embedding in G channel).

4   Conclusion

In this paper, three different SVD-based watermarking schemes were tested and evaluated to be used with colour images to construct a colour image watermarking schemes. Two colour models, RGB and YCbCr colour models; were used in the experiments. Three different standard colour image which are Lena, Baboon and Peppers images were used as testing images. For each watermarking scheme, the image is divided into the color channels (R, G, and B) or (Y, Cb, and Cr). Then, each colour channel is considered as a separate host image and the embedding of the watermark is done in each channel. Different experiments had been done to evaluate RDWT-SVD, IWT-SVD and IWT-SVD-AT watermarking schemes using several attacks. Similar to grey images, RDWT-SVD, IWT-SVD and IWT-SVD-AT watermarking schemes showed high imperceptibility and good robustness against attacks when the colour image are used. Different performance had been obtained based on the colour model and its colour channels.

Acknowledgment. This work is supported by Universiti Malaysia Pahang RDU180365.

References

1. Abdulrahman, A.K., Ozturk, S.: A novel hybrid DCT and DWT based robust watermarking algorithm for color images. Multimed. Tools Appl. **78**(12), 17027–17049 (2019)
2. Ali, M., Ahn, C.W., Pant, M.: A robust image watermarking technique using SVD and differential evolution in DCT domain. Optik-Int. J. Light Electron Opt. **125**(1), 428–434 (2014)
3. Aslantas, V.: An optimal robust digital image watermarking based on SVD using differential evolution algorithm. Opt. Commun. **282**(5), 769–777 (2009)
4. Bhatnagar, G.: A new facet in robust digital watermarking framework. Int. J. Electron. Commun. (AEU) **66**(4), 275–285 (2012)
5. Chang, C.C., Tsai, P., Lin, C.C.: SVD-based digital image watermarking scheme. Pattern Recogn. Lett. **26**(10), 1577–1586 (2005)
6. Cox, I., Miller, M., Bloom, J., Fridrich, J., Kalker, T.: Digital Watermarking and Steganography, 2nd edn. Morgan Kaufmann Publishers Inc., San Francisco (2007)
7. Ganic, E., Eskicioglu, A.M.: Robust embedding of visual watermarks using discrete wavelet transform and singular value decomposition. J. Electron. Imaging **14**(4), 043004-9 (2005)
8. Giri, K.J., Bashir, R.: A block based watermarking approach for color images using discrete wavelet transformation. Int. J. Inf. Technol. **10**(2), 139–146 (2018)
9. Hartung, F., Kutter, M.: Multimedia watermarking techniques. Proc. IEEE **87**(7), 1079–1107 (1999)
10. Lagzian, S., Soryani, M., Fathy, M.: A new robust watermarking scheme based on RDWT-SVD. Int. J. Intell. Inf. Process. (IJIIP) **2**(1), 22–29 (2011)
11. Lai, C.C.: A digital watermarking scheme based on singular value decomposition and tiny genetic algorithm. Digit. Signal Proc. **21**(4), 522–527 (2011)

12. Lai, C.C., Tsai, C.C.: Digital image watermarking using discrete wavelet transform and singular value decomposition. IEEE Trans. Instrum. Measur. **59**(11), 3060–3063 (2010)
13. Liu, R., Tan, T.: An SVD-based watermarking scheme for protecting rightful ownership. IEEE Trans. Multimed. **4**(1), 121–128 (2002)
14. Loukhaoukha, K., Chouinard, J.Y., Taieb, M.H.: Optimal image watermarking algorithm based on LWT-SVD via multi-objective ant colony optimization. J. Inf. Hiding Multimed. Signal Process. **2**, 303–319 (2011)
15. Loukhaoukha, K., Chouinard, J.Y.: Hybrid watermarking algorithm based on SVD and lifting wavelet transform for ownership verification. In: Canadian Workshop on Information Theory, pp. 177–182 (2009)
16. Maity, S., Kundu, M.: Perceptually adaptive spread transform image watermarking scheme using Hadamard transform. Inf. Sci. **181**(3), 450–465 (2011)
17. Makbol, N.M., Khoo, B.E.: A hybrid robust image watermarking scheme using integer wavelet transform, singular value decomposition and arnold transform. In: Zaman, H.B., Robinson, P., Olivier, P., Shih, T.K., Velastin, S. (eds.) IVIC 2013. LNCS, vol. 8237, pp. 36–47. Springer, Cham (2013). https://doi.org/10.1007/978-3-319-02958-0_4
18. Makbol, N.M., Khoo, B.E.: Robust blind image watermarking scheme based on redundant discrete wavelet transform and singular value decomposition. AEU-Int. J. Electron. Commun. **67**(2), 102–112 (2013)
19. Makbol, N.M., Khoo, B.E.: A new robust and secure digital image watermarking scheme based on the integer wavelet transform and singular value decomposition. Digit. Signal Process. **33**, 134–147 (2014)
20. Makbol, N.M., Khoo, B.E., Rassem, T.H.: Block-based discrete wavelet transform-singular value decomposition image watermarking scheme using human visual system characteristics. IET Image Process. **10**, 34–52(18) (2016)
21. Makbol, N.M., Khoo, B.E., Rassem, T.H.: Security analyses of false positive problem for the SVD-based hybrid digital image watermarking techniques in the wavelet transform domain. Multimed. Tools Appl. **77**(20), 26845–26879 (2018)
22. Makbol, N.M., Khoo, B.E., Rassem, T.H., Loukhaoukha, K.: A new reliable optimized image watermarking scheme based on the integer wavelet transform and singular value decomposition for copyright protection. Inf. Sci. **417**, 381–400 (2017)
23. Pérez-Freire, L., Comesaña, P., Troncoso-Pastoriza, J.R., Pérez-González, F.: Watermarking security: a survey. In: Shi, Y.Q. (ed.) Transactions on Data Hiding and Multimedia Security I. LNCS, vol. 4300, pp. 41–72. Springer, Heidelberg (2006). https://doi.org/10.1007/11926214_2
24. Singh, P., Chadha, R.: A survey of digital watermarking techniques, applications and attacks. Int. J. Eng. Innov. Technol. (IJEIT) **2**(9), 165–175 (2013)

Privacy Preserving Threat Hunting in Smart Home Environments

Ahmed M. Elmisery[1]([⊠]) and Mirela Sertovic[2]

[1] Faculty of Computing, Engineering and Science,
University of South Wales, Pontypridd, UK
`ahmedmisery@gmail.com`
[2] Faculty of Humanities and Social Sciences, University of Zagreb,
Zagreb, Croatia
`msertovic@yahoo.com`

Abstract. The recent proliferation of smart home environments offers new and transformative circumstances for various domains with a commitment to enhancing the quality of life and experience of their inhabitants. However, most of these environments combine different gadgets offered by multiple stakeholders in a dynamic and decentralized manner, which in turn presents new challenges from the perspective of digital investigation. In addition, a plentiful amount of data records got generated because of the day-to-day interactions between smart home's gadgets and homeowners, which poses difficulty in managing and analyzing such data. The analysts should endorse new digital investigation approaches and practices to tackle the current limitations in traditional digital investigations when used in these environments. The digital evidence in such environments can be found inside the records of log-files that store the historical events and various actions occurred inside the smart home. Threat hunting can leverage the collective nature of these gadgets, the vengeful artifacts observed on smart home environments can be shared between each other to gain deeper insights into the best way for responding to new threats, which in turn can be valuable in reducing the impact of breaches. Nevertheless, this approach depends mainly on the readiness of smart homeowners to share their own personal usage logs that have been extracted from their smart home environments. However, they might disincline to employ such service due to the sensitive nature of the information logged by their personal gateways. In this paper, we presented an approach to enable smart homeowners to share their usage logs in a privacy-preserving manner. A distributed threat hunting approach has been developed to elicit the various threat reputations with effective privacy guarantees. The proposed approach permits the composition of diverse threat classes without revealing the logged records to other involved parties. Furthermore, a scenario was proposed to depict a proactive threat Intelligence sharing for the detection of potential threats in smart home environments with some experimental results.

Keywords: Smart home · IoT · Secure-multiparty computation · Privacy · Threat hunting · Digital investigations

M. Anbar et al. (Eds.): ACeS 2019, CCIS 1132, pp. 104–120, 2020.
https://doi.org/10.1007/978-981-15-2693-0_8

1 Introduction

The emergence of smart connected things that contain resource-constrained embedded systems with autonomous capabilities to enable connecting with other surrounding things and be self-aware of their internal states or external environment, has recently evolved into what is recently recognized as the internet of things. With the various wired and wireless communication technologies currently exist to facilitate connectivity between these heterogeneous devices, an increasing number of resource-constrained objects are getting connected with each other. These objects also have the capability of interacting with people, where they can collect data from people's everyday activities, then the collected data got exchanged with each other or remote services on the internet. Because of this feature, these objects are often titled "smart" and can be used as basic building blocks for smart automation systems. The smart home is one of the domains of IoT, that is composed of an IoT network of connected systems that facilitate connectivity between electronic sensors, analytical software and mechanical actuators inside the physical home environment [1]. The kind of setup, empower the smart homeowners with the ability to get notifications, to apply control and automate various activities performed within the home's perimeter. This also has an impact on enhancing the quality of daily chores from anywhere at any time through a smartphone application and an internet connection [2]. The progress of IoT-based smart home environments is currently gaining an increased momentum due to the wide range of improvements in the development of wireless protocols, embedded systems, cloud technologies, and the availability of internet-enabled smartphones. Most large businesses launching their own products to gain a share in this potential market and to inspire the advance of the next smart home ecosystem e.g., Nest smart thermostat, Apple HomeKit, Siri and Alexa enabled devices. These smart devices hold valuable digital data [3], potentially targeted by invasion attacks from external actors. Additionally, Smart home environments are frequently being targeted as well. It has been noticed a gradual increase in practices and available resources in relation to exploiting the vulnerabilities within smart home' devices. Since most of The IoT devices within Smart homes have a large number of vulnerabilities in their protocols, firmware, and software. Attackers are always ready to abuse these vulnerabilities to gather, alter or delete private information of smart-home owners or damage their IoT systems. The current security techniques are not 100% effective in the face of these increasing attacks. The threats dynamics for the smart home environment are very high, almost new vulnerabilities or unusual exploits are getting discovered daily in these systems. Data from different IoT systems of a smart home can be logged in different formats. From a threat hunting perspective, such logged data about various events in the IoT systems can give an indication about the behaviors and functionalities of these systems. In our work, we refer to IoT-based smart home environments as smart home.

Digital investigations are scientifically proven methods concerned with examination and analysis of digital evidence. The success of these tasks is highly depending on the ability of the forensic investigators to analyze large volumes of digital forensic data to locate suitable evidence. This, in turn, will require massive computational resources because of the size of the involved data. With the increasing cases of cybercrimes utilizing IoT devices [4], the need for applying digital investigations into IoT domain became indispensable. Since, the new IoT paradigm has been exposed to various vulnerabilities, which can induce a new type of cybercrimes that is accomplishable through these devices. However, it is necessary to adapt the processes of digital investigations when being applied into IoT scenarios, due to certain characteristics imposed by the IoT paradigm that make it different from other contexts, such as the increasing number of connected devices, the heterogeneity, diversity of collected data formats, and proprietary protocols of connected devices requires type-specific evidence retrieval tools, and the resource-constrained nature of these connected devices. Hence, existing digital investigations tools cannot successfully be applied to this paradigm without considering these features. IoT Forensics [5] is a relatively new term that characterizes a new paradigm in the digital investigations committed to implementing forensic practices for the collection and analysis of evidence from the peculiarities of Internet of Things (IoT) infrastructure. This new paradigm follows the well-established principles of traditional computer forensics, particularly targeting identification, acquisition, preservation, analysis, and reporting of digital evidence. Nonetheless, IoT forensics faces many challenges due to the inadequacy of currently usable computer forensics tools and methodologies in the IoT realms [6]. Furthermore, the tremendous amount of diversified data generated by the IoT devices poses a substantial challenge for the digital investigators to smoothly determine the precise portion of crucial data required for further analysis and examinations [7]. The potential evidence source in IoT forensics may include household appliances, health and fitness devices, entertainment systems, connected home hubs, Home monitoring/security systems, and outdoor gadgets, among others. While, in traditional computer forensics the potential evidence source can be computers, main servers, networking devices or mobile phones. In respect of the particular kind of the digital evidence that can be found, in IoT forensics, the digital evidence can exist in a standard or proprietary format, unlike the traditional computer forensics where the digital evidence mostly exists in standard formats. The last challenging factor in IoT forensics is the complex hardware architecture and diverse operating systems these gadgets have, along with monopolistic protocols and hardware that are subject to unclear standards.

One of the recent emerging themes in digital investigations is threat hunting, which is a preemptive cyber-defense activity that involves iterative searching through networks to detect sophisticated threats or potential vulnerabilities that elude existing security solutions, which differs from the current approaches that depend on passive waiting for cyber threats that might be detected if a violation in the previously configured conditions occurred inside any of the deployed network security solutions (IDS, IPS, SIEMS). The proactive approach can profoundly support the creation of a strong digital perimeter that continuously tracks pieces of evidence of new penetrative threats or malicious activities on the smart home environment. The threat hunting activity crucially relies on the cooperation between various groups of smart home's gadgets to repeatedly collect data to hunt for evidence regarding potential vulnerabilities without halting the functions of a smart home environment. The success of threat hunting activity highly depends on the ability of the system to execute threat-based security analysis approaches on large volumes of incomplete data from smart home's gadgets to locate suitable evidence, this, in turn, will require a lot of computational resources due to the volume of the data involved. The main objective of this research is to propose a collaborative threat hunting platform, which aims to share pieces of evidence with other smart home environments to facilitate prompt detection of attacks against the smart-home owners, or the infrastructure of the smart environment and for mitigation. The proposed platform can have a vast impact on alleviating the need for high computational resources, since only high confidence rules and artifacts related to attacks observed on other smart home environments will be shared. Furthermore, this approach can assist to overcome the complexity of evidence acquisition which might be incomplete or inaccurate when getting extracted from a single source. Finally, logs from several smart environments' gadgets collectively support each other since recording the same data in two different logs makes the extracted evidence stronger and can guarantee the genuineness of the threat to particular systems. An additional important requirement for threat hunting that the evidence data collected from various smart home environments are going to be processed collaboratively. Hence, scalability is essential in order to support the construction of large threat reputations groups with semantically enriched information. In order to prevent malicious entities from participating in the formation of threat reputations groups, tampering the results or compromising smart-home infrastructure to launch other attacks; every smart home environment needs to provide a set of credentials or prove identity during any of the steps required for the formation of threat reputations groups.

Most of the threat hunting solutions proposed so far have undervalued the demands to protect the privacy of end-users during the whole process of digital investigations. This situation has noticed real and significant implications for privacy concerns with the advent of IoT devices as an essential part of our daily activities as these gadgets are able to harvest and transmit personally identifiable information from every angle of our day-to-day activities. Thus, smart-home owners might be reluctant to participate in threat hunting activity, especially if they feel their own privacy is at stake by sharing data within their smart-home environment. These privacy issues that are related to threat hunting need to be taken into consideration for the advance of this kind of approaches. Most of privacy issues are related to how the data will be distributed and which laws govern the sharing of data. Thus, it is necessary to provide a technical assurance to smart-homeowners that privacy is guaranteed at all times and the sharing of information will not adversely affect their personal and professional reputation [8]. It is important that the proposed platform be able to enforce privacy principles in each of the phases of threat hunting approach and to provide initial functionality related to applying group-based access control and reputation mechanisms, to promote the establishment of trust between the various unnamed participants.

In this work, a threat hunting approach was proposed to implicitly elicit the relevant threat reputations groups from the multiple feeds of event logs. This process has been designed to be carried at the smart homeowner side. The presented system will attain security, privacy for event logs and will help smart homeowners to easily adopt a proactive approach for threat hunting. Any event logs collected from smart-home environments and shared with our system will be camouflaged using two-stage concealment protocols to preclude any potential risk of data breaches. This proposed approach also maintains the privacy of the data influx within the smart home such as sensitive usage patterns, events, and conditions, since any released data for threat hunting process will be concealed, and the original raw data will be stored in an encrypted form and only available for its owner. When the two-stage concealment protocols handle the records within the event logs, any beneficial patterns for the threat hunting will be eliminated. Therefore, to support the analysis phase of threat hunting process on the concealed logs, some selective properties in the collected records have to be maintained to ease the ranking process related to threat reputations. This paper has been organized as follows, In Sect. 2, related works were summarized. Section 3 the proposed system that envisioned at the smart homeowner's side was outlined. The proposed adversary model was presented in Sect. 4. Essential definitions related to the problem formulation along with the two-stage concealment protocols realized for the ranking process of threat reputations were explicated in Sect. 5. Section 6, experimental results were depicted. Finally, the conclusions and future directions were given in Sect. 7.

2 Related Works

At present, digital investigation is a well-established technical aspect used by almost all big business. The processes of digital investigation begin only after a breach occurs. Lately, the attention has deviated from a reactive manner to a more proactive one, where security solutions will hunt for threats and vulnerabilities in the system to thwart breaches from occurring. The earlier detection of malicious activities or potential flaws, the better chance of reducing or avoiding future damages that may occur. This approach is what is known as threat hunting, which has recently emerged as a hot topic in the domain of cyber-security. However, there is a notable lack of literature review on this new approach. Each cyber-security vendor tends to promote its own definition of threat hunting to differentiate their own product as a threat hunting solution. In turn, this leads to ambiguity related to this concept. There are many different definitions to explain this term formulated based on its perception within the cyber-security community. For example, threat hunting can be defined as the process of seeking out adversaries before they can successfully execute an attack [9]. Sqrrl refers to threat hunting as a proactive and iterative searching through networks and datasets to detect threats that evade existing automated tools [10]. For the purpose of this research, threat hunting can briefly be defined as a preemptive activity that seeks for indicators of compromise in smart-home environments. The work in [11] proposed a framework that models multi-stage attacks in a way that describe the attack methods and the expected consensuses of these attacks. The groundwork of their research is to model behaviors using an Intrusion Kill-Chain attack model and defense patterns. The implementation of their proposed framework was employed using Apache Hadoop. The authors in [12] presented framework that utilizes text mining techniques to actively correlate information between the security-related events and the catalogue of attack patterns. The foundation of this work is to reduce analysis time and enhance the quality of attack identification. The work in [13] proposed a methodology that combines structural anomaly detection from information networks and psychological profiling of individuals. The structural anomaly detection uses graph analysis and machine learning to identify structural anomalies in various information networks, while the psychological profiling dynamically assembles individuals' psychological profiles from their behavioral patterns. The authors proceed to identify threats through by linking and ranking of the varied results obtained from structural anomaly detection and psychological profiling. In [14] an aspect of threat detection was introduced, which relies on identifying unexpected changes in edges' weights over time. Wavelet decomposition method was employed to differentiate the transient activity from the stationary activity in the edges. The authors in [15] proposed the usage of data mining techniques through visual graphical representation to overcome different threats. In their research, two new visualization schemes were proposed to visualize threats. In [16], a botnet detection framework has been developed, which utilizes cluster analysis to characterize similarity patterns of C&C communication and activities flows. The proposed framework sniffs the network traffic then executes two types of parallel analyses, one analysis is performed for detecting a cluster of hosts with similar communication patterns, and the other inspects the packet payloads to detect anomalous activities. The activities are later grouped to detect a cluster of hosts with similar malicious behavior. A cross-correlation process is utilized to merge the results of preceding analyses to produce meaningful groups of malicious hosts that might be forming a Botnet. The trade-off between digital investigation and privacy was discussed in [17], where the authors proposed privacy preserving forensic attribution layer to attain a balance between privacy and digital investigation processes. Group-based signatures were utilized as a part of their proposed solution to achieve the previous goal. Finally, the authors in [18] studied privacy issues in digital investigation and assumed that the forensics investigation process may violate the privacy of truthful users. The research work has proposed a protocol to offer privacy to these users while holding malicious users liable.

3   The Proposed System

The general approach of threat hunting is to log any and all events in its environment for further analysis. This allows forensic investigators to have more data during the correlation analysis of patterns in order to discover malicious behaviors. When the amount of collected data increases, this task becomes cumbersome and difficult to manage. Within smart home environments, the massive amount of generated data poses a restriction on any human-based analysis and calls for new automated approaches for threat hunting. In this work, clustering analysis will be utilized to infer potential future vulnerabilities and to rapidly label events on the smart home to cut down on detection time. The cooperative approach was utilized to get more threats related data and understand the whole context from nearby smart home environments. This in turn, vastly reduces the threat window which needs a further investigation. Moreover, the proposed platform actively mitigates these threats using immediate notification to the smart homeowner that contains the recommended remediation procedures along with automatically generating new detection and prevention rules for the deployed security solutions at smart homeowner's side. This offers a complete security solution that can be used to benefit new smart homeowners.

The research conducted on this paper aims to realize privacy by design approach [19] in which a middleware was proposed for governing the data privacy during the ranking process of threat reputations groups. The homeowners will not be forced to follow a binary subscription system, either to participate in the threat hunting by releasing their raw event logs or opt-out from the whole process. With the proposed system, the homeowners now have the capability to sanitize the sensitive information in any released event logs. In such a procedure, they will be empowered to disclose their data gradually. The proposed system can enable the homeowners to control their data that need to be shared with various threat hunting processes. Hence, they have the choice to enroll in any threat hunting group with a crafted version of their event logs. The key motivation behind our system is to apply a user-centric principle that follows the safest approach to preserve the sensitive records at the homeowners' gateways and to not release them in a raw form. Nonetheless, in order to participate in threat hunting and to obtain the related set of threat reputations groups, the homeowners should disclose their event logs in a specific way to facilitate the ranking process. Our proposed system relies on a middleware approach, that we named a cognitive middleware for cooperative threat hunting (CMCTH). Our middleware is composed of multiple cooperative agents and is being hosted in the smart home gateways. The collaboration between these different agents is essential to achieve privacy for the homeowners' data. Within CMCTH, every agent has a certain task; a local concealment agent executes a baseline concealment process which generates a sanitized event log by segregating the sensitive events based on end-user's policies. The local masking agent receives the sanitized event log then engages in the execution of the two-stage concealment protocols required for the ranking process of threat reputations groups.

The first stage protocol proposed in this research was entitled the secure threat ranking (STR), which is a distrusted cryptographic protocol, that is used to compose generalize virtual threat groups based on the individual event logs collected from different smart home systems. The second stage protocol was named the secure threat insights (STI), which takes as an input the virtual threat groups extracted from the first stage protocol then proceed to detect a set of real threat groups in every and all virtual threat groups. Aggregation topologies were employed in CMCTH to manage the data collection process from homeowners' gateways. The first stage protocol utilizes a simple ring formation topology for its processes and the second stage protocol uses a complex hierarchical formation topology for extracting precise real threat groups. The selection of these two aggregation topologies is adequate to the different steps in every protocol. Our proposed system relies on the existence of a centralized threat intelligence server (CTI). CTI is a centralized element on the proposed system responsible for initiating the ranking process and storing the final groups extracted after every run. CTI also offers a virtual workplace and a proxy for facilitating the interaction between smart homes' gateways of different vendors that might have uncommon communication protocols. The scenario presented in this research is the following: based on the several threat categories, CTI generate initial threat reputation groups then submit data related to these groups to the smart home's gateways to verify if the event logs might have occurrences of these threats. Every gateway is running its own CMCTH. CMCTH start the threat hunting process by inciting the local concealment agent to produce a sanitized event log that contains only generalized events that are related to their logs while segregating any sensitive events. Since this step cannot guarantee full privacy, CMCTH attempts to conceal these sanitized events by executing two-stage concealment protocols during the threat categorization process. The final threats ranking get offered based on the relevancy of the published events to different extracted threats. At the end of the threat hunting, CTI will permit the smart home's gateways to participate in a pertinent threat reputation group which will present a set of countermeasures to prevent these threats from occurring.

4 The Assumed Adversary Model

Our proposed system attains privacy for the sensitive records in the event logs. Every entity participating in the threat hunting process is following the semi-honest model. Hence, it is obliged to behave in accordance with the processes of the two-stage concealment protocols, but any intermediate data received from other entities could be stored for further investigation. In our model, we considered the centralized threat intelligence server (CTI) to act as an untrusted adversary that aims to gather the sensitive records in the event logs to be able to infer activities of various homeowners and to trace them back. We don't assume CTI to be an entirely malicious adversary which is a practical assumption. CTI is aiming to attain some business goals as well in order to boost their profits and reputations in the threat hunting industry. As a measure for the usefulness of our system, the achieved privacy is considered high only if the CTI can't infer activities of various homeowners from their event logs released for the threat hunting process.

5 The Proposed Concealment Procedure in CMCTH

We will start this section with outlining a set of significant notions used during this research work based on our previous research in [20, 21]. The event logs within our system are being presented in two forms, a sanitized event log and a sensitive event log. On one hand, the sanitized event log is a generalized version of the sensitive event log, where sensitive events get suppressed and other non-sensitive events get replaced with a set of hypernym phrases that are in the same semantic level of these non-sensitive events. The sanitized event logs can be considered the public data the smart home-owners agreed to disclose and released by CMCTH for the threat hunting process. On the other hand, the sensitive event logs stores records of personal events that smart homeowners avoid publishing in a raw form for other external entities. Privacy should be maintained when performing the ranking process related to threat reputations groups. Privacy should also be preserved when the final threats ranking get offered to a new entity on the system. The collected event logs used in threat hunting processes should also be preserved from CTI and/or any external entities involved in the whole procedure. In this paper the term "virtual threat group" can be defined:

Definition 1. A virtual threat group is the set $VC = \{RC_1, RC_2, \ldots, RC_n\}$, where n is the number of real threat groups in VC, the virtual threat group has the following properties: (1) Each $\forall_{i=1}^n RC_i \in VC$ has a 3-element tuple $RC = \{I_{sg}, V_{sg}, d_{sg}\}$ such that $I_{sg} = \{i_1, i_2, \ldots, i_l\}$ presents the set of sanitized events, $V_{sg} = \{v_1, v_2, \ldots, v_k\}$

corresponds to the set of gateways, and $d_{sg} \in I_{sg}$ is the main- defining event of RC. (2) For every gateway $\forall_{i=1}^l v_i \in V_{sg}$, v have the events V_{sg}. (3) d_{sg} is the most frequent event in V_{sg} events log, and this event considered as the "core-point" of this real threat group RG. (4) For any two real threat groups RC_a and $RC_b (1 \leq a, b \leq n$ and $a \neq b)$ the following conditions are satisfied: $V_{sg_a} \cap V_{sg_b} = \emptyset$ and $I_{sg_a} \neq I_{sg_b}$.

5.1   The Two-Stage Concealment Protocols

This work presents two-stage concealment protocols that will be used for masking the event logs of smart homeowners when being released for threat hunting. The CMCTH is the element that is hosted on the gateways of smart homeowners and enforces the privacy preservation of the sensitive records on the event logs [22–29]. CMCTH will also execute the proposed cryptographic concealment protocols. The first stage concealment protocol was named secure threat ranking (STR) and the second stage concealment protocol was termed secure threat insights (STI). These protocols will facilitate the secure ranking extraction of threat groups from the masked event logs. These protocols will privately offer a ranked list of potential threats to new participants based on the relevancy of their released event logs to the different extracted threat reputation groups. Hence, any newly registered gateway can participate in any real threat group in a secure and private manner. The members of the same real threat group can share their systems configurations to prevent the occurrence of these threats and share information that can aid in handling a certain chain of threats facing their crucial systems.

Secure Threat Ranking (STR) Protocol

The first stage concealment protocol aims to categorize different event logs into multiple virtual threat groups. CMCTH will face two challenges when categorizing those virtual threat groups. The first challenge is related to the representation of this threat group, i.e., an accurate intra-group closeness and a precise intra-group separation need to be clear in every extracted virtual threat group. The second challenge is related to attaining high privacy level for the sensitive records inside the event logs. Therefore, STR takes as an input the sanitized event log that was previously preprocessed by local concealment agent. This is a crucial step to maintain higher privacy levels for any published records. The sanitized event log is usually formed using public information by mapping any released event logs with a set of hypernym phrases obtained through taxonomy trees and/or public dictionaries that produce alternative events in the same semantic level of the original sensitive events. This process will form what is known as a sanitized event log as previously proposed in [20, 21].

After generating sanitized event logs, CMCTH invokes the masking agent to run the distributed STR protocol to start building virtual threat groups based on the sanitized event logs that were submitted by smart homes' gateways. After running the STR protocol, every created virtual threat group will hold the set of smart homes' gateways who are largely sharing a similar set of events in their published event logs. The STR protocol gets executed in a distributed way. This protocol starts by organizing smart homes' gateways in a ring topology. STR protocol utilizes sanitized records published by gateway V_c to create an event vector $V_c = (e_c(w_1), \ldots, e_c(w_m))$, such that m represents the number of unique events in the event log, and $e_c(w_1)$ describes the significance weight of such event w_1 in gateway V_c (weighted frequency). The next computation steps utilizes the concept of term frequency inverse log frequency model that was presented in [30] as follows:

$$Term - frequency_{V_c}(w_i) = \#w_i \text{ in } V_c \log/\#events \text{ in } V_c \log, \text{ and}$$
$$inverse - log - frequency_{V_c}(w_i)$$
$$= \log(\#gateway/\#logs \text{ contain event } w_i), \text{ where}$$
$$e_c(w_1) = Term - frequency_{V_c}(w_i) * inverse - log - frequency_{V_c}(w_i)$$

The selection of similarity metric is an important step in STR protocol. Since an appropriate metric will be able to capture the hidden similarity between all sanitized records of every gateway. For this reason, we employed the Dice similarity metric. Let $V_c(V_d)$ to be two event vectors respectively for two gateways C and D then:

$$GatewaysSimilarity(V_c, V_d) = 2|V_c \cap V_d|/|V_c|^2 + |V_d|^2$$

In simple words, every two gateways C and D can be considered similar to each other if they are sharing many sanitized records with each other. Accordingly, the STR protocol should be able to infer that these two gateways should be belonging to the same virtual threat group. It is worth mentioning that any sensitive events will not be published and will be stored in an encrypted form at the smart homeowner side. The processes for the STR can be described as follows:

- For each threat hunting procedure, every two gateways $C, D \in V$ own a set of event vectors $e_c(w_i)$ and $e_d(w_i)$. Each one of them executes a predefined hash function denoted by h on its own set of event vectors to generate new hashed sets $V_c = h(e_c(w_i))$ and $V_d = h(e_d(w_i))$ respectively. *CMCTH* hosted on the gateway C will generate a two pair of encryption key E and decryption key U. *CMCTH* shares this encryption key E with the other gateway D. Computing the similarity between every two gateways is done by calculating two steps. The first one, is to compute the numerator, and the second one is to compute the denominator.
- For the correct execution of the STR protocol, one of the smart home's gateways should be selected as a trusted node for the aggregation process. Thereafter, topological ring formation is built between all of these gateways who decided to participate in the threat hunting in order to receive the calculated numerator values.
- The masking agent running on gateway D starts to hide V_d by executing $B_d = \{e_d(w_i) \times r^D | w_i \in V_d\}$ where r is a random number for every event in its event log w_i. After finishing this step, the gateway D sends its B_d to the gateway C.
- After the gateway C receives correctly B_d. The masking agent at gateway C starts to sign B_d using its private key to obtain the signature S_d. Gateway C sends S_d again to the gateway D in the same order as it has received it before. The *CMCTH* running at the gateway D start the process of divulging the received event set S_d by utilizing its r values to obtain the real signature SI_d of the gateway D. The gateway C starts to

implement the predefined hash function h on the real signature SI_d to obtain the set $SIH_d = H(SI_d)$.

- The masking agent running on the gateway C also signs the event set V_c to get the signature set SI_c. Additionally, masking agent implements the same predefined hash function h on the signature set SI_c to form a new set $SIH_c = H(SI_c)$. The *CMCTH* on the gateway C submits the calculated values back to the gateway D.
- The masking agent at the gateway D initiates a comparison process between the two hashed sets SIH_d and SIH_c based on the knowledge it previously owns from V_d. The gateway D obtains the result of the intersection process between the two sets $IN_{C,D} = SIH_c \cap SIH_d$ which presents the interaction set between the two event sets of both of the gateways C, and D which will be denoted by $|V_c \cap V_D|$. *CMCTH* at the gateway D applies the predefined hash function h on the interaction set $IN_{C,D}$. After finishing the previous step, the gateway D encrypts with the public key of the trusted node the calculated hashed set along with the size of two sets $|V_D|$, $|V_C|$ and the gateways' pseudonyms identities. This encrypted data is later will be sent to the trusted node of this threat group.
- Finally, after collecting all of these intermediate results from every pairs of gateways at the trusted node. The trusted node starts the process of decrypting them, then after runs cluster analysis on these values using the S-seeds clustering algorithm [20] to order to obtain different virtual threat groups.

The presented STR protocol performs all of these steps on m hashed sanitized records that are distributed across m parties without disclosing any of the raw values of these sanitized records.

Secure Threat Insights (STI) Protocol

The masking agent is the component within the *CMCTH* that is also responsible for implementing the second stage concealment protocol (STI protocol) on the extracted virtual threat groups obtained from the first stage concealment protocol (STR protocol). The idea of the STI protocol is to infer in a bilateral manner the set of correlated events exists between the sanitized records of event logs. The final output of this protocol aids in detecting the pertinent real-threat groups that exist within every virtual threat group. STI protocol is mainly based on our previous research work presented in [20, 21]. The main intuition of the STI protocol is to utilize the sets of frequent events that commonly exist between the event logs of multiple smart homes' gateways. If one of these frequent sets is large enough, a real threat group is formed that has this set a main/core topic. For the correct execution of the STI protocol, a topological hierarchical formation should be built between all of these gateways who decided to participate in the threat hunting. This topological formation aids in finding similar real threat groups spanned around the various virtual threat groups. The processes for the STI can be described as follows:

- The STI protocol is usually started after the termination of the first stage concealment protocol. However, it can also start by an indication from the CTI. The gateways in each virtual threat group confer together to elect one of them to act as a trusted node. The trusted node will be responsible for distributing its own catalog of 1-candidate frequent events. Upon receiving the 1-candidate frequent events, the gateways designate a local function hosted on the *CMCTH* to calculate their local frequent events on their sensitive event logs utilizing their own support and closure parameters. The algorithm discussed in [31] can run locally on every event logs to extract global & local frequent events of all event logs for the gateways within every virtual threat group.

- For the gateways in the same virtual threat group $\forall_1^n P_i$, the gateway P_i start encrypting with its own key the locally extracted list of frequent events then sends this list to the second member P_{i+1} in its virtual threat group, and so on for all gateways.

- This process got repeated for all gateways until the last gateway in the virtual threat group P_{n-1} submits all the collected lists to the elected trusted node of this virtual threat group. The trusted node begins to calculate the global support for the global frequent events by simply aggregating all the received local supports from the different gateways. Moreover, the global closure for the global frequent events can also be calculated by finding the intersection between all the received local closures from the different gateways.

- The trusted node starts to encrypt and distribute the catalogs of global supports & closures in random order to the gateway P_{n-1}. The first gateway P_{n-1} that receives these catalogs begins decrypting its own encrypted contribution using its own private key. After that, the gateway P_{n-1} forwards these catalogs to another gateway P_{n-2} also in random order. Finally, the trusted node gets back these catalogs, but this time these catalogs are only encrypted with the trusted node's own key. Therefore, final results can be generated.

- The trusted node initializes a real-threat group *RC* for every adjacent set of global frequent events. These initial real-threat groups comprise all gateways that have these global frequent events in their event logs. In the beginning, these initial real-threat groups could be overlapped between multiple virtual threat groups. However, the continuous progress of STI, they will be merged together such that every set of global frequent events will be representative for one real-threat group.

- For the event log of gateway V_i, the masking agent will need to assign an appropriate initial real-threat group $RC(c_i)$ by utilizing the following scoring function: $\text{SimilarityScore}(RC_i \leftarrow V_i) = \left[\sum_{w_i} e_r(w_i) * RC\_support(w_i) \right] - \left[\sum_{w_i'} e_r(w_i') * VC\_support(w_i') \right]$. Where w_i represent the global frequent event in the event log r also this global frequent event is common in an initial real-threat group RC_i. The w_i' is representing the global frequent event in the event log r and is not frequent in this initial real-threat group RC_i. After applying this scoring function on all event log of all gateways. At this point, every gateway will be able to determine its membership to an exactly one real-threat group. The representative of each real-threat group gets re-calculated based on the event logs of its current members.

- Inside every virtual threat group VC, the elected set of trusted nodes collaborate together to assemble a hierarchical structure of the real-threat groups, that have been extracted from the event logs of their members' gateway. Each real-threat group can now be represented using the set of global frequent k-events, in such case; it will act as a main/core topic or simply a representative. In the hierarchical structure, the real-threat group owns k-frequent events will be placed at level k of this structure. The parent of this real-threat group at level k−1 will own k−1 frequent events, which is also a subset of the frequent events owned by its child at level k. We have utilized the previously mentioned scoring function to derive the nominee parent for every child real-threat group. In the end of the step, the list of extracted real-threat groups got distributed between all the trusted nodes. This crucial step enables the integration of real-threat groups that own similar frequent events based on the inter-real threat group similarity and removes the restrained threat groups based on the intra- threat group separation. The proposed new similarity metric for this task is similar to the scoring function used in the STR protocol. The only new variation introduced in here in the normalization process that is employed to exclude the effect of the size of the real-threat group on the final result. This new utilized metric can be expressed as follows:

$$RC_{\text{Similarity}(RC_i \leftarrow RC_j)} = \left[\frac{\text{SimilarityScore}(RC_i \leftarrow \forall_{x=1}^{n} V_x \in RC_j)}{\left[\sum_{w_j} e(w_j) + \sum_{w_j'} e\left(w_j'\right) \right]} \right] + 1$$

The *Inter* $RC\_similarity(RC_i \leftrightarrow RC_j) = [RC\_Similarity(RC_i \leftarrow RC_j) * RC\_Simila rity(RC_j \leftarrow RC_i)]$. Where RC_i and RC_j are two real-threat groups; $\forall_{x=1}^{n} V_x \in RC_j$ represents a single conceived event log for the real-threat group RC_j that contain all the event logs of its current members. w_j stands for a global frequent event exists in both of RC_i and RC_j while the w_j' stands for a global frequent event exists only in the real-threat groups RC_j but not in RC_i. Finally, $e(w_j)$ and $e\left(w_j'\right)$ represent the weighted frequency of both of w_j and w_j' in the real-threat group RC_j.

- Finally, when a new smart homeowner decides to participate in a threat hunting process, He/she invokes his/her own CMCTH to download from the CTI the catalog of core points for the available real-threat groups. Later, CMCTH begins the execution of the two-stage concealment protocols on the sensitive event logs stored at the smart homeowner's gateway. The similarity between the owner's sensitive event logs and the representatives of the real-threat groups can be computed locally at the homeowner's side. In the end, the CMCTH ranks all the similarity values then enroll its smart home's gateway in the real-threat group with the highest similarity value. the CMCTH will start receiving information related to the threat reputations of its owner usage events, the technical systems configurations of its owner will be automatically adjusted to prevent the occurrence of these threats and finally a set of threat analysis information will be provided to aid the smart homeowner in handling a certain chain of threats facing their crucial systems. Additionally, the smart homeowner can now get a detailed instruction related to mitigation and remediation procedures in the case of the occurrence of these threats. Finally, the CMCTH utilize the cooperative nature of the real-threat groups to automatically generate new detection and prevention rules for the current security solutions deployed at the smart homes.

6 Experiments and Results

The experiments presented in this research were performed on two Intel® machines connected using a local network. The Server has an Intel® Core i7 and the other machine has an Intel® Core 2 Duo. A data storage was done using a MySQL database for saving a set of event logs from various gateways. The CTI entity has been implemented as a web service. The *CMCTH* has been built as an applet to manage the various communications between the gateways themselves, and the interaction between the CTI and other gateways. The proposed two-stage concealment protocols were implemented using Java and BouncyCastle© library, RSA algorithm was used in encryption with key length of 512 for all experimental scenarios. The experiments have proceeded on a real smart home network that contains different IoT devices. In order to mimic a normal usage log, a dataset was pulled from an IPTV network which has been linked to another dataset containing 54 threat services of 30 IoT devices. The sanitized event logs were created based on recorded events. In order to measure the accomplished privacy level and the accuracy of results obtained using our system. We used precision and recall metrics as shown in Fig. 1. As noticed in the figure, good quality is attained when our solution identifies virtual threat groups first. These virtual threat groups will contain multiple sets of real-threat groups. With this way, our solution will be able to extract accurate information from the gateways who share the same data. Additionally, the impact of every sensitive event within the real threat group can be easily calculated. This will permit the *CMCTH* to extract and remove anomalies that are far from the common sanitized events.

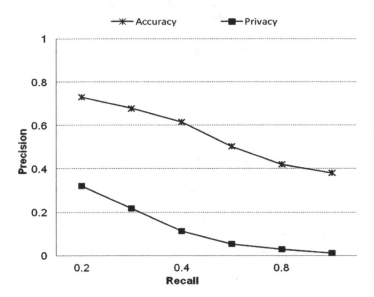

Fig. 1. Accuracy and privacy of the extracted threat reputations groups

We have also measured the impact of leaked sensitive events from different gateways on privacy levels during the run of the two-stage concealment protocols. We assumed a set gateways intentionally disclosed a portion of their sensitive events in the sanitized event logs released for threat hunting. For every set of sensitive events; the attack procedure mentioned in threat model was conducted with the aim of revealing other sensitive events stored in their sensitive event logs and based on the real-threat group they are belonging to. The obtained sensitive events were quantified and the results are shown in Fig. 1. As seen from the results, the proposed system can significantly reduce privacy leakages of the exposed sensitive events, However, the exposed sensitive events will only be hashed hypernym phrases that are in the same semantic level of non-sensitive events. The real sensitive events of other smart homeowners have already been suppressed from being released.

7 Conclusions and Future Directions

In this research work, a cognitive middleware for cooperative threat hunting (CMCTH) was presented which is hosted at the homeowners' gateways. CMCTH enroll the smart homeowners' gateways in a specialized threat hunting groups that permit the sharing of threat related information related to mitigation and remediation procedures in the case of the occurrence of these threats and also facilities the automatic re-configurations of smart homeowners' systems to prevent the occurrence of these threats. The formation of threat hunting groups is done without revealing any sensitive events logs to external entities. An overview of the two-stage concealment protocols was given. The performance of our solution was tested on a real dataset. The experimental results and the analysis clearly demonstrate that achieving higher privacy levels during the threat reputations processes is possible using our solution without the need to reduce the accuracy of the extracted threat reputations. A future research agenda for this research will include utilizing game theory to better compose virtual threat groups, multiple events publications and its impact on the privacy of the smart homeowners.

References

1. Seralathan, Y., et al.: IoT security vulnerability: a case study of a Web camera, pp. 172–177 (2018)
2. Boztas, A., Riethoven, A., Roeloffs, M.: Smart TV forensics: digital traces on televisions. Digit. Investig. **12**, S72–S80 (2015)
3. Gao, C., Chandrasekaran, V., Fawaz, K., Banerjee, S.: Traversing the quagmire that is privacy in your smart home, pp. 22–28 (2018)
4. Biswas, K., Muthukkumarasamy, V.: Securing smart cities using blockchain technology, pp. 1392–1393 (2016)
5. Chandok, P., Shin, C., Liu, R., Nielson, S.J., Leschke, T.R.: Potential forensic analysis of IoT data: an overview of the state-of-the-art and future possibilities. In: 2017 IEEE International Conference on Internet of Things (iThings) and IEEE Green Computing and Communications (GreenCom) and IEEE Cyber, Physical and Social Computing (CPSCom) and IEEE Smart Data (SmartData), Exeter (2017)

6. Ryu, J.H., Sharma, P.K., Jo, J.H., Park, J.H.: A blockchain-based decentralized efficient investigation framework for IoT digital forensics, pp. 1–16 (2019)
7. Adedayo, O.M.: Big data and digital forensics. In: 2016 IEEE International Conference on Cybercrime and Computer Forensic (ICCCF), Vancouver, BC, Canada, pp. 1–7 (2016)
8. KPMG Australia: Cyber Threat Intelligence and the Lessons from Law Enforcement. KPMG Australia (2015)
9. Lord, N.: What is threat hunting? The emerging focus in threat detection. Digit. Guard. (2018)
10. Sqrrl. Cyber Threat Hunting. www.sqrrl.com
11. Bhatt, P., Yano, E.T., Gustavsson, P.: Towards a framework to detect multi-stage advanced persistent threats attacks, pp. 390–395 (2014)
12. Scarabeo, N., Fung, B.C., Khokhar, R.H.: Mining known attack patterns from security-related events. PeerJ Comput. Sci. 1, e25 (2015)
13. Mahyari, A.G., Aviyente, S.: A multi-scale energy detector for anomaly detection in dynamic networks, pp. 962–965 (2013)
14. Miller, B.A., Beard, M.S., Bliss, N.T.: Eigenspace analysis for threat detection in social networks, pp. 1–7 (2011)
15. Bhardwaj, A.K., Singh, M.: Data mining-based integrated network traffic visualization framework for threat detection. Neural Comput. Appl. 26(1), 117–130 (2015)
16. Gu, G., Perdisci, R., Zhang, J., Lee, W.: Botminer: clustering analysis of network traffic for protocol-and structure-independent botnet detection (2008)
17. Afanasyev, M., et al.: Privacy-preserving network forensics. Commun. ACM 54(5), 78–87 (2011)
18. Antoniou, G., Sterling, L., Gritzalis, S., Udaya, P.: Privacy and forensics investigation process: the ERPINA protocol. Comput. Stand. Interfaces 30(4), 229–236 (2008)
19. Rubinstein, I.S.: Regulating privacy by design. Berkeley Technol. Law J. 26(3), 1409–1456 (2011)
20. Elmisery, A.M., Doolin, K., Botvich, D.: Privacy aware community based recommender service for conferences attendees. IOS Press (2012). https://doi.org/10.3233/978-1-61499-105-2-519
21. Elmisery, A.M., Doolin, K., Roussaki, I., Botvich, D.: Enhanced middleware for collaborative privacy in community based recommendations services. In: Yeo, S.S., Pan, Y., Lee, Y., Chang, H. (eds.) Computer Science and its Applications. Lecture Notes in Electrical Engineering, vol. 203, pp. 313–328. Springer, Dordrecht (2012). https://doi.org/10.1007/978-94-007-5699-1_32
22. Beil, F., Ester, M., Xu, X.: Frequent term-based text clustering. In: Proceedings of the Eighth ACM SIGKDD International Conference on Knowledge Discovery and Data Mining, Edmonton, Alberta, Canada, pp. 436–442 (2002)
23. Fung, B.C.M.: Hierarchical document clustering using frequent item sets. Master's thesis, Simon Fraser University (2002)
24. Elmisery, A.M., Rho, S., Botvich, D.: Privacy-enhanced middleware for location-based sub-community discovery in implicit social groups. J. Supercomput. 72(1), 247–274 (2015). https://doi.org/10.1007/s11227-015-1574-x
25. Elmisery, A.M., Rho, S., Botvich, D.: Collaborative privacy framework for minimizing privacy risks in an IPTV social recommender service. Multimedia Tools Appl. 75(22), 14927–14957 (2016). https://doi.org/10.1007/s11042-014-2271-0
26. Elmisery, A.M.: Private personalized social recommendations in an IPTV system. New Rev. Hypermedia Multimedia 20(2), 145–167 (2014). https://doi.org/10.1080/13614568.2014.889222

27. Elmisery, A., Botvich, D.: Enhanced middleware for collaborative privacy in IPTV recommender services. J. Converg. **2**(2), 10 (2011)
28. Elmisery, A.M., Botvich, D.: Agent based middleware for maintaining user privacy in IPTV recommender services. In: Prasad, R., Farkas, K., Schmidt, A.U., Lioy, A., Russello, G., Luccio, F.L. (eds.) MobiSec 2011. LNICST, vol. 94, pp. 64–75. Springer, Heidelberg (2012). https://doi.org/10.1007/978-3-642-30244-2_6
29. Elmisery, A.M., Botvich, D.: An agent based middleware for privacy aware recommender systems in IPTV networks. In: Watada, J., Phillips-Wren, G., Jain, L.C., Howlett, R.J. (eds.) Intelligent Decision Technologies. Smart Innovation, Systems and Technologies, vol. 10, pp. 821–832. Springer, Heidelberg (2011). https://doi.org/10.1007/978-3-642-22194-1_81
30. Sebastiani, F.: Machine learning in automated text categorization. ACM Comput. Surv. **34**(1), 1–47 (2002)
31. Cheung, D.W., Han, J., Ng, V.T., Fu, A.W., Fu, Y.: A fast distributed algorithm for mining association rules. In: Proceedings of the Fourth International Conference on Parallel and Distributed Information Systems, Miami Beach, Florida, United States, pp. 31–43 (1996)

Digital Forensics and Surveillance, Botnet and Malware, and DDoS and Intrusion Detection/Prevention

Performance Analysis of EMM an EDoS Mitigation Technique in Cloud Computing Environment

Parminder Singh[1], Shafiq Ul Rehman[2(✉)],
and Selvakumar Manickam[1]

[1] National Advanced IPv6 Centre (Nav6), Universiti Sains Malaysia (USM),
George Town, Penang, Malaysia
{parminder,selva}@nav6.usm.my
[2] ST Engineering Electronics - SUTD Cyber Security Laboratory,
Singapore University of Technology and Design (SUTD), Singapore, Singapore
shafiq_rehman@sutd.edu.sg

Abstract. As many organizations are adopting cloud computing as this allows them to be more agile, flexible and efficient. Nevertheless, as with any new technologies, cloud computing also suffers from various issues especially in security and privacy. Distributed Denial of Service (DDoS) attack saturates server resources, e.g. web server, by flooding it with fake requests. This renders the server inaccessible to legitimate users. Nevertheless, if the server is hosted as a cloud service, DDoS attack will not be effective due to the elasticity nature of the cloud server. Thus, a new variant of the DDoS attack, called Economic Denial of Sustainability (EDoS) attack, has emerged. Since the cloud service is based on "pay-per-use" model, EDoS attack endeavors to scale up the resource usage over time to the point the purveyor of the server is financially incapable of sustaining the service due to the incurred unaffordable usage charges. The implication of EDoS attack is a major security implication as more elastic cloud services are being deployed. A new mechanism, EDoS Mitigation Mechanism (EMM), is proposed to address these shortcomings using OpenFlow and statistical techniques, i.e. Hellinger Distance and Entropy. The experiments clearly showed that EMM is able to detect and mitigate EDoS attacks effectively without the need for additional resource requirements.

Keywords: Anomaly detection technique · Cloud computing · DDoS attack · EDoS attack · Mitigation mechanisms · Cyber security

1 Introduction

Cloud Computing (CC) [1, 2] has revolutionized the Information and Communication Technology (ICT) field [3]. This model delivers the computing resources as commodity services like water, electricity, and/or telecommunication. CC provides various service models such as infrastructure, software, platform, function etc., these services are provided on-demand based where the consumers pay as per their usage [4]. However, CC is found vulnerable to security threats that inhibit its development [5, 6].

© Springer Nature Singapore Pte Ltd. 2020
M. Anbar et al. (Eds.): ACeS 2019, CCIS 1132, pp. 123–137, 2020.
https://doi.org/10.1007/978-981-15-2693-0_9

Economic Denial of Sustainability (EDoS) is considered a new form of security threat to the CC environment [5–7]. In contrast to the conventional distributed denial of service (DDoS) attack [8] which takes down the services by consuming the resources of a targeted server in a traditional setup. EDoS attack uses the elasticity feature provided as a cloud service [8, 9] which induces the resources to dynamically scale to fulfill the demand thus leading in a hefty bill for the customer [7]. As a result, many organizations are reluctant to migrate their data or operations to cloud environment as EDoS attack targets such financial components of the cloud service providers which can have severe impact on them.

In this research, we explore and analyze the mitigation performance of EMM through a series of carefully planned experiments. The effectiveness of the EMM is verified based on its capability of handling the various scenarios whereby different types of attack traffic is generated from various tools with random packet size and throughput. This includes application layer hypertext transfer protocol (HTTP) and user datagram protocol (UDP) attack traffic besides a flow of legitimate traffic (normal traffic). Based on the evaluation results, it has been shown that EMM is able to handle the attacks efficiently by ensuring that attack traffic is dropped as soon as being detected by sending updated flow table rules to Open Virtual Switch (OVS) to block packets originating from the attacker for a fixed interval. During this period, only legitimate traffic is allowed to pass or request the resources of the cloud server.

Rest of the paper is structured as follows: Sect. 2 describes some of the most relevant state-of-the-art EDoS mitigation techniques and their limitations. The proposed EMM technique is mentioned in Sect. 3. The experimental design and results are presented in Sect. 4. And finally, the conclusion and future works are outlined in Sect. 5.

2 State of the Art

Most of the current literature available addresses mainly on DDoS protection emphasizing on techniques for preventing of apparently malicious traffic at the network or application layer [9–12]. There is limited number of literatures that are available to provide deployable solutions specifically for mitigating EDoS attacks in Cloud Computing environment. Some of the well-known EDoS mitigation techniques are as follows:

In 2009 self-verifying proof of work (sPoW) was proposed by Khor and Nakao [13]. The authors attempted to distinguish the EDoS attack, on-demand network filter and prioritize the legitimate traffic from network level DDoS traffic. To do so, sPoW does two things: first, it does packet pattern matching to distinguish and filter the DDoS network traffic. Second, it allows the legitimate traffic to go through the network. This mechanism does packet filtering based on cryptography puzzles methodology. By applying such algorithm, it allows legitimate traffic while discards the malicious network-level DDoS traffic. However, it possesses certain drawbacks. Firstly, asymmetric computational power consumption for the clients. Solving computational puzzles require more CPU power and suitable only to faster CPUs. Therefore, mobile devices with less processing power will not be able to resolve the puzzles, thus unable to access the cloud resources [14]. Secondly, the Server must create separate channels to address each request. In case of large number of incoming requests, server will generate number of puzzles which leads to puzzle accumulation attack if puzzles do not resolve in time.

Later in 2011, Sqalli et al. proposed another mitigation technique called EDoS-Shield [15]. This technique distinguishes the legitimate and malicious requests by checking the user's presence at client-side machine. EDoS-Shield architecture consists of Virtual Firewall (VF) and Verifier Nodes that functions in tandem to execute the EDoS mitigation tasks. Nevertheless, the proposed technique has certain constraints. First, it is vulnerable to spoofing attack. By performing IP address spoofing, attacker can use IP address belonging to the white list of the verifier node to carry out an EDoS attack that would remain undetected. Second, due to its designed mechanism it can possess higher false positive rate by blocking of many IP addresses belonging to the legitimate users, as the two lists are not updated in a timely and accurate manner.

In-cloud scrubber service is another mechanism proposed to mitigate the EDoS attack [16]. This mechanism uses on-demand web service (Scrubber Service) to address such attack by using crypto puzzle approach to validate the legitimate users request [13]. This mechanism offers two modes namely; normal mode and suspected mode. Based on the requirement service providers can choose the one accordingly. But there are certain limitations with this mechanism such as: it can only detect and mitigate HTTP attacks, also it depends on third party application for authentication purpose.

In 2013, Masood et al. proposed an EDoS mitigation framework known as EDoS Armor [17] specifically meant for E-Commerce applications. It uses two-step approach, comprises of admission control and congestion control. At first, when user initiates a session, the server sends a challenge to the user, it could be an image or a cryptographic puzzle to be resolved, in case user resolves the challenge, the request is being directed to admission control. Otherwise, the session of the user gets dropped and the number of connections to the server are limited for the user. This technique applies port hiding approach to restrict the users, as attack cannot be initiated in the absence of a valid port number. Next, the behavior of the user browsing is consistently being traced. whenever an abnormal behaviour is detected, service priority is being set for that particular user based on his previous records. Thus, in this manner, EDoS Armor can mitigate EDoS application. However, in e-commerce applications new users may find it complicated system due to its complexity in design. Therefore, in practice, the implementation of this method seems to be doubtful.

Recently, Chowdhury et al. proposed a new approach known as EDoS Eye to counter the EDoS attack [18]. This model applies game theory approach to mitigate the EDoS traffic. Authors claimed to develop a Game Based Decision Module (GBDM) that can get threshold values to restrict the incoming traffic. Similarly, another technique proposed by Shawahna et al. known as EDoS Attack Defense Shell (EDoSADS) [19]. According to the authors, this technique is applicable to Network Address Translation (NAT) based networks where it gets triggered if it sniffs any incoming abnormal traffic. For instance, in attack scenario, it triggers a checking component to differentiate between legitimate users and attackers. However, both techniques were evaluated in simulation environments that have their own limitations as well as are not closely representing the real-world scenario.

In the context of this work, a summary of previous efforts and research has been done in the area of network worm, network scanning and signature automation approaches. The main observations that can be derived from the related works are:

- EDoS attack affects the financial aspect of hosting a service on a CC environment.
- An appropriate testbed that can enable real-time and hi-speed analysis of a network is lacking.
- A more robust approach is required to ensure EDoS can be mitigated effectively.

3 Proposed Mechanism

In this section, we present our proposed mechanism for Cloud Computing (CC) environments known as EDoS Mitigation Mechanism (EMM) [20]. The aim of this mechanism is to be effective enough to mitigate different type of EDoS attacks while consume less resources. Due to space constraints, only the main functionalities of the EMM are presented here. For more details, readers can refer to our previous article [20] to attain the clarity. It consists of three major modules namely *Data preparation, Detection,* and *Mitigation,* to fulfill its objectives.

In data preparation module, the network traffic is sampled using sFlow agents and sent for analysis to sFlow collector. Network statistics are generated using the inputs received by the sFlow collector and traffic is then segregated based on *source IP, source port, destination IP, destination port,* and *counter.*

In the detection module, network statistics are compared against the threshold value defined using Hellinger's distribution [21] and classified for suspicious behaviours based on an entropy analysis [22].

Finally, in mitigation module, Open Flow (OF) controllers [23] drop the network traffic of suspicious source IP addresses by updating switching rules and continue monitoring the network for anomalies.

4 Experimental Design and Results

Before going to the results of the evaluation, it is imperative to understand the design of the experiments upfront. They are detailed as follows:

4.1 Test-Bed Environment Setup

The performance of any cloud mitigation technique can be best evaluated on an existing CC environment. However, access to such an environment is often not possible due to the usage of propriety tools or service provider organization's policies. Although there are solutions using simulation tools such as Mininet [24], only limited evaluation can be performed. For this purpose, a standard benchmark for CC environment is developed as a testbed using OpenStack cloud computing environment with

OpenDay Light (ODL) as Open Flow Controller (OFC) [23]. This allows the possibility to create network topologies and to carry out various tests.

OpenDaylight (ODL) controller is the most recent addition to OpenFlow controllers and is written in Java. It is meant to be a common platform for all SDN users. Recently, ODL pronounced its second release, *Helium*. ODL support most of the operating systems, i.e., Linux, Mac, and Windows, and it has the feature of topology discovery. ODL uses *karaf* framework, which makes it modular, besides enabling plug-in of various application modules developed in Java.

The developed testbed enables the opportunity for one to utilize a modern platform to design the topology with any number of virtual machines, OpenFlow controllers, virtual routers, and firewalls. With the implemented testbed, virtual machines can be launched with various web applications (web server). The testbed also consists of target machine, which primarily experience the large volume of attach/user traffic.

At first instance, all new traffic will pass through OFC, which will update all the network switches to perform basic forwarding functions. However, all switches and components are configured with sFlow agents to periodically update the monitoring agent with the current network statistics. Once traffic exceeds a defined threshold, the decision engine will update the OFC about the network condition and in return, OFC updates the flow table of switches to instruct the devices to drop the traffic from a specific attacker host. The rest of the traffic from other nodes will not be affected by the new flow update. The design of this testbed allows efficient monitoring process without introducing latencies or overhead to the underlying cloud computing network.

The specification of the utilized hardware (servers) is provided as below and in Table 1:

Blade Chassis M100OC with Power Edge M 610 Server.

- M610, Dual Quad Core Processor/16 GB/1 TB HDD.
- 720xd, Dual Hex Core Processor/64 GB/4 TB HDD.

Table 1. Hardware specification.

Number of machines	Operating systems	Hardware details	Purpose
1	Ubuntu14.04 x64	1 TB HDD, 16 GB RAM	Controller
1	Ubuntu14.04 x64	1 TB HDD, 16 GB RAM	Network
1	Ubuntu14.04 x64	1 TB HDD, 16 GB RAM	OpenFlow Controller
1	Ubuntu14.04 x64	1 TB HDD, 16 GB RAM	Compute-1
1	Ubuntu14.04 x64	1 TB HDD, 16 GB RAM	Compute-1
1	Ubuntu14.04 x64	1 TB HDD, 16 GB RAM	Compute-1
1	VMware ESXi 6	4 TB HDD, 64 GB RAM	Various VM

4.2   Performance Evaluation

All conducted experiments are carried out for a duration of 5 min. The duration of 5 min is used because the auto scaling timers used for the upper threshold is assumed to be duration of 5 min [25]. Specifically, the evaluation is performed to answer the following research question:

What is the influence of network traffic from different communication protocols, i.e., HTTP, transmission control protocol (TCP) and UDP in the effectiveness of EMM in a cloud computing environment?

The network topology for all the evaluation consists of five nodes that generate (pushes) normal traffic to the target machine and one host is dedicated for inducing and generating attack traffic to the target machine. Victim's network bandwidth is fixed at 10Mbps so that any variation in network can be easily measured.

Evaluation Metrics

The core idea behind the proposal of a mechanism i.e. EMM is to quickly detect and mitigate an ongoing EDoS attack as soon as possible to reduce the incurred damage to the cloud service/user. As such, the experiments that are conducted in evaluating EMM uses the standard metrics which measures the consumed resources, such as CPU, Memory, and Network bandwidth utilization rates.

The evaluation metrics are to be interpreted as following: the closer the resource consumption pattern to the baseline (or normal traffic), the better the performance of the evaluated mechanism. This is also applicable to the costs incurred by the cloud user; whereby, the lower the costs incurred, the better the performance of the mechanism in place.

Use Case 1: Influence of TCP (HTTP) Flooding Attack as an EDoS Attack.

The first set of experiments are conducted to investigate the influence of HTTP traffic flooding attack as an EDoS attack. HTTP flooding attack is the most common application layer attack (OSI Layer 7). This attack is volumetric in nature and uses legitimate protocol's GET or POST requests to retrieve information from the URL data.

In the first experiment, the victim machine is flooded with HTTP GET requests using the BoNeSi botnet DDoS HTTP flood simulator. The network and computer's network utilization are constantly being monitored via the monitoring tools.

At the same time, network traffic of random HTTP GET requests are generated using scripts that are running on five participating nodes to generate normal traffic to the webserver. The command line for the script is executed as shown below:

```
root@ubuntu:$perl httpflooder.pl -a GF -h 192.168.200.53 -t 400
```

Use Case 2: Influence of UDP Flooding Attack as an EDoS Attack.

A UDP flooding attack is another most common volumetric attack in the network. Attackers craft large-sized UDP packets and direct them to the victim. As the UDP protocol is "connectionless", it can be exploited to launch quick and massive attacks as it does not require any handshakes as it is with TCP sessions.

In fact, UDP attacks on network time protocol (NTP) service are observed to have reached a peak of 500 Gbps [26]. Domain name system (DNS) amplification attack is another example of UDP attack also known as the alphabet soup attack. As there is no specific packet format defined for UDP, attackers can craft large packets, fill it with junk text or numbers ("alphabet soup"), and redirect them to the victim of their choice.

The victims usually have to receive the packets and analyze them manually one by one before discarding useless packets.

Such a UDP attack is used to evaluate the effectiveness of EMM to mitigate such attacks. For that, IPerf is used to generate UDP streams of 20 Mb of random size packets to the victim IP as the attack traffic. The attack is repeated with an interval of 400 s using command as:

```
root@ubuntu:$ iperf -c 192.168.200.53 -v -b 20M -t 400
```

In addition to the attack traffic, normal UDP traffic is also generated using 10 Mb as bandwidth for a 300 s interval using IPerf command line as shown below:

```
root@ubuntu:$ iperf -c 192.168.200.53 -u -b 10M -t 300
```

Figures 1 and 2 depicts the normal HTTP and UDP traffic patterns before the attacker starts flooding the victim machine respectively. These represent the incoming packets per second in dependence to the time. Once the attack is initiated, the monitoring agent will detect the spike of traffic as an ongoing attack if the traffic exceeds the calculated dynamic threshold value based on the rate of incoming normal traffic.

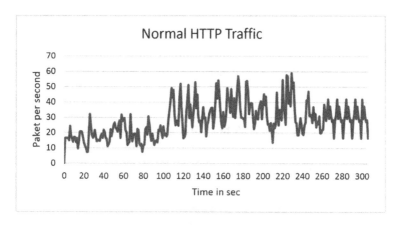

Fig. 1. HTTP traffic in normal condition.

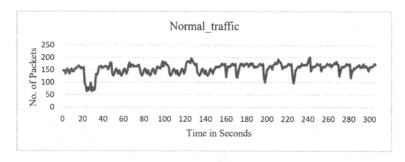

Fig. 2. UDP traffic in normal condition.

Figures 3 and 4 indicate the combined HTTP and UDP network traffics of both the normal as well as the attack traffic before the deployment of EMM into the network in dependence to the time. The Fig. 3 depicts the attacker generating HTTP traffic above 4Kpps in the network. Attack was initiated at 5 s and stopped at 300 s. Whereas Fig. 4 shows the attacker generates attack traffic above 3Kpps in the network starting from 3 s and ending at 270 s.

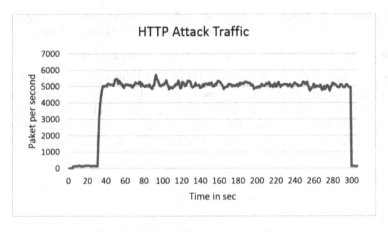

Fig. 3. HTTP traffic in attack condition.

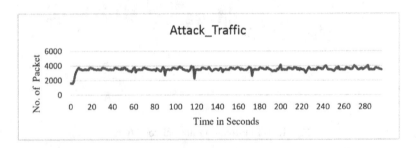

Fig. 4. UDP traffic in attack condition.

Next, EMM is deployed in the network and the same experiments are repeated once more. Figures 5 and 6 depict the observed HTTP and UDP network traffics in dependence to time that are delivered to the victim node in network after EMM implementation. Once EMM gets introduced in the network and attack breaches the defined dynamic threshold, the monitoring agent generates a call to OFC to push an updated rule to OVS to block the attacker's source IP for period defined by the administrator. In our experiment, we defined the block time as 30 min. This duration is chosen based on the reports of the average duration of a DDoS attack observed in the Internet. It was reported that 85% of DDoS attacks last for less than 30 min [27]. It is clearly visibly that surge of traffic perceived at the victim node is reduced significantly after the deployment of EMM.

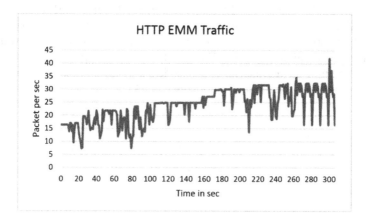

Fig. 5. HTTP traffic after EMM deployment.

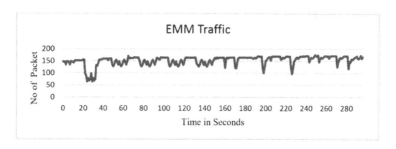

Fig. 6. UDP traffic after EMM deployment.

As soon as the blocking time expires, the monitoring agent call OFC to delete the rule from the OVS and continue to monitor the network. If the monitoring system detects that the attack is still in progress, it adds another new rule to OVS via Open-Flow controller to drop the packets of the attackers.

As aforementioned, DDoS or EDoS attacks cause the overall system resources utilization to increase proportionally. The resource utilization analysis of the attacker machine under attack is presented in Figs. 7, 8, 9, 10, 11, 12, 13 and 14:

Figures 7 and 8 represent the comparison of the HTTP and UDP network traffic patterns of the victim's machine under several scenarios in dependence to time. The first scenario which is depicted in blue line is the normal traffic in which no attack is taking place. The second scenario depicts the scenario of an ongoing attack to the victim by indicating the combined network traffic pattern that is being delivered to the victim. Finally, the plot in red depicts the network traffic pattern when the proposed EMM is in place.

The comparison indicates that without any mitigation mechanism in place, the victim suffers from non-legitimate HTTP network traffic pattern that is between 10000% higher than the HTTP normal traffic and from non-legitimate UDP network traffic pattern that is between 2300% higher than the normal UDP traffic. With the proposed EMM in place, the delivered network traffic patterns are reduced significantly, and are closely matching with the rate of normal traffic. However, it is noted that a minor amount of the legitimate HTTP traffic is also dropped, i.e., false positives, due to the design of the mechanism that considers a deviation of network traffic from the observed dynamic threshold as an ongoing attack.

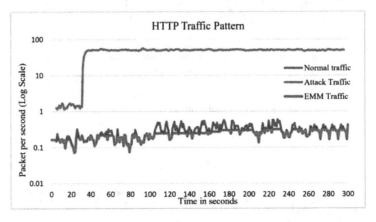

Fig. 7. Network traffic pattern comparison in HTTP traffic conditions.

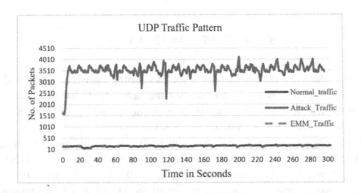

Fig. 8. Network traffic pattern comparison in UDP traffic conditions.

When comparing the CPU utilization rate of the three scenarios mentioned above, it is evident that an ongoing attack also consumes the resources of CPU utilization tremendously. As shown in Fig. 9, the utilization rate of the victim machine under attack HTTP traffic is 600% higher than the HTTP normal traffic. Similarly, Fig. 10

depicts the CPU utilization rate of the victim machine under UDP attack traffic is around 200% higher than the normal UDP traffic. However, when comparing to the proposed EMM in place, no additional significant CPU utilization is measured (even under the attack scenario) in comparison to the utilization during normal HTTP and UDP traffics. This indicates that the proposed EMM is not only able to help the victim from having spike in its resources, but also strengthen the point that implementation of EMM itself is lightweight in terms of the consumed CPU utilization.

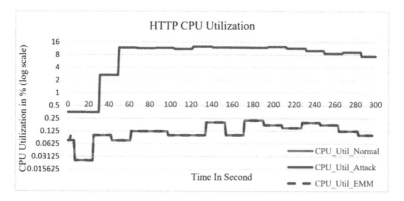

Fig. 9. CPU utilization comparison in HTTP traffic conditions.

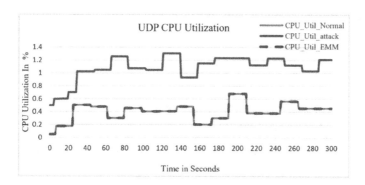

Fig. 10. CPU utilization comparison in UDP traffic conditions.

Similar observations can also be derived from Figs. 11 and 12 in terms of the memory utilization of the victim machine. In the scenario of an ongoing attack, the memory utilization rate of the victim machine increased up to about 33% compared to the rate with normal HTTP and UDP traffics. In comparison, both scenarios of normal traffic and as well as the one attack traffic (with EMM) remains constant throughout the experiment. This exhibits the effectiveness of EMM in mitigating the EDoS/DDoS attack rendered on the victim machine. Most importantly, it should be noted that EMM brings almost no additional overhead to the victim's machine after implementation.

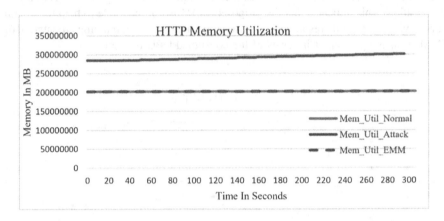

Fig. 11. Memory utilization comparison in HTTP traffic conditions.

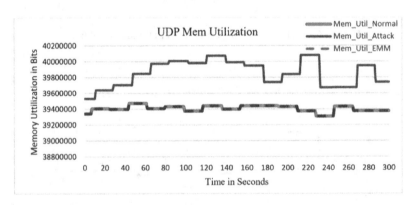

Fig. 12. Memory utilization comparison in UDP traffic conditions.

Finally, the total network utilization of the victim machine is compared based on the three scenarios. The results which are plotted in Figs. 13 and 14 respectively, indicates that the victim machine consumes network resources up to 350 Mb against the (initially) dedicated bandwidth of 10 M, resulting in over utilization of resources by 3000% (without any mitigation mechanism). In the conducted experiment, EMM successfully blocked the attacker in real-time and no more malicious traffic reaches the victim host after the block rule is pushed. Therefore, consumption of expensive bandwidth that will result in exhaustion of system resources or EDoS is alleviated.

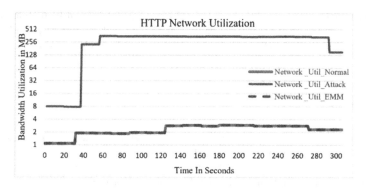

Fig. 13. Network utilization comparison in HTTP traffic conditions.

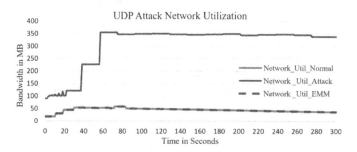

Fig. 14. Network utilization comparison in UDP traffic condition.

5   Conclusion and Future Works

In this study, the proposed EDoS detection and mitigation mechanism called EMM is evaluated. EMM detects an ongoing EDoS attack by conducting network monitoring. Because of the design, EMM requires very minimal overhead in deploying it in cloud environment. In addition, EMM takes a more generic approach in detecting an ongoing attack by observing the rate of network traffic that is being delivered to the protected server. The goal of this research is to ensure cloud users are not affected by a hefty bill due to EDoS attack.

EMM which is an automated detection and mitigation mechanism, demonstrated its ability to accurately detect and mitigate EDoS attack against cloud infrastructure through a set of carefully planned experiments that was done to evaluate it. The evaluation is performed in a real-time testbed environment that closely resembles a commercial cloud computing environment setup. EMM also fulfils its objectives of this study in coming up with an efficient EDoS detection and mitigation mechanism. For future works, we will compare the performance of EMM with existing mechanisms in terms of resource utilization and we will also investigate the feasibility of extending EMM to detect and mitigate EDoS/DDoS attacks as a SaaS model in cloud environment.

Acknowledgments. This research was supported by National Advanced IPv6 Centre (NAv6), Universiti Sains Malaysia (USM), Malaysia. In collaboration with ST Engineering Electronics-SUTD Cyber Security Laboratory, Singapore University of Technology and Design (SUTD), Singapore.

References

1. Strømmen-Bakhtiar, A.: Digital economy, business models, and cloud computing. In: Global Virtual Enterprises in Cloud Computing Environments, pp. 19–44 (2019)
2. Brintha, N.C., Winowlin Jappes, J.T., Sukumaran, J.: Integrating SMEs through cloud: an industrial revolution. In: Organizational Transformation and Managing Innovation in the Fourth Industrial Revolution, pp. 143–164 (2019)
3. Adamov, A., Erguvan, M.: The truth about cloud computing as new paradigm in IT. In: IEEE International Conference on Application of Information and Communication Technologies, pp. 1–3 (2009)
4. Bhardwaj, S., Jain, L., Jain, S.: Cloud computing: a study of infrastructure as a service (IAAS). Int. J. Eng. Inf. Technol. **2**(1), 60–63 (2010)
5. Ficco, M.: Could emerging fraudulent energy consumption attacks make the cloud infrastructure costs unsustainable? Inf. Sci. **1**(476), 474–490 (2019)
6. Bhushan, K., Gupta, B.B.: Network flow analysis for detection and mitigation of fraudulent resource consumption (FRC) attacks in multimedia cloud computing. Multimedia Tools Appl. **78**(4), 4267–4298 (2019)
7. Singh, P., Manickam, S., Rehman, S.U.: A survey of mitigation techniques against economic denial of sustainability (EDoS) attack on cloud computing architecture. In: 3rd IEEE International Conference on Reliability, Infocom Technologies, and Optimization (ICRITO) (Trends and Future Directions), pp. 1–4 (2014)
8. Hoff, C.: Cloud Computing Security: From DDoS (Distributed Denial of Service) To EDoS (Economic Denial of Sustainability). Blog (2008). Accessed 27 November 2008
9. Swami, R., Dave, M., Ranga, V.: Software-defined networking-based DDoS defense mechanisms. ACM Comput. Surv. (CSUR) **52**(2), 28 (2019)
10. Chaudhary, D., Bhushan, K., Gupta, B.B.: Survey on DDoS attacks and defense mechanisms in cloud and fog computing. Int. J. E-Serv. Mobile Appl. (IJESMA) **10**(3), 61–83 (2018)
11. Joshi, A., Vijayan, S., Joshi, B.K.: Securing cloud computing environment against DDoS attacks. In: IEEE International Conference on Computer Communication and Informatics (ICCCI), pp. 1–5 (2012)
12. Chapade, S.S., Pandey, K.U., Bhade, D.S.: Securing cloud servers against flooding-based DDoS attacks. In: IEEE International Conference on Communication Systems and Network Technologies, pp. 524–528 (2013)
13. Khor, S.H., Nakao, A.: sPoW: on-demand cloud-based eDDoS mitigation mechanism. In: HotDep (Fifth Workshop on Hot Topics in System Dependability) (2009)
14. Green, J., Juen, J., Fatemieh, O., Shankesi, R., Jin, D.(Kevin), Gunter, C.A.: Reconstructing hash reversal based proof of work schemes. In: LEET (2011)
15. Sqalli, M.H., Al-Haidari, F., Salah, K.: EDoS-shield a two-steps mitigation technique against EDoS attacks in cloud computing. In: Fourth IEEE International Conference on Utility and Cloud Computing, pp. 49–56, (2011)

16. Kumar, M.N., Sujatha, P., Kalva, V., Nagori, R., Katukojwala, A.K., Kumar, M.: Mitigating economic denial of sustainability (EDoS) in cloud computing using in-cloud scrubber service. In: Fourth International Conference on Computational Intelligence and Communication Networks, pp. 535–539 (2012)
17. Masood, M., Anwar, Z., Raza, S.A., Hur, M.A.: EDoS Armor: a cost-effective economic denial of sustainability attack mitigation framework for E-commerce applications in cloud environments. In: 16th IEEE International Multi Topic Conference (INMIC), pp. 37–42 (2013)
18. Chowdhury, F.Z., Idris, M.Y.I., Kiah, M.L.M., Ahsan, M.M.: EDoS eye: a game theoretic approach to mitigate economic denial of sustainability attack in cloud computing. In: 8th IEEE Control and System Graduate Research Colloquium (ICSGRC), pp. 164–169 (2017)
19. Shawahna, A., Abu-Amara, M., Mahmoud, A., Osais, Y.E.: EDoS-ADS: an enhanced mitigation technique against economic denial of sustainability (EDoS) attacks. IEEE Trans. Cloud Comput. (1), 1 (2018)
20. Bawa, P.S., Rehman, S.U., Manickam, S.: Enhanced mechanism to detect and mitigate economic denial of sustainability (EDoS) attack in cloud computing environments. Int. J. Adv. Comput. Sci. Appl. 8(9), 51–58 (2017)
21. Sengar, H., Wang, H., Wijesekera, D., Jajodia, S.: Detecting VoIP floods using the Hellinger distance. IEEE Trans. Parallel Distrib. Syst. 19(6), 794–805 (2008)
22. Shannon, C.E.: A note on the concept of entropy. Bell Syst. Tech. 27(1), 379–423 (1948)
23. Shalimov, A., Zuikov, D., Zimarina, D., Pashkov, V., Smeliansky, R.: Advanced study of SDN/OpenFlow controllers. In: Proceedings of the 9th Central & Eastern European Software Engineering Conference, Russia, p. 1, ACM (2013)
24. De Oliveira, R.L.S., Schweitzer, C.M., Shinoda, A.A., Prete, L.R.: Using mininet for emulation and prototyping software-defined networks. In: IEEE Colombian Conference on Communications and Computing (COLCOM), pp. 1–6 (2014)
25. Baig, Z.A., Sait, S.M., Binbeshr, F.: Controlled access to cloud resources for mitigating economic denial of sustainability (EdoS) attacks. Comput. Netw. 97(1), 31–47 (2016)
26. Hulboj, M.M., Jurga, R.E.: Packet Sampling and Network Monitoring (2007)
27. ARBOR Networks: Worldwide Infrastructure Security Report XI (2016). https://www.arbornetworks.com/images/documents/WISR2016_EN_Web

Detection Mechanisms of DDoS Attack in Cloud Computing Environment: A Survey

Mohammad Abdelkareem Alarqan[1], Zarul Fitri Zaaba[1]([✉]),
and Ammar Almomani[2]

[1] School of Computer Sciences, Universiti Sains Malaysia,
11800 Minden, Pulau Pinang, Malaysia
zarulfitri@usm.my
[2] Department of Information Technology, Al-Huson University College,
Al-Balqa Applied University, Irbid, Jordan

Abstract. Distributed Denial of Service (DDoS) attack is considered as one of the major security threats to the cloud computing environment. This attack hampers the adoption and deployment of cloud computing. DDoS Attack is an explicit attempt by an attacker to prevent and deny access to shared services or resources on a server in a cloud environment by legitimate users of cloud computing. This kind of attack targets victim servers by sending massive volumes of traffic from multiple sources to consume all the victim server resources. This paper discussed various defense mechanisms for defending DDoS. The main objective of this paper is to evaluate different mechanisms that help to defend DDoS attacks. This paper highlights the importance of statistical anomaly-based approaches in detecting DDoS attacks.

Keywords: DDoS · Cloud computing · Anomaly detection · Defense taxonomy

1 Introduction

Cloud computing is a strong rival to traditional computing systems [1]. It has become an appropriate means of accessing services, resources, and applications via the Internet [2]. Cloud computing supports easy data access between cloud service providers and cloud computing clients from anywhere, anyhow and anytime by using different network access techniques. It has the ability to allocate resources and release them efficiently, and it allows users to pay only for consumed resources [3]. Therefore, governments, industries, and organizations have migrated their entire or most of IT infrastructures to the cloud [1, 4–6]. However, there are numerous cloud computing security issues which hamper cloud computing adoption and deployment [3, 5]. Since the cloud computing allows users to access services and resources via the Internet, this makes cloud computing environment prone to security issues that may lead to poor quality of service [7].

DDoS attacks have become one of the major threats to the cloud computing environment. DDoS attacks are causing havoc by exploiting threats to cloud computing services [1, 2, 8–19]. Denial of Service (DoS) attack is an attacker's explicit attempt to

M. Anbar et al. (Eds.): ACeS 2019, CCIS 1132, pp. 138–152, 2020.
https://doi.org/10.1007/978-981-15-2693-0_10

prevent and deny legitimate users' access to shared resources or services on a server in the cloud computing environment. This type of attack targets a victim server by sending huge traffic to consume all the victim server resources [1, 20]. On the other hand, when the incoming DoS attack packets arrive on the victim server from various resources it is called a Distributed Denial of Service (DDoS) attack [20].

The number of reported DDoS incidents has increased considerably. This makes it one of the critical security issues that threaten the cloud computing environment among many security issues. In early 2015, a large DDoS attack was carried out on Amazon's Elastic Compute Cloud (EC2) and Rackspace server that are cloud service providers. In 2015, a heavy DDoS attack targeted Greatfire.org costing Greatfire.org a high bill of $30,000 a day on Amazon's Elastic Computing Cloud (EC2) [1]. In 2016, a two-hour DDoS attack was carried out on Amazon, Twitter, and Spotify resulting in huge financial losses due to service interruptions [9].

According to Arbor Networks report [21], the scale of the DDoS attacks has increased. The largest attack reported by a service provider in 2017 was 600 Gbps. This increase of packet scale for using IoT devices help the attackers to generate huge packet floods. Figure 1 illustrates that the size of DDoS attacks was continuously increasing between 2008 and 2016. However, in 2017 there was a decline in the scale of the attack that is, to some degree, a surprise given the latent capability within some of the weaponized DDoS services and botnets are currently active across the Internet.

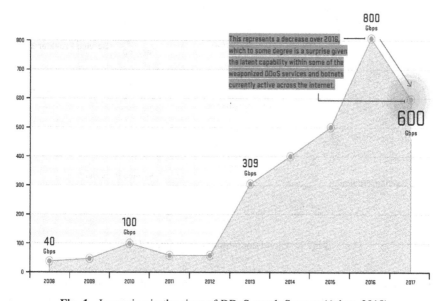

Fig. 1. Increasing in the sizes of DDoS attack Source: (Arbor, 2018)

As illustrated in Fig. 1, DDoS attacks are continuously increasing in size. Therefore, there is no indication that we can effectively defend such attacks in the near future. Hence, defense mechanisms become one of the key concerns for safeguarding the cloud computing environment [22].

This paper is organized as follows. Section 2 explains DDoS attacks in the cloud computing environment. Section 3 discusses methods of defense and detection of DDoS attacks in cloud computing environment. Section 4 describes the importance of statistical-based anomaly detection in the detection of DDoS attacks. Section 5 concludes our work on the future plan.

2   DDoS Attacks in Cloud Computing Environment

2.1   Cloud Computing Environment

Cloud computing environment is vulnerable to security threats. These threats include all areas of the environment where a malicious or unauthorized user can attempt to access cloud computing and damage the environment [23]. Cloud computing platform consists of servers, storages, and networks [7]. Figure 2 represents the cloud computing environment that has many servers, and each server runs a number of Virtual Machines (VMs).

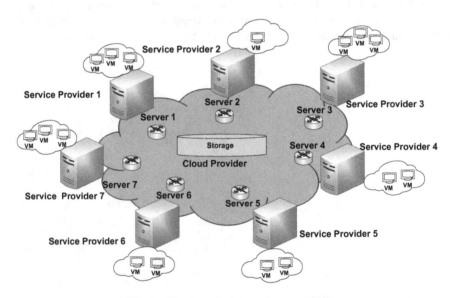

Fig. 2. Cloud computing environment [1].

Cloud computing uses the pay-as-you-go basis to provide available resources as an on-demand utility. An Infrastructure as a Service (IaaS) is provided by the cloud provider which provides virtual machines (VMs) on demand to service providers. IaaS provides the use of basic computing infrastructure of servers, software, and network equipment and other fundamental computing resources. Whereas, a service provider places the web services as a set of Virtual Machines (VM) in the cloud infrastructure which has been provided by the cloud provider [1].

2.2 Features of Cloud Computing

Cloud computing has five features, namely, on-demand self-service; broad network access; shared resources; elasticity; and pay-as-you-go model. The main reasons for cloud computing success trends depend on these cloud computing features. In contrast, an attacker may exploit these features to launch DDoS attack in cloud computing environment [3]. Table 1 shows the advantages of cloud computing feature and role of features that an attacker can exploit to launch DDoS attack in the cloud environment.

Table 1. Advantages of Cloud Computing Features and their role in DDoS Attacks.

Cloud computing feature	Advantages	The role of feature in DDoS attacks
On-demand self-service	Help legitimate users to obtain extra resources as they need	Attacker exploits this feature to consume resources by DDoS attack
Broad network access	Allow legitimate users to access the cloud using heterogeneous devices from anywhere	Allow attackers to compromise heterogeneous devices from anywhere to launch DDoS attack
Shared resources	Cloud resources are shared among several legitimate users	Attacker exploits shared resources and plants the attack code in resources to launch DDoS attack
Elasticity	Legitimate user efficiently allocates and release resources	Attacker allocates resources through DDoS attack to consume it
Pay-as-you-go	Allow legitimate users to use resources without physically buying them	Attacker exhausts the VM's resources to cause a denial of service

2.3 DDoS Attack Scenario

Usually, the launching of a DDoS attack is done by using a botnet. A botnet is a huge network of compromised machines called bots controlled and managed by the botnet master [12, 25]. The attack procedure is coordinated in advance [1, 10, 11, 15, 22, 24, 26]. Therefore, the botnet master, i.e., the attacker needs to prepare a botnet to launch a DDoS attack. Then, a botmaster begins to attack. As shown in Fig. 3, four basic steps are taken to prepare a botnet, namely, agent selection; compromise; communication; and attack [12].

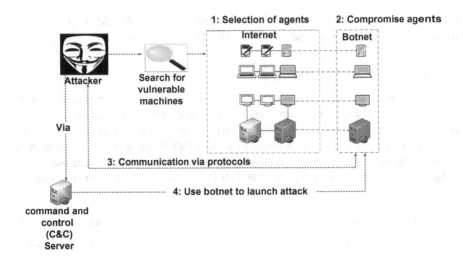

Fig. 3. Steps to prepare a botnet

The attacker uses different kinds of techniques to find vulnerable machines to work as agents that have abundant resources based on vulnerabilities in these machines. The attacker compromises these machines and plants the attack code, i.e., malware which is used as attack tools [24]. Then the attacker communicates with these machines via a protocol by using botnet and command and control server to attack victim's server [22]. Figure 4 shows the DDoS attack scenario in cloud computing infrastructure.

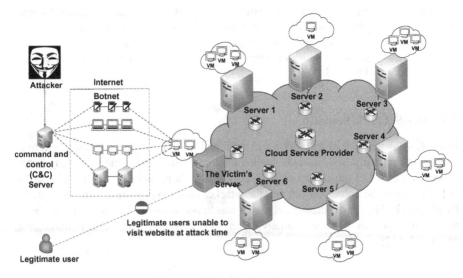

Fig. 4. DDoS attack scenario in cloud computing infrastructure [1].

As illustrated in Fig. 4, cloud infrastructure has a wide range of servers which can operate Virtual Machines (VMs) based on virtualized environments characterized by multi-tenant [1]. A DDoS attacker will use the botnet to launch an attack. An attacker uses the Command and Control (C&C) server to manage its network and to execute its attacks [20, 27]. An attacker would send enough fake requests to the victim's server by using a botnet [1]. Therefore, virtual machine resources running on the victim server will be heavily utilized.

Elasticity feature of cloud computing is activated to allocates resources from another virtual machine on the victim server once a virtual machine resource is consumed [28]. The elasticity feature will choose one of VM resource allocation strategies, such as migration to another VM, or placement to another VM [29].

Let's assume that all the victim server resources are consumed. In this case, the cloud computing elasticity feature is activated to allocate resources from another server, and then, the pay-as-you-go model is activated. It is a method that requires the service providers to pay for the cloud service provider before allocating resources from another server. This situation lasts until payment is made by the service provider or all resources of the cloud service provider are consumed [1]. As a result, if there is no defense system to stop this situation it will cause Distributed Denial of Service. Consequently, legitimate users are prevented from accessing the victim server, i.e., legitimate users are unable to visit the website of the victim server [9].

3   Taxonomy of DDoS Attack Defense Methods in Cloud Computing

Mostly, defense methods of DDoS attacks in cloud computing are segmented into three methods, namely, attack prevention; attack detection; and attack mitigation [1, 16, 22, 29].

Figure 5 demonstrate defense methods of DDoS attacks in cloud computing.

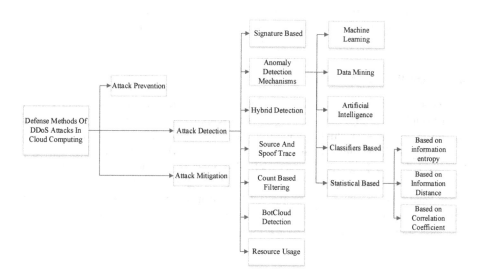

Fig. 5. Defense methods of DDoS attacks in cloud computing

4 Defense Methods of DDoS Attacks

A. Attack Prevention

Preventing cloud attacks is a proactive step in filtering or dropping requests from suspicious attackers before affecting the server [1]. This prevention is an appropriate system to safeguard data and services from DDoS attacks at various places. This system is deployed to work as monitoring tools that collect host or network information against DDoS attacks and also keep track of prevention system execution [16]. For example, such monitoring tools are Firewalls, Proxy server, Switches, and Application front end hardware [22].

B. Attack Detection

Attack detection includes analysis of running systems to identify malicious sources that lead to DDoS attacks or identify malicious packets in network traffic [16], though the attack prevention technique is used to defend against DDoS attacks. Nevertheless, attack detection is one of the most important techniques to defend against DDoS attacks than other defensive techniques [26]. The attack prevention has a usability issue, because it is applied to all users. This leads to additional server overhead when prevention is applied to legitimate users [1]. Therefore, attack detection mechanisms play an important role in the detection of DDoS attacks [12].

C. Attack Mitigation

At the time of the attack, a victim server may continue serving the user's requests by using attack mitigation techniques [1]. Since, the victim server resources are not fully consumed at the beginning of the attack DDoS mitigation completes the defense by evaluating the strength of the attack and selecting the right response at the right time. Moreover, a response system deals with suitable countermeasures appropriate to the type of attack [16]. Attack mitigation includes strategies, such as traceback techniques and filtering of packets [22]. On the other hand, multiple elements, such as servers, router, switch, protocols, and applications are involved in a security architecture [29].

4.1 Detection Mechanisms

The DDoS attack is one of the cyber threats to cloud computing, it aims to compromise the principle of availability, i.e., legitimate users are unable to use the services and resources available in cloud computing. Therefore, detection mechanisms of DDoS attack play an important role in cybersecurity against cyber adversaries [30].

According to [2], DDoS attack detection mechanisms are classified into three subcategories, namely signature based; anomaly based; and hybrid detection. On the other, [1] classified DDoS attack detection mechanisms are classified into five subcategories, namely anomaly detection; Source and spoof trace; count-based filtering; BotCloud detection; and resource usage.

A. Signature-Based Detection Mechanisms

Detection based on the signature involves a set of attack signatures of different patterns of known attacks. The attack pattern signatures will be stored in a database. Any incoming traffic is compared to existing signatures that are stored in the database to detect patterns of attack traffic [31–33]. These mechanisms are to accurately detect known attacks if the database is always updated [2]. Due to the easiness to reconfigure, the rules are needed to update the signatures in the database for unknown attacks. However, unknown attacks cannot be detected if signatures are not updated [32]. As a result, any variation in known stored attack signature or obscure attacks will cause high false negative rate [2, 32, 33]. Furthermore, updating signatures for each attack is not feasible as attacks change from time to time, which also leads to time and resource consumption [33].

B. Anomaly-Based Detection Mechanisms

Anomaly detection involves identifying patterns in data which are incompatible with expected behaviour. These patterns which are not compatible are called anomalies patterns [34]. These mechanisms aim to identify events that seem anomalous in the normal behavior of the system [35]. Normally, traffic behavior is collected over a certain period of time to compare with incoming network traffic [2]. Nowadays, anomaly detection mechanisms are being used to detect DDoS attacks on cloud computing [36].

C. Hybrid Detection

The combination of two or more mechanisms is used by hybrid detection. Such mechanisms of hybrid detection include the use of both mechanisms- signature and anomaly-based detection to increase the detection rate [2]. The strengths and limitations of these detection mechanisms depend on the algorithm used by such detection mechanisms [32]. These detection mechanisms are capable of classifying rules accurately, due to combined advantage of multiple techniques [31]. However, the performance and computational cost of these detection mechanisms depends on the number of combined detection techniques [31, 33].

D. Source and Spoof Trace Detection

The traceback technique is useful in finding the source from which DDoS attacks are generated. These attacks tend to use spoof addresses to launch DDoS attacks. A reflector attack is an example of this attack [2]. Source traceback and spoofing are extremely important for detection mechanisms. However, this process requires service providers support and several network components, such as servers, and edge routers. Additionally, it is not easy to design a defense system in cloud computing against large-scale botnets with spoofed IP addresses, as this detection mechanism requires a great deal of effort between service providers [1].

E. Count Based Filtering

The network resource parameters are utilized to indicate the start of attack in count-based filtering and later are used to detect an attack occurrence such as hop-count, connections number, and requests number for a single source in a unit time. The main strength of these detection mechanisms can be easily deployed, these mechanisms allow administrators to quickly monitor the situation. However, it requires a database to be continuously updated and also have a variety of heterogeneous applications in different systems that cause issues while using these methods, and it also requires a false alarm rate calibration [1]. In addition, it also suffers from IP spoofing which leads to problems of integrity and accuracy [37].

F. BotCloud Detection

An attacker may exploit cloud computing features to create bots in the cloud instead of infecting user machines [38]. Therefore, the cloud becomes a platform for malicious users to launch attacks. These bots are called BotCloud [39]. BotCloud's detection mechanisms aim to detect or find an attack targeting the virtual machine in the cloud. The main strength of these mechanisms is their deployment location at the end of the cloud service provider. However, these mechanisms cannot detect all types of attacks. Furthermore, only the edge of the cloud that originates the attack can operate with such a detection mechanism. If cloud service providers do not support such detections, these attacks could become large, due to the use of heavy cloud computing resources [1].

G. Resource Usage (Resource Consumption)

Cloud computing environment uses a virtualized server called a hypervisor running a virtual operating system platform to run a guest machine, such as a virtual machine or server. The hypervisor has the ability to manage the resources available in each guest machine. This method uses incoming traffic features such as throughput, CPU usage, and memory usage as a DDoS attack detection metric [40]. When the virtual machine or server reaches the specified limit of resource usage, this indicates the suspicion that an attack happened. As a result, the consumption of various virtual machine or server resources is capable of providing vital information about the expectation or occurrence of the DDoS attack [1]. Table 2 illustrate the discussed attack detection mechanisms alongside their strengths and limitations.

Table 2. Attacks detection mechanisms strengths and limitations.

Detection mechanism	Strengths	Limitations
Signature - based	• Accuracy in detecting known attack signatures as long as the database is always up to date • Easily to reconfigure rules that are required for updating the signatures of unknown attacks in database	• Cannot detect unknown attacks • Unknown attacks or variation of known attack signatures lead to high false negatives rate • Infeasible to update signatures for all attacks
Anomaly-based	• Effective against unknown attacks • Discriminate anomalous patterns of DDoS from legitimate network traffic patterns • Helps the security analysts to identify and detect any possible threats	• The computation cost for training is high • Need matching and statistical analysis of traffic features
Hybrid	• Have ability to classify rules accurately	• The performance depends on the numbers of combined detection techniques • The computational cost depends on the combined detection techniques
Source and Spoof Trace	• Important for all the detection methods	• Require support from many networks • Need much effort between service providers
Count Based Filtering	• Easy deployment • Give administrators fast control over the situation	• Requires a user database which has the actual hop count/TTLs • Variety of heterogeneous implementations of hop-count in different systems • Difficult to ensure of the source IP addresses and their corresponding hops from the victim
BotCloud Detection	• Easy to deploy this detection mechanisms • Cloud service provider has ability to control and monitor any incoming anomaly traffic	• Unable to detect all types of attacks • Can only work at the edge of attack originating cloud • May become massive using the heavy resources of cloud computing
Resource Usage	• Indicates the suspicion of occurrence an attack	• Throughput of incoming traffic cannot be used as the only evidence of a DDoS attack • CPU and memory utilization depend on fine tuning of the threshold values to detect an attack traffic effectively

4.2   Classes of Anomaly Detection Mechanisms

Anomaly detection mechanisms are classified into five classes based on the algorithms used in the detection process, namely machine learning; data mining; artificial intelligence; classifiers; and statistical-based [2].

Anomaly detection based on machine learning includes the construction of a system to enhance performance based on previous results [2]. Data mining involves processes of knowledge extraction such as clustering and classification. Whereas, detection mechanisms based on artificial neural networks can classify behaviors as normal or intrusive by using generalized data from incomplete data [35]. Classifiers are methods to classify a test instance into a class from several labeled data instances. These methods normally work in two stages, namely the training and the testing [2]. In statistical-based anomaly detection, the statistical characteristics of normal traffic are analyzed to create a normal traffic pattern which is compared with incoming traffic to detect anomalous packets [2, 35]. Table 3 shows a comparison of anomaly detection classes based on the algorithms used in the detection process alongside their strengths and limitations.

Table 3. Comparisons the Classes of Anomaly Detection Mechanisms

Class	Strengths	Limitations
Based on Machine Learning	• Detection of DDoS attack patterns with high efficiency • it can change their execution strategy throughout detection	• Significant computing resources are required during training and testing • High overhead leads to performance declining
Based on Data Mining	• Increase the speed of detection processes • Low computation cost • It can deal with a huge database • Helps network administrators to discriminate attacks traffic from legitimate traffic	• Inefficient in case of a high volume of incoming network traffic • Missing values from the dataset will influence the detection processes
Based on Artificial Intelligence	• Classify behaviors as normal or intrusive • Detecting DDoS attacks Effectively	• Detection accuracy depends on the training profile • Scalability issues
Based on Classifier	• Detection rate depends on threshold settings • High adoption rate to update detection strategies	• detection of unknown attacks needs adequate training • Resource consumption is high
Statistical Based	• Learning of expected behavior from observations without prior knowledge of normal activities • Accurate detection of malicious activity	• Difficulty of setting an optimal threshold • Need to justify assumptions which are needed to determine the classification rate

5   Discussion

The detection of anomalies is a vital issue that has been discussed in different studies, fields and applications [34]. Therefore, anomaly detection mechanisms are increasingly popular, because these mechanisms can effectively detect known and unknown patterns of attack [2]. In addition, anomaly detection mechanisms are used to discriminate anomalous DDoS patterns from legitimate network traffic patterns. It also has more powerful detection than other mechanisms [20, 40]. Furthermore, detection of anomalies is used for both attack prevention and detection [1]. In addition, anomaly detection is one of the strong methods for identifying and detecting potential threats to safeguard the network. Indeed, anomaly-based detection can detect irrelevant patterns or abnormal events in the network at an early stage [34].

In the case of DDoS attacks, statistical-based anomaly detection is vitally important, because some statistical features can be used as an indicator for suspicion of attack traffic [41, 42].

The current research trend shows that many researchers tend to use information entropy and information distance as detection metrics for statistical-based anomaly detection, These detection metrics can be used to detect DDoS attacks and to discriminate anomalous patterns of DDoS attacks from legitimate network traffic, due to the following major advantages (a) with few packet header features, it can effectively identify the various types of network traffic, (b) low computation costs due to the use of only packet header information to calculate entropy or distance, (c) low false positive rate, (d) high sensitivity and (e) high scalability [8, 9, 25].

6   Conclusion

This paper mainly characterizes the DDoS attack in the cloud computing environment. DDoS attacks have become one of the critical security issues that threaten the cloud computing. DDoS is a security issue that hampers the adoption and deployment of the cloud computing. It also discusses how DDoS attackers can achieve success in the cloud computing environment by exploiting the features of the cloud computing environment to launch a DDoS attack. It also addresses the various existing defense mechanisms that help detect DDoS attacks and discusses their advantages and disadvantages. It also deals with the different classes of anomaly detection mechanisms based on the algorithms used in the detection process alongside their strengths and limitations.

Even though, there are many detection mechanisms in the cloud computing to detect DDoS attacks. In this paper, we focused on anomaly detection mechanisms, because the following key advantages of using anomaly detection mechanisms are- (a) they can detect known and unknown attacks; (b) they can discriminate attack traffic from legitimate traffic; (c) they can be used for detection and prevention; (d) help identify and detect potential threats (f) help detect irrelevant patterns or uncommon network events early. However, the anomaly-based detection mechanisms require matching and statistical analysis of traffic features to discriminate attack traffic from legitimate traffic.

The current research trend shows that many researchers are inclined to use information entropy and information distance as detection metrics for statistical anomaly detection. Therefore, in our future work, we will conduct a detailed study of statistical-based anomaly detection based on different detection metrics, such as information entropy and information distance.

References

1. Somani, G., Gaur, M.S., Sanghi, D., Conti, M., Buyya, R.: DDoS attacks in cloud computing: issues, taxonomy, and future directions. Comput. Commun. **107**, 30–48 (2017)
2. Osanaiye, O., Choo, K.-K.R., Dlodlo, M.: Distributed denial of service (DDoS) resilience in cloud: Review and conceptual cloud DDoS mitigation framework. J. Netw. Comput. Appl. **67**, 147–165 (2016)
3. Kaaniche, N., Laurent, M.: Data security and privacy preservation in cloud storage environments based on cryptographic mechanisms. Comput. Commun. **111**, 120–141 (2016)
4. Arjun, U., Vinay, S.: A short review on data security and privacy issues in cloud computing. In: 2016 IEEE International Conference on Current Trends in Advanced Computing (ICCTAC), Bangalore, India, pp. 1–5. IEEE (2016)
5. Khalil, I.M., Khreishah, A., Azeem, M.: Cloud computing security: a survey. Computers **3**(1), 1–35 (2014)
6. Sharma, R., Trivedi, R.K.: Literature review: cloud computing–security issues, solution and technologies. Int. J. Eng. Res. **3**(4), 221–225 (2014)
7. Khan, M.A.: A survey of security issues for cloud computing. J. Netw. Comput. Appl. **71**, 11–29 (2016)
8. Behal, S., Kumar, K.: Detection of DDoS attacks and flash events using information theory metrics–an empirical investigation. Comput. Commun. **103**, 18–28 (2017)
9. Behal, S., Kumar, K.: Detection of DDoS attacks and flash events using novel information theory metrics. Comput. Netw. **116**, 96–110 (2017)
10. Bhatia, S.: Ensemble-based model for DDoS attack detection and flash event separation. In: 2016 Future Technologies Conference (FTC), San Francisco, CA, USA, pp. 958–967. IEEE (2016)
11. Bhatia, T., Verma, A.K.: Data security in mobile cloud computing paradigm: a survey, taxonomy and open research issues. J. Supercomput. **73**(6), 2558–2631 (2017)
12. Bhuyan, M.H., Bhattacharyya, D.K., Kalita, J.K.: E-LDAT: a lightweight system for DDoS flooding attack detection and IP traceback using extended entropy metric. Secur. Commun. Netw. **9**(16), 3251–3270 (2016)
13. Mansfield-Devine, S.: The growth and evolution of DDoS. Netw. Secur. **2015**(10), 13–20 (2015)
14. Sachdeva, M., Kumar, K., Singh, G.: A comprehensive approach to discriminate DDoS attacks from flash events. J. Inf. Secur. Appl. **26**, 8–22 (2016)
15. Saravanan, R., Shanmuganathan, S., Palanichamy, Y.: Behavior-based detection of application layer distributed denial of service attacks during flash events. Turk. J. Electr. Eng. Comput. Sci. **24**(2), 510–523 (2016)
16. Shameli-Sendi, A., Pourzandi, M., Fekih-Ahmed, M., Cheriet, M.: Taxonomy of Distributed Denial of Service mitigation approaches for cloud computing. J. Netw. Comput. Appl. **58**, 165–179 (2015)

17. Shifali, C., Sachdeva, M., Behal, S.: Discrimination of DDoS attacks and flash events using Pearsons product moment correlation method. Int. J. Comput. Sci. Inf. Secur. **14**(10), 382–389 (2016)
18. Xiao, P., Qu, W., Qi, H., Li, Z.: Detecting DDoS attacks against data center with correlation analysis. Comput. Commun. **67**, 66–74 (2015)
19. Yan, R., Xu, G., Qin, X.: Detect and identify DDoS attacks from flash crowd based on self-similarity and Renyi entropy. In: 2017 Chinese Automation Congress (CAC), Jinan, China, pp. 7188–7194. IEEE (2017)
20. Bhandari, A., Sangal, A.L., Kumar, K.: Characterizing flash events and distributed denial-of-service attacks: an empirical investigation. Secur. Commun. Netw. **9**(13), 2222–2239 (2016)
21. Arbor Network. https://pages.arbornetworks.com/rs/082-KNA-087/images/13th_Worldwide _Infrastructure_Security_Report.pdf. Accessed 21 Dec 2018
22. Gupta, B.B., Badve, O.P.: Taxonomy of DoS and DDoS attacks and desirable defense mechanism in a Cloud computing environment. Neural Comput. Appl. **28**(12), 3655–3682 (2017)
23. Iqbal, S., et al.: On cloud security attacks: a taxonomy and intrusion detection and prevention as a service. J. Netw. Comput. Appl. **74**, 98–120 (2016)
24. Bhuyan, M.H., Bhattacharyya, D.K., Kalita, J.K.: An empirical evaluation of information metrics for low-rate and high-rate DDoS attack detection. Pattern Recognit. Lett. **51**, 1–7 (2015)
25. Almomani, A.: Fast-flux hunter: a system for filtering online fast-flux botnet. Neural Comput. Appl. **29**(7), 483–493 (2018)
26. Tao, Y., Yu, S.: DDoS attack detection at local area networks using information theoretical metrics. In: 2013 12th IEEE International Conference on Trust, Security and Privacy in Computing and Communications, Melbourne, VIC, Australia, pp. 233–240. IEEE (2013)
27. Prasad, K.M., Reddy, A.R.M., Rao, K.V.: Afr. J. Comput. ICT **6**(2), 53–62 (2013). 2017 Chinese Automation Congress (CAC)
28. Stillwell, M., Schanzenbach, D., Vivien, F., Casanova, H.: Resource allocation algorithms for virtualized service hosting platforms. J. Parallel Distrib. Comput. **70**(9), 962–974 (2010)
29. Bonguet, A., Bellaiche, M.: A survey of denial-of-service and distributed denial of service attacks and defenses in cloud computing. Future Internet **9**(3), 43 (2017)
30. Moustafa, N., Hu, J., Slay, J.: A holistic review of Network Anomaly Detection Systems: a comprehensive survey. J. Netw. Comput. Appl. **128**, 33–55 (2019)
31. Alzahrani, S., Hong, L.: A survey of cloud computing detection techniques against DDoS attacks. J. Inf. Secur. **9**, 45–69 (2018)
32. Bakshi, A., Sunanda, : A comparative analysis of different intrusion detection techniques in cloud computing. In: Luhach, A., Singh, D., Hsiung, P.A., Hawari, K., Lingras, P., Singh, P. (eds.) Advanced Informatics for Computing Research, vol. 956, pp. 358–378. Springer, Singapore (2018). https://doi.org/10.1007/978-981-13-3143-5_30
33. Modi, C.N., Acha, K.: Virtualization layer security challenges and intrusion detection/prevention systems in cloud computing: a comprehensive review. J. Supercomput. **73**(3), 1192–1234 (2017)
34. Ariyaluran Habeeb, R.A., Nasaruddin, F., Gani, A., Targio Hashem, I.A., Ahmed, E., Imran, M.: Real-time big data processing for anomaly detection: a Survey. Int. J. Inf. Manag. **45**, 289–307 (2019)
35. Modi, C., Patel, D., Borisaniya, B., Patel, H., Patel, A., Rajarajan, M.: A survey of intrusion detection techniques in cloud. J. Netw. Comput. Appl. **36**(1), 42–57 (2013)
36. Katiyar, P., Senthil Kumarn, U., Balakrishanan, S.: Detection and discrimination of DDoS attacks from flash crowd using entropy variations. Int. J. Eng. Technol. **5**(4), 3514–3519 (2013)

37. Zargar, S.T., Joshi, J., Tipper, D.: A survey of defense mechanisms against distributed denial of service (DDoS) flooding attacks. IEEE Commun. Surv. Tutor. **15**(4), 2046–2069 (2013)

38. Khattak, S., Ramay, N.R., Khan, K.R., Syed, A.A., Khayam, S.A.: A taxonomy of botnet behavior, detection, and defense. IEEE Commun. Surv. Tutor. **16**(2), 898–924 (2014)

39. Hammi, B., Rahal, M.C., Khatoun, R.: Clustering methods comparison: application to source based detection of botclouds. In: 2016 International Conference on Security of Smart Cities, Industrial Control System and Communications (SSIC), Paris, France, pp. 1–7. IEEE (2016)

40. Chen, C., Chen, H.: A resource utilization measurement detection against DDoS attacks. In: 2016 9th International Congress on Image and Signal Processing, BioMedical Engineering and Informatics (CISP-BMEI), Datong, China, pp. 1938–1943 IEEE (2016)

41. Xiang, Y., Li, K., Zhou, W.: Low-rate DDoS attacks detection and traceback by using new information metrics. IEEE Trans. Inf. Forensics Secur. **6**(2), 426–437 (2011)

42. Sahoo, K.S., Puthal, D., Tiwary, M., Rodrigues, J.J.P.C., Sahoo, B., Dash, R.: An early detection of low rate DDoS attack to SDN based data center networks using information distance metrics. Future Gener. Comput. Syst. **89**, 685–697 (2018)

Overview of IPv6 Based DDoS and DoS Attacks Detection Mechanisms

Abdullah Ahmed Bahashwan[1]([✉]), Mohammed Anbar[1]([✉]),
and Sabri M. Hanshi[2]

[1] National Advanced IPv6 Centre (NAv6), Universiti Sains Malaysia (USM),
11800 Gelugor, Penang, Malaysia
bahashwan@student.usm.my, anbar@usm.my
[2] Seiyun Community College, Hadhramaut, Yemen
smhanshi@ieee.org

Abstract. In recent years, the number of Internet users and devices are rapidly increased. For this reason, the Internet Assigned Number Authority (IANA) launched a new protocol called Internet Protocol version six (IPv6) next generation. The IPv6 provides new features that fit the internet revolution. IPv6 is equipped with new protocols such as Neighbor Discovery Protocol (NDP) and Internet Control Messages protocol version six (ICMPv6). In fact, ICMPv6 is considered as the backbone of the IPv6 protocol since it is responsible for many key functions like the NDP process. In addition, the NDP protocol is a stateless protocol that gives the lack of authentication to NDP messages, which is vulnerable to many types of attacks such as Distributed Denial of Services (DDoS) and Denial of Services (DoS) flooding attacks. In this type of attacks, the attacker sends an enormous volume of abnormal traffic to increase network congestion and break down the network. Under those circumstances, the first line of defense in a network has been supplemented by additional devices and tools that supervise the network activities and monitor the network traffic behaviors as well as to stop unauthorized intrusions. Overall, the aim of this review paper is to give pure thoughts about the IPv6 features and the most important related protocols like ICMPv6 protocol and NDP protocol. Also, this article discusses DDoS and DoS attack based on ICMPv6 protocol. Likewise, this article gives a comprehensive review of the IPv6 Intrusion Detection Systems based on DDoS & DoS attacks with their features and security limitations.

Keywords: IPv6 · ICMPv6 · NDP · ICMPv6 based DDoS & DoS utilization · IDS

1 Introduction

In the previous years, the number of Internet users and devices are rapidly increased which led to consume the Internet Protocol Version 4 (IPv4). The main reasons of that during the rise of current technologies such as the Internet

© Springer Nature Singapore Pte Ltd. 2020
M. Anbar et al. (Eds.): ACeS 2019, CCIS 1132, pp. 153–167, 2020.
https://doi.org/10.1007/978-981-15-2693-0_11

of thing (IoT), cloud computing, and wireless technology are getting severe [1]. Even though by implementing Network Address Translation (NAT) in order to reserve IPv4 addresses which at the same time is not secure enough. According to a study at the end of 2011 IPv4 public addresses will be exhausted because of the speedy evolution of Internet usage [2]. To defeat this major issues of IPv4 addresses consumption, the IPv6 is introduced as the next generation protocol and it is considered as the successor to IPv4 protocol [3].

Furthermore, IPv6 comes out with some key function and protocols. For example, Internet Control Message protocol (ICMPv6) is an integrated part of IPv6 and gives feedback in case any error happens to other nodes. Other key function protocol is Neighbor discovery protocol (NDP). It is a new protocol that derived with IPv6 and depend on ICMPv6 protocol. The NDP main function is to discover the other nodes on the same link local address [4]. Moreover, there are some other features in IPv6 like IPv6 address Autoconfiguration, Router discovery, successful transmission and mobility. All recent features of IPv6 get the opportunity to be totally enforced in any IPv6 nodes. Additionally, these days many enterprise companies added to their services the IPv6 support and started to give IPv6 connectivity, such as Facebook and Google [5].

Towards this end, this paper is organized as follow in Subsect. 1.1 addressing IPv6 protocol features, Subsect. 1.2 covers the ICMPv6 protocol, Subsect. 1.3 is about Neighbor Discovery Protocol (NDP), Subsect. 1.4 discuss DDoS & DoS Attacks established on ICMPv6 protocol utilization, Sect. 2 underling the related work, Sect. 3 having a discussion about this comprehensive study and finally Sect. 4 is the conclusion of this review paper.

1.1 Internet Protocol Version Six (IPv6)

The successor of IPv4 protocol is IPv6 next generation Internet protocol. It is defined in RFC 2460 [3]. IPv6 is the savior protocol to fulfill the IPv4 gaps include the exhausting IP address and lack of security. The IPv6 address is increasing the size of addressing pool from 32 bits to 128 bits, In addition, There are some built in features in IPv6 protocol such as Dynamic Host Configuration Protocol Version 6 (DHCPv6), IPSec, Autoconfiguration [6]. Moreover, IPv6 is surrounded by some technical benefits that simplify the header of packet in order to reduce the CPU and save the bandwidth. However, IPv6 has been upgraded in terms of security, but still there are doubtless areas where security issues are still stumbling block, such as ICMPv6 DDoS & DoS flooding attacks [7].

1.2 Internet Control Messages Protocol Version Six (ICMPv6)

The ICMPv6 is defined in RFC 2463 [8]. ICMPv6 is a fundamental part of IPv6 protocol since it is encapsulated with the IPv6 packet and it is responsible for many key functions. One of these functions the ICMPv6 is an intermediate director between a router and a host or hosts and routers. Another feature that associated with the ICMPv6 protocol is delivers a feedback about any issues that occurred on the routing path of destination. For an instant, a router may not forward a packet because of a packet is too big. Other feature of ICMPv6 messages which has been mainly used to report errors that happen, like destination host unreachable [9]. In brief, the ICMPv6 protocol have two types of messages, the ICMPv6 Informational Messages that start from 1 to 127 and ICMPv6 error messages that start from 128 to 255 messages [10]. The following Table 1 abstract these two types of ICMPv6 messages.

Table 1. ICMPv6 Types

Code	ICMPv6 informational messages	Code	ICMPv6 error messages
1	Destination Unreachable	128	Echo Request
2	Packet is Big	129	Echo Reply
3	Time Exceeded	133	Router Solicitation
4	Parameter Problem	134	Router Advertisement
100	Private Experimentation	135	Neighbor Solicitation
101	Private Experimentation	136	Neighbor Advertisement
127	Reserved for expansion	137	Redirect
		200	Private Experimentation
		255	Reserved for Expansion

1.3   Neighbor Discovery Protocol (NDP)

Previously, in IPv4 network any host needs to communicate with any host in the local Area Network (LAN), it is required to know the MAC address of the target host, which is conceivable through Address Resolution Protocol (ARP), this process is a stateless protocol and associated with many attacks such as request spoofing, response spoofing, Man in the Middle (MiTM) and Denial-of-service (DoS) attack [7]. NDP protocol is defined as (RFC 2461). The NDP protocol has been replaced the ARP protocol of IPv4 [11]. Similarly, NDP protocol is working on the top (ICMPv6) protocol to discover the nodes in IPv6 networks. The NDP protocol reserve five information messages from ICMPv6 protocol are listed out as following [12].

– Router Advertisement (RA) messages are initiated by routers that sent periodically or referred in response to Router Solicitation (RS). Routers use RA to inform the others about his existing on a network and send exact parameters such as maximum transmission unite (MTU), Router Prefix, lifetime for each prefix, and hop limits.
– Router Solicitation (RS) messages are initiated by all routers while startup, then Sent RS asking other routers on the attached link to send router advertisement (RA) message.
– Neighbor Solicitation (NS) messages are initiated by hosts, which tries to pick up the link-layer addresses of other nodes on the same LAN, or originated

use in duplicate address detection (DAD) to verify the address uniqueness, or trying to verifying the reachability of a neighbor.

- Neighbor Advertisement (NA) type of messages that contains information about any changes of the nodes such as Media Access Control (MAC) address and IP address or ask response to NS messages.
- Redirect Messages (RM) are working to forward traffic from one router to another Router [9].

Additionally, the NDP protocol allows any nodes on an IPv6 network to generate their IP addresses and initiate communication with each other without any authentication in the same network. NDP is stateless protocol given lacking authentication process makes NDP messages exposed to several types of attacks [13]. Consequently, NDP protocol supplied with a basic defense mechanism, like Secure Neighbor Discovery (SEND), which became a standard. SEND uses cryptographically generated addresses (CGA), a digital signature, and an X.509 certification to shield NDP [51]. The purpose of SEND was to provide message integrity, prevent IPv6 address spoofing and offer a perfect way to verify routers' authority. Also, SEND itself can be vulnerable to a number of attacks [14,15] Additionally, this shield is not filled full the equipment to wholly protect IPv6 local networks.

1.4 DDoS and DoS Attacks Established on ICMPv6 Protocol Utilization

The ICMPv6 protocol is exposed to diverse kinds of attacks. For example, Distributed Denial of Services (DDoS) attacks and Denial of Services (DoS) flooding attacks, which are grounded on ICMPv6 messages [16]. It is one of the greatest common serious issues of these days in Internet attacks [17]. Within the same manner, the DDoS attack is giving the commands to attacks remotely then the attacker controls the infect systems. In the light of, ICMPv6 DDoS attack is a cyber-attack where a perpetrator seeks to make the network resource unavailable. It is accomplished by streaming of superfluous request to attempt overload the victim from different sources addresses, unlike the ICMPv6 DoS attacks is performed from single source address. In addition, the flooding attack goal is to stop the authorized individual from being fulfilled the requirements. These attacks initiated from fabricating source address, in order to make it difficult to detect and track. Moreover, in the above scenario the attacker takes advantage of the exploit vulnerabilities circumstances of the ICMPv6 messages to attempt such attacks [18].

Additionally, for more technical details of DDoS & DoS flooding attacks. For example, the attacker can produce an ICMPv6 flooding attack by utilizing one of it is messages. In this example the attacker uses Router Advertisement (RA) message. RA is a type of ICMPv6 messages used by routers to advertise their existence on the network segment and RA message offers assistance to hosts in the link-local network by providing them with network prefix and routing information [19]. Unfortunately, RA messages are spoofed by the attacker and flood the victim nodes with RA malicious traffic and the victim nodes update their neighbor table accordingly till the target nodes exhausted and stop its services. In short, DDoS attacks are attempted by sending a flood of malicious RA massages from several sources to make it more harder to detect, whereas DoS attacks performed by sending the malicious RA traffic from single source targeting the victim nodes [20].

2   Related Work

There are a number of Intrusion detection systems (IDSs) that are projected to spot ICMPv6 DDoS&DoS attacks. This section lists out an overview of existing IDSs with their capacitance to detect ICMPv6 attacks [21]. The Intrusion detection systems (IDSs) are protection management system, that detects the incoming and outgoing network traffic and identifies suspicious forms that may break into the network. IDS aim is to safeguard systems or networks from a variety of attacks that threatening their confidentiality, integrity, and availability. The IDSs are destined to spot abnormal activities from a normal behavior and it work to discover malicious attacks then give alert about any hostile activities [22].

Consequently, a variety of IDSs is projected to detect IPv6 and ICMPv6 attacks. Moreover, there are two main types according to detecting approaches, Signature-based IDSs (sometimes remarked as Misuse Detection Systems) and Anomaly-based IDSs (sometimes called profile-based detection) [16]. Figure 1 illustrates the taxonomy of existing IDSs, that will be described in following subsections.

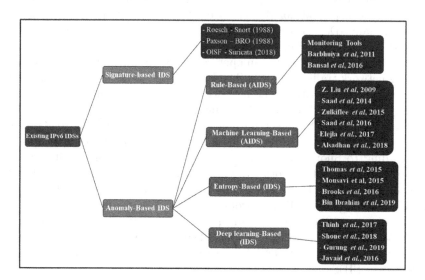

Fig. 1. Taxonomy of existing IDSs based DDoS&DoS attacks

2.1   Signature-Based IDS

The majority of IDS are grounded on Signature-based Intrusion Detection Systems (SIDS). The SIDS rely on particular patterns that match a specific type of attacks. Additionally, the misused detection systems mechanism is accountable for the detecting a predefined attack based on previous signatures that stored in SIDS. Moreover, the most features of the signatures based are to having knowledge about network behavior. For example, by using signature that looks for specific threads within exploit a particular buffer-overflow weakness [23]. In addition, a number of IPv4 IDSs and new signatures are updated and extended in order to detect IPv6 attacks. In the same way, those SIDSs are not effective enough to spot ICMPv6 attacks, since of their detection limitation and earlier signature attacks that stored in their databases [24]. In this subsection concentrates on evaluating these existing signatures-based IDS in such a way to understand their approaches, their advantages and disadvantages.

Furthermore, one of the most obstacles confronted by signature-based IDS is that all signatures must be entered and stored in their database. So, it contains hundreds or thousands of signatures entries. Identically, the signature-based approach detects the network traffic and compare them with associated signature in the database of SIDS. By this way extremely highly resource consuming and it will slow down the productivity of detecting attacks and making the IDS vulnerable to variety of attacks. In another word, one of the IDS elision tools uses this exploit by flooding the signature with thousands of packets till the IDS cannot deal with the traffic then making the IDs is unreachable and drop the packets. As a result, malicious traffic bypass the network. Moreover, this category of IDS is remain defenseless since it depends on signatures that present in database to detect attacks [25]. Additionally, signature-based systems procedure has been applied in many IDSs in order to detect explicit IPv6 attacks. There are some Signature-based IDSs are introduced as follow.

According to, BRO [26] it is an open-source SIDS and standalone system for detecting network traffic intrusion. The BRO intrusion detecting systems is just for monitoring and notifying the network admin in case there are intrusions is matching. The major drawback of this mechanism is not sufficient for the IPv6 network and not able to detect zero-day attacks. Also, according to a previous study Gehrke et al., [29] BRO unable to detect 8% for detection IPv6 attacks.

According to Snort [27] is an open source SIDS. The Snort offers a layer of protection that just to notify the admin in case there are abnormal traffic detected. The drawback of Snort is that it is no capable to detect IPv6 attacks since it was designed for IPv4 network.

According to Suricata [28] is an open source SIDS, that uses IPv4 specification to detect IPv6 attacks. These SIDSs have low detection accuracy for detecting ICMPv6-based DDoS&DoS attacks. The Table 2 is summarized and listed out the SIDSs.

2.2   Anomaly-Based IDS (AIDS)

AIDS relies on knowledge of the network behavior and based on prior defined behavior, then it triggers the event in anomaly detection. Furthermore, Anomaly detection becomes abroad topic in intrusion detection studies. There are several anomaly-based detections approaches are projected and applied to detect IPv6 attacks. Also, the majority of anomaly-based are based on supervised algorithms. In addition, the anomaly-based AIDS has a principal benefit in detecting new (zero-day) attacks [30]. Overall, anomaly-based AIDS can be grouped into four species. The first is rule-based AIDS, which predefines rules to detect network traffic, the second is Learning-based AIDS which uses machine learning algorithm to inspire their detection models [31], the third is entropy-based IDS and the last is deep learning-Based IDS.

Rule-Based AIDS are planned to observe the network traffic and alert the network admin about any suspicious behavior associated with the ICMPv6 messages. There are some popular tools that are grounded on rule based IDS such as NDP Monitoring by Beck et al., [32], that only gives the admin alert if any changes in NDP messages and it suffers from lack of scalability. Another monitoring tool is Ndpwatch, 2018 [33]. It provides security for NDP messages by combine IPv6 and MAC address. As a result, it will notify the administrator if any suspicious happen.

Also, there is one more tool for monitoring RA messages Morse, 2018 [34] that only monitors the RA message. However, the above monitoring tools are just notifying the admin in case of any changes happen in network and they are not able take any action against these types of attacks. Therefore, the previous monitoring tools are never be considered as self-sufficient IDS. In addition, most of the mention tools having an issue with the change in network interface controller (NIC) that drives to clash between the MAC and IPv6 addresses and cause false alarms [35].

Correspondingly, there are a lot of Rule-based IDS that has been introduced. But this sub-section will mention some of them. The first, rule-based was proposed by Barbhuiya et al., [36] is proposing a technique to detect Man-in-the-middle attack (MiTM) and DoS attacks that generated by NS and NA message spoofing massage. This technique gives promising that no spoofing occurs among the MAC and IPv6 address, by forwarding a probe packet for this objective. The drawback of this approach is that the probe packets will consume the network bandwidth, particularly in case of DDoS attacks. The Bansal et al., [37] is an improved and extent of the Barbhuiya et al., [36] approach. The above two approaches have drawbacks like using the probe packet that will consume the network bandwidth and they are limited to NS and NA messages spoofing attack and it is not perfect enough to detect ICMPv6 attacks.

Machine Learning AIDS. As alternatively of using manually outlined rules to detect any possible attacks the learning-based are utilized automatically to build advance detection model by using machine learning that added to the IDS.

Learning-based techniques is sophisticated method to learn the attacks behaviors based on record data-set to detect similar behaviors such as Data mining. It is an efficient approach that applied in ADSs to detect IPv6 DDoS &DoS attacks. Moreover, there are many researchers tried to find out an accurate approach to detect, mitigate and classify such horrible attacks.

According to Saad et al., [38] by using fuzzy logic was successfully implemented to detect ICMPv6 Echo request DoS flooding attack only. Another learning technique Saad et al., [39] used Back-Propagation algorithm to detect ICMPv6 echo request DDoS flooding attack and had a 98.3% detection accuracy. However, the drawback of this technique is limited to ICMPv6 echo request flooding attack. One more Learning method was proposed by Zulkiflee et al., [1] using Support Vector Machine (SVM) to detect ICMPv6 RA DoS flooding attacks. The accuracy rate is high 99.95%. The machine drawback is just for detection RA attack only.

According to Alsadhan et al., [13] is used machine learning to detect DDoS attack based on NDP protocol. The experimental was grounded on GNS3 simulator and Virtual machines and the experimental result as mentioned is good. Another research, according to Elejla et al., [18] is proposed a set of features for detecting Router Advertisement (RA) flooding attack by using many types of classification. and the detection accuracy is acceptable between 60% to 79%. One more research, according to Liu et al., [40] is used machine learning to detect DDoS attack based in IPv6 and the detection rate is 72.2%. In Table 2 is Summaries machine learning IDSs for detection ICMPv6 DDoS & DoS attacks.

Entropy-Based IDS. This is a totally different technique from the previous ones. In this technique, entropy captures the most important features in network traffic distribution. The features that are selected used to detect the normal and abnormal in network traffic. In another word, the entropy technique has the ability to select large number of attributes of network traffic flow records that play a vital role in intrusion detecting system [41]. There are many researchers who tried to find out an accurate approach to detect such attacks.

According to Thomas et al., [42] is used Fast entropy approach to detect DDoS attack based on flow-based network traffic in order to select large number of attributes from the flow records. Also, the researcher used adaptive threshold algorithm to detect abnormality that based on variation of network traffic changes. The detection accuracy rate of this technique is good and the drawback of this detection mechanism the experiment was implemented in IPv4 network environment.

According to Mousavi et al., [43] using the entropy approach to spot DDoS attack in Software Defined Network (SDN). The research approach uses the entropy technique since it has shown efficient result and got high accuracy rates. The research used window size of 50 packets than the entropy calculated each window size and then compare it to threshold algorithm. The detection result was 96%. The drawback of this approach was implemented in IPv4 network.

According to Brooks et al., [44] is used a combination of cumulative sum (CUSUM) algorithm and entropy-based approach to detect DDoS attacks and getting high accuracy rate detection. The researcher improves the detection effectiveness by adding signal processing on entropy of the packet header field with help of wavelet filtering. The experimental of this research has just utilized the entropy of source IP address. The result showed high detection 95% and low false positive rates. The drawback of this approach implements the in IPv4 network environment.

One more research Bin Ibrahim et al., [45] propose a combination approach of entropy-based technique with the adaptive threshold algorithm to detect RA DoS flooding attack only and this technique archives 98% detection accuracy. As can be seen, most of the recent IDSs techniques are rely on a packet-based traffic. The drawbacks of packet-based traffic representation is that it takes more processing time and more complexity method to analysis a huge amount of data. The following Table 2 is summaries the entropy-based IDSs that proposed to detection ICMPv6 attacks.

Deep Learning- Based IDS. The deep learning is a subcategory of machine learning which in turn is a part of artificial intelligent. Also, artificial intelligent is a technique that allow the machine to mimic the human behaviors [46]. Moreover, the deep learning algorithm is a new advanced technique that has been emerged recently. The deep learning approach has the ability to use big Data with lowest minimum training time and extremely high accuracy rate by its characteristic learning mechanism. Similarly, the operation of deep learning technique uses many interconnected sequential layers. Every layer is collecting the output of previous layer as input. In addition, deep learning technique is playing a vital role in hierarchical features extraction [47]. The deep learning is successively implemented in intrusion detection systems that shown an effective and efficient detection accuracy rates in many different types of attacks. There are number of researchers that used deep learning for network intrusion detection systems.

According to Shone et al., [46]who proposed a Network Intrusion Detection System using deep learning classification model constructed using non-symmetric deep autoencoder (NDAE). In addition, the dataset that was used is the KDD Cup '99 and NSL-KDD benchmark datasets since it was broadly used and showed very promising result. The security drawback is not using real time network traffic.

According to Javaid et al., [48] who has proposed an efficient and flexible Network Intrusion Detection System using Self-taught Learning (STL) which is a deep learning techniques. The proposed system implements the NSL-KDD dataset for training and tested data. The dataset has 21 attacks classes, 16 novel attacks include DoS attacks and 1 normal class whereas the dataset have 38 traffic classes. As mentioned, the proposed NIDS approach gained extremely high accuracy rate with minimum false alarm.

According to Thinh et al., [49] used two deep learning techniques "Restricted Boltzmann Machines (RBM) and Autoencoder" to pre-training and to come

Table 2. Summarization of IDSs Based in DDoS&DoD Attacks

Mechanism	Mechanisms properties	Security drawbacks
Signature-Based Intrusion detecting systems		
Snort [27]	It is an open source By applying IPv4 policies for IPv6 traffic and IPv4 values with their IPv6 values	Unable to understand the IPv6 features Powerless to spot the zero-day attack Unable to detect DDoS attacks
BRO [26]	It is an open source SIDS By applying IPv4 policies for IPv6 traffic and IPv4 values with their IPv6 values, an administrator can write BRO script rules	Unlimited up-to-date signatures Unable to the understanding of IPv6 features Powerless to detect zero-day attacks Unable to detect all DDoS & DoS attacks
Suricata [28]	It is an open source It is multi-threading IDS Fasted IDS the same IPv4 policies for IPv6 traffic	Unable to understand IPv6 features Unqualified to detect zero-day attacks Consuming machine memory
Anomaly-Based Intrusion Detection Systems		
Zulkiflee et al., [1]	Detect IPv6 attacks including DDoS attack Learning-based AIDS Use SVM algorithm High accuracy (99.95%)	Detect RA DoS flooding attack only
Barbhuiya et al., [36]	A Mechanism to detect MiTM and DoS attacks of NS and NA spoofing attack	Using the probe packets that will consuming the network bandwidth
Bansal et al., [37]	Detect MiTM and DoS attacks of NS & NA spoofing messages An improved version of [36]	Consuming more resources Limited to NS and NA attacks DoS
Saad et al., [38]	Detect ICMPv6 DoS flooding attack Use Fuzzy Logic algorithm High accuracy rate	Detect ICMPv6 ECHO Request only
Saad et al., [39]	Learning-based AIDS Detect ICMPv6 Echo request DDoS attack. Use Back-Propagation Neural Network algorithm The accuracy is (98.3%).	Only detect ICMPv6 Echo request DDoS attack
Z. Liu et al., [40]	Detect DDoS attacks in IPv6 network It is learning-based AIDS used Apriori algorithm	Medium accuracy rate (72%)
Entropy-Base Intrusion Detecting systems		
Mousavi et al., [43]	Using entropy approach to spot the DDoS attack in (SDN) The detection result was 96%	Implemented in IPv4 network

(continued)

Table 2. (*continued*)

Mechanism	Mechanisms properties	Security drawbacks
Brooks et al., [44]	Used a combination of the cumulative sum (CUSUM) algorithm and entropy approach to detect network anomalies DDoS attacks High detection 95% and low fals positive rates	Using IPv4 network environment
Thomas et al., [42]	Used Fast entropy and adaptive threshold algorithm to detect DDoS attacks	Implement the experiment in IPv4 network environment
Bin Ibrahim et al., [45]	Using a hybrid approach of entropy-based technique and adaptive threshold algorithm to detect DoS RA High accuracy rate 98%	Only detecting RA DoS flooding attack
Deep Learning- Based Intrusion Detection Systems		
Shone et al., [46]	It is NIDS using deep-learning classification model. Detect various types of attack class include DoS attack. Used is the KDD Cup '99 and NSL-KDD datasets The accuracy rate is high	Not implemented in real time network traffic
Javaid et al., [48]	It is Deep learning NIDS to detect DoS attacks and different types Using NSL-KDD dataset High accuracy rate	Not implemented in real network
Thinh et al., [49]	It is anomaly-based NIDS. Detect and classify attacks into groups normal or DoS attacks The dataset was KDDCup99. The accuracy rat is high	Taking more time for training and detecting The classifying of attacks is slow
Gurung et al., [50]	It is NIDS using deep learning to detect any possible intrusion Using NSL-KDD dataset The accuracy of proposed model was 87.2%	The proposed model was compared with signature-based IDS

out with anomaly based network intrusion detecting system. The experimental dataset was KDDCup99 network traffic connections that shown low error rate. The anomaly-based NIDS is able to detect and classify attacks into groups such as Normal or DoS attacks. The accuracy rate is high as it mentioned of detecting and classifying network activities based on data sources. The drawback of this system is taking more time for training detecting and classifying of attacks is slow.

According to Gurung et al., 2019 [50] who proposed a network intrusion detection system using deep learning technique. The proposed system uses the pattern of anomalies and deep network to identify any intrusions as well as to classify network traffic in case of normal or abnormal traffic. The proposed system trained NSL-KDD dataset and the accuracy of the proposed model was 87.2%. Overall, the proposed model was compared with signature- based IDS approaches, the proposed model gets higher accuracy rates than signature-based IDS. The following Table 2 is summaries all the above deep learning IDSs that underlined in this subsection.

3 Discussion

In the final analysis, IPv6 is the most essential protocol at the present time since it accommodates the extreme increase in IP address demands. Henceforth, the IPv6 protocol is insecure and the attackers take advantages of this breaches to attempt DDoS & DoS attacks. These attacks are one of the powerful weapons that the attacker uses to target Vital facilities such as online shopping servers in order to make the services unavailable or to stop the authorized individuals from being accessing these services. Those type of attacks are considered as one of major issues in Internet cyber-security, since there is no countermeasure placed at first line of defense to stop such a grave attack. Under those circumstances, there are many researchers who try to find out an accurate way to detect, mitigate and classify such horrible attacks. After all, the DDoS & DoS attacks were not fully covered by any one of the existing intrusion detection systems. For this reason, these IDSs are suffers from security limitations to detect such attacks.

4 Conclusion

In the long run, the aim of this review paper is to provide a clear understanding and uncomplicated overview of IPv6 features and associated protocols. As the result, ICMPv6 and NDP have the same vulnerabilities that can be exploited by the attackers. These attacks happen during the exchange messages which are not fully secured and there are no sophisticated countermeasures against such horrible attacks. In short, this article reviews a number of mechanisms that have been projected to find out an accurate way to detect, to mitigate, and to classify the IPv6 attacks. These mechanisms are effectively summarized with their advantages and disadvantages.

Acknowledgment. The authors would like to thank Hadhramout Establishment For Human Development. Yemen-Hadramout-Mukalla for finalacial support of this research work.

References

1. Zulkiflee, M., Azmi, M., Ahmad, S., Sahib, S., Ghani, M.: A framework of features selection for ipv6 network attacks detection. WSEAS Trans. Commun. **14**(46), 399–408 (2015)
2. Mali, P., Phadke, R., Rao, J., Sanghvi, R.: Mitigating IPv6 Vulnerabilities (2015)
3. Deering, S., Hinden, R.: Internet protocol, version 6 (IPv6) specification (No. RFC 8200) (2017)
4. Mun, Y., Lee, H.K.: Understanding IPv6. Springer, Heidelberg (2005). https://doi.org/10.1007/b135746
5. Saad, R.M., Anbar, M., Manickam, S., Alomari, E.: An intelligent ICMPv6 DDoS flooding-attack detection framework (V6IIDS) using back-propagation neural network. IETE Tech. Rev. **33**(3), 244–255 (2016)
6. Radhakrishnan, R., Jamil, M., Mehfuz, S., Moinuddin, M.: Security issues in IPv6. In: International Conference on Networking and Services (ICNS 2007), pp. 110–110. IEEE (2007)
7. Tian, J., Li, Z.: The next generation Internet protocol and its test. In: ICC 2001. IEEE International Conference on Communications. Conference Record (Cat. No. 01CH37240), Vol. 1, pp. 210–215. IEEE (2001)
8. Conta, A., Gupta, M.: Internet control message protocol (ICMPv6) for the internet protocol version 6 (IPv6) specification (2006)
9. Najjar, F., Kadhum, M.M.: Reliable behavioral dataset for IPv6 neighbor discovery protocol investigation. In: 2015 5th International Conference on IT Convergence and Security (ICITCS), pp. 1–5. IEEE (2015)
10. Arjuman, N.C., Manickam, S.: A review on ICMPv6 vulnerabilities and its mitigation techniques: classification and art. In: 2015 International Conference on Computer, Communications, and Control Technology (I4CT), pp. 323–327. IEEE (2015)
11. Osman, A.: Improvement of Address Resolution Security in IPv6 Local Network using Trust-ND (2015)
12. Anbar, M., Abdullah, R., Saad, R., Hasbullah, I.H.: Review of preventive security mechanisms for neighbour discovery protocol. Adv. Sci. Lett. **23**(11), 11306–11310 (2017)
13. Alsadhan, A.A., Hussain, A., Baker, T., Alfandi, O.: Detecting distributed denial of service attacks in neighbour discovery protocol using machine learning algorithm based on streams representation. In: Huang, D.S., Gromiha, M., Han, K., Hussain, A. (eds.) Intelligent Computing Methodologies, vol. 10956, pp. 551–563. Springer, Cham (2018). https://doi.org/10.1007/978-3-319-95957-3_58
14. Zhang, T., Wang, Z.: Research on IPv6 neighbor discovery protocol (NDP) security. In: 2016 2nd IEEE International Conference on Computer and Communications (ICCC), pp. 2032–2035. IEEE (2016)
15. Saad, R.M., Anbar, M., Manickam, S.: Rule-based detection technique for ICMPv6 anomalous behaviour. Neural Comput. Appl. **30**(12), 3815–3824 (2018)
16. Saad, R., Manickam, S., Alomari, E., Anbar, M., Singh, P.: Design & deployment of testbed based on ICMPv6 flooding attack. J. Theoret. Appl. Inf. Technol. **64**(3), 795–801 (2014)
17. Mowla, N.I., Doh, I., Chae, K.: Multi-defense mechanism against DDoS in SDN based CDNi. In: 2014 Eighth International Conference on Innovative Mobile and Internet Services in Ubiquitous Computing, pp. 447–451. IEEE (2014)

18. Elejla, O.E., Anbar, M., Belaton, B.: ICMPv6-based DoS and DDoS attacks and defense mechanisms. IETE Tech. Rev. **34**(4), 390–407 (2017)
19. Anbar, M., Abdullah, R., Al-Tamimi, B.N., Hussain, A.: A machine learning approach to detect router advertisement flooding attacks in next-generation IPv6 networks. Cogn. Comput. **10**(2), 201–214 (2018)
20. Elejla, O.E., Belaton, B., Anbar, M., Smadi, I.M.: A new set of features for detecting router advertisement flooding attacks. In: 2017 Palestinian International Conference on Information and Communication Technology (PICICT), pp. 1–5. IEEE (2017)
21. Anbar, M., Abdullah, R., Hasbullah, I.H., Chong, Y.W., Elejla, O.E.: Comparative performance analysis of classification algorithms for intrusion detection system. In: 2016 14th Annual Conference on Privacy, Security and Trust (PST), pp. 282–288. IEEE (2016)
22. Papamartzivanos, D., Mármol, F.G., Kambourakis, G.: Dendron: genetic trees driven rule induction for network intrusion detection systems. Future Gener. Comput. Syst. **79**, 558–574 (2018)
23. Jyothsna, V.V.R.P.V., Prasad, V.R., Prasad, K.M.: A review of anomaly based intrusion detection systems. Int. J. Comput. Appl. **28**(7), 26–35 (2011)
24. Moore, N.: Optimistic duplicate address detection (DAD) for IPv6 (No. RFC 4429) (2006)
25. Uddin, M., Rahman, A.A., Uddin, N., Memon, J., Alsaqour, R.A., Kazi, S.: Signature-based Multi-layer distributed intrusion detection system using mobile agents. IJ Netw. Secur. **15**(2), 97–105 (2013)
26. Paxson, V.: Bro: a system for detecting network intruders in real-time. Comput. Netw. **31**(23–24), 2435–2463 (1999)
27. Roesch, M.: Snort: lightweight intrusion detection for networks. In: Lisa, vol. 99, no. 1, pp. 229–238 (1999)
28. Suricata: Suricata—Open Source IDS/IPS/NSM engine. https://suricata-ids.org. Accessed 02 Apr 2019
29. Gehrke, K.A.: The unexplored impact of ipv6 on intrusion detection systems. Naval Postgraduate School, Monterey, CA, Department of Computer Science (2012)
30. Patcha, A., Park, J.M.: An overview of anomaly detection techniques: existing solutions and latest technological trends. Comput. Netw. **51**(12), 3448–3470 (2007)
31. Aydın, M.A., Zaim, A.H., Ceylan, K.G.: A hybrid intrusion detection system design for computer network security. Comput. Electr. Eng. **35**(3), 517–526 (2009)
32. Beck, F., Cholez, T., Festor, O., Chrisment, I.: Monitoring the neighbor discovery protocol. In: 2007 International Multi-Conference on Computing in the Global Information Technology (ICCGI 2007), pp. 57–57. IEEE (2007)
33. Lecigne, C.: Ndpwatch, Ethernet/IPv6 address pairings monitor. http://ndpwatch.sourceforge.net/. Accessed 19 Apr 2018
34. Morse, J.: Router Advert MONitoring Daemon. http://ramond.sourceforge.net/. Accessed 19 Apr 2018
35. Elejla, O.E., Belaton, B., Anbar, M., Alnajjar, A.: Intrusion detection systems of ICMPv6-based DDoS attacks. Neural Comput. Appl. **30**(1), 45–56 (2018)
36. Barbhuiya, F.A., Biswas, S., Nandi, S.: Detection of neighbor solicitation and advertisement spoofing in IPv6 neighbor discovery protocol. In: Proceedings of the 4th International Conference on Security of Information and Networks, pp. 111–118. ACM (2011)
37. Bansal, G., Kumar, N., Nandi, S., Biswas, S.: Detection of NDP based attacks using MLD. In: Proceedings of the Fifth International Conference on Security of Information and Networks, pp. 163–167. ACM (2012)

38. Saad, R.M., Almomani, A., Altaher, A., Gupta, B.B., Manickam, S.: ICMPv6 flood attack detection using DENFIS algorithms. Indian J. Sci. Technol. **7**(2), 168 (2014)
39. Saad, R.M.A.: ICMPv6 echo request DDoS attack detection framework using back-propagation neural network, Doctoral dissertation, Universiti Sains Malaysia (2016)
40. Liu, Z., Lai, Y.: A data mining framework for building intrusion detection models based on IPv6. In: Park, J.H., Chen, H.H., Atiquzzaman, M., Lee, C., Kim, T., Yeo, S.S. (eds.) ISA 2009. LNCS, vol. 5576, pp. 608–618. Springer, Heidelberg (2009). https://doi.org/10.1007/978-3-642-02617-1_62
41. Umer, M.F., Sher, M., Bi, Y.: Flow-based intrusion detection: techniques and challenges. Comput. Secur. **70**, 238–254 (2017)
42. David, J., Thomas, C.: DDoS attack detection using fast entropy approach on flow-based network traffic. Procedia Comput. Sci. **50**, 30–36 (2015)
43. Mousavi, S.M., St-Hilaire, M.: Early detection of DDoS attacks against SDN controllers. In: 2015 International Conference on Computing, Networking and Communications (ICNC), pp. 77–81. IEEE (2015)
44. Özçelik, İ., Brooks, R.R.: Cusum-entropy: an efficient method for DDoS attack detection. In: 2016 4th International Istanbul Smart Grid Congress and Fair (ICSG), pp. 1–5. IEEE (2016)
45. Shah, S.B.I., Anbar, M., Al-Ani, A., Al-Ani, A.K.: Hybridizing entropy based mechanism with adaptive threshold algorithm to detect RA flooding attack in IPv6 networks. In: Alfred, R., Lim, Y., Ibrahim, A., Anthony, P. (eds.) Computational Science and Technology, vol. 481, pp. 315–323. Springer, Singapore (2019). https://doi.org/10.1007/978-981-13-2622-6_31
46. Shone, N., Ngoc, T.N., Phai, V.D., Shi, Q.: A deep learning approach to network intrusion detection. IEEE Trans. Emerg. Top. Comput. Intell. **2**(1), 41–50 (2018)
47. Karatas, G., Demir, O., Sahingoz, O.K.: Deep learning in intrusion detection systems. In: 2018 International Congress on Big Data, Deep Learning and Fighting Cyber Terrorism (IBIGDELFT), pp. 113–116. IEEE, December 2018
48. Javaid, A., Niyaz, Q., Sun, W., Alam, M.: A deep learning approach for network intrusion detection system. In: Proceedings of the 9th EAI International Conference on Bio-Inspired Information and Communications Technologies (formerly BIO-NETICS), pp. 21–26. ICST (Institute for Computer Sciences, Social-Informatics and Telecommunications Engineering) (2016)
49. Van, N.T., Thinh, T.N., Sach, L.T.: An anomaly-based network intrusion detection system using deep learning. In: 2017 International Conference on System Science and Engineering (ICSSE), pp. 210–214. IEEE (2017)
50. Gurung, S., Ghose, M.K., Subedi, A.: Deep learning approach on network intrusion detection system using NSL-KDD dataset. Int. J. Comput. Netw. Inf. Secur. **11**(3), 8 (2019)
51. AlSa'deh, A., Meinel, C.: Secure neighbor discovery: review, challenges, perspectives, and recommendations. IEEE Secur. Priv. **10**(4), 26–34 (2012)

Performance Evaluation for Four Supervised Classifiers in Internet Traffic Classification

Alhamza Munther[1(⊠)], Imad J. Mohammed[2], Mohammed Anbar[3], and Anwer Mustafa Hilal[4(⊠)]

[1] IT Department, Sur College of Applied Science, Ministry of Higher Education, Sur, Sultanate of Oman
alhamza.sur@cas.edu.om
[2] Department of Computer Science – College of Science, University of Baghdad, Baghdad, Iraq
dr.imadjm@scbaghdad.edu.iq
[3] National Advanced IPv6 Centre of Excellence, Universiti Sains Malaysia, Penang, Malaysia
anbar@nav6.usm.my
[4] Department of Computer and Self Development, Prince Sattam Bin Abdulaziz University, Kharj, Kingdom of Saudi Arabia
a.hilal@psau.edu.sa

Abstract. Supervised machine learning is a method to predict a class for labeled data, to improve different QoS metrics of several scopes such as educational, industrial and medical etc. This paper presents in-deep study focusing on four supervised classifiers were used widely to distinguish or categorize TCP/IP network traffic model and how they can be employed, these four are Naïve Bayes, Probabilistic Neural Network, Support Vector Machine and C4.5 decision tree. The classifiers are compared with regard to three significant metrics namely classification accuracy, classification speed and memory consumption. The implementation results of simulation and comparisons show that C4.5 decision tree introduce best results with high accuracy up to 99.6% using the benchmark dataset consist of 24863 packets compared to the rest three tested classifiers.

Keywords: Network machine learning · Supervised learning · Internet traffic engineering · Internet traffic classification

1 Introduction

Network traffic engineering is one of the most vital technologies that have witness a fast growing in the revolution of worldwide technologies. Network traffic identification and classification have newly added considerable interest as an important network engineering tool for network security, network design, as well as network monitoring and management. Network traffic classification is a process of categorizing the network traffic into several application classes such as (P2P, WWW, Mail, etc.) [1, 2].

With data in hand, many of network operators have been started to inspect and analyze network traffic but they faced some incoming challenges. The vast volume of

M. Anbar et al. (Eds.): ACeS 2019, CCIS 1132, pp. 168–181, 2020.
https://doi.org/10.1007/978-981-15-2693-0_12

classified data traffic and the diversity of applications are two significant questions among these challenges. As a result, numerous of studies have been proposed to encounter the above-mentioned challenges and started to consider competitive and sometimes contrary factors in terms of QoS such as accuracy of classification, memory consumption, CPU consumption and time complexity [3–5]. The port-based classification (IANA) [6] is the first approach that is proposed as a traditional method used to classify network traffic by examining the port numbers of transport protocol headers but no longer to use because some application doesn't follow the well-known port for hiding its behavior from monitoring (e.g. some VOIP application used port 23 that allocated for Telnet). Signature-based classification is another solution suggested by [7, 8] where the payload of packets are examined to determine whether or not contain signature of known application. For example, web traffic packet contains (.'\GET'). Although this method achieved good performance in term of accuracy, but the complex computation of this solution contributed negatively with encrypted traffic. A behaviour-based analysis is proposed as economizing process of resources usage compared with signature-based method [9, 10]. However, this method suffers from the time consuming to analyze the host statistical behavior besides the difficulty in the applying of real time. At the time being, it has been notes that more interest research is given to employ automated machine learning techniques in network traffic classification domain. Generally, machine learning [11] is categorized into two types supervised and unsupervised. Supervised learning requires training data to be labeled in advance (i.e., the class of each traffic flow must be known before learning). Unsupervised algorithms are able to cluster traffic flows into different classes according to similarities in their statistical properties (feature values).

In this paper we are focusing on supervised learning by studying in details classification process based on four types of supervised namely Naïve Bayes (NB) [12], Probabilistic Neural Network (PNN) [13], Support Vector Machine (SVM) [14] and C4.5. Moore dataset will use for evaluation. The classifiers will assess based on three main factors memory consumption, classification speed and classification accuracy in order to introduce an enough insight for researches. Section 2 explains the taxonomy of classifiers and how are employed for network traffic classification. Section 3 evaluates the performance based on different significant parameters for each classifier. Section 4 introduces the conclusion for this paper.

2   Research Method

This section presents the necessary analytical details that helps and simplify the understanding of the four supervised learning classifiers by discussing their mechanisms, advantages, limitations and to prepare for the implementation and performance evaluation. Moreover, how to employ each classifier for network flow classification is targeted as well:

2.1 Naïve Bayes

Moore and Zuev [8] employed the Naïve Bayes method as a supervised machine learning to categorize Internet traffic according to the type of applications. The packets that flow in the dataset are classified manually depending on the source application, to allow for very accurate evaluation. Moore adopted 248 features that were taken out in [15, 16] as input dataset for the classifier. Some of the traffic for the internet applications were categorized under different labels in order to facilitate classification, for instances: bulk data transfer, database, interactive, mail, services, www, p2p, attack, games and multimedia. Moore and his team applied naïve bayes using entire features set leading to the overall accuracy up to 65%. The successful employment of Naïve Bayes Kernel Estimation (NBKE) and Fast Correlation-Based Filter (FCBF) methods contributed in the reduction of feature space. Consequently, it improved the classifier performance in terms of overall accuracy.

Needless to say, Naïve bayes classifier makes an estimation of the class conditional probability through a presumption that the attributes independent conditionally. The terms P(c), P(x) and P(x|c) are employed by Naïve Bayes to calculate the value of posterior probability P(c|x) as formulated in Eq. 1. According to this classifier, a certain feature value effect of a predictor (x), on a given class (c) is not dependent on other predictors' values. "Class Conditional Independence" is the term given to this presumption. In other words, Naïve Bayes classifier presumes the value of one specific feature does not depend on the value of other features, given the class variable. For instance, an object can be considered as a formal soccer ball if it is spherical in shape, black and white in color and having a radius of 4.3–4.5 in. Naïve Bayes classifier would always adopt such features pertaining to any object sample to be contributing independently to a probability of being a soccer ball, as long as it is having these vary features.

$$P(c/x) = \frac{P(x|c)P(c)}{P(x)} \qquad (1)$$

where,

- P(c|x) is the posterior probability of class (target) given predictor (attribute).
- P(c) is the prior probability of class.
- P(x|c) is the likelihood which is the probability of predictor given class.
- P(x) is the prior probability of predictor.

For more understandable form, the above Bayesian probability equation is reformulated using plain English text as follows:

$$Posterior\ Probability = \frac{Likelihood \times class\ prior\ probability}{Predictor\ prior\ probaibilty\ (evidence)} \qquad (2)$$

Another technique is called Kernel estimator technique [11] which is used to study and analyze the relationship between each attribute and the class of instance by deriving a conditional probability for these relationships. Considering a typical case, the Naïve Bayes classifier has to make an estimation of the probabilities of a feature that has some feature value. For continuous features almost an infinite number of values can be available. Still, the probability estimation using the frequency distribution is not feasible. Modeling features with a continuous probability distribution function can be expressed using continuous probability distribution or Gaussian distribution.

2.2 Probabilistic Neural Network

Sun [13] suggested Probabilistic Neural Network (PNN) method for the network traffic classification. PNN commonly used for pattern classification by estimating the probability that an instance input i pattern belongs to a class. PNN considered as a kind of neural network that uses Bayes decision rule for Bayes inference. Using PNN, the operations are organized into a multilayered feed forward (i.e. the information moves unidirectional, forward, from the input nodes to the nodes in the next layer, no cycles or back propagation in the network) as shown in Fig. 1.

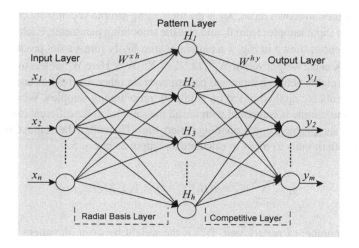

Fig. 1. Probabilistic neural network architecture [10]

The principle idea of PNN work is, once an input is entering into the first layer the distance is measured from the input vector to the training input vectors and yields a vector with elements indicate the closest training input to that input. The second layer sums these outputs for each class of inputs to yield as its net output with multi probabilities. Finally, compare transfer function of the output for second layer and selects the maximum of these probabilities, and exclusively produces a 1 for a certain class that holds the maximum probability and produces a 0 for the rest classes. Mathematically could be expressed as follow: Assumes a classification task of m categories for which $\theta 1, \theta 2, \ldots, \theta m$ belongs to class is defined. The decision of objective θ is based on a set of measurements denoted as n-dimensional vector $X^T = [x\_1, x\_2, x\_3, ..., x\_n]$. Then for a category θ_q, the Bayes decision rule is:

$$d(x) = \theta_q \quad if \quad h_q l_q f_q(X) > h_k l_k f_k(X), \ k \neq q \tag{3}$$

where $f_q(X)$ and $f_k(X)$ are the Probability Density Functions (PDF) of category q and k respectively. PDF is a function that describes the relative likelihood for random instances to take on a given value. Parameter h, is prior probability of an unknown sample being drawn from a particular population, l_q denotes the misclassification cost. These density functions correspond to the concentration of category (class) c instances around the unknown instance. The main target to use the Bayes decision rule is to estimate the probability density functions based on training patterns. An extensively and operative estimator proposed by Parzen is formulated as follows:

$$f_q(X) = \frac{1}{(2\pi)^{n/2}\sigma^n n_q} \sum_{i=1}^{n_q} \left[-\frac{(X - X_{qi})^T (X - X_{qi})}{2\sigma} \right] \tag{4}$$

where X denotes unknown input, X_{qi} is the ith training sample vector from class θ_q, n_q is the number of input samples from θ_q and σ is the smoothing parameter. Each pattern unit is a pattern neuron shown in Fig. 1 a pattern neuron firstly forms a dot product Z_i using input vector X and a weight vector W_i^{xh}, i.e. $Z_i = X \cdot W_i^{xh}$. Here W_i^{xh} refers to W_{xh} which is the set of weights between input and pattern layer. In other words, the classification of dataset elements are applied based on similarity ratio among samples. Weighting how much alike the sample is compared with the all the samples in the different classes. After each training sample has a corresponding pattern unit. Thereafter, the output unit uses the outputs of pattern units as input to calculate its output as in Eq. 5.

$$y_i = \sum_{i=1}^{h} W_{ij}^{hy} net(H_i), \quad j = 1, 2, 3, \dots, m \tag{5}$$

where h the number of pattern unit, W_{ij}^{hy} is the weight between ith pattern unit and jth output. The output y_j indicate the probability of X from category θ_j. $net(H_i)$ is calculated using Eq. 6 and representing the nonlinear operator (already applied in the pattern neuron using radial basis function that is formulated in Eq. 2).

$$net(H_i) = e^{-\frac{(w_i^{xh}-X)^T(w_i^{xh}-X)}{2\sigma^2}} \tag{6}$$

2.3   Support Vector Machine

Network traffic is an important carrier that records and reflects Internet and user activities. This parameter is also an important composition of network behavior. Through the analysis of traffic indicators, we can master network statistical behavior directly. This approach studies the behavior of each application flow independently and attempts to find discriminate by extracting the common behavioral information of the hosts (e.g., BLINC).

Zhu Li proposed a Support Vector Machine (SVM) method for network flow classification. The implemented SVM designed to compose seven classes of applications namely (Bulk, Interactive, www, Services, P2P, Mail and Services). SVM considered as one of the most famous supervised machine learning methods distinguished by the construction of an optimal separating hyperplane using binary labeled training data in which a maximum margin between two classes can be obtained. SVMs can learn a larger set of patterns and be able to better scale, because the classification complexity does not depend on the dimensionality of the feature space. SVMs also could update the training traffic dynamically especially in the online classification [17, 18]. Furthermore, SVM has been achieved fairly good separation by the hyperplane having the greatest distance to the nearest training data point within a class that is termed (Maximum Margin Hyperplane), and it has been noticed that the greater the margin, the less generalization error of the classifier can be realized. For more clarification, Fig. 2 shows an example for multi hyperplanes probably usage to separate two classes of information, where the circle denotes a Mail and the square represents P2P for linear dataset. The objective of SVM classifier is to select the best hyperplane in order to represent the decision boundaries and their margins (Figs. 2 and 3).

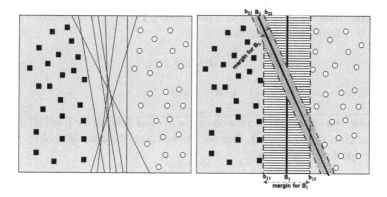

Fig. 2. SVM decision boundaries and margins

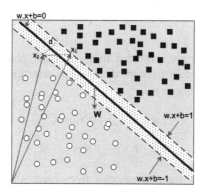

Fig. 3. Two different decision boundaries in SVM

To get a clearer picture of how to select the best hyperplane and the selection effect on the generalization error. Figure 3 shows two different decision boundaries B_1 and B_2 both can split the training samples (traffic packets) into their respective categories or application classes avoiding any misclassification percentage. Each decision boundary B_i is linked to a pair of hyperplanes, denoted b_{i1} and b_{i2} respectively. b_{i1} is found to touch the closest square by moving the hyperplane parallelly far away the decision boundary. While b_{i2} is moved parallelly until hits the nearest circles. The distance between these two hyperplanes is called the margin of classifier. From the figure exposed, the margin for B_1 is considerably bigger than that for B_2. Based on this example, B_1 is considered as a maximum margin hyperplane of the training samples. Therefore, linear dataset with the maximum margin can be classified as follow: assume each one of the training samples denoted by pair (x_i, y_i) where $i = 1, 2, 3, 4, ..., N$, and $xi = (xi1, xi2, ..., xid)T$ refers to the traffic features set for the ith example while y_i denotes application class $y_i \in [-1, 1]$ so decision boundary can be expressed as following:

$$w.x + b = 0 \qquad (7)$$

where w and b are parameters of the model. Figure 3 depicts decision boundary and the margin for two dimensional dataset with two classes. The margin for decision boundary $w.x + b = 0$ is formulated as follows:

$$w.xs + b = 1 \qquad (8)$$

$$w.xc + b = -1 \qquad (9)$$

This means that if we label all the squares s as class denoted by 1 and all the circles c as another class denoted by -1, then we can calculate the class labeled by y for any test sample (packet) z as follows:

$$y = \begin{cases} -1, & \text{if } w.z + b < 0 \\ 1, & \text{if } w.z + b > 0 \end{cases} \qquad (10)$$

Note that the margin of the decision boundary is expressed in terms of the distance between two hyperplanes for two alternate points x_1, x_2 and can be expressed as $d = \frac{2}{||W||}$.

Both w and b criteria are estimated in the training phase of SVM in order to calculate the decision boundary from the dataset. The selection of the parameter should be subjected to the following terms

$$w.x_i + b \geq 1 \text{ if } y_i = 1 \qquad (11)$$

$$w.x_i + b \leq -1 \text{ if } y_i = -1 \qquad (12)$$

Which implies that all training samples from class y = 1, namely the squares, should be located above or equal to the hyperplane $w.x + b = 1$ whereas the location of all samples from class y = −1, namely the circles, ought to be below or equal the hyperplane w.x + b = −1. These two equations may be reduced and grouped as one equation, as in the following equation:

$$y_i(w.x_i + b) \geq 1, i = 1, 2, 3, \ldots, N \tag{13}$$

In addition, there is an additional requisite as mentioned above; regarding maximizing the margin for decision boundary, which is equal to minimizing f(x):

$$f(x) = min \frac{||W^2||}{2} \tag{14}$$

2.4   C4.5 Decision Tree

C4.5 is another widespread method within the field of supervised machine learning used for network traffic classification [19–22]. It was developed by Ross Quinlan [23] and used for generating a decision tree. C4.5 is considered as an extension to ID3 algorithm [24], characterized by the ability to classify instances that carried either continuous or discrete attributes. It follows the divide-and-conquer approach to solve the classification problem of learning from a set of independent inputs (instances). Generally, decision tree uses divide-and-conquer approach to solve the classification problem through asking a set of sequences questions about the attributes of the test instance (input). The instance under questions goes iteratively into a subtree, until it reaches leaf node according to the predicted class [25]. These set of questions and answers are arranged in a hierarchy structure that is comprised of nodes and directed edges. C4.5 algorithm is grown recursively by dividing the training instances (inputs) into purer subsets (sub-trees). The tree structure of C4.5 algorithm consists of test nodes, each of them represents a feature, with branches representing possible values that connect the features.

C4.5 takes into account the information gain ratio in selecting the decision nodes (attributes) as alternative to the information gain that is used in ID3 that caused high error classification [26]. C4.5 uses gain ratio which applies normalization on information gain (difference in entropy [27]) using a value defined in Eq. 16. The feature with the highest normalized information gain is promoted to make the splitting decision process ongoing until reaches the leaf node (the class label).

$$Gainratio(F) = \frac{Gain\,(S,F)}{Entropy\,(S)} \tag{15}$$

$$Gain(S,F) = Entropy(S) - \sum_{v \in V(F)} \frac{|S_V|}{|S|} Entropy(S_V) \tag{16}$$

The Gain (S, F) refers to the information gain that is generated through fragmenting the training dataset S into v partitions corresponding to v outcomes of a test on the feature F

$$Entropy(S) = \sum_{i=1}^{m} -P_i \log_2 P_i \qquad (17)$$

where P_i refers the percentage of instances in set S that belongs to class i, m refers to total number of classes.

3 Performance Evaluation and Comparison

The implementation of the four classifiers is developed using Weka software version 3.7.10 based on the benchmark Moore dataset [12]. Moore dataset represent flow of TCP segments between client and server, its consist of 24863 instances, 248 attributes, and 11 classes namely WWW, FTP-CONTROL, MAIL, FTP-PASV, P2P, ATTACK, FTP-DATA, DATABASE, SERVICES, MULTIMEDIA, and INTERACTIVE. The dataset is divided into two parts; one as a training data with 14918 instances and the rest as testing data with 9945 instances. The features selection technique which is used for classifier is correlation feature selection and the search method is best first filter which are identify by default in Weka. As we alluded to earlier in the paper, the classifiers performances are compared using three parameters; classification accuracy, classification speed and memory consumption. These significant parameters are widely considered for classifiers evaluation especially in online and real time environments. These three parameters are elaborated with some details in the following subsections.

3.1 Classification Accuracy

The classification accuracy (the overall accuracy) is one of the most important metrics used to measure both supervised and unsupervised learning capabilities. Overall accuracy can be is defined as the sum of all True Positives (TP) over the sum of all the True Positive (TP) and False Positive (FP) for all classes as in Eq. 18 which explains the metrics combination for overall accuracy evaluation. Figure 4 shows the simulation results for the four classifiers; while NB realized lower percent of accuracy with only 57.8%, C4.5 decision tree achieved superior percent with 99.6%. Whereas SVM ranked second at 99.1% and PNN occupied third at 87%.

$$overall\ accuracy = \frac{\sum_{i=1}^{n} TP_i}{\sum_{i=1}^{n} (TP_i + FP_i)} \qquad (18)$$

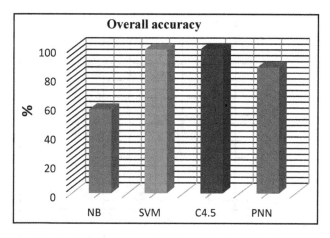

Fig. 4. Overall accuracy for four supervised classifiers.

3.2   Classification Speed

For time evaluation and comparison of the four tested classifiers, two types of time measures are considered namely build model time and total processing time. Build model time represents the needed time to build the classifier structure based on each classifier rules using training data only as discussed above. The total processing time quantifies the summation of classifying time of the testing data added to the building model time. Figure 5 highlights the Build model time for the four supervised classifiers. The results show that Naïve bays behaves the best and took time up to 3 s to build the model since it used simple probability function for classification. On contrary, PNN got more time consumption reached to 187 s due to the complexity of PNN classifier model. C4.5 build the model with 35 s while SVM took 114 s. Figure 6 demonstrates the total processing time to classify the descriptive dataset. C4.5 needed only 56 s compared to 170 s for SVM. Whilst PNN shows the highest consuming time up to 199 s. It is noted that both PNN and SVM took the most time during the model construction, conversely NB and C4.5 consumed the major time during the classification phase of testing data.

In overall result, from Fig. 5, it can be noted that NB and C4.5 competed to get the first rank position when the build model time is considered, NB wins the competition with significant difference from C4.5 time even from the rest two classifiers. Comparatively using the total processing time (as shown in Fig. 6) C4.5 behaved the best in terms of time processing leaving the second rank position to NB method with sound difference. Furthermore, the two competitors for the rear positions (third and fourth) occupied by SVM and PNN respectively.

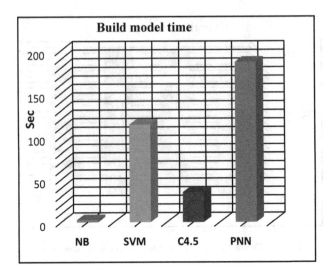

Fig. 5. Build model time for four classifiers.

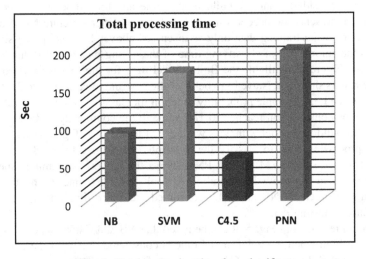

Fig. 6. Total processing time four classifiers.

3.3 Memory Consumption

Typically network traffic classification needs enough memory space to process (classify) and store the huge data traffic generated by the increasing number of applications. This metric occupies the significant role during real time and online classification. Figure 7 shows the results of memory consumption occupied by the four classifiers. Using 8 GB RAM memory, C4.5 decision tree shows less occupation (reach to 7%) of the RAM to deal with the dataset. Whilst NB utilized 9%. SVM exploited 14% of memory while PNN used 16%. Finally, it can be derived that the percentages of memory consumption kept the same ranks of the four classifiers when the total processing time is considered but with less average difference.

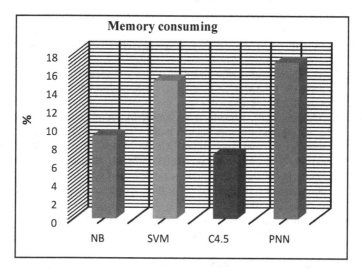

Fig. 7. Memory consumption for four supervised classifiers.

4   Conclusion

This paper focused analytically and validated practically the performances of the four supervised machine learning methods namely Naïve bayes (NB), Probabilistic Neural Network (PNN), C4.5 decision tree and Support Vector Machine (SVM). The methodologies and how are they employed to classify network flow are explained analytically, examined practically and compared quantitatively in-depth. The results are evaluated based on three important metrics namely classification accuracy, classification speed and memory consumption. The classification speed metrics is evaluated using two sub metrics; build model time and total processing time. The results show C4.5 is the best in accuracy classification reach to 99.6%, faster, and less memory consumption compared to the three others. While NB presented good results in terms of speed classification and memory consumption, but it failed in classifying the network traffic accurately. SVM shows pronounced result as classification accuracy up to 99.1% but it consumed extra time as well as memory space significantly. PNN is ranked the last because of the method complexity. Additionally, in practice, measured results usually emerge further questions and existing extra measurement may help in prompt replies. Therefore, as a future work we hope to extend the test evaluation of the four classifiers using huge dataset and how it can to be fit with online and real time network classification through measuring another QoS parameters as jitter and throughput.

References

1. Callado, A., Kamienski, C., Fernandes, S., Sadok, D.: A survey on internet traffic identification and classification (2009)
2. Munther, A., et al.: Active build-model random forest method for network traffic classification. Int. J. Eng. Technol. (IJET) **6**(2), 796–804 (2014)
3. Karagiannis, T., Broido, A., Faloutsos, M.: Transport layer identification of P2P traffic. In: Proceedings of the 4th ACM SIGCOMM Conference on Internet Measurement, pp. 121–134 (2004)
4. Munther, A., et al.: Network traffic classification—a comparative study of two common decision tree methods: C4.5 and random forest. In: 2014 2nd International Conference on Electronic Design (ICED). IEEE (2014)
5. Munther, A., Othman, R.R., Alsaadi, A.S., Anbar, M.: A performance study of hidden Markov model and random forest in internet traffic classification. In: Kim, K., Joukov, N. (eds.) Information Science and Applications (ICISA) 2016. LNEE, vol. 376, pp. 319–329. Springer, Singapore (2016). https://doi.org/10.1007/978-981-10-0557-2_32
6. Sen, S., Spatscheck, O., Wang, D.: Accurate, scalable in-network identification of P2P traffic using application signatures. In: Proceedings of the 13th International Conference on World Wide Web, pp. 512–521 (2004)
7. Williams, N., Zander, S., Armitage, G.: A preliminary performance comparison of five machine learning algorithms for practical IP traffic flow classification. ACM SIGCOMM Comput. Commun. Rev. **36**, 5–16 (2006)
8. Moore, A.W., Zuev, D.: Internet traffic classification using bayesian analysis techniques. In: ACM SIGMETRICS Performance Evaluation Review, pp. 50–60 (2005)
9. Liu, Y., Li, W., Li, Y.: Network traffic classification using k-means clustering. In: Second International Multi-Symposiums on Computer and Computational Sciences, IMSCCS 2007, pp. 360–365 (2007)
10. Li, Z., Yuan, R., Guan, X.: Accurate classification of the internet traffic based on the svm method. In: IEEE International Conference on Communications, ICC 2007, pp. 1373–1378 (2007)
11. Fu, L., Tang, B., Yuan, D.: The study of traffic classification methods based on C4.5 algorithm (2012)
12. IANA: Internet Assigned Numbers Authority
13. Dreger, H., Feldmann, A., Mai, M., Paxson, V., Sommer, R.: Dynamic application-layer protocol analysis for network intrusion detection. In: USENIX Security Symposium, pp. 257–272 (2006)
14. Moore, A.W., Papagiannaki, K.: Toward the accurate identification of network applications. In: Dovrolis, C. (ed.) PAM 2005. LNCS, vol. 3431, pp. 41–54. Springer, Heidelberg (2005). https://doi.org/10.1007/978-3-540-31966-5_4
15. Erman, J., Mahanti, A., Arlitt, M.: Qrp05-4: internet traffic identification using machine learning. In: Global Telecommunications Conference, GLOBECOM 2006, pp. 1–6. IEEE (2006)
16. Li, W., Moore, A.W.: A machine learning approach for efficient traffic classification. In: 15th International Symposium on Modeling, Analysis, and Simulation of Computer and Telecommunication Systems, MASCOTS 2007, pp. 310–317 (2007)
17. Hao, S., et al.: Improved SVM method for internet traffic classification based on feature weight learning. In: 2015 International Conference on Control, Automation and Information Sciences (ICCAIS). IEEE (2015)

18. Sivaprasad, A., et al.: Machine learning based traffic classification using statistical analysis. Int. J. Recent Innov. Trends Comput. Commun. **6**(3), 187–191 (2018)
19. Kim, H., Claffy, K.C., Fomenkov, M., Barman, D., Faloutsos, M., Lee, K.: Internet traffic classification demystified: myths, caveats, and the best practices. In: Proceedings of the 2008 ACM CoNEXT Conference, p. 11 (2008)
20. Haffner, P., Sen, S., Spatscheck, O., Wang, D.: ACAS: automated construction of application signatures. In: Proceedings of the 2005 ACM SIGCOMM Workshop on Mining Network Data, pp. 197–202 (2005)
21. Ma, J., Levchenko, K., Kreibich, C., Savage, S., Voelker, G.M.: Unexpected means of protocol inference. In: Proceedings of the 6th ACM SIGCOMM Conference on Internet Measurement, pp. 313–326 (2006)
22. Karagiannis, T., Papagiannaki, K., Faloutsos, M.: BLINC: multilevel traffic classification in the dark. In: ACM SIGCOMM Computer Communication Review, pp. 229–240 (2005)
23. Clarke, B.S., Fokoue, E., Zhang, H.H.: Principles and Theory for Data Mining and Machine Learning. Springer, Heidelberg (2009). https://doi.org/10.1007/978-0-387-98135-2
24. Mitchell, T.M.: Machine Learning. WCB. McGraw-Hill, Boston (1997)
25. Fagan, T.J.: Letter: nomogram for Bayes theorem. New Engl. J. Med. **293**, 257 (1975)
26. Bennett, K.P., Campbell, C.: Support vector machines: hype or hallelujah? ACM SIGKDD Explor. Newsl. **2**, 1–13 (2000)
27. Breiman, L.: Random forests. Mach. Learn. **45**, 5–32 (2001)

Mobile Authentication Using Tapping Behavior

Vasaki Ponnusamy$^{(\boxtimes)}$, Chan Mee Yee, and Adnan Bin Amanat Ali

Faculty of Information and Communication Technology,
Universiti Tunku Abdul Rahman Kampar, Kampar, Malaysia
vasaki@utar.edu.my,
{meeyee95,adnanbinamanat}@lutar.my

Abstract. Mobile phones or smartphones are rapidly becoming the primary and essential communication device in people's lives that cannot be replaced by other communication devices, because of the portability, the size, and the multifunctionality provided in it. Nowadays, mobile phones are being used in almost every aspect of life and work as your personal assistant e.g. meeting reminders. It monitors your daily activities and gives suggestions accordingly e.g. health applications. With the help of smartphone online transactions can be performed, meetings can be conducted via video conferencing. It contains your personal files, emails, bank information, and your social network accounts record. It also contains information related to the credentials, which are stored in its memory. Despite all the benefits, there is a great threat to private information, in the case when mobile is snatched, misplaced, or in the use of an unauthorized user. An attacker can steal the user's private data and can misuse it without the owner's consent. Although the traditional authentication methods are in use, they have several limitations. In this paper, an authentication system is proposed that uses a combination of user behavior and touchscreen which can seamlessly capture the user's tapping behavior. The information obtained from the touch screen sensors reflects the unique tapping behavior of each user. Moreover, machine learning is utilized to perform the classification for the user's authentication.

Keywords: Tapping behavior · Machine learning · Mobile authentication · Behavior-based authentication

1 Introduction

Smartphones with touchscreen have revolutionized and dominated the user input technologies because of portability and usability. Today's mobile devices have more storage capacity, rich functionalities and have great computational power because of powerful processors. Many of the applications for which we were dependent on the desktop computers/laptops are now available on a smartphone. Also, nowadays many health-related applications are available on the smartphone that monitors your routine and gives suggestions accordingly. These things fascinate the user to use the smartphone for daily activities. According to a recent study conducted by the Deloitte Global Mobile Consumer Survey of 2016 [1], there are 61% of people who check their phones 5 min after waking up, meanwhile, 88% are those who check their phones within

M. Anbar et al. (Eds.): ACeS 2019, CCIS 1132, pp. 182–194, 2020.
https://doi.org/10.1007/978-981-15-2693-0_13

30 min, and 96% within an hour. This study shows that smartphone usage has greatly increased.

The more services we use, the more passwords are forced to be remembered and it is becoming a nuisance with a large number of accounts. It is evident that users have many passwords for devices and for different accounts, for instance, bank account, e-commerce site, and social media. Remembering a large number of passwords jumble up, difficult passwords are hard to remember, easy passwords can easily be hacked, keeping one password for all the applications is also a threat to the security of all the applications. According to the study reported by Buzz Feed News [16], 37% of people forget their password at least once a week. If a password is not used regularly it will have a higher tendency to be forgotten. Biometric authentication is vulnerable to brute force attack and dictionary attack as shown in Table 1. Hence, integrating these two types of authentication is not adequate in terms of security with high risks.

Table 1. Level of security for different smartphone authentication techniques [2]

Technique name	Brute force	Shoulder surfing	Smudge attack	Dictionary attack	Spyware
Slide lock	Yes	Yes	Yes	Yes	Not defined
PIN/password	Yes	Yes	Yes	Yes	Yes
Finger print	Yes	No	No	Yes	Yes
Speaker recognition	Yes	No	No	Yes	Not defined
Iris recognition	Yes	No	No	Yes	Not defined
Face recognition	Yes	No	No	No	Not defined

To overcome the problem mentioned above, a system is proposed which will capture user's tapping behavior [3, 4] on mobile devices that rely on standard machine learning techniques to perform user authentication. The user tapping behaviors features consists of x-coordinate, y-coordinate, pressure, size, tapping time and releasing time. It is assumed that different people will have different behavior when interacting with a mobile device. Based on the features extracted, the machine learning technique is applied which is the major contribution of the user verification system. This approach will ensure a strong user authentication process hence free from the above-mentioned attacks.

The objectives of this research are: to identify and explore the characteristic/ features of user taping behavior. To verify the identity of the user by classifying the tapping behavior when they interact with the mobile phone. The decision score from the classifier will be used by the decision maker to make a final decision and further action will be taken accordingly.

2   Related Work

Authentication is the process of comparing the user's credentials with the credentials are kept in the database of an authorized user. The current authentication techniques are categorized in the knowledge base (i.e. PIN, password, pattern), token base (i.e. smart card or Token based but this is not applicable for a smartphone.), and biometrics. Biometrics is further categorized in physical biometrics (i.e. fingerprint, iris) and behavioral biometrics (i.e. keystroke dynamics, touch dynamics, gait, etc.). This research is related to behavioral biometrics, so the authentication methods related to behavioral biometrics are discussed in the literature.

2.1 Behavioral Biometrics Authentication

Behavioral biometrics is how a user interacts with the mobile device i.e. holding method, typing, taping, and swipe behavior. These approaches are based on the users' behavioral actions and the authentication may happen implicitly. According to [5], an efficient mobile device authentication system should improve security beyond point-of-entry methods, reduce authentication attempts via transparent authentication, provide continuous authentication throughout the entire session of use, and maintain functionality across all mobile platforms regardless of hardware, software, and networking differences [6].

Behavioral biometrics is more suitable, as they meet all of the requirements without the need for specific or additional hardware and the user is unaware of the authentication process because the authentication process is being done on the background of the application. Moreover, behavioral biometrics allow protection during "user abandonment" [7], or the time in which the owner of the device is not present while the device remains unlocked.

Another research [8] is done on behavioral biometrics by observing the hand movements of the user using accelerometer and gyroscope. The author proposed an authentication mechanism by shaking the mobile device and collected the sensors data. From the experiments, he found an EER of 1.2%. To provide an extra level of security for user authentication on mobile devices, different biometric approaches have been explored. An author in [9] introduced a biometric technique based on hand gesture recognition. User is identified by a 3-D gesture when he/she moves one of his/her hands holding an accelerometer-embedded mobile device. After repeating his/her 3-D hand gesture three times, the user is able to enter the system. Multiple sets of samples will be produced when the user performs the same gestures continuously. In order to find the best alignment between two samples, a signal preprocessing algorithm, based on sequence alignment was introduced by [9].

Walking is a rhythmic pattern and everyone has a different walking style due to different body posture. Research [10] is done on walking pattern identification using accelerometer and gyroscope data. For the data collection, the user has to walk some steps by putting the mobile in the front pocket of the trouser. The EER achieved under zero factor attack was 13%. For the testing purpose, some professional actors were hired to impersonate the legitimate user but 29% attackers lose the rhythm. Another researcher [11] presented a method for gait-based user identity verification using smartphone sensor data. Gait-based user identity verification depends on the biometric specificity of human activity traits. It realized that gait analysis has a great potential to improve the user's identity. The proposed method is based on selected statistical and heuristic gait features and application of Random Projections method for reduction of feature dimensionality. An estimate of probability density function (PDF) of the low-dimensional feature vector is used to match the user in question with the PDF of the valid user.

2.2 Behavioral Biometrics Authentication Using Touchscreen

Using touchscreen a user can perform certain operations like tap, double tap, scroll, swipe, drag, and pinch. Due to different body structure and behavior, everyone uses touchscreen different from another user. e.g. touch size is different among different persons, have different sizes of the fingertips. These features can be used for the authentication purpose with slide lock, pattern lock or with pin/password to provide a
The behavior pattern can be classified into many categories as discussed below:
Slide Lock is a Lock Screen, it is a "touch–horizontal slide" form of screen. It does not serve as a security system and necessitates extra security applications. Pattern Lock consists of nine dots on the screen, each of which can be touched and dragged one dot at a time to form a password which is well matched with the user interface. Users may enter an easy pattern for convenience, as a result, it is weak security power. However, the scheme will not be comfortable to use if the users enter a more complicated pattern. Pattern lock is a scheme similar to pattern recognition [12] techniques used for authentication.
Personal Identification Number (PIN) is numeric only [13]. Users are required to exactly enter four digits long [0–9]. The most frequently used pin code is 1234. Some of the pin codes are easily predictable, such as 0000, 4321, and 1010. In addition, hackers can successfully guess if users are using the keypad to create pin code like 2580 going straight down. Moreover, most of the users select their birthdate as the pin code (e.g., MMDD), so that it can be easily remembered. But birthdate can be known by everyone from many sources such as social networks etc. Passwords include letters, numbers and special characters; usually, there is no limit in length. This is much more secure compared to pin code, slide lock, and pattern lock but the disadvantage is that it will take slightly longer to access the phone [14].
Using touchscreen, a research is done by doing swipe movements, the swipe behavior data is tested under five different classifiers and best 94.97% accuracy was achieved using random forest classifier [15].
Compared to knowledge-based methods, behavioral biometrics decrease the need for the legitimate owner of the device to authenticate by 67% [16], indicating a significant increase in usability. Hence, several behavioral modalities, such as motion, keystroke dynamics, gait, touch gestures, voice, and profiling, have been extensively analyzed for mobile device security. In this paper, touch gestures, specifically on tapping behavior is analyzed for user authentication.

3 Methodology

From the methodology shown in Fig. 1, when the user taps the screen, the system will automatically collect tapping raw data of users. The out of range data are filtered from the collected raw data. From the collected tapping raw data, 7 sets of features: x-coordinate, y-coordinate, tapping time, releasing time, pressure, touched size and action were obtained. The features result is then stored into the database and used to perform classification. The decision-maker makes a final decision, perform labeling whether the user tapping action belongs to the device owner itself or an imposter based on the decision score.

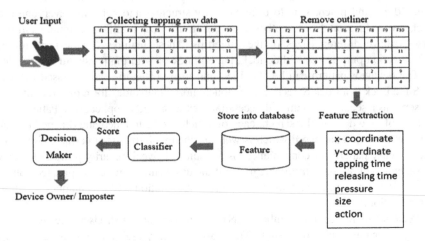

Fig. 1. Mobile user authentication system architecture

3.1   Enrolment Phase

Figure 2 shows the initial screen, to begin with, the application. It consists of two options, the login option for existing users and the register option for the new users.

Fig. 2. Register and login

After the successful login, users are required to click on the enrollment tap, followed by 10 taps of the user and the intruder subsequently. The information such as x-coordinate, y-coordinate, size, tapping time and releasing time will be displayed on the screen. These tapping data are stored in the database Fig. 3.

Fig. 3. Enrolment phase

3.2 Prediction Phase

In the prediction phase, verification will be performed whereby the user is asked to tap once and the application will be able to predict whether it is the device owner or an imposter as shown in Fig. 4.

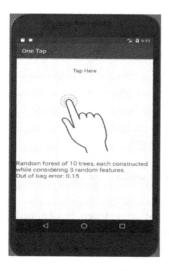
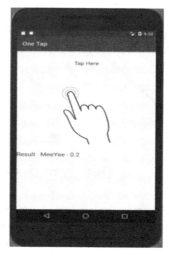

Fig. 4. Prediction phase

4   Simulation Results

Figures 5, 6 and 7 shows different training data sets such as 50 data set, 100 data set and 200 data set. Each of the training data sets includes two different participants, user A and user B. The output of the training data set is used as model to predict 10 testing data which is obtained from user A and user B. Among the variety of classifiers, 8 classifiers were chosen, such as Naive Bayes (NB), Naive Bayes Multinomial (NBM), Decision Table (DT), Decision Stump (DS), Random Forest (RF), Multilayer Perceptron (MLP), IBk and KStar. These classifiers were used in performing prediction with the testing data. The testing was conducted from 50 data sets, 100 data sets and 200 data sets to observe how accurately the classifier can differentiate between two users. The number of data provided will affect the prediction result.

In Fig. 5, 50 training data and 10 testing data were utilized, in which those training data and testing data are different. The y-axis represents the accuracy, the x-axis represents 8 types of selected classifiers. The results of each classifier are divided into two categories include correctly classified instances (percentage of correct prediction with the actual data) and incorrectly classified instances (percentage of incorrect prediction with the actual data). NB and NBM obtained 100% correctly classifier instances. DT, DS, and RF get 60% correct classified instances and 40% incorrectly classified instances. Meanwhile, MLP, IBk as well as KStar produced the same result which is 50% correctly classified instances and 50% incorrectly classified instances.

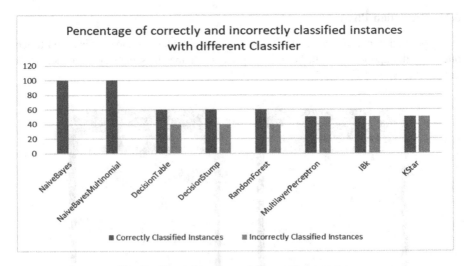

Fig. 5. 50 training data and 10 supplied test data

Table 2 shows the prediction for 10 sets of data which is obtained from two participants User A and User B. The output from the table shows the number of data for User A and User B which correctly and incorrectly predicted from the actual data.

Based on the output, NB and NBM produced better results. The classifier can accurately predict the data among User A and User B.

Table 2. Prediction of 10 testing data with 50 training data

Classifier	Correctly predict User A	Correctly predict User B	Error predicted user A as User B	Error predicted user B as User A
NB	5	5	0	0
NBM	5	5	0	0
DT	5	1	0	4
DS	5	1	0	4
RF	5	1	0	4
MLP	0	5	5	0
IBk	0	5	5	0
KStar	5	0	0	5

As shown in Fig. 6, 100 training data and 10 testing data for the test were used, in which those training data and testing data are different. NBM, DT, DS, RF, and IBk obtained 100% correctly classified instances. Whereas the remaining classifiers obtained 50% correctly classified instances and 50% incorrectly classified instances.

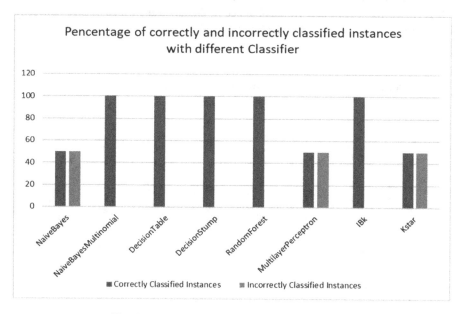

Fig. 6. 100 training data and 10 supplied test data

Table 3 shows the prediction results with 10 datasets which comes from two participants, user A and user B. The table shows a number of data for User A and User B correctly and incorrectly predicted from the actual data. From the current results, NBM, DT, DS, RF, and IBk obtained better results compared to other classifiers.

Table 3. Prediction of 10 data with 100 training data

Classifier	Correctly predict User A	Correctly predict User B	Error predicted user A as User B	Error predicted user B as User A
NB	5	0	0	5
NBM	5	5	0	0
DT	5	5	0	0
DS	5	5	0	0
RF	5	5	0	0
MLP	0	5	5	0
IBk	5	5	0	0
KStar	5	0	0	5

As in Fig. 7, 200 training datasets and 10 testing datasets were used. From the results, NBM and IBk obtained 100% correctly classified instances. On the other hand, NB, DT, DS, RF, MLP, and KStar obtained a similar result which is 50% correctly classified instances and 50% incorrectly classified instances.

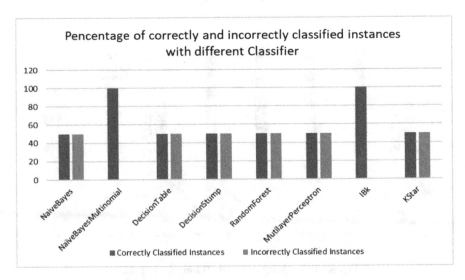

Fig. 7. 200 training data and 10 supplied test data

Table 4 shows the prediction with the 10 datasets of user A and user B correctly and incorrectly predicted from the actual data. NBM and IBK were able to accurately predict which data belongs to which user compared to other classifiers.

Table 4. Prediction of 10 data with 200 training data

Classifier	Correctly predict User A	Correctly predict User B	Error predicted user A as User B	Error predicted user B as User A
NB	5	0	0	5
NBM	5	5	0	0
DT	0	5	5	0
DS	0	5	5	0
RF	0	5	5	0
MLP	0	5	5	0
IBk	5	5	0	0
KStar	5	0	0	5

In these 3 scenarios, 3 different data size from 50 training data, 100 training data, and 200 training data with 10 testing data to identify the two participants were used. It is evident that the data size of the training data can affect the accuracy in prediction for the classifiers. The most constant classifier is NBM, it produces 100% correctly classified instances for all 3 scenarios which can successfully identify User A and User B clearly shown in Table 5.

Table 5. Results

	NB	NBM	DT	DS	RF	MLP	IBk	KStar
10/50	100%	**100%**	60%	60%	60%	50%	50%	50%
10/100	50%	**100%**	100%	100%	100%	50%	100%	50%
10/200	50%	**100%**	50%	50%	50%	50%	100%	50%

Thus, NBM is suitable for these three scenarios. There are possibilities that features will affect the result. In order to achieve high accuracy in order to identify two participants, it is strongly recommended to obtain more features and more training data to test with different classifiers.

5   Conclusion and Future Work

Smartphones have become an essential part of our everyday life. Due to the ample use of the mobile device, there is a need for a more secure authentication system. A large number of authentication problems are being raised to secure sensitive data and researchers have been implementing many authentication methods using behavior biometrics to resolve these issues. In this paper, we proposed an authentication method based on tapping behavior. We collected the tap behavior data (i.e. position, press time, release time, touch duration, and pressure) and tested this data on 8 different classifiers. Experimental results show that NBM gave 100% accuracy when tested on 3 different sets based on a different number of training samples. For future work, there is also a need to check the other conditions that must be considered e.g. the quantity of training and testing data, training and testing time consumed. Also other touch dynamics i.e. double tap, swipe, and pinch should also be included instead of tapping alone. Then, there will be additional features like x-coordinate, y-coordinate of second tap, duration, and speed between two taps and acceleration [17]. These additions would definitely affect the results and can give a better prediction of the legitimate and illegitimate user. Besides that, other modalities for implicit authentication [18] such as keystroke and touch dynamics [19–29], touch gesture [30–32], gait [8, 33–38] based recognition can also be integrated to improve the results further.

References

1. Lee, T.: Study finds 61% of people check their phone 5 minutes after waking up. https://www.ubergizmo.com/2016/12/study-61-percent-check-phones-5-mins-waking-up/. Accessed 21 Nov 2019
2. Shafique, U., et al.: Modern authentication techniques in smart phones: security and usability perspective. Int. J. Adv. Comput. Sci. Appl. (IJACSA) 8(1), 331–340 (2017)
3. Miluzzo, E., Varshavsky, A., Balakrishnan, S., Choudhury, R.R.: Tapprints: your finger taps have fingerprints. In: Proceedings of the 10th International Conference on Mobile Systems, Applications, and Services - MobiSys 2012, p. 323 (2012)
4. Xu, Z., Bai, K., Zhu, S.: TapLogger: inferring user inputs on smartphone touchscreens using on-board motion sensors. In: Proceedings of the Fifth ACM Conference on Security and Privacy in Wireless and Mobile Networks - WISEC 2012, p. 113 (2012)
5. Clarke, N.L., Furnell, S.M.: Advanced user authentication for mobile devices. Comput. Secur. 26(2), 109–119 (2007)
6. Clarke, N.L., Furnell, S.M.: Authenticating mobile phone users using keystroke analysis. Int. J. Inf. Secur. 6(1), 1–14 (2006)
7. Schaffer, K.B.: Expanding continuous authentication with mobile devices. Computer 48(11), 92–95 (2015)
8. Zhu, H., Hu, J., Chang, S., Lu, L.: ShakeIn: secure user authentication of smartphones with single-handed shakes. IEEE Trans. Mob. Comput. 16(10), 2901–2912 (2017)
9. Guerra-Casanova, J., Sánchez-Ávila, C., Bailador, G., de Santos Sierra, A.: Authentication in mobile devices through hand gesture recognition. Int. J. Inform. Secur. 11(2), 65–83 (2012)
10. Muaaz, M., Mayrhofer, R.: Smartphone-based gait recognition: from authentication to imitation. IEEE Trans. Mob. Comput. X(X), 1 (2017)
11. Damaševičius, R., et al.: Smartphone user identity verification using gait characteristics. Symmetry 8(10), 100 (2016)
12. Neal, T., Woodard, D.: Surveying biometric authentication for mobile device security. J. Pattern Recognit. Res. 11(1), 74–110 (2016)

13. Pinola, M.: The most (and least) common PIN numbers and numeric passwords. is yours one of them? https://lifehacker.com/the-most-and-least-common-pin-numbers-and-numeric-pas-5944567. Accessed 21 Nov 2018
14. Bernstein, J.: Survey says: people have way too many passwords to remember (2016). https://www.buzzfeednews.com/article/josephbernstein/survey-says-people-have-way-too-many-passwords-to-remember#.mm4e5jJ7Q. Accessed 23 Nov 2018
15. Ali, A.B.A., Ponnusamay, V., Sangodiah, A.: User behaviour-based mobile authentication system. In: Bhatia, S.K., Tiwari, S., Mishra, K.K., Trivedi, M.C. (eds.) Advances in Computer Communication and Computational Sciences. AISC, vol. 924, pp. 461–472. Springer, Singapore (2019). https://doi.org/10.1007/978-981-13-6861-5_40
16. Crawford, H., Renaud, K., Storer, T.: A framework for continuous, transparent mobile device authentication. Comput. Secur. **39**, 127–136 (2013)
17. Owusu, E., Han, J., Das, S., Perrig, A., Zhang, J.: ACCessory: password inference using accelerometers on smartphones. In: Proceedings of the Twelfth Workshop on Mobile Computing Systems and Applications - HotMobile 2012, p. 1 (2012)
18. Jakobsson, M. Shi, E., Golle, P., Chow, R.: Implicit authentication for mobile devices. In: Proceedings of the 4th USENIX Conference on Hot Topics in Security, p. 9 (2009)
19. Bergadano, F., Gunetti, D., Picardi, C.: User authentication through keystroke dynamics. ACM Trans. Inform. Syst. Secur. **5**(4), 367–397 (2002)
20. Monrose, F., Rubin, A.: Authentication via keystroke dynamics. In: Proceedings of the 4th ACM Conference on Computer and Communications Security, pp. 48–56 (1997)
21. Krishnamoorthy, S., Rueda, L., Saad, S., Elmiligi, H.: Identification of user behavioral biometrics for authentication using keystroke dynamics and machine learning. In: Proceedings of the 2018 2nd International Conference on Biometric Engineering and Applications - ICBEA 2018, pp. 50–57 (2018)
22. Monrose, F., Reiter, M.K., Wetzel, S.: Password hardening based on keystroke dynamics. Int. J. Inf. Secur. **1**(2), 69–83 (2002)
23. Killourhy, K.S., Maxion, R.A.: Comparing anomaly-detection algorithms for keystroke dynamics. In: 2009 IEEE/IFIP International Conference on Dependable Systems and Networks, pp. 125–134 (2009)
24. Cai, L., Chen, H.: TouchLogger: inferring keystrokes on touch screen from smartphone motion. HotSec **11**(2011), 9 (2011)
25. Karatzouni, S., Clarke, N.: Keystroke analysis for thumb-based keyboards on mobile devices. In: IFIP International Federation for Information Processing, vol. 232, pp. 253–263 (2007)
26. Zahid, S., Shahzad, M., Khayam, S.A., Farooq, M.: Keystroke-based user identification on smart phones. In: Kirda, E., Jha, S., Balzarotti, D. (eds.) RAID 2009. LNCS, vol. 5758, pp. 224–243. Springer, Heidelberg (2009). https://doi.org/10.1007/978-3-642-04342-0_12
27. Tasia, C.-J., Chang, T.-Y., Cheng, P.-C., Lin, J.-H.: Two novel biometric features in keystroke dynamics authentication systems for touch screen devices. Secur. Commun. Netw. **7**(4), 750–758 (2014)
28. Sen, S., Muralidharan, K.: Putting 'pressure' on mobile authentication. In: 2014 7th International Conference on Mobile Computing and Ubiquitous Networking, ICMU 2014, pp. 56–61 (2014)
29. Buschek, D., De Luca, A., Alt, F.: Improving accuracy, applicability and usability of keystroke biometrics on mobile touchscreen devices. In: Proceedings of the 33rd Annual ACM Conference on Human Factors in Computing Systems - CHI 2015, pp. 1393–1402 (2015)
30. Antal, M., Szabó, L.Z., Bokor, Z.: Identity information revealed from mobile touch gestures. Stud. Univ. Babes-Bolyai Inform. **59** (2014)

31. Zhang, H., Patel, V.M., Fathy, M., Chellappa, R.: Touch gesture-based active user authentication using dictionaries. In: 2015 IEEE Winter Conference on Applications of Computer Vision, pp. 207–214 (2015)
32. Sae-Bae, N., Memon, N., Isbister, K., Ahmed, K.: Multitouch gesture-based authentication. IEEE Trans. Inf. Forensics Secur. **9**(4), 568–582 (2014)
33. Muaaz, M., Mayrhofer, R.: Smartphone-based gait recognition: from authentication to imitation. IEEE Trans. Mob. Comput. **16**(11), 3209–3221 (2017)
34. Ferrero, R., Gandino, F., Montrucchio, B., Rebaudengo, M., Velasco, A., Benkhelifa, I.: On gait recognition with smartphone accelerometer. In: 2015 4th Mediterranean Conference on Embedded Computing (MECO), pp. 368–373 (2015)
35. Al-Naffakh, N., Clarke, N., Li, F., Haskell-Dowland, P.: Unobtrusive gait recognition using smartwatches. In: 2017 International Conference of the Biometrics Special Interest Group (BIOSIG), pp. 1–5 (2017)
36. Fernandez-lopez, P., Sanchez-casanova, J., Tirado-martin, P., Liu-jimenez, J.: Optimizing resources on smartphone gait recognition. In: International Joint Conference on Biometrics, pp. 1–6 (2017)
37. Laghari, A., Waheed-ur-Rehman, Memon, Z.A.: Biometric authentication technique using smartphone sensor. In: 2016 13th International Bhurban Conference on Applied Sciences and Technology (IBCAST), pp. 381–384 (2016)
38. Maghsoudi, J., Tappert, C.C.: A behavioral biometrics user authentication study using motion data from android smartphones. In: 2016 European Intelligence and Security Informatics Conference (EISIC), pp. 184–187 (2016)

The Impact of Different Feature Scaling Methods on Intrusion Detection for in-Vehicle Controller Area Network (CAN)

Siti-Farhana Lokman[1](✉) ⓘ, Abu Talib Othman[1],
Muhamad Husaini Abu Bakar[1], and Shahrulniza Musa[2]

[1] System Engineering and Energy Laboratory, Universiti Kuala Lumpur,
Malaysian-Spanish Institute, Kulim, Malaysia
farhana.lokman@s.unikl.edu.my
[2] Universiti Kuala Lumpur, Malaysian Institute of Information Technology,
Kuala Lumpur, Malaysia

Abstract. Numerous security researchers have a growing interest in the vulnerabilities of the in-vehicle Controller Area Network (CAN) bus system to cyber-attacks. The adversaries can leverage these vulnerabilities in manipulating vehicle functions and harming the drivers' safety. Some security mechanisms proposed for CAN bus in detecting anomalies have favoured over the one-class classification, where it constructs a decision boundary from normal instances. Nevertheless, the accuracy performance of the classifier is highly influenced by the data representation. Judging from this fact, this paper analyses the advantage of utilizing different feature scaling technique as in to obtain higher classification accuracy of the classifier algorithms. To serve this purpose, the CAN bus datasets in this paper are scaled using standardization, min-max, and quantile, and are evaluated using one-class classifier model used in automotive CAN bus. The results exhibit that integrating different feature scaling techniques could greatly enhance the classification accuracy of the classifiers.

Keywords: Anomaly-based detection · Neural network · Controller Area Network · Feature scaling · One-class classification

1 Introduction

Cybersecurity in vehicles will become more essential due to the rising of wireless technology embedded in the vehicle system [1]. Many security researchers have demonstrated the vulnerabilities of vehicles that focused on leveraging CAN bus network which eventually compromises the entire internal vehicle system [2]. As a result, the vehicle could be controlled by attackers to prevent it from functioning in a normal way and finally could harm the safety of the driver. One of the attack techniques called fuzzy attack showed by Koscher et al. is intended to make cyber-physical effects on the vehicle [3]. The authors aimed to take over various Electronic Control Unit (ECUs) by flooding the bus with a combination of CAN bus messages. They discovered that by performing little reversed engineering on how vehicle functions work and randomly fuzzed the CAN bus data could gain legitimate access on the entire ECUs.

© Springer Nature Singapore Pte Ltd. 2020
M. Anbar et al. (Eds.): ACeS 2019, CCIS 1132, pp. 195–205, 2020.
https://doi.org/10.1007/978-981-15-2693-0_14

With the emerging attacks occurring in the CAN bus network, numerous researchers have proposed intrusion detection mechanisms in vehicles as a last line of defence. One of the promising security approaches is anomaly detection [4]. The inclination towards the anomaly detection approach over other approaches is due to limitations and constraints that the CAN bus system possesses. In contrast to signature-based IDS that operates in the IT desktop domain, the attack signatures are not established and documented publicly in the CAN bus field by scientific researchers of automotive manufacturers [5]. The uncertainty in predicting future and unknown attack demand makes the detection in CAN bus domain difficult. Judging from this face, thus, encourages several scholars to exploited one-class classification methods [6–10]. This method is useful when dealing with CAN bus environment where the only large corpus of normal data is available.

In the case of the CAN bus, the broadcasted CAN bus data from various ECUs are comprised of string and numeric data types and lengths, which make the packet features to have different scales. As a result, the features with larger scales dominate the small ones, thus minimizing the positive impact. Further, it has been discovered that choosing the right pre-processing techniques for data specifically feature scaling [11, 12] will make the gradient descent converge quickly, hence reduce computational cost and improve high classification accuracy performance. Based on these findings, thus encourage feature scaling steps in the model to make the classifier performance-enhanced remarkably.

To the best of our knowledge, comparing different feature scaling methods in analyzing detection rate performance has not yet been examined in the CAN bus environment. Subsequently, in this paper, we explore and analyze three different scaling methods applied on CAN bus data, and study the performance using one-class classification model. We applied standard scaling feature methods that have been widely used in CAN bus domain i.e., min-max and standardization [8, 13–15]. We compared against quantile normalization which has been effectively used to eliminate unwanted technical variation in DNA sequence domain [16, 21]. The advantage of quantile normalization could be a potential feature scaling candidate for CAN bus environment which it can remove any systematic variations in the CAN bus network [17]. We captured CAN data from Toyota Camry in order to accomplish the comparisons. Next, we study the scaled data feature results using one-class classification (OCSVM) model proposed in [8, 10, 18]. The model used to evaluate feature scaling methods in this paper is chosen based on its effectiveness in generalize, able to learn and perform rapid decisions in one-class problem in CAN bus domain.

Finally, this paper is organized into 4 sections; Sect. 1 introduces some related works on algorithms optimization specifically in the classification task. We explained the overall learning procedure in Sect. 2. As well, we described three types of feature scaling methods used to transform CAN bus datasets are presented along with the one-class classifier algorithm, the experimental setup and the CAN bus datasets used in order to validate the pre-processing techniques. Section 3 exhibits the overall detection rate results of three feature scaling techniques on four different types of attacks. Finally, we summarized the conclusions of this paper and presented some future works in Sect. 4.

2   Materials and Methods

This research undergoes six stages. The illustration depicted in Fig. 1 summarizes entire procedure. In this section, we demonstrate different approach performed in each step.

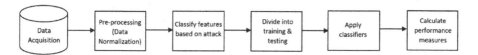

Fig. 1. Flowchart of the entire learning procedure.

2.1   Data Acquisition

In this stage, we obtained raw CAN data from Toyota Camry at low and high-speed driving. The CAN bus data acquisition process is illustrated in Fig. 2. During CAN bus data acquisition, we plugged the cable into OBD-II port which usually located under the steering wheel. The cable is also connected to the CAN bus sniffer hardware in order to communicate with the CAN bus system. We logged the CAN bus data through our laptop nearly 15 min of driving including braking, speeding, idling, and parking.

Fig. 2. Data acquisition setup through OBD-II port of Toyota Camry with CANTact device.

The structure of CAN data features (see Fig. 3) extracted from Toyota Camry are basically encompassed of CAN ID (identifier), timestamp, Cyclic Redundancy Check (CRC), Data field (with the fixed of size from 2 to 8 bytes in this paper) and finally Acknowledge (ACK) field. Nevertheless, the scope of this paper is only focused on the CAN ID and Data field. The CAN ID is used to indicate the vehicle functions e.g., steering, braking. Whereas the CAN Data field encompasses information used by the specific vehicle function, e.g., rotating steering anticlockwise, pushing and releasing the brake.

Arbitration				Control	Data	CRC		ACK	
S O F	ID	R T R	I D E	R B 0	DLC	DATA	CRC	CRC DeL	A C K	ACK DeL	E O F

Fig. 3. CAN bus data structure [19]

To have better insight into how CAN bus traffic works, we explored and analyzed CAN data traces logged from a real vehicle. The understanding of the behaviour of CAN data is useful in order to measure how far the variance is spread out and how feature scaling can help in removing unwanted variation that exist in CAN data.

There are 103 distinct CAN IDs were found (for ease of illustration purposes we assign each ID using the numeric value from 0 to 103 shown in Fig. 4) in Toyota Camry. Nearly 2,000,000 data were transmitted (estimated data collected from 30 min of driving) at a fixed period, varying from 4 ms to 10 ms while the vehicle is moving. Figure 4 showed the different occurrences or frequencies of each ID ranging from 20 to 112,000 times throughout 30 min of driving. Meanwhile. Figure 5 exhibited the variation of Data field belong to each ID (for ease of comparison and readability, only several real IDs can be displayed in the Fig. 5). Some IDs like ID 047 and ID 300 have constant values, meaning their Data words value are always the same. However, the rest of the IDs produced multi-value of Data words. Some of the multi-value produced by ID 5AB, ID 110 and ID 609 contains an abundance and unique Data words, whereas ID 121 and ID 30C generate a smaller variation of data.

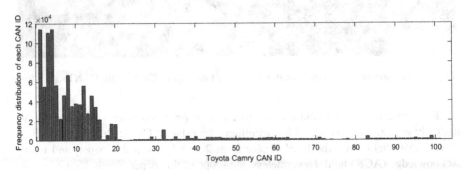

Fig. 4. The distribution of each CAN ID during 30 min of driving

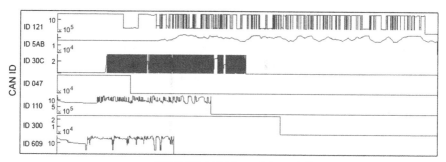

The variation of Data words for each ID

Fig. 5. The variation of Data words distributed from each CAN ID

Judging from this fact, CAN ID and Data words with small variability be swamped by the high variability, and eventually may lead to misclassification. Thus, the feature scaling method is essential to ensure the data is processed in a standard range. Besides, it also can assure the small variation introduced by some IDs due to rarely occurred in CAN bus traffic can still be distinguishable from any types of attack.

2.2   Data Pre-processing

In this stage, we scaled the CAN data using three feature scaling techniques; min-max, standardization and quantile normalization. Besides reducing dominancy impact among data features and improving training convergence, min-max and standardization methods have been commonly used in CAN bus environment as it is simple to be implemented while at the same time provide good classification results in anomaly detection problem [8, 13–15]. However, judging from the nature of CAN data behaviour motivate this study to adopt quantile normalization [20] in the CAN bus environment. Besides the increasing rate of new CAN Data words produced by a single ID that will be increasing in the future, there is also technical variation occurred caused by the signaling and clock drift in the CAN bus traffic [22]. Consequently, it induces the variation of unique CAN Data words that may slightly differ from normal. Hence, the quantile normalization proposed in this paper may be suitable in dealing with noisy environment occurred in the CAN bus in order to ensure unwanted variation can be compared with other normal features.

The necessity of proposed quantile normalization method to be used in this paper can be judged according to the preliminary data analysis such as the construction of the boxplots presented in Fig. 6. Boxplots can be effectively used in revealing similarities and difference of patterns found in the sets of observations [23]. Figure 7 compared the raw and scaled CAN data distribution throughout 30 min of driving. A large number of variations in raw CAN data distribution due to rarely occurred in the bus traffic are indicated as outliers in the boxplot.

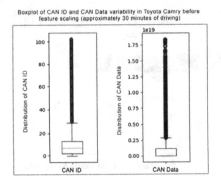

Fig. 6. Boxplots of raw CAN ID and CAN data before feature scaling methods

The figure below presented boxplots of CAN data after scaled into min-max, standardization and quantile normalization method. Based on the observation, there is a significant difference among data after feature scaling methods were applied. Min-max and standardization are very sensitive to the existence of outliers in both features. However, it may not be guaranteed whether the presence of outliers especially in CAN Data features balanced through standardization method. Nonetheless, it is worth examining the effect of this feature scaling method on a classification problem. In addition to the boxplots exhibited below, quantile normalization is robust to the presence of outliers where removing or adding outliers will still yield nearly the same transformation on the data to a defined boundary.

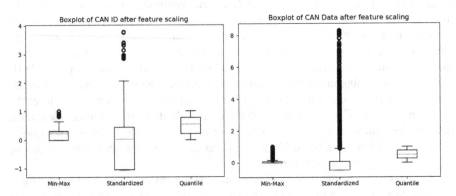

Fig. 7. Boxplots of raw CAN ID and CAN data after feature scaling methods are applied

The formulas for each scaling methods used in this paper are presented in Table 1; where x_i^j denotes as the beginning value of jth feature within the ith sample, whereas σ^j signifies as standard deviation, μ^j represents mean, and finally min^j max^j indicate as minimum and the maximum value of jth feature calculated on all samples.

Table 1. Formulas for different scaling feature methods.

Method	Abbreviation	Formula	Function
Min-Max normalisation	Min-Max	$\dfrac{x_i^j - min^j}{max^j - min^j}$	Subtracts the minimum from all instances values and makes them scale from minimum to maximum. Then it divides the difference between maximum and minimum of each feature instances
Standardization	Standardized	$\dfrac{x_i^j - \mu^j}{\sigma^j}$	Eliminates the mean, while at the same time scales the input data into unit variance
Quantile normalisation	Quantile	$inf\{x \in \mathbb{R} : p \geq F(x)\}$	Implements a non-linear transformation where the function of a continuous random variable of each feature is mapped to the same distribution

2.3 Classification Algorithm

In this section, we discussed the one-classification algorithm used in this paper. We choose One-Class Support Vector Machine (OCSVM) [24] to study the impact of different feature scaling methods applied on the Toyota Camry data. OCSVM algorithm is considered in this paper as it has been commonly used in several works found in [8, 10, 18] and therefore offer a good baseline. Moreover, OCSVM is one of the boundary-based methods that utilize a decision function through the optimum separating margin. We employed this one class algorithm on the CAN bus data where only normal data is used during the training. As stated earlier, this type of algorithm is suitable for CAN bus problem where generally only non-anomalous CAN data is available. Thus, OCSVM can utilize its kernel function in making decision functions on complex data in the CAN bus environment. We set the algorithm to use non-linear kernel; Radial Basis Function and optimum settings of hyperparameters based on work in [25].

3 Experiment and Result

3.1 Experimental Data

In this study, we injected the CAN bus traffic with three types of attacks, the explanation of each attack is described as below:

DoS attack: this attack aims to occupy the dominant state in the CAN bus traffic by injecting higher priority of CAN data. In CAN bus domain, the priority of the data payload is determined by the CAN ID. The lower the CAN ID value indicates the higher priority of the packet. As a result, the legitimate data with lower priority ID will drop. In this case, we continuously inserted new high priority CAN ID and CAN Data every 1 ms with the smallest constant values of '0x000' to preempt legitimate data.

Fuzzy attack: we altered both CAN Data field and CAN ID field with random values. In this case, we randomly choose CAN data in Toyota Camry and altered the ID as well as the content of the data every 3 ms.

Impersonate attack: we spoofed the CAN Data field that is related to gear and RPM with constant values of '0x000' and '0xfff' every 4 ms.

Next, we did labelling on the captured CAN bus data into normal and attack dataset. Table 2 exhibits CAN bus datasets that are used to conduct our experiment. The datasets are divided into training and test dataset.

Table 2. Formulas for different scaling feature methods.

Vehicle	CAN dataset	Attack type	CAN normal data	CAN attack data
Toyota Camry	Training	Normal	900,000	N/A
	Testing	DoS	900,000	223,430
		Impersonate (Gear)	900,000	225,144
		Impersonate (Brake)	900,000	225,046
		Fuzzy	900,000	225,156

3.2 Performance Measure

In this paper, we compared the effects of algorithm's performance on each feature scaling method in Sect. 3.3 using four performance measures; precision, recall and Receiver Operating Characteristics (ROC). The precision and recall used in this work are one of the common basic evaluation metrics in order to measure the robustness and the reliability of the anomaly-based detection model. Precision is a proportion of true positive (anomalies) divided by true positive and false positive. It shows how far the model can predict the positive class. among the samples which are indicated as a true anomaly. Whereby Recall which is known as sensitivity denotes as the proportion of relevant instances detected among the entire number of relevant instances. F-measure summarizes the trade-off between precision and recall using a various number of thresholds. The value of precision, recall and F-measure that approximately to 100% indicates the best performance of the detection model with zero false-negative and zero false-positive rates.

Meanwhile, ROC represents a diagram of a true positive rate against false positive rate based on a various number of thresholds. The ideal percentage of ROC is also 100% detection along with zero false-positive rates.

3.3 Feature Scaling Experiment

The primary focus of this work is to enhance the classification accuracy performance of the classifier algorithms using three different feature scaling techniques. Table 3 shows the overall detection rate results obtained with three feature scaling techniques (we used the abbreviation for feature scaling methods with 'MM' for min-max, 'SS' for standardization and 'QT' as quantile normalization) using OCSVM algorithm. We also used a naming convention for impersonate attack as 'imp' for brake and gear.

The values highlighted with bold typeface specifies the best classification accuracy results. From the results shown below, some preliminary remarks can be concluded. Among the dataset, at least one feature scaling technique showed better average detection rate performance approximately 100% detection rate on DoS and impersonate attack as compared with others, which in this case, the QT method.

Table 3. The overall detection rates of OCSVM with MM, SS and QT scaling techniques applied on Toyota Camry against DoS, fuzzy and impersonate attacks.

Model	Attack	Scaling	ROC	Precision	Recall	F1_measure	Average detection rate
OCSVM	DoS	SS	100.00%	100.00%	100.00%	100.00%	100.00%
		MM	100.00%	100.00%	100.00%	100.00%	100.00%
		QT	100.00%	100.00%	100.00%	100.00%	100.00%
	Fuzzy	SS	29.00%	88.60%	64.30%	68.70%	62.65%
		MM	57.60%	86.70%	34.50%	34.90%	53.43%
		QT	**89.00%**	**92.80%**	**87.30%**	**88.50%**	**89.40%**
	Imp Break	SS	100.00%	100.00%	100.00%	100.00%	100.00%
		MM	100.00%	100.00%	100.00%	100.00%	100.00%
		QT	100.00%	100.00%	100.00%	100.00%	100.00%
	Imp Gear	SS	89.20%	68.00%	74.30%	71.00%	75.63%
		MM	44.60%	68.00%	74.30%	71.00%	64.48%
		QT	**100.00%**	**100.00%**	**100.00%**	**100.00%**	**100.00%**

It can be seen that QT normalization achieved the overall highest percentage precision, recall, F-measure and ROC for the majority of attacks after MM and followed by SS. But, its performance slightly degraded when tested on the fuzzy attack. In contrast to MM and SS method, they may perform well when injected with DoS and impersonate attack, however, they performed poorly on impersonate (gear) and fuzzy attack with an average detection rate of nearly 60% and 65%. Generally, we would say that all feature scaling methods are more affected when tested on Fuzzy attack as the randomness in the attack may have similar values like the normal data, which may, in turn, make the model confuse and lead to misclassification. However, all feature scaling techniques showed good performance on DoS and impersonate (brake) attack as these types of attack were injected with constant values that are not similar like normal data. Another important observation, the OCSVM classifier that relies heavily on distance-based calculations are affected on feature scaling, thus scaling the data with an appropriate method like QT helps in eliminating any biases that exist in raw data. Another important observation, QT normalization helps the OCSVM to converge especially when dealing with CAN bus dataset that has larger variability. Finally, the detection rate can still be improved by some tunings of the model hyperparameters. In general, we can conclude that the consequence of pre-processing step such as feature scaling relies on the characteristics of the data features and also the classifier models.

4 Conclusion

This paper examined the detection rate performance of various feature scaling techniques in CAN bus datasets from real vehicle model. When quantile normalization is used, the OCSVM, the distance-based approach is significantly improved especially when the CAN data has a large number of variabilities. Lastly, all feature scaling methods performance degraded when tested on the fuzzy attack since the attack may contain variations that similar to normal data. However, the proposed feature scaling method in this paper, quantile normalization is still robust on different types of attack. quantile normalization can be a potential candidate for pre-treatment method for CAN bus data as it showed its effectiveness in compressing the outliers in normal data and eventually make the unwanted variation comparable with normal features and still can be distinguishable from attack data.

As future work, although quantile normalization presented in this paper showed a good performance, however, we can find and analyze other potential pre-processing techniques like feature selection, feature cleaning and feature conversion to different characteristics and higher dimensional of CAN bus datasets in order to study which method improves the detection rate results. Further, regardless of the higher detection accuracy, the scaling method, as well as the algorithm, is still lacking in terms of attack patterns in automotive CAN bus domain. Thus, increasing the number of fuzzy attacks during experiment makes the performance assessment to be more precise since many possibilities of attack patterns are revealed.

References

1. Sakiz, F., Sen, S.: A survey of attacks and detection mechanisms on intelligent transportation systems: VANETs and IoV. Ad Hoc Netw. **61**, 33–50 (2017)
2. Miller, C., Valasek, C.: Remote exploitation of an unaltered passenger vehicle. Black Hat USA (2015)
3. Koscher, K., et al.: Experimental security analysis of a modern automobile. In: 2010 IEEE Symposium on Security and Privacy (SP), pp. 447–462 (2010)
4. Hoppe, T., Kiltz, S., Dittmann, J.: Security threats to automotive CAN networks – practical examples and selected short-term countermeasures. In: Harrison, M.D., Sujan, M.-A. (eds.) SAFECOMP 2008. LNCS, vol. 5219, pp. 235–248. Springer, Heidelberg (2008). https://doi.org/10.1007/978-3-540-87698-4_21
5. Hoppe, T., Kiltz, S., Dittmann, J.: Applying intrusion detection to automotive it-early insights and remaining challenges. J. Inform. Assur. Secur. (JIAS) **4**(6), 226–235 (2009)
6. Martinelli, F., Mercaldo, F., Nardone, V., Santone, A.: Car hacking identification through fuzzy logic algorithms. In: IEEE International Conference on Fuzzy Systems, Naples (2017)
7. Tomlinson, A., Bryans, J., Shaikh, S.A.: Using a one-class compound classifier to detect in-vehicle network attacks. In GECCO 2018 Companion: Genetic and Evolutionary Computation Conference Companion. ACM, Kyoto (2018). https://doi.org/10.1145/3205651.3208223
8. Weber, M., Klug, S., Sax, E., Zimmer, B.: Embedded hybrid anomaly detection for automotive CAN communication (2018)

9. Xing, Y., Lv, C., Wang, H., Cao, D. Recognizing driver braking intention with vehicle data using unsupervised learning methods (2017)
10. Loukas, G., Vuong, T., Heartfield, R., Sakellari, G., Yoon, Y., Gan, D.: Cloud-based cyber-physical intrusion detection for vehicles using deep learning. IEEE Access 6, 3491–3508 (2017)
11. Nawi, N.M., et al.: The effect of pre-processing techniques and optimal parameters selection on back propagation neural networks. Int. J. Adv. Sci. Eng. Inform. Technol. 7(3), 770–777 (2017)
12. Kumar, D.A., Venugopalan, S.: The effect of normalization on intrusion detection classifiers (Naïve Bayes and J48). Int. J. Future Revolut. Comput. Sci. Commun. Eng. 3, 60–64 (2017)
13. Kang, M.J., Kang, J.W.: Intrusion detection system using deep neural network for in-vehicle network security. PLoS One 11(6), e0155781 (2016)
14. Wasicek, A., Weimerskirch, A.: Recognizing manipulated electronic control units (No. 2015-01-0202). SAE Technical Paper (2015)
15. Taylor, A., Leblanc, S., Japkowicz, N.: Anomaly detection in automobile control network data with long short-term memory networks. In: 2016 IEEE International Conference on Data Science and Advanced Analytics (DSAA), pp. 130–139 (2016)
16. Pan, M., Zhang, J.: Quantile normalization for combining gene-expression da-tasets. Biotechnol. Biotechnol. Equip. 32(3), 751–758 (2018)
17. Upender, B.P., Dean, A.G.: Variability of CAN network performance. In: Proceedings of the 3rd International CAN Conference ICC (1996)
18. Taylor, A., Japkowicz, N., Leblanc, S.: Frequency-based anomaly detection for the automotive CAN bus. In: 2015 World Congress on Industrial Control Systems Security (WCICSS), pp. 45–49. IEEE (2015)
19. Lokman, S.F., Othman, A.T., Bakar, M.H.A., Razuwan, R.: Stacked sparse autoencoders-based outlier discovery for in-vehicle controller area network (CAN). Int. J. Eng. Technol. 7 (4.33), 375–380 (2018). https://doi.org/10.14419/ijet.v7i4.33.26078
20. Hicks, S.C., Okrah, K., Paulson, J.N., Quackenbush, J., Irizarry, R.A., Bravo, H.C.: Smooth quantile normalization. Biostatistics 19(2), 185–198 (2017)
21. Hansen, K.D., Irizarry, R.A., Wu, Z.: Removing technical variability in RNA-seq data using conditional quantile normalization. Biostatistics 13(2), 204–216 (2012)
22. Monot, A., Navet, N., Bavoux, B.: Impact of clock drifts on CAN frame response time distributions. In: ETFA2011, pp. 1–4. IEEE (2011)
23. Potter, K., Hagen, H., Kerren, A., Dannenmann, P.: Methods for presenting statistical information: the box plot. Vis. Large Unstr. Data Sets 4, 97–106 (2006)
24. Moya, M.M., Hush, D.R.: Network constraints and multi-objective optimization for one-class classification. Neural Netw. 9(3), 463–474 (1996)
25. Ghafoori, Z., Erfani, S.M., Rajasegarar, S., Bezdek, J.C., Karunasekera, S., Leckie, C.: Efficient unsupervised parameter estimation for one-class support vector machines. IEEE Trans. Neural Netw. Learn. Syst. 29(10), 5057–5070 (2018)

STEM: Secure Token Exchange Mechanisms

Maneesh Darisi[✉], Janhavi Savla, Mahesh Shirole, and Sunil Bhirud

CE & IT Department, Veermata Jijabai Technological Institute,
Mumbai 400019, India
{mdarisi_b15,jnsavla_b15,mrshirole}@it.vjti.ac.in, sgbhirud@ce.vjti.ac.in

Abstract. With the flooding of a large variety of isolated blockchain solutions into the technological world, one major challenge is to enable efficient interoperable interchain and intrachain exchanges. The dearth of inter-operating among these eclectic tokens is hindering the profits that can be earned by potential investors. The myriads of tokens that are flooding into the blockchain ecosystem need to interoperate amongst each other. This paper proposes a mechanism to provide better atomic intrachain token swaps. Our blockchain solution can assist the exchange of these eclectic heterogeneous tokens securely, using digital signatures and hashed time lock contracts, which reduces the problem of interoperability. This paper presents a solution which is token standard agnostic and provides effective intrinsic smart contracts facilitating token exchange and thus reducing the counterparty risk.

Keywords: Blockchain · Interoperability · Atomic swaps · Token exchange

1 Introduction

Blockchain is a sequential chain of immutable data structures called blocks that encompass a set of valid transactions, which are transparent to the participants of the blockchain. Blockchains have entities known as miners who perform suitable consensus algorithms to append blocks onto the chain. With the emergence of blockchain ecosystems, the means of completing a trustless transaction between two parties has become very lucid. Blockchain is yet in its embryonic stage of development and requires amelioration on several inchoate usecases on which amelioration is required. In the present blockchain world, there exists no blockchain solution which addresses all these problems, thus hindering blockchains adaptability. Blockchain 3.0 aims to achieve improvements in the regions of scalability, interoperability and governance. Presently most of the blockchains and tokens are independent of each other and do not transact among each other easily. Therefore the future of the distributed internet thrives on the ability of blockchains to interoperate with each other.

Interoperability is the ability of several blockchains to exchange their data seamlessly among each other. Interoperability in blockchains is required at both:

© Springer Nature Singapore Pte Ltd. 2020
M. Anbar et al. (Eds.): ACeS 2019, CCIS 1132, pp. 206–219, 2020.
https://doi.org/10.1007/978-981-15-2693-0_15

interchain and intrachain levels. In the present interchain solutions, the exchange occurs between two independent blockchains. If both the chains that are interacting are of the same type, then they are known as *homogenous interchains*, and if two disparate chains are interacting, then they are known as *heterogeneous interchains*. Granularity of interoperability is defined as the level at which blockchains can interoperate. We have two levels of Interoperability: (a)Blockchain Interoperability (b)Token Interoperability. The interoperability among chains can take place either through the base currencies or through the exchange of tokens. Popular homogenous and heterogenous interchain frameworks are PeaceRelay [1], Polkadot [2] and Cosmos [3]. Xclaim and WBTC [4] are innovative projects which facilitate interoperability among Bitcoin [5] and Ethereum [6] blockchains. Xclaim facilitates the interoperability among the two chains through their base currencies ETH and BTC whereas WBTC facilitates the interoperability among the chains with support of $WBTC$ tokens.

With the proliferation of blockchains, the tokenisation of traditional assets into crypto-based assets has gained immense popularity. The myriad tokens which are present in the crypto world can be broadly classified into either fungible or non-fungible tokens. Fungible Tokens are tokens which have currency like properties and are interchangeable, uniform across platforms and are divisible into units. Non-fungible tokens are uniquely identifiable during interaction and circulation, and these tokens are non-interchangeable, unique in nature and non-divisible. These tokens are used to represent potpourri assets, research projects and business processes. If we notice in the present blockchain systems, there is an acute shortage of interoperability at the intrachain level. At the intrachain level, there are no efficient methods to provide proper interoperability among the different tokens.

This paper's main contribution is providing solutions to the currently hindering intrachain interoperability problem. This paper offers two approaches to solve these intrachain problems: (a)Central Contract Based Technique (b) Atomic Swap Based Technique.

Rest of the paper is organised as follows: Sect. 2 discusses related work in the field of blockchain interoperability, Sect. 3 gives an overview of the basic concepts which will be used in this paper, Sect. 4 describes the proposed solution. Finally, Sect. 5 concludes the paper.

2 Related Work

The development of blockchain solutions began with the inception of rudimentary systems like Interchain [7], which employed three handshaking method to facilitate asset transfers between isolated blockchains. However, they did not provide efficient consensus algorithms to settle cross chain transfers. As time progressed the blockchain community witnessed the emergence of new consensus algorithms like Byzantine Fault Tolerance [8] and Proof of Stake [9] which aimed to replace the current consensus algorithms to enhance the scalability and interoperability of blockchain systems.

These new consensus algorithms paved the way to several solutions like two pegged Sidechains [10] and Strong Federations [11]. Sidechains pioneered the concepts of interoperability to the blockchain world, which was the critical step to abate the inability of isolated blockchains to communicate with each other. Sidechains enabled cryptocurrencies such as Bitcoins and Altcoins to be transferred between myriad blockchains using a two-way peg. Tokens from one chain (e.g. Bitcoin) held on behalf of a side-chain are secured only by the side-chains ability to incentivise miners to canonicalise valid transitions. It did not provide a protocol to validate the sidechain transactions. With the inception of sidechains with mining, fees have caused a grave resource pressure on miners, thus creating centralisation risks on the blockchain systems. Strong federations proposed a Byzantine-robust interoperable blockchain solution which facilitated the movement of assets between diverse markets, using federated-peg mechanism for two-way transfer of assets between the Mainchain and Sidechain. Strong Federations proposed multi-signature addresses, where assets are locked in and could be unlocked if only enough key holders would agree onto the fact that the payment is valid. The authors claimed that the participants in a Strong Federations would be naturally incentivised to take greater care of access to the federated signers under their control. However, none of this could be proved rigorously and is potentially not even real. Both Strong Federations and Sidechains could come up with exciting concepts to facilitate cross chain transfers, but none could provide effective governance for the consensus mechanisms used in their systems, which was a significant drawback in their proposals.

The shortcomings were a learning trajectory for many heterogeneous interchain interoperability projects like Polkadot [2] and Cosmos [3]. Both the projects starkly addressed the scalability and interoperability problems in the existing blockchain solutions and worked to provide robust frameworks to tackle these issues using interesting methodologies. Polkadot's architecture revolves around two major components; one is the relay chain, which is responsible for facilitating interoperability among different chains, and the second is the parachains which improve the present torpid blockchain transaction rate. Cosmos proposes an interesting star topology which connects heterogenous blockchains using a central hub and is backed up by the high-performance Tendermint [12] cores, efficient consensus algorithms like DPoS [13] to address the scalability hindering the current blockchain systems. However, both Polkadot and Cosmos, do not envision to support the deployment of customised blockchain smart contracts.

With substantial growth in the popularity of tokens, several protocols like 0x [14] and LoopRing [15] came into the blockchain world providing promising open exchange protocols for the exchange of these multifarious tokens. 0x and LoopRing are open protocol standards for facilitating intrachain symmetric and asymmetric decentralised transactions of eclectic tokens on the ethereum blockchain. 0x aims to delineate a learning trajectory for programmers to develop an interoperable token exchange solution by providing a robust baseline framework. 0x offers dual benefits of not only enabling transfer between fungible tokens but also between fungible and non-fungible tokens.

On the other hand, LoopRing excels in building standards and contracts which facilitate low gas cost, trustless, anonymous intrachain transfers by using off chain set of actors for agglomeration. LoopRing is a blockchain agnostic protocol which only requires the blockchain to support the deployment of smart contracts. Other decentralised exchange protocols are starkly juxtaposed with 0x and LoopRing. 0x and LoopRing protocols have addressed the intrachain interoperability but have not still shed light on the interchain token interoperability.

XClaim [16] and Wrapped Bitcoins [4] are practical implementation papers demonstrating the exchanges between the two popular blockchains, Ethereum and Bitcoin. XClaim and Wrapped Bitcoins provide protocols for minting, burning, transferring and swapping tokens securely on the existing blockchain. Both XClaim and Wrapped Bitcoins use two different methodologies to achieve these cross chain transfers. Xclaim uses low-cost atomic cross chain swaps to transfer cryptocurrency backed assets among the two blockchains whereas Wrapped Bitcoins uses a central authority to mitigate these transfers between the blockchains. Xclaim presently doesn't facilitate the exchange of fungible and non-fungible tokens.

Aion network [17] is an innovative project, which incorporates efficient design patterns in its tiered architecture to enable disparate systems to communicate by employing a Connecting Network, a Participating Network and a Bridge protocol that paves the path for the transparent communication between the two networks using its own set of validators. It maintains accountability across networks using a light-weighted BFT-based agreement algorithm that approves transactions when $2/3^{rd}$ of the validators vote. Stakeholders of the connecting networks assign people who act as bridge validators.

3   Basic Concepts

Interoperability solutions require some basic concepts understanding such as, Hashed TimeLock Mechanism and Atomic Swap Mechanism. Consider two parties A having token of type t_1 and B having token of type t_2. The ability to exchange among t_1 and t_2 is known as token interoperabiity.

3.1   Hash Time Lock Contracts

Hash Time Lock Contracts (HTLC) are special contracts that are used to lock the assets of the participants. The locked assets can be redeemed by a mutually decided secret and are accompanied with expiration time. To deploy an HTLC, the transmitter of the token will first create a secret s, LockPeriod L and then calculates the hash H of this secret:

$$H = sha256(s) \tag{1}$$

As any person with the secret s can claim the assets, we sign the assets with the *public key* (Pu_R) of the receiver so that only the intended receiver can unlock the resources using his *private key* (Pr_R). However, if the secret is not revealed in the intended expiration time, then these assets are refunded to their respective owners.

There are two types of timelocks: (a) *Absolute Timelock Contracts*: In these time lock contracts, the tokens will be locked for a fixed amount of time. (b)*Relative Timelock Contracts*: In these time lock contracts, the tokens will be locked after the time when the transaction has been confirmed.

$$H_1 = Encrypt(Pu_R(H)) \tag{2}$$

The exchange occurs if the receiver has the secret s, H_1 and decrypts it using his private key (Pr_R) .

$$f(H_1, S) = Equal(decrypt(Pr_R(H_1)), sha256\ (s)) AND(LocktimePeriod < block.timestamp) \tag{3}$$

$$f(H_1, S) = \begin{cases} 1, & \text{Exchange occurs} \\ 0, & \text{Exchange does not occur and respective assets are refunded} \end{cases}$$

Timelock Contracts are used to lock the resources (assets) for the LockTimePeriod (L) specified by the Transmitter until the transfer of ownership of the assets takes place.

3.2   Atomic Swaps

The interactions between the two parties involved in the transaction of tokens must be atomic. Partial execution of transfers should be reverted. Hash time lock contracts is the method used to achieve atomic exchange of tokens t_1 of party A with tokens t_2 of party B on the same chain as shown in Fig. 1.

Suppose we have two parties, A and B (Refer Fig. 1), who hold tokens on different accounts. The atomic swap algorithm facilitates A to exchange its tokens for B's tokens as follows:

1. First, party A generates a random secret s and then computes the hash H of the secret, $H = \text{hash}(s)$. After that, A shares H with B.
2. A first locks its tokens t_1 by moving them to a temporary output Q_1 for N seconds.
3. Similarly, party B locks its tokens t_2 by moving them to a temporary output Q_2 for 2 N seconds after seeing that A has locked his tokens and has sent secret of H
4. A passes this transaction to B for it to be signed. B then claims tokens t_1 using its signature and secret s.
5. A claims tokens t_2 using B's signature and its own signature.
6. A then creates another transaction which returns tokens t_1 from Q_1 to A with a lock-time of N *seconds* stating that if secret s for H is revealed within N *seconds* by B, then ownership of the token will be transferred to B;otherwise, the asset will be unlocked after N seconds.

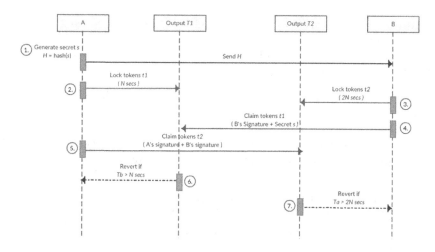

Fig. 1. Atomic Swap of tokens between parties A and B

7. Similarly, B creates another transaction which returns tokens t_2 from Q_2 to B, with a lock time of *2N seconds* stating that if secret s for H is revealed within *2N seconds* by A, then ownership of the asset will be transferred to A; otherwise, the token will be unlocked after *2N seconds*.

4 Proposed System

4.1 Definitions

Below we provide the definitions for blockchain interoperability, token, and token interoperability.

Blockchain. Each blockchain is defined as "tuple (G, B) where G is a genesis state and B $= [\beta_1, \beta_2, \beta_3...]$ is an ordered list of blocks. A blockchain is valid if every $\beta \in$ B is valid, and so G $+ \beta_0 + \beta_1 + ... = \sigma_f$ is a valid state. A block β is a package containing a list of transactions T, a reference to a parent block and auxiliary verification data" [18].

Blockchain Interoperability. Blockchain interoperability can be defined as a two-tuple (S, D) where S is the source blockchain and D is the destination chain with which it wants to interoperate.

For a cross chain transfer with the transaction $T_I \in T_S, T_D$ to occur, we need to ensure that the states of both the blockchains interoperating change as

- $C_S(\sigma(S) + T_I) = \sigma_{I+1}(S)$ in the context of σ of source chain using consensus algorithm C_S
- $C_D(\sigma(D) + T_I) = \sigma_{I+1}(D)$ in the context of σ of destination chain using consensus algorithm C_D

Where σ is used to denote the current state of the blockchain and σ_{I+1} is used to denote the next state of the blockchain. C_D and C_S are used to verify and validate the Transaction T on their respective chains.

If (S,D) are of the same chains then they are known as homogenous chains. If (S,D) are of different chain then they are known as heterogeneous chains.

Token. A token T is defined by a five tuple <S, N, T, I, P> where S is the Token Symbol, N is the Token Name, T is the Token Type, I is the initial supply of the token and P is Precision of the Token supply.
Properties

- Both S and N must be unique in a blockchain.
- Token type can be either fungible (F) or non-fungible (NF).
- Precision of the token is a positive number.For example a number ranging between [0–18].

Token Interoperability. For a given blockchain B which consists of a list of Tokens $T = [t_1, t_2, t_3...t_n]$, exchange among any two token T_S and T_D is defined using a four tuple $<T_S, N_S, T_D, E>$, where T_S is defined as the source token, N_S is the number of the source tokens to be exchanged, T_D is defined as the destination token and E as the Exchange Rate.

4.2   Exchange Scenario

The actors of the proposed solution are:

1. Token Trader: Token traders are user accounts who trade and buy tokens from user accounts.
2. Token Owner: Token Owners are user accounts which deploy token contracts with an initial supply. These are the account holders which can mint the new supply of tokens.

Consider several ICOs that have been launched since 2010. Tokenization has become a vital source of funding for research projects. With these many tokens into the crypto world, we have an urgent need to interoperate among them. Consider two ICO's I_A and I_B who are the token contract owners who have deployed a token contract with an initial supply of N tokens each to get funds for their project. Each of the ICOs has sold N_s to token traders who are investors that invest in potential projects to gain profits. These investors aspire to maximize their profit. So these token traders keep exchanging tokens among themselves based on the growth of the ICOs. The problem that is hindering these token

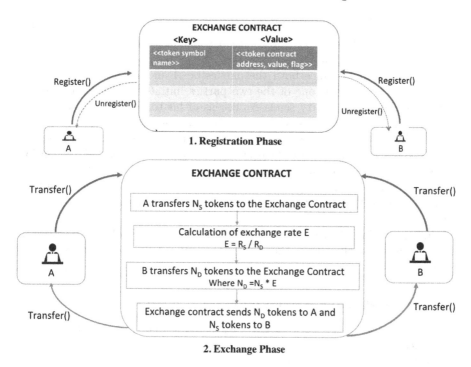

Fig. 2. Exchange of tokens between parties A and B using intermediate Exchange Contract

traders from maximizing their profit is the inability of these token traders to exchange between the two different tokens.

This paper presents two solutions to resolve the above problem. For each of the solutions mentioned below, the contract interface and the implementation details have been provided.

Consider A and B as potential Token Traders who want to exchange tokens among themselves to maximize their profit. So the exchange of these eclectic tokens can be enabled using Central Contract exchange mechanism and Atomic Swap exchange mechanism.

4.3   Using Central Contract Exchange

In this approach we maintain a single intermediate *Exchange Contract* which will interact with the users A and B (Refer Fig. 2). This solution mainly consists of three phases:

1. **Registration phase:** All intrachain transfers can occur only after the tokens have been registered to the *Exchange Contract*. Each token trader provides a three tuple (A, S, R) to the *Exchange Contract* during the registration phase

where A denotes the address of the token contract that is deployed, S denotes the token symbol name and R the rate at which he would like to trade in the base blockchain currency.

2. **Exchange Phase:** Once both the parties(i.e A and B) have registered to the exchange contract, one of the two parties initiates the intrachain token transfer. The source party sends N_s tokens of his to obtain N_d tokens from the destination party. The *Exchange Contract* facilitates this exchange by calculating the exchange rate E for the exchange of the two tokens as $E = R_s/R_d$ where R_s and R_d are the exchange rates of the source and destination parties. Once the exchange rate E is calculated, $N_d = N_s * E$ tokens are sent from the destination party to the exchange contract. The *Exchange Contract* then forwards N_d tokens to the source party and N_s tokens to the destination party.

3. **Unregistration Phase:** Once the exchange is complete both the parties can unregister themselves from the *Exchange Contract* or remain registered for further transactions.

Contract Interface: interface CentralTokenContract {

```
function deRegister (string memory symbol) public returns (bool
success)
function Register(address address, uint256 saleValue, string
memory symbol) public returns (bool success)
function getOwner(string memory symbol) public view returns
(address TokenOwner)
function NativeToken(string memory SrcSym,string memory DestSym,
uint256 Qty) public returns (uint256 success)
function getTokenValues() public view returns(ValueDisplay[]
memory Table)
```

}

- **deRegister:** Given the Token Symbol, the Token Contract is unregistered from the *Exchange Contract*. This function returns a *boolean* value which states whether the de-registration was successful or not.
- **Register:** Given the address of the token contract, the value at which the token must be sold and the Token Symbol, a *boolean* value is returned which states whether the registration was successful or not.
- **getOwner:** Given the Token Symbol, the *address* of the Token Owner is returned.
- **NativeToken:** Given the Source Token Symbol, Destination Token Symbol and Quantity of Native tokens to be exchanged, Returns a *boolean* value which shows if the exchange was successful or not.
- **getTokenValues:** Displays a two-tuple Table indicating the Sale Value and the Token Symbol of all the tokens which are registered to the *Exchange Contract*. Returns an array of type *ValueDisplay*.

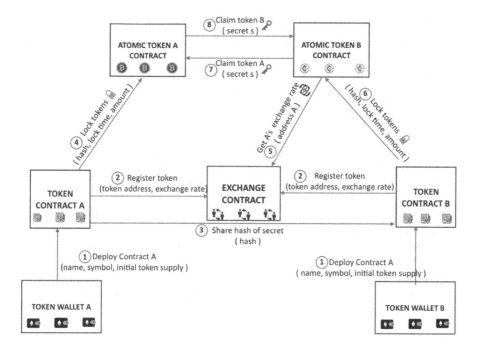

Fig. 3. Atomic Swap of tokens between parties A and B

4.4 Using Atomic Swap Exchange

Atomic Swap is a common mechanism used in interoperability solutions. The exchanges in these solutions take place without the involvement of intermediate entities. The atomicity of the intrachain transactions must be maintained i.e. the partial execution of the atomic swap transactions should result in the reversion of the transactions. Atomic swap exchanges primarily use *HTLC Contracts* to lock their assets. These assets can be claimed by revealing the secret within the expiration time. Most of the atomic swap solutions involve 1:1 backing up of tokens and do not involve oracles to aid them during execution. The process is as follows (Refer Fig. 3):

STEP 1. Wallet *A* deploys *Token Contract A* with a predefined initial supply, name and symbol of the token. Similarly, Wallet *B* deploys a *Token contract B* with a predefined initial supply, name and symbol of the token. The balances of user accounts and token contracts is maintained using a hash-map data structure.

STEP 2. *Token Contract A* and *Token Contract B* then register to the Exchange Contract and specify the rate at which they want to sell their corresponding tokens.

STEP 3. *Token Contract A* subscribes to an oracle [19] and generates a random number s which is hashed ($H=$ hash(s)) and is shared with *Token Contract B.*

STEP 4. Now *Token Contract A* locks N_A tokens of its wallet with a time stamp of N seconds, signs it with the *public key* of B (PK_B) and transfers it to *Atomic Token A Contract* for the intrachain exchange.

STEP 5. Similarly, *Token Contract B* calculates the exchange rate E by interacting with the Exchange Contract. E is calculated as Ra/Rb where Ra and Rb represent the exchange rates of tokens A and B respectively.

STEP 6. *Token Contract B* then locks N_B tokens where $N_B = N_A * E$ with a timestamp of *2N seconds*, signs it with the public key of A (Pka) and transfers it to the *Atomic Token B Contract.*

STEP 7. *Atomic Token B Contract* first claims N_A tokens it by decrypting using its private key Pr_B and secret s. If the contract fails to claim A's tokens within the designated timestamp (N seconds), the transaction is reverted.

STEP 8. Similarly, *Atomic Token A Contract* can claim N_B tokens by unlocking them using its private key Pr_A and secret s. If the contract fails to redeem B's tokens within the required timestamp (*2N seconds*), the transaction is reverted.

Contract Interface

```
interface AtomicSwap {
    function lock(address to, bytes32 hash, uint lockExpiryMinutes,
    uint amount) public view returns (boolean success)
    function unlock(bytes32 hash) public returns (boolean success)
    function claim(bytes32 secret) public returns (boolean success)
}

interface ExchangeContract{
    function deRegister(string memory symbol) public returns (bool
    success)
    function Register(address address,uint256 saleValue,string memory
    symbol) public returns (bool success)
    function getExchangeRate(address TokenAddress) public returns (uint
    rate)
}
```

5   Implementation

We have implemented both the approaches of the token exchange mechanisms in Solidity. The detailed data structures are given in the following subsections:

5.1   Central Exchange Contract

For the implementation of the Central Exchange Contract we have used the following data structures.

```
struct registerParam{
    address TokenContractAddress;
    uint256 valueInEther;
    String TokenSymbol;
}
 struct ValueDisplay{
    string TokenSymbol;
    uint256 saleValue;
 }


mapping(string=>registerParam) tokenLookup;
```

This is a global mapping of all the tokens that are registered to the *Exchange Contract* where *TokenSymbol* is the key of the mapping.

This implementation uses *ERC 777* [20] tokens to reduce the gas cost and these tokens are backward compatible with *ERC20* [21] tokens. It allows symmetric (where one token of A is exchanged with one token of B) and asymmetric transfers (where X tokens of A are exchanged with Y tokens of B) to take place easily. This process is token standard agnostic and easy to extend. However, since the deployment of the contract is by a third party, he can include functions like *destroy()* in the implementation of the *Exchange Contract*. Thus, there can be a loss of tokens because we have to depend on a third party to keep the exchange running when a transaction is taking place.

5.2   Atomic Swap

For the implementation of the Atomic Swap Contract we have used the following data structures.

```
Struct AtomicTransactions{
    from address;
    to address;
    amount uint64;
    lockPeriod uint64;
}
mapping (bytes32 => AtomicTransactions) transactions;
mapping (address => uint256) public balanceOf;
mapping (address tokenOwner, uint256 rate) public exchangeRate;
```

This implementation uses *ERC 777* [20] tokens to reduce the gas cost and these tokens are backward compatible with *ERC20* [21] tokens. It enables efficient low cost intrachain transfers. Atomic swaps eliminate the need of intermediate parties, thus enabling trustless, anonymous, decentralized fee-less, less attack prone exchanges among the parties.This mechanism is currency, token and platform standard agnostic.

5.3   Contracts Execution

The above contracts were implemented using solidity programming language .The contracts were intially deployed on remix and subsquently deployed on rinkeby using metamask. We have observed that atomic swap is more efficient than central contract exchange.Excluding contract deployment time and cost we contract execution details in Table 1.

Table 1. Cost comparision of central contract and atomic swap mechanism

	Central contract	Atomic Swap contract
#Transactions	6	6
Execution cost (ETH)	0.000613948	0.00043875

Although both the contracts require equal number of transactions internally, atomic swap is 25% cost efficient than central contract exchange. Morever atomic swap contracts are more scalable than central contract contracts.

6   Conclusion

Blockchain is now being viewed as a potential technology of the future, replacing the current centralised architectures. Some of the key industries which have dire need of interoperability among their businesses are healthcare and supply chain. This paper can be viewed as a baseline mechanism for many blockchain use cases of these industries where interoperability is the key issue. This paper explores secure token exchange methodologies which decrease the intrachain interoperability problem among heterogeneous tokens. The mechanisms proposed are generic and thus provide the flexibility to the user to change the token standards without affecting the procedures of these mechanisms.

References

1. Luu, L.: Peacerelay: connecting the many ethereum blockchains (2017)
2. Wood, G.: Polkadot: vision for a heterogeneous multi-chain framework (2017)
3. Kwon, J., Buchman, E.: A network of distributed ledgers (2018)
4. Wrapped Bitcoin (WBTC) an ERC20 token backed 1:1 with Bitcoin
5. Satoshi, N.: Bitcoin: a peer-to-peer electronic cash system. Bitcoin (2008)
6. Buterin, V.: Ethereum white paper: a next generation smart contract & decentralized application platform (2013)
7. Ding, D.: InterChain: a framework to support blockchain interoperability (2018)

8. Veronese, G.S., Correia, M., Bessani, A.N., Lung, L.C., Verissimo, P.: Efficient byzantine fault-tolerance. IEEE Trans. Comput. **62**(1), 16–30 (2013)
9. Buterin, V.: Proof of stake: how i learned to love weak subjectivity (2014)
10. Back, A., et al.: Enabling blockchain innovations with pegged sidechains (2014). http://cs.umd.edu/projects/coinscope/coinscope.pdf
11. Dilley, J., Poelstra, A., Wilkins, J., Piekarska, M., Gorlick, B., Friedenbach, M.: Strong federations: an interoperable blockchain solution to centralized third party risks (2016)
12. Kwon, J.: TenderMint: consensus without mining (2014)
13. Larimer, D.: Delegated proof-of-stake (DPoS). Bitshare whitepaper (2014)
14. Warren, W., Bandeali, A.: 0x: an open protocol for decentralized exchange on the Ethereum blockchain. Technical report (2017)
15. Wang, D., Zhou, J., Wang, A., Finestone, M.: Loopring: a decentralized token exchange protocol. Technical report (2018)
16. Zamyatin, A., Harz, D., Lind, J., Panayiotou, P., Gervais, A., Knottenbelt, W.: XClaim: trustless, interoperable, cryptocurrency-backed assets, March 2019
17. M. Spoke and Nuco Engineering Team. Aion: The thirdgeneration blockchain network
18. Buterin, V.: Notes on scalable blockchain protocols (2015)
19. Andreas, A., Wood, G.: Mastering Ethereum : Building Smart Contracts and DApps. Orielly, Newton (2018)
20. ERC777. https://eips.ethereum.org/eips/eip-777
21. ERC20 (2015). https://github.com/ethereum/eips/issues/20

On Way to Simplify the Reverse Engineering of UEFI Firmwares

Philip Lebedev, Konstantin Kogos[(⊠)], and Egor Vasilenko

National Research Nuclear University MEPhI,
Kashirskoe Sh. 31, 115409 Moscow, Russia
lfv002@campus.mephi.ru, kgkogos@mephi.ru

Abstract. In this paper authors introduce an algorithm to simplification of UEFI firmware reverse engineering via limiting the amount of code examined on Intel-based systems, which is based on proprietary UEFI protocols searching. The provided implementation of the algorithm is tested on few platforms that are Gigabyte BRIX, Razer Blade Stealth and Intel NUC based on 7th Generation Intel(R) Processor Families. As a result, UEFI modules that contain references to proprietary protocols were defined.

Keywords: Firmware · Reverse engineering · UEFI

1 Introduction

BIOS firmware is where CPU performs its first instructions beginning with CPU reset vector, chipset initialization, enumerating PCIe devices and many more. PC firmware vulnerabilities enable the malware to persist in the system across OS reinstalls, interfere with the boot process and lets an attacker stay unseen. The main reason why security issues occur in BIOS image is the existence of firmware bugs, errors and insecure hardware configuration.

The history of BIOS is full of firmware vulnerabilities and security issues: BIOS code reflashing [1], System Management Mode security issues [2–4], UEFI rootkits [5, 6], DCI enabled interface [7] and etc.

UEFI firmware is now widely deployed and has become a target for security researchers. The way to minimize firmware bugs roots at perfect understanding of UEFI procedures which can be achieved by source codes audit, reverse engineering techniques and hardware debugging, e.g. via DCI interface. But it is hard to investigate all UEFI images manually, there is why it is important to find a method to choose UEFI modules that you need to look at first. The good thing is that the most of UEFI firmwares are based on open source project called EDK that makes development process much easier, developers just need to add proprietary modules in existing source code. Such proprietary modules bring more interest in information security research field due to closed source codes. In this paper we talk about a possible way to identify proprietary functions located in UEFI firmware with the help of UEFI internal structures.

© Springer Nature Singapore Pte Ltd. 2020
M. Anbar et al. (Eds.): ACeS 2019, CCIS 1132, pp. 220–231, 2020.
https://doi.org/10.1007/978-981-15-2693-0_16

2 Related Works

While UEFI firmwares are developing, security assessment methods and reverse engineering techniques are also growing. For example, starting from 2014 CHIPSEC framework [8] provides a set of modules, including hardware protection and correct configuration test, tests for vulnerabilities in firmware and platform components, fuzzing tools for various platform devices and many more. From the big set of CHIPSEC modules SMI tool for pointer validation vulnerabilities is more interesting in context of current work. Using this utility we can minimize code analysis space, relying only on potentially-vulnerable SMI handlers. Current work has similar mission which is achieving minimization of code analysis space by searching for interfaces of proprietary protocols.

3 UEFI Applications and Their Structure

There are 7 common types of UEFI images:

- PEI modules
- PEI/DXE combined modules
- UEFI applications
- DXE drivers
- UEFI OS loaders
- SMM drivers
- SMM/DXE combined drivers.

Each type is represented by PE/COFF image. It is unnecessary to investigate all types of UEFI images, on the contrary in the current work that is enough to consider the structure of a simple UEFI application presented in Listing 1.

Listing 1. Simple UEFI application

```
#include <Uefi.h>
#include <Library/UefiLib.h>
#include <Library/DebugLib.h>
#include <Library/MemoryAllocationLib.h>
#include <Library/BaseMemoryLib.h>
#include <Library/UefiBootServicesTableLib.h>
#include <Library/ShellLib.h>

EFI_STATUS
EFIAPI
UefiMain(
    IN EFI_HANDLE ImageHandle,
    IN EFI_SYSTEM_TABLE *SystemTable
) {
    EFI_STATUS efiStatus = EFI_SUCCESS;
    return efiStatus;
}
```

Most of UEFI applications involve an entry point function with two arguments being ImageHandle and SystemTable. Their types definition are shown in Listing 2.

Listing 2. System table and UEFI handle types definition

```
typedef struct {
  EFI_TABLE_HEADER  Hdr;
  CHAR16 *FirmwareVendor;
  UINT32 FirmwareRevision;
  EFI_HANDLE ConsoleInHandle;
  EFI_SIMPLE_TEXT_INPUT_PROTOCOL *ConIn;
  EFI_HANDLE ConsoleOutHandle;
  EFI_SIMPLE_TEXT_OUTPUT_PROTOCOL *ConOut;
  EFI_HANDLE StandardErrorHandle;
  EFI_SIMPLE_TEXT_OUTPUT_PROTOCOL *StdErr;
  EFI_RUNTIME_SERVICES *RuntimeServices;
  EFI_BOOT_SERVICES *BootServices;
  UINTN NumberOfTableEntries;
  EFI_CONFIGURATION_TABLE *ConfigurationTabl2e;
} EFI_SYSTEM_TABLE;

typedef VOID *EFI_HANDLE;
```

These definitions correspond with EDK repository. There are two types of services maintained by UEFI firmware:

- Boot Services
- Runtime Services

The main difference between them is that Boot Services are not longer in use after the system passes control to the OS kernel meaning the end of DXE phase, but Runtime Services should communicate with OS during its execution. Device access is partially abstracted via protocols. Boot services give an ability to link devices and system functionality during boot time. UEFI Boot services are represented by a table that contains pointers to all of the boot services. The definition of the table could be found in EDK repository.

All elements in the table are prototypes of function pointers except the table header. An access to boot services is provided through a set of protocol interfaces [9]. UEFI firmware scalability is partially achieved by selecting a wide range of protocol interfaces. As the matter of fact, some UEFI protocols come from specific implementations by different OEMs for new platform devices, e.g. new boot media types. That is why it is a challenge to identify such protocol interface for further investigation and reverse engineering.

4 UEFI Protocols

UEFI protocols consist of next elements:

- Protocol name:
  - Brief description of the protocol interface
  - GUID (Globally Unique Identifier) - identifier for the protocol interface

- Protocol Interface:
  - Data structure definition containing the procedures and data fields produced by the protocol interface
  - Description of each field in the protocol interface
  - Interface functionality description
  - The type declaration and constants that are used in the protocol interface structure

To understand how these protocols are used in UEFI firmware it is needed to extend simple UEFI application by next view, which is presented in Listing 3.

Listing 3. Extended UEFI application

```
#include <Uefi.h>
#include <Library/UefiLib.h>
#include <Library/DebugLib.h>
#include <Library/MemoryAllocationLib.h>
#include <Library/BaseMemoryLib.h>
#include <Library/UefiBootServicesTableLib.h>
#include <Library/ShellLib.h>

EFI_STATUS
EFIAPI
UefiMain (
    IN EFI_HANDLE ImageHandle,
    IN EFI_SYSTEM_TABLE* SystemTable
    )
{
EFI_SYSTEM_TABLE *ST = SystemTable;
EFI_BOOT_SERVICES *BT = ST->BootServices;
EFI_LOCATE_PROTOCOL LP = BT->LocateProtocol;
EFI_STATUS efiStatus = TRUE;
EFI_GUID gopGuid = {
    0x9042a9de,
    0x23dc,0x4a38,
    0x96,0xfb,0x7a,0xde,
    0xd0,0x80,0x51,0x6a
};
EFI_GRAPHICS_OUTPUT_PROTOCOL *gop = NULL;
efiStatus = LP(&gopGuid, NULL, (VOID**)gop);
ASSERT_EFI_ERROR(efiStatus);
efiStatus = gop->SetMode(gop, 0x1337);
if (efiStatus == EFI_UNSUPPORTED) {
    Print(L"Video is not supported\n");
}
else {
    Print(L"Video is supported\n");
}
ASSERT_EFI_ERROR(efiStatus);
return efiStatus;
}
```

In this example UEFI application tries to set graphics device video mode specifying number 0x1337 through boot services table. The algorithm of this program is the following:

- Define protocol GUID
- Get protocol interface via specified GUID
- Invoke protocol interface
- Check return value

To obtain protocol interface it's necessary to call LocateProtocol function, which declaration is shown below in Listing 4.

Listing 4. LocateProtocol function declaration

```
typedef
    EFI_STATUS
    (EFIAPI *EFI_LOCATE_PROTOCOL)(
    IN  EFI_GUID  *Protocol,
    IN  VOID      *Registration, OPTIONAL
    OUT VOID      **Interface
    );
```

According to the declaration it is clear that only UEFI GUID is required to get protocol interface. In example above it equals Graphics Output Protocol from the UEFI 2.7 specification. In practice OEM modules are closed and the only way to find LocateProtocol call is to disassemble UEFI binary and do its reverse engineering.

5 UEFI Image Reverse Engineering

As said before each UEFI application is a simple PE/COFF image. Let's disassemble UEFI application presented above and consider machine instructions used to call LocateProtocol. Figure 1 provides the disassembled view of UEFI application presented in Listing 3.

According to Fig. 1:

- lines 1–4: function prolog
- line 5: obtaining RuntimeServices table pointer
- line 7: storing the value of the ImageHandle
- line 8: obtaining BootServices table pointer
- line 9: storing the pointer of the RuntimeServices table
- line 10: storing the pointer of the SystemTable
- line 11: storing the pointer of the BootServices table
- line 13: obtaining LocateProtocol function pointer
- line 14: setting first argument value
- line 15–18: storing protocol GUID value on stack
- line 19: invoking LocateProtocol function

```
 1    mov     %rbx,0x8(%rsp)
 2    push    %rbp
 3    mov     %rsp,%rbp
 4    sub     $0x30,%rsp
 5    mov     0x58(%rdx),%rax
 6    xor     %r8d,%r8d
 7    mov     %rcx,0x175d(%rip)
 8    mov     0x60(%rdx),%rcx
 9    mov     %rax,0x1762(%rip)
10    mov     %rdx,0x1743(%rip)
11    xor     %edx,%edx
12    mov     %rcx,0x174a(%rip)
13    mov     0x140(%rcx),%rax
14    lea     -0x10(%rbp),%rcx
15    movl    $0x9042a9de,-0x10(%rbp)
16    movl    $0x4a3823dc,-0xc(%rbp)
17    movl    $0xde7afb96,-0x8(%rbp)
18    movl    $0x6a5180d0,-0x4(%rbp)
19    callq   *%rax
20    mov     $0x1337,%edx
21    xor     %ecx,%ecx
22    callq   *0x8
23    mov     %rax,%rbx
24    lea     0x11b9(%rip),%rcx
25    movabs  $0x8000000000000003,%rax
26    cmp     %rax,%rbx
27    je      0x30d
28    lea     0x11d3(%rip),%rcx
29    callq   0x3ac
30    mov     %rbx,%rax
31    mov     0x40(%rsp),%rbx
32    add     $0x30,%rsp
33    pop     %rbp
34    retq
```

Fig. 1. Disassembled extended UEFI application

- line 22: invoking SetMode function
- line 24: getting the address of the string («Video is not supported»)
- line 26: comparing efiStatus value with defined value
- line 28: getting the address of the string («Video is supported»)
- line 29: printing corresponding message

Mind that LocateProtocol pointer is located at fixed offset along Boot services table and register RBX keeps System table pointer. It means that final algorithm of UEFI protocols identification could be achieved if next conditions are met:

- The calling instruction is identified, that stores LocateProtocol pointer offset
- The first argument value is identified which points to GUID value

In most cases the GUID value will be stored in RCX register because of UEFI applications calling convention. Those conditions could also be achieved because the System table pointer is passed as an argument to UEFI application entry point through RBX register.

In presented application GUID value stored on stack memory, but in reality firmwares maintain System table and Boot services with the help of global memory. Therefore, let's change Listing 3 into the form as presented in Listing 5.

Listing 5. Extended UEFI application with protocol GUID passed via global memory

```
#include <Uefi.h>
#include <Library/UefiLib.h>
#include <Library/DebugLib.h>
#include <Library/MemoryAllocationLib.h>
#include <Library/BaseMemoryLib.h>
#include <Library/UefiBootServicesTableLib.h>
#include <Library/DebugLib.h>
#include <Library/ShellLib.h>

EFI_STATUS
EFIAPI
UefiMain (
    IN EFI_HANDLE ImageHandle,
    IN EFI_SYSTEM_TABLE* SystemTable
    )
{
EFI_SYSTEM_TABLE *ST = SystemTable;
EFI_BOOT_SERVICES *BT = ST->BootServices;
EFI_LOCATE_PROTOCOL LP = BT->LocateProtocol;
EFI_STATUS efiStatus = TRUE;
EFI_GRAPHICS_OUTPUT_PROTOCOL *gop = NULL;
EFI_GUID g = gEfiGraphicsOutputProtocolGuid;
efiStatus = LP(&g, NULL, (VOID**)gop);
ASSERT_EFI_ERROR(efiStatus);
efiStatus = gop->SetMode(gop, 0x1337);
if (efiStatus == EFI_UNSUPPORTED) {
    Print(L"Video is not supported\n");
}
else {
    Print(L"Video is supported\n");
}
ASSERT_EFI_ERROR(efiStatus);
return efiStatus;
}
```

The disassembled view of application presented in Listing 5 is shown in Fig. 2.

```
1    push    %rbx
2    sub     $0x30,%rsp
3    mov     0x58(%rdx),%rax
4    xor     %r8d,%r8d
5    movups  0x112c(%rip),%xmm0
6    mov     %rcx,0x174d(%rip)
7    mov     0x60(%rdx),%rcx
8    mov     %rax,0x1752(%rip)
9    mov     %rdx,0x1733(%rip)
10   xor     %edx,%edx
11   mov     %rcx,0x173a(%rip)
12   mov     0x140(%rcx),%rax
13   lea     0x20(%rsp),%rcx
14   movdqu  %xmm0,0x20(%rsp)
15   callq   *%rax
16   mov     $0x1337,%edx
17   xor     %ecx,%ecx
18   callq   *0x8
19   mov     %rax,%rbx
20   lea     0x11be(%rip),%rcx
21   movabs  $0x8000000000000003,%rax
22   cmp     %rax,%rbx
23   je      0x2f8
24   lea     0x11d8(%rip),%rcx
25   callq   0x394
26   mov     %rbx,%rax
27   add     $0x30,%rsp
28   pop     %rbx
29   retq
```

Fig. 2. Disassembled extended UEFI application with protocol GUID passed via global memory

According to Fig. 2:

- lines 1–2: function prolog
- line 3: obtaining RuntimeServices table pointer
- line 5: storing protocol GUID value
- line 6: storing the value of the ImageHandle
- line 7: obtaining BootServices table pointer
- line 8: storing the pointer of the RuntimeServices table
- line 9: storing the pointer of the SystemTable
- line 11: storing the pointer of the BootServices table
- line 12: obtaining LocateProtocol function pointer
- line 13: setting first argument value

- line 15: invoking LocateProtocol function
- line 18: invoking SetMode function
- line 20: getting the address of the string («Video is not supported»)
- line 22: comparing efiStatus value with defined value
- line 24: getting the address of the string («Video is supported»)
- line 25: printing corresponding message

6   Proprietary UEFI Protocols Identification Algorithm

Previous sections give an idea about action taken to collect protocols existing in the UEFI firmware. EDK repository keeps a big set of GUID values which could be used as generally known. With this set you can identify protocols developed by OEM by discarding EDK protocols. The proposed algorithm is presented below.

Data: Disassembled UEFI image
$instructions$ = set of disassembled instructions in UEFI image;
$instLength$ = number of disassembled instructions in UEFI image;
$uefiCalls$ = set of UEFI functions processing the given protocol (GUID value);
$edkGuids$ = set of public UEFI protocols (GUID values);
$proprietaryGuids = \varnothing$;
$i = 0$;
while $i < instLength$ **do**
    if $instructions[i] \in uefiCalls$ **then**
        $guid$ = GUID value of UEFI protocol;
        if $guid \notin edkGuids$ **then**
            $proprietaryGuids = proprietaryGuids \cup guid$;
        end
    end
    $i = i + 1$;
end
Output: $proprietaryGuids$
Algorithm 1: Proprietary UEFI protocols identification algorithm

It should be noted that the algorithm of proprietary protocols finding can be implemented for all UEFI-compatible architectures, e.g. ARM, because it does not depend on architectural features. All possible values for the variable uefiCalls could be identified by functions which are presented in the Table 1. Each function prototype could be found in official EDK repository.

Table 1. Set of protocol handler functions.

Function
EFI INSTALL PROTOCOL INTERFACE
EFI REINSTALL PROTOCOL INTERFACE
EFI UNINSTALL PROTOCOL INTERFACE
EFI HANDLE PROTOCOL
EFI OPEN PROTOCOL
EFI CLOSE PROTOCOL
EFI OPEN PROTOCOL INFORMATION
EFI PROTOCOLS PER HANDLE
EFI REGISTER PROTOCOL NOTIFY
EFI LOCATE HANDLE
EFI LOCATE DEVICE PATH
EFI LOCATE HANDLE BUFFER
EFI LOCATE PROTOCOL

7 Experimental Results

The algorithm of proprietary GUID records was implemented with the help of Python programming language [10]. The final software solutions consists of multiple modules, which are responsible for UEFI image parsing, DXE and SMM drivers extracting and processing. Each extracted image is independent executable file, there is why it's much convenient to use special API for their analysis, e.g. IDA Python or radare2 API. The developed software package allows you to get a list of GUID-records of proprietary protocols for any UEFI firmware, including the following information:

- the name of the executable image where the proprietary protocol is found
- the name of the service that processes the GUID record of the UEFI protocol
- the address of the GUID record of the protocol in the memory of the executable image

The developed software module has been tested on Gigabyte BRIX, Razer Blade Stealth and Intel NUC based on 7th Generation Intel(R) Processor Families platforms.

UEFI modules presented in Tables 2, 3 and 4 with nonzero values of proprietary protocols are of interest for further research, e.g. fuzz testing or deep reverse engineering.

Table 2. Number of proprietary UEFI protocols in Gigabyte BRIX for some DXE and SMM drivers.

UEFI module	Number of proprietary protocols
Bds.efi	3
CpuSpSMI.efi	2
CryptoSMM.efi	2
RomLayoutDxe.efi	0
SmmAccess.efi	0
SmramSaveInfoHandlerSmm.efi	0

Table 3. Number of proprietary UEFI protocols in Intel NUC for some DXE and SMM drivers.

UEFI module	Number of proprietary protocols
AcpiDebugTable.efi	0
NbDxe.efi	0
DxeOverClock.efi	3
OverclockInterface.efi	1
OemEventDxe.efi	2

Table 4. Number of proprietary UEFI protocols in Razer Blade Stealth for some DXE and SMM drivers.

UEFI module	Number of proprietary protocols
SecureEraseDxe.efi	2
BiosExtensionLoader.efi	4
AMITSE.efi	4
IntegratedTouch.efi	1

The total results are presented in Tables 5 and 6 providing the full info about the amount of proprietary functions in considered UEFI firmwares.

Table 5. Number of identified proprietary protocols in considered UEFI firmwares.

Platform	Number of proprietary protocols
Gigabyte BRIX	341
Razer Blade Stealth	267
Intel NUC	274

Table 6. Percentage of identified proprietary protocols in considered UEFI firmwares.

Platform	Number of proprietary protocols
Gigabyte BRIX	24%
Razer Blade Stealth	22%
Intel NUC	21%

8 Conclusions

UEFI firmware shows opportunities in scalable development allowing OEMs to add new hardware features and devices. However, larger code causes a bigger set of possible binary vulnerabilities. The proposed algorithm showed, that UEFI firmwares keeps significant number of modules that is not studied yet, therefore, security issues may also occur.

Further research can aim at extending and upgrading the algorithm by considering other boot services that depend on UEFI protocols and developing fuzzing algorithms for testing the extracted proprietary protocols routines.

References

1. Wojtczuk, W., Tereshkin, A.: Attacking Intel BIOS. https://www.blackhat.com/presentati ons/bh-usa-09/WOJTCZUK/BHUSA09-Wojtczuk-AtkIntelBios-SLIDES.pdf. Accessed 20 July 2019
2. Duflot, L., Etiemble, D., Grumelard, O.: Using CPU system management mode to circumvent operating system security functions. https://pdfs.semanticscholar.org/62be/ ba49b7a9eb50c0a860547cceb2863e994aa2.pdf. Accessed 20 July 2019
3. System Management Mode Hack: Using SMM for Other Purposes. http://phrack.org/issues/ 65/7.html. Accessed 20 July 2019
4. Duflot, L., Levillain, O., Morin, B., Grumelard, O.: Getting into the SMRAM: SMM Reloaded. https://cansecwest.com/csw09/csw09-duflot.pdf. Accessed 20 July 2019
5. Lin, P.: Hacking team uses UEFI BIOS Rootkit to Keep RCS 9 agent in target systems. https://blog.trendmicro.com/trendlabs-securityintelligence/hacking-team-uses-uefi-bios-rootkit-to-keep-rcs-9agent-in-target-systems. Accessed 20 July 2019
6. Matrosov, A., Rodionov, E.: UEFI firmware rootkits: myths and reality. https://www. blackhat.com/docs/asia17/materials/asia-17-Matrosov-The-UEFI-Firmware-Rootkits-Myths-AndReality.pdf. Accessed 20 July 2019
7. Goryachy, M., Ermolov, M.: Where there's a JTAG, there's a way: obtaining full system access via USB. https://www.ptsecurity.com/upload/corporate/ww-en/analytics/Where-theres-a-JTAG-theres-a-way.pdf. Accessed 20 July 2019
8. Loucaides, J., Bulygin, Y.: Platform security assessment with CHIPSEC. https://cansecwest. com/slides/2014/PlatformFirmwareSecurityAssessmentwCHIPSEC-csw14-final.pdf. Accessed 20 July 2019
9. UEFI Specification Version 2.7. http://www.uefi.org/sites/default/files/resources/UEFISpec 2_7_ASept6.pdf. Accessed 20 July 2019
10. UEFI firmware analyser tool. https://github.com/yeggor/UEFI_RETool. Accessed 20 July 2019

Ambient Cloud and Edge Computing, Wireless and Cellular Communication

Comparison Between BlindLogin and Other Graphical Password Authentication Systems

Yean Li Ho[1]($\boxtimes$) (iD), Siong Hoe Lau[1] (iD), and Afizan Azman[2]

[1] Multimedia University, Jalan Ayer Keroh Lama, 75450 Melaka, Malaysia
ylho@mmu.edu.my
[2] Melaka International College of Science and Technology, Aras 6,
Bangunan Graha Maju, Jalan Graha Maju, 75300 Melaka, Malaysia

Abstract. This pilot study was done to evaluate the picture superiority effect on the memorability and usability of BlindLogin based on the Usability-Deployability-Security (UDS) Model and to compare the results with other graphical password authentication systems found in literature. The results from this pilot study indicated that the visually impaired users generally thought that BlindLogin was better than the textual password based on all the UDS Model usability criteria. The results further indicated that BlindLogin was significantly better than textual passwords in four usability criteria (Memorywise Effortless, Infrequent Errors, Efficient to Use and Physically Effortless). For Memorywise-Effortless, BlindLogin ($p < 0.012$) is more significant than Image PassTiles ($p < 0.013$) and much more significant than Object PassTiles ($p < 0.045$). For Infrequent Errors, BlindLogin ($p < 0.015$) is almost as significant as Passpoints ($p < 0.013$). The security of BlindLogin was also assessed by tabulating the password space and launching a dictionary attack and a brute-force attack using the capabilities of the cloud. The results showed that it would take about 48188.59 years to brute-force a BlindLogin password using the capabilities of the cloud, which is better than DAS (541.8 years) and Grid Selection (541.8 years). As currently graphical authentication systems designed for the visually impaired have yet to be found in literature, BlindLogin has been shown to be a memorable and usable graphical authentication system for visually impaired users as compared to other graphical password systems which was designed only for sighted users on the mobile platform.

Keywords: Visually impaired · Blind · Authentication · Graphical passwords · Human computer interaction security · Usability · Mobile · Smartphone

1 Introduction

Graphical password authentication systems were introduced by Blonder [1]. It was proposed as a more user-friendly alternative to the common textual password authentication system. Thorpe and van Oorschot [2] held that people in general remember pictures better than words. Subsequently, it was shown that most people remember objects better than pictures [3–7]. This is known as the picture superiority effect [8–11]. This is due to the fact that text is coded is a single form in memory while

© Springer Nature Singapore Pte Ltd. 2020
M. Anbar et al. (Eds.): ACeS 2019, CCIS 1132, pp. 235–246, 2020.
https://doi.org/10.1007/978-981-15-2693-0_17

pictures are usually stored in dual coding in the brain through name labelling and pictures [3, 12].

Ho et al. [13] contains a taxonomy of existing graphical password authentication systems. There are generally four major categories of graphical passwords, namely Recognition, Recall, Recognition-Recall and Textual-Graphical password authentication systems. Recognition password authentication systems depend on the user to recognize certain objects or pictures in a certain fashion. Recall password authentication systems depend on the user to remember and recall their graphical password. Recognition-Recall password authentication systems have both features of recognition as well as recall properties. Finally, Textual-Graphical password authentication systems combine the properties of a textual password with a graphical password.

In general, it is observed that these graphical password authentication systems are not universally usable because they were not designed with the needs of the blind and visually-impaired in mind. BlindLogin, which is a Recognition-based graphical password authentication system was proposed in Ho et al. [14] to address this issue. A pilot user study was done to assess the memorability of the BlindLogin password and its usability and compare the usability of BlindLogin with the common textual password and with some graphical password authentication systems.

2 Literature Review

2.1 Graphical Password Systems

In 2000, Dhamija and Perrig [15] proposed a Recognition-based graphical password using hash visualization techniques while Brostoff and Sasse [16] proposed Passfaces, which allows you to select a sequence of faces from a keypad of faces. Then, Jansen et al. proposed the Picture password in 2003 [17] which is essentially a tiled picture for mobile devices.

In 2005, Wiedenbeck et al. [18] introduced a Single-Image Locimetric Cued-Recall Graphical password system called Passpoints, which is made up of sequential location points in a single picture. This was followed by PassMap (proposed by Yampolskiy in 2007 [19]) which required a user to trace a series of locations while using a map as a cue.

In Passpoints [18], an image is displayed on the screen by the system. The image is not secret and has no role other than helping the user to remember the click points. Any pixel in the image is a candidate for a click point. To log in, the user has to click close to the chosen points, in the chosen sequence. Since it is almost impossible for human users to click repeatedly on exactly the same point, the system allows for an error tolerance r in the click locations (e.g., a disk with radius r = 10 or 15 pixels). The system allows any common image format to be used and the images could be provided by the system or chosen by the user. The password space is large as compared to alphanumeric passwords and there is no need for artificial predefined click regions with well-marked boundaries. The drawback of this scheme is that the number of available click regions is small, perhaps only dozens in an image; thus a password has to be rather long to be secure. Also, people tend to forget the exact loci they chose previously. Furthermore, people tend to point inaccurately at the chosen location with the mouse. In addition to that, the locations chosen can be predictable based on user patterns (Hotspots).

Multiple-images Locimetric Cued-Recall graphical password systems include Persuasive Cued Click-Point (PCCP) [20] in which a user is required to choose a click point in each picture in a sequential series and Click Buttons according to Figures in Grids (CBFG) [21]. In 2012, another graphical password system called Passmap was introduced by Sun et al. [22] which is an extension of Passpoints using a map as a base picture.

For PCCP [20], a user is first presented with some images in a sequence. The user must choose one click-point per image while avoiding hot-spots. The system assigns the first image but each subsequent image is determined by the user's previous click. If different locations on an image are clicked, it results in different subsequent images. This allows the users to get feedback about the correctness of their password entry attempt. If they see the correct image, they will know that they have clicked on the correct click-point on the previous image. Thus, the attacker will not be able to know if the images presented at each stage are the correct images, only the user will know. During the password creation stage, the system displays "persuasive" properties by displaying a random viewport which is not a hotspot. The user is required to click within the viewport or shuffle to another randomly generated viewport. Larger images provide greater security because increased click-points provide greater security. However, increasing the size of the image and increasing the number of click-points will decrease usability. A weakness which has been detected is that hotspots and patterns reduce the effective password space in click-based graphical passwords. Also, remembering a password for one account can disrupt the memory of a password for another account. This psychological phenomenon is known as interference.

The Free-Recall graphical password methods include grid-based drawmetric systems like Draw a Secret (DAS) [23], Grid Selection [2], Pass-go [24] and DAS with Rotation (RDAS) [25] while Non grid-based Free-Recall graphical password mechanisms like pinPass.js [26] was also introduced as well.

Inspired by an old Chinese game, Go, Pass-Go [24] can be considered as an improvement of DAS [23], as it keeps most of the advantages of DAS and achieves stronger security and better usability. Pass-Go [24] requires a user to touch (or select) intersections, instead of cells, as a way to input password. Consequently, the coordinate system refers to a matrix of intersections, rather than cells as in DAS [23]. This method offers an extremely large password space (256 bits for the most basic scheme) and supports most application environments and input devices. However, the final form of a graphical password produced does not provide sufficient information about how the password is actually drawn.

For the pinPass.js [26] method, a user is required to draw a path through the pins to form a password which will be appended to a salt and hashed using SHA-1 to form the final password which will be sent through the web browser. This method is commonly used in smartphones as a login option for activating the smartphone. This method is simple and easy to use. However, this method is not protected from spyware or man-in-the-middle attacks.

PassTiles [7] is a Recognition-recall based graphical password which consists of cued recall, free recall and recognition properties. This method consists of 3 models: recall, cued recall and recognition schemes. The Blank PassTiles is a recall method. The Image PassTiles is a cued-recall method and the Object PassTiles is a recognition method. The users are supposed to select five PassTiles as their password for authentication. The order is not important. This method is easy to use. However, the average login time for Object PassTiles was about 30 s, which is too slow for widespread use and the password space is small.

Several Textual-Graphical password mechanisms were also introduced including SS7.0 [27], Hybrid Password [28], Advance Secure Login [29] and Text-based Shoulder Surfing Resistant Graphical Password Scheme [30].

2.2 Usability-Deployability-Security (UDS) Model

The BlindLogin app was evaluated through a user study survey which was designed according to the UDS Model which was proposed by Bonneau et al. [31] as shown in Fig. 1. The sample consisted of 46 Visually Impaired participants (20 Female and 26

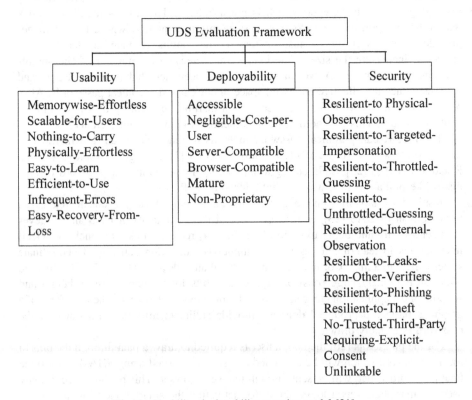

Fig. 1. Usability-deployability-security model [31] .

Male participants). Participants were from the age range of 18 years of age until 75 years of age. It took about half an hour for the users to be trained to use BlindLogin and complete the survey questions posed to them.

3 BlindLogin

While there are several virtual keyboard systems available for the sighted and the blind or visually impaired, BlindLogin was designed based on the No-Look-Notes virtual keyboard system proposed by Bonner et al. [32]. This design takes into consideration the habit of most blind and visually impaired to recognize location of objects based on a clock interface. Each object pie slice was designed according to the findings of Grussenmeyer and Folmer [33] that target size be between 9.2 mm and 9.6 mm for optimal comfort and usability for pointing tasks.

As the shoulder-surfing concern is important for the visually impaired, this obstacle is mitigated in BlindLogin with the use of the screen curtain app which causes the whole smartphone screen to be black so direct physical surveillance is not possible. Due to the fact that BlindLogin also uses audio and vibrational feedback, the visually impaired and blind users can still use this together with a headphone without any concern for direct physical observation.

Figure 2 shows some samples of the BlindLogin interface. The details of the design was covered in Ho et al. [14].

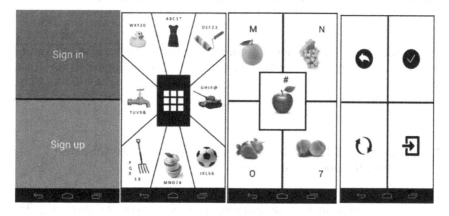

Fig. 2. Screen layout design of the BlindLogin app interface [14].

4 Comparison Between BlindLogin and Reviewed Literature

4.1 One-Sample T-Test

A One-sample T-Test was conducted to compare BlindLogin with the textual password on the visually impaired as well as sighted users using a survey with a 5-point Likert scale based on the UDS Model [31]. The scale was set with the value 1 signifying

BlindLogin was much worse than Textual Password, the Test Value 3 signifying BlindLogin was equivalent to the Textual Password and the value 5 signifying BlindLogin was much better than the Textual Password.

Table 1. One-sample T-test to determine the significance of the results for the relevant usability criteria [31]

| | Test Value = 3 | | | | | |
| | | | | | 95% Confidence Interval of the Difference | |
Usability Benefits	t	df	Sig. (2-tailed)	Mean Difference	Lower	Upper
U_Memorywise_Effortless	-2.608	45	.012	-.457	-.81	-.10
U_Scalable_For_Users	-1.658	45	.104	-.304	-.67	.07
U_Physically_Effortless	-2.197	45	.033	-.413	-.79	-.03
U_Easy_To_Learn	-1.522	45	.135	-.283	-.66	.09
U_Efficient_To_Use	-2.752	45	.009	-.565	-.98	-.15
U_Infrequent_Errors	-2.520	45	.015	-.500	-.90	-.10
U_Easy_Recovery_From_Loss	.123	45	.903	.022	-.34	.38

The results from Table 1 shows that the following usability criteria are significant and supports the hypothesis that BlindLogin is significantly better than the Textual Password in terms of Usability ($\mu < 3$): Memorywise Effortless ($t(45) = -2.608$, $p < 0.05$), Physically Effortless ($t(45) = -1.658$, $p < 0.05$), Efficient To Use ($t(45) = -2.752$ $p < 0.05$) and Infrequent Errors ($t(45) = -2.520$, $p < 0.05$).

4.2 Comparison of T-Test Results for Usability with Other Graphical Password Schemes in Literature

Table 2 displays the comparison of the results for T-Tests conducted on Passpoints, PassTiles and BlindLogin. From the literature surveyed, the sample sizes of the T-Tests conducted were 81 (PassTiles) and 20 (Passpoints). The sample size for BlindLogin is an average in between the two authentication systems: 46 (BlindLogin).

Table 2. Comparison of BlindLogin with other graphical passwords in terms of usability based on results obtained from literature.

Graphical Password	Authors	Method	Sample Size	Comparison	Criteria	Df	T value	Sig
Passpoints	Wiedenbeck et al., 2005	T-Test	20	Alphanumeric and Graphical	Number of incorrect submissions	38	-2.73	p<0.013
					Total practice time (seconds)	38	-4.24	p<0.0001
	Chiasson, Biddle and van Oorschot, 2007	T-Test	43 (Lab Study) 191 (Field Study)	Field Study and Lab Study	Click-Times for login phase	3403	2.02	p<0.05
Passtiles	Stobert and Biddle, 2013	One-sided T-Test	81	Chosen Text and Blank PassTiles	Memory time (hours)	29	2.6	0.007
				Chosen Text and Image PassTiles		29	2.34	0.013
				Chosen Text and Object PassTiles		29	1.76	0.045
BlindLogin	Ho et al, 2017	One-sided T-Test	46	Textual Password and Graphical	Memorywise Effortless (Usability)	45	-2.608	0.012
					Physically Effortless (Usability)	45	-2.197	0.033
					Efficient to Use (Usability)	45	-2.752	0.009
					Infrequent Errors (Usability)	45	-2.52	0.015

Furthermore, all the criteria used to measure these systems consisted of only usability criteria.

Stobert and Biddle [7] carried out a one-sided T-Test on PassTiles and compared it with Chosen Text and Assigned Text. Similarly, BlindLogin was assessed and compared with the Textual Password using a one-sided T-Test. PassTiles was evaluated based on memory time (in hours) and the "Memorywise-Effortless" criterion is the only criterion comparable to this for BlindLogin. However, the results supporting the memorability of the BlindLogin password (p < 0.012) is more significant than Image PassTiles (p < 0.013) and much more significant than Object PassTiles (p < 0.045). At worst, BlindLogin is less significant than Blank PassTiles (p = 0.007). This shows that the picture superiority effect [8–11] is relatively strong in BlindLogin which supports greater memorability for the BlindLogin password and contributes to the usability and recall of the BlindLogin password for visually impaired users.

Wiedenbeck et al. [17] and Chiasson, Biddle and van Oorschot [34] also conducted T-Tests on Passpoints. Of the three criteria evaluated for Passpoints, only "Number of incorrect submissions" is equivalent to the "Infrequent Errors" criterion used to evaluate the usability of BlindLogin (p < 0.015) and shown to be almost the same as Passpoints (p < 0.013).

4.3 Comparison of Security Testing of BlindLogin with Other Password Schemes in Literature

Table 3 summarizes the results comparing the Password Space, Brute Force Attack and Dictionary Attack resiliency between BlindLogin and several other password schemes in literature.

Table 3. Comparison of password space, brute force attack and dictionary attack between BlindLogin and other password schemes found in literature

Graphical Password	Authors	Method	Alphabet	Password length	Pasword Space	Time to crack password
BlindLogin	Ho et al. (2017)	Calculate Password Space	40	10 (chars)	1.048576×10^{16}	
		Brute Force Attack using 1 machine				48188.59 years
		Dictionary attack using 1 machine				4 hours 24 minutes 21 seconds
Text-based shoulder surfing resistant Graphical Password Scheme	Chen et al. (2013)	Calculate Password Space	64	15(chars)	1.006×10^{28}	
Advance Secure Login	Imran and Nizami (2011)	Calculate Password Space	48	10(chars)	6.4925×10^{16}	
Click Buttons according to Figures in Grids(CBFG)	Liu et al. (2011)	Calculate Password Space		7 (clicks)	2.3×10^{15}	
Passpoints	Liu et al. (2011)	Calculate password space on Lmax=12	373	5 (clicks)	7.2×10^{12}	
Hybrid Password	Zheng et al. (2010)	Calculate Password Space	25	13(chars)	1.5×10^{18}	
SS7.0	Mahansaria et al. (2009)	Calculate Password Space	48	10(chars)	6.4925×10^{16}	
PassPhrase	Yampolskiy (2007)	Calculate Password Space	50000	5 (words)	3.1×10^{23}	
			95	10 (chars)	5.987×10^{19}	
			64	8 (chars)	2.8×10^{14}	
Textual password	Yampolskiy (2007)	Calculate Password Space	96	8(chars)	7.2×10^{14}	
Pin Number	Yampolskiy (2007)	Calculate Password Space	10	4(numbers)	1×10^{4}	
Text with Graphical Assistance	Yampolskiy (2007)	Calculate Password Space	10(spaces)	8(chars)	2×10^{6}	
Déjà vu	Yampolskiy (2007)	Calculate Password Space	20	5(images)	1.5×10^{4}	
PassFace	Yampolskiy (2007)	Calculate Password Space	9	5(faces)	5.9×10^{4}	
Check-Off Password	Yampolskiy (2007)	Calculate Password Space	16	4(check-offs)	1.2×10^{4}	
PassThought	Yampolskiy (2007)	Calculate Password Space	95	8(chars)	6.6×10^{15}	
			10	2(changes)	3.5×10^{13}	
PassMap	Yampolskiy (2007)	Calculate Password Space	25	3(changes)	2×10^{00}	
	Yampolskiy (2007)	Calculate Password Space	30	8(selections)	6.5×10^{11}	
Picture Password	Jansen et al. (2003)	Calculate Password Space	930	7(chars)	6.017009×10^{20}	
	Yampolskiy (2007)	Calculate Password Space	6 x 5 grid	7(elements)	6×10^{8}	
	Jermyn et al.(1999)	Calculate Password Space	5 x 5 grid	12(elements)	2.8823×10^{17}	
Draw-a-Secret (DAS)	Chakrabarti, Landon and Singhal(2007)	Dictionary attack using 1 machine	Lmax=4	4(elements)		1.1 days
	Chakrabarti, Landon and Singhal(2007)	Dictionary attack using 1 machine	Lmax=12	12(elements)		541.8 hours
	Tao (2006)	Brute Force Attack using 1 machine				541.8 years
Pass-Go	Tao (2006)	Brute Force Attack using 1 machine on Lmax=16				1.2×10^{12} years
Grid Selection	Thorpe and van Oorschot (2004)	Brute Force Attack using 1 machine				541.8 years
Rotation Draw-a-Secret (RDAS)	Chakrabarti, Landon and Singhal(2007)	Dictionary attack using 1 machine	Lmax=12	12(elements)	$2 \wedge 141.7$	1.05×10^{38} years

Table 3 shows that BlindLogin (10^{16}) is better than a 96-alphabet 8-character Textual password (10^{14}) but worse than a 95-alphabet 10-character Textual password (10^{19}) in terms of password space. Yet, the security of BlindLogin is almost equivalent to a 40-alphabet 10-character Textual password. In addition to that, the calculated password space of BlindLogin (10^{16}) is better than the following graphical password systems: CBFG (10^{15}), PassThought (10^{15}), PassMap with 10 alphabets and 2 changes (10^{13}), Passpoints (10^{12}), Picture Password with 30 alphabets and 8 selections (10^{11}), DAS with 6×5 grid and 7 elements (10^{8}), Text with Graphical Assistance (10^{6}), Pin Number (10^{4}), Passfaces (10^{4}), Déjà vu (10^{4}) and Check-Off password (10^{4}). Conversely, the calculated password space of BlindLogin (10^{16}) is worse than the following graphical password systems: Text-based shoulder surfing resistant graphical password scheme (10^{28}), PassPhrase (10^{23}), Hybrid Password (10^{18}), Advance Secure Login (10^{16}) and SS7.0 (10^{16}).

A dictionary attack which was conducted on BlindLogin using the cloud (4 h 24 min 21 s) shows that it is weaker than RDAS (10^{28} years) and DAS (541.8 h and 1.1 days). However, in terms of a Brute-force attack, BlindLogin (48188.59 years) performs better than DAS (541.8 years) and Grid Selection (541.8 years), which are Drawmetric password schemes. Thus, BlindLogin can be considered to be reasonably secure in comparison to other password authentication schemes.

5 Conclusion

Table 4 summarizes the comparison of the UDS Model Usability Features Between BlindLogin with other authentication schemes which have been compared by Marchetto [21]. The overall results for BlindLogin shows a positive support for all the usability features of the UDS model as compared to the textual password. The results also show that the BlindLogin password is more memorable than the Object Passtiles and Image Passtiles graphical password. Hence, the initial results of this pilot study shows that the picture superiority effect also applies to the visually impaired on a graphical authentication system for the mobile platform.

The drawback of the BlindLogin prototype is that it was designed and developed as a proof of concept just to reach the objectives and obtain results to the research questions of this pilot study. Therefore, one improvement would be to create a usable Android system for everyday use as a companion to use the BlindLogin authentication function for further repeatable within-subject testing and evaluation on a wider scale. Furthermore, a password recovery feature would also be a good improvement to the system. As it stands, the current system does not support password recovery as it is only a proof-of-concept prototype for a pilot study. Therefore, further study to implement the best way to recover a lost or forgotten password could be done. Further upgrades could also be done to cater to support more languages in the audio feedback for BlindLogin.

Table 4. Comparison of UDS model features between BlindLogin versus other authentication schemes from reviewed literature [21].

	Authentication Schemes				
		Other Password Schemes			
	BlindLogin	Textual			
Usability Benefits		Passwords	PassGo	PCCP	pinPass
Memorywise Effortless	Better	No	No	No	No
Scalable for Users	No	No	No	No	Better
Nothing To Carry	Yes	Yes	Yes	Yes	Yes
Physically Effortless	Better	No	No	No	No
Easy To Learn	No	Yes	Yes	Yes	Yes
Efficient To Use	Better	Yes	Worse	Worse	Yes
Infrequent Errors	Better	Almost	Almost	Almost	Almost
Easy Recovery from Loss	No	Yes	Yes	Yes	Yes

References

1. Blonder, G.: Graphical password. US patent 5,559,961, field, 30 Aug 1995, and issued 24 Sept 1996 (1996)
2. Thorpe, J., van Oorschot, P.C.: Towards secure design choices for implementing graphical passwords. In: 20th Annual Computer Security Applications Conference, pp. 50–60 (2004)
3. Paivio, A., Rogers, T.B., Smythe, P.C.: Why are pictures easier to recall than words? Psychon. Sci. 11(4), 137–138 (1968)
4. Lin, P.L., Weng, L.T., Huang, P.W.: Graphical passwords using images with random tracks of geometric shapes. In: Proceedings - 1st International Congress on Image and Signal Processing, CISP 2008, vol. 3, pp. 27–31 (2008)
5. Khan, W.Z., Aalsalem, M.Y., Xiang, Y.: A graphical password based system for small mobile devices. Int. J. Comput. Sci. Issues 8(5), 145–154 (2011)
6. Ray, P.P.: Ray's scheme: graphical password based hybrid authentication system for smart hand held devices. J. Inf. Eng. Appl. 2(2), 1–12 (2012)
7. Stobert, E., Biddle, R.: Memory retrieval and graphical passwords. In: Proceedings of the Ninth Symposium on Usable Privacy and Security - SOUPS 2013 (2013)
8. Gehring, R.E., Toglia, M.P., Kimble, G.A.: Recognition memory for words and pictures at short and long retention intervals. Mem. Cogn. 4(3), 256–260 (1976)
9. De Angeli, A., Coventry, L., Johnson, G., Renaud, K.: Is a picture really worth a thousand words? Exploring the feasibility of graphical authentication systems. Int. J. Hum Comput Stud. 63(1–2), 128–152 (2005)
10. Crutcher, R.J., Beer, J.M.: An auditory analog of the picture superiority effect. Mem. Cogn. 39(1), 63–74 (2014)
11. Gloede, M.E., Paulauskas, E.E., Gregg, M.K.: Experience and information loss in auditory and visual memory. Q. J. Exp. Psychol. 70(7), 1344–1352 (2017)

12. Oates, J.M., Reder, L.M.: Memory for pictures: sometimes a picture is not worth a single word. In: Benjamin, A.S. (ed.) Successful Remembering and Successful Forgetting: A Festschrift in Honor of Robert A. Bjork, pp. 447–462 (2010)
13. Ho, Y.L., Azman, A., Lau, S.H.: An analysis of graphical user authentication systems. In: 9th International Conference on IT in Asia (CITA 2015) (2015)
14. Ho, Y.L., Bendrissou, B., Azman, A., Lau, S.H.: BlindLogin: a graphical authentication system with support for blind and visually impaired users on smartphones. Am. J. Appl. Sci. **14**, 551–559 (2017)
15. Dhamija, R., Perrig, A.: Déjà Vu : a user study using images for authentication. In: Human Factors (2000)
16. Brostoff, S., Sasse, M.A.: Are passfaces more usable than passwords? Field Trial Invest. HCI **2000**, 1–20 (2000)
17. Jansen, W., Gavrila, S., Korolev, V., Ayers, R., Swanstrom, R.: Picture password: a visual login technique for mobile devices. NISTIR 7030 (2003)
18. Wiedenbeck, S., Waters, J., Birget, J.-C., Brodskiy, A., Memon, N.: Authentication using graphical passwords : effects of tolerance and image choice. In: Proceedings of the 2005 Symposium on Usable Privacy and Security (SOUPS 2005), pp. 1–12 (2005)
19. Yampolskiy, R.V.: User authentication via behavior based passwords. In: Systems, Applications and Technology Conference, 2007. LISAT 2007. IEEE Long Island, pp. 1–8 (2007)
20. Stobert, E., Forget, A., Chiasson, S., Van Oorschot, P.C., Biddle, R.: Exploring usability effects of increasing security in click-based graphical passwords. In: ACSAC 2010, pp. 79–88 (2010)
21. Liu, X., Qiu, J., Ma, L., Gao, H., Ren, Z.: A novel cued-recall graphical password scheme. In: 2011 Sixth International Conference on Image and Graphics, pp. 949–956 (2011)
22. Sun, H.-M., Chen, Y.-H., Fang, C.-C., Chang, S.-Y.: PassMap: a map based graphical-password authentication system categories and subject descriptors. In: ASIACCS 2012, pp. 2–6 (2012)
23. Jermyn, I., Mayer, A., Monrose, F., Reiter, M.K., Rubin, A.D.: The design and analysis of graphical passwords. In: Proceedings of the 8th USENIX Security Symposium (1999)
24. Tao, H.: Pass-Go, a new graphical password scheme. Master's thesis, School of Information Technology and Engineering, University of Ottawa (2006)
25. Chakrabarti, S., Landon, G.V., Singal, M.: Graphical passwords: drawing a secret with rotation as a new degree of freedom. In: Proceedings of the Fourth IASTED Asian Conference on Communication Systems and Networks (AsiaCSN 2007), pp. 114–120 (2007)
26. Marchetto, J.: pinPass.js: Easy to Use, Easy to Deploy Graphical Passwords, pp. 3–5 (n.d.)
27. Mahansaria, D., Shyam, S., Samuel, A., Teja, R.: A fast and secure software solution [SS7.0] that counters shoulder surfing attack. In: Proceedings of the 13th IASTED International Conference Software Engineering and Applications (SEA 2009), pp. 190–195 (2009)
28. Zheng, Z., Liu, X., Yin, L., Liu, Z.: A hybrid password authentication scheme based on shape and text. J. Comput. **5**(5), 765–772 (2010)
29. Imran, Z., Nizami, R.: Advance secure login. Int. J. Sci. Res. Publ. **1**(1), 1–4 (2011)
30. Chen, Y.-L., Ku, W.-C., Yeh, Y.-C., Liao, D.-M.: A simple text-based shoulder surfing resistant graphical password scheme. In: 2013 International Symposium on Next-Generation Electronics, pp. 161–164 (2013)
31. Bonneau, J., Herley, C., Van Oorschot, P.C., Stajano, F.: The quest to replace passwords: a framework for comparative evaluation of web authentication schemes. In: 2012 IEEE Symposium on Security and Privacy (SP), pp. 553–567 (2012)

32. Bonner, M.N., Brudvik, J.T., Abowd, G.D., Edwards, W.K.: No-look notes: accessible eyes-free multi-touch text entry. In: Floréen, P., Krüger, A., Spasojevic, M. (eds.) Pervasive 2010. LNCS, vol. 6030, pp. 409–426. Springer, Heidelberg (2010). https://doi.org/10.1007/978-3-642-12654-3_24
33. Grussenmeyer, W., Folmer, E.: Accessible touchscreen technology for people with visual impairments: a survey. J. ACM Trans. Accessible Comput. (TACCESS) 9(2), Article no. 6 (2017)
34. Chiasson, S., Biddle, R., van Oorschot, P.C.: A second look at the usability of click-based graphical passwords. In: Symposium on Usable Privacy and Security (SOUPS) 2007, pp. 1–12 (2007)

Bluetooth Low Energy 5 Mesh Based Hospital Communication Network (B5MBHCN)

Muhammad Rizwan Ghori[1(✉)], Tat-Chee Wan[1,2], and Gian Chand Sodhy[1]

[1] School of Computer Sciences, Universiti Sains Malaysia, Penang, Malaysia
mrizwanghori@student.usm.my, sodhy@usm.my
[2] National Advanced IPv6 Centre, Universiti Sains Malaysia, Penang, Malaysia
tcwan@usm.my

Abstract. Currently, the Wireless Ad-Hoc Networks (WAHN) are becoming very common due to the advancements in the Internet of Things (IoT) technologies. For WAHN, there are many available technologies such as ZigBee, Z-Wave, Threads, Bluetooth Low Energy (BLE) etc. Despite of the improvements in IoT technologies, multicasting pure mesh-based routing is still a major problem that needs to be resolved. In view of the aforesaid, this research will propose a multicast mesh-based communication network architecture and protocol having topology auto-configuration features. Subsequently, for this study, the use case will be the hospital (being the most critical place dealing with emergencies). Furthermore, for the aforesaid use case, the BLE is supposed to be the most suitable technology being low power and easily available (in smart phone and gadgets). Initially, the BLE was introduced in Bluetooth version 4.0 and its features got matured in the advance version 4.2 and 5. BLE 5 has the capability for mesh topology that has increased the network coverage and enhanced end to end diversity of the Bluetooth based ad-hoc networks. Likewise, in this paper, the emphasis will be on proposing a pure mesh-based routing protocol capable of multicasting and topology autoconfiguration for BLE 5 enabled network for the hospital.

Keywords: Bluetooth Low Energy (BLE) · BLE 5 · Ad-hoc network · Mesh network · Hospital

1 Introduction

Bluetooth Low Energy (BLE) has emerged to be the foremost low power wireless technology. Moreover, BLE technology was introduced in Bluetooth 4.0 version in which BLE network design followed the star topology. However, this version suffered range limitation problem due to lack of mesh topology support. Moreover, in the absence of the aforesaid feature, the technology such as IEEE 802.15.4 (ZigBee etc.) has been utilized to support the mesh network. Nevertheless, Bluetooth Sig launched Bluetooth 5.0 provisioned with mesh capability in

© Springer Nature Singapore Pte Ltd. 2020
M. Anbar et al. (Eds.): ACeS 2019, CCIS 1132, pp. 247–261, 2020.
https://doi.org/10.1007/978-981-15-2693-0_18

race with other mesh technologies to support long range communication (Darroudi and Gomez 2017). Nowadays, the technologists are more biased towards the technologies supporting mesh topologies and low power consumption for better network efficiency. In view of the aforesaid, in this paper, we are proposing and discussing the BLE 5 Mesh Based Hospital Communication Network (B5MBHCN) protocol to support the staff as well as an indoor and outdoor patient.

The rest of the paper is organized in a way that in Sect. 2, the use case for B5MBHCN is discussed. In Sect. 3, the related works are discussed while Sect. 4 will debate on the potential available technologies for B5MBHCN. Furthermore, Sect. 5 is about the proposed network architecture for B5MBHCN protocol. Moreover, Sect. 6 is related to the security in IoT technologies. Subsequently, in Sect. 7, Security in BLE Networks is discussed. Also, in Sect. 8 B5MBHCN protocol security features are described. Finally Sect. 9 will conclude the paper.

2   Use Case B5MBHCN

Wireless Ad-hoc Network (WAHN) is becoming popular day by day due its unique features such as it requires no infrastructure and low power for the communication. Moreover, due its exceptional characteristics, the communication can be possible in difficult situations like earthquake, fire or in case of other accidents. Additionally, in case of the hospitals, this infrastructure less communication is necessary to cater for with the emergency situations for example to call the staff in emergency or normal condition from one location to another, medical equipment authentication, message transfer, patient convenience for getting different kinds of information after entering the hospital vicinity. Subsequently, in the event of any disaster, the communication in the hospital becomes the most important to deal with the injured people or others. For making the WAHN possible for the hospitals, there are many available technologies such as ZigBee, Z-Wave, Threads, BLE etc. (as discussed in Sect. 4). In view of the aforesaid, after the detailed research, in this paper, we have found Bluetooth Low Energy 5 (BLE 5) to be the best suited technology for the proposed B5MBHCN due to its easy availability in mobile devices, low power, low cost and mesh support characteristic. Also, after deep literature review, we have come up with the conclusion that till to date there is no Pure Mesh Solution using BLE is available. In view of the aforesaid, we are proposing a pure mesh based BLE protocol targeting the hospital (being the most critical place dealing with emergencies) where efficient and reliable communication is required.

To ensure pure mesh B5MBHCN we will focus on mesh nodes mobility, message transmission controlling, topology auto-configuration, mesh connection stability and fast handovers.

3   Related Works

The use of wireless devices and equipment has increased enormously due to rapid progression in wireless technologies. Moreover, with the passage of time, the WAHN is becoming very popular as it does not require infrastructure and thus low cost for design and development. New technologies such as ZigBee, XBee, LoRA, WiMax, BLE etc are being introduced in the market to get more efficiency.

Talking of the efficient communication, hospital is the most crucial and sensitive place. Due to its critical nature, the communication network must be user friendly, efficient and fast enough to cater for different alarming situations. In view of the aforesaid, the idea of smart hospitals came into being. According to the literature, there is not much work done for putting IoT technology in the field of smart hospitals.

There are few researches that exists in the field of IoT based smart hospitals. Iqbal et al. (2018) proposed the IoT based system capable of monitoring the hygiene and cleanliness of the hospital. Moreover, Zhang et al. (2018) introduced the IoT system capable of monitoring the real time drop rate as well as volume of drug during intravenous infusion. Also, Zilani et al. (2018) developed smart system to measure the patient ECG, respiration airflow and send the data to the remote server. Yattinahalli and Savithramma (2018) developed an IoT based system model using Raspberry Pi 3 for the provision of information related to current health status of the patient. Naik et al. (2018) proposed a system for the attendee to deal with the patient who require more attention. The system shows the stability of the patient on the smartphone with the help of flex sensor installed on patient gloves. Furthermore, Udawant et al. (2017) developed the smart ambulance system with the IoT technology to monitor the patient's critical health parameters such as ECG, heart rate etc. and send the data to the hospital with the help of GPRS. More so, Kassem et al. (2017) introduced the smart medical bed with the help of IoT technology to recognize the patient condition. Also, Cabra et al. (2017) proposed a system based on wireless sensor network for electronic health monitoring. Moreover, Dubey et al. (2017) introduced the IoT based design of digital drug administration in the hospitals. Subsequently, Thangaraj et al. (2015) proposed the IoT system that can manage and send the hospital general data.

After the detailed literature review related to the smart hospitals, up till now no work has yet been done for the IoT based communication network for smart hospitals. In view of the aforesaid, this paper will propose an IoT communication network for the hospital. Moreover, the technology being chosen for the network is BLE due to its more prominent features such as easy availability in the smart phone and other gadgets, very low power consumption, proximity control and accurate localization. Also, to make system reliable there is a requirement of mesh-based topology support that exists in BLE 5 technology which makes it a stronger candidate for this network.

BLE mesh has been introduced in many areas such as homes, factories, parking lots etc. Moreover, this section will discuss the related research works done in the past in the field of BLE mesh network design.

In 2013, Mikhaylov and Tervonan (2013) introduced for the first time the multi-hop data transfer mechanism in BLE networks. Moreover, as per the author, the solution discussed in the paper, supposed to be the first one that has been implemented and tested in practical. Also, the writer's depicted system has some limitations like security as well as the mobility of nodes. Guo et al. (2015). developed a BLE multi-hop routing protocol based on the scatter net topology features of Bluetooth 4.1 version and implemented on real hardware to get the results. According to the author, the protocol performed well in terms of delay and resource utilization. According to Balogh et al. (2015), due to the incorporation of scatter-net topology in Bluetooth 4.1, it can support long range communication. Therefore, the technology can be used in more applications as compared to its predecessor's version. In the paper, the author introduced the concept of service mediation created on Named Data Networking (NDN) concept by working on GAT and ATT layers. Furthermore, Kim et al. (2015) developed an opportunistic routing protocol for BLE mesh. Moreover, the writer compared the results with flooding and conventional routing. Subsequently, the researcher concluded that the proposed protocol works well in contrast with other routing techniques. Sirur et al. (2015) proposed a BLE Mesh Network to support mobility feature. The author developed a protype of Android Operating System for BLE Mesh Network to optimize the data routing by considering residual energy, hop count and degree. Lindemann et al. (2016) compared the BLE and Wi-Fi technology in the scenario to monitor the disoriented people movement by following the region monitoring approach. Moreover, the technique was actualized as an application for android based phones. Gogic et al. (2016) introduced a system capable of disaster prediction and monitoring by using Wireless Sensor Network technologies. Also, the author designed an improved and abridged WSN routing protocol that is developed on top of trickling routing algorithm. Moreover, the protocol was deployed utilizing BLE protocol to accomplish low power consumption. Subsequently, the writer did performance analysis of the designed algorithm in disaster situation. Furthermore, the study has given acceptable outcomes related to the performance of the system. However, according to the author, there are some limitations in the system that can be improved by using 3G cellular for long distance data transfer. Hussain et al. (2018) investigated a problem that IoT devices do not connect to multiple gateways smoothly. However, after an in-depth research, the author proposed the gateway selection mechanism for the transmission of connection associated information to the optimum gateways. Moreover, the analysis has shown reduced overhead and low latency. Jung et al. (2017) developed the Cluster Based on Demand Routing Protocol to support multi hop communication in BLE networks. Moreover, the author concluded that the energy consumption has reduced due to the adoption of the aforesaid routing technique. Leonardi et al. (2018) did research for developing the first multi-hop real time protocol on top of the BLE for the industrial purpose. Moreover, the author adopted the connection-oriented approach for the utilization of all 37 data channel for the communication. The main idea in the design of the protocol was to break (subdivide) a network into clusters (small networks). The protocol was created for Industrial Wireless Sensor Networks (IWSN) to enable the BLE mesh network for provision of bounded packet delays to support real time communication. Celia

Table 1. BLE comparative study

Ref	Year	Works	BLE 4	BLE 5	Topology			
					Beacon (Only)	Simple M-Hop	Star Mesh	Pure Mesh
Mikhaylov	2013	BLE MHDTS	Yes	No	No	Yes	No	No
Guo et al.	2015	BLE-based AODMHRP	Yes	No	No	No	Yes	No
Kim et al.	2015	BLE Mesh	Yes	No	No	Yes	No	No
Lindemann et al.	2016	A Comparison of Wi-Fi and BLE for Region Monitoring	Yes	No	Yes	No	No	No
Gogic et al.	2016	Performance Analysis of BLE Mesh Routing Algorithm	Yes	No	No	No	Yes	No
Jung et al.	2017	Topology Configuration and Multi-Hop RP for BLE	Yes	No	No	No	Yes	No
Leonardi et al.	2018	Multi-Hop Real-Time Communications Over BLE Industrial WMN	Yes	No	No	No	Yes	No
Celia et al.	2018	Heterogeneous IoT Mesh Network Deployment for Industry 4.0	No	No	No	No	Yes	No
		B5MBHCN	No	Yes	No	No	No	Yes

et al. (2018) developed a heterogeneous network with the combination of BLE and LoRa for the security of the operators in the industrial environment. In the paper, the author has investigated to explore key empowering IoT technologies for collaborative network in Industry 4.0 conditions.

Moreover, after the detailed discussion on available literature, the Table 1 is showing the results of comparative study.

4   Potential Available IoT Mesh Based Technologies for B5MBHCN System

This section will discuss the potential available technologies that can be utilized for designing of B5MBHCN system.

4.1   ZigBee

ZigBee is a wireless mesh supported technology based on IEEE standard 802.15.4. Moreover, it is cost-effective with the capacity to work for months or years on batteries. Also, the technology is being utilized throughout the world in various applications due its reliability and low-cost (Ghori et al. 2018). ZigBee devices can be configured as ZigBee End Device (ZED), ZigBee Router (ZR) and ZigBee Coordinator (ZC).

4.2 WiFi

Wi-Fi is a widespread wireless technology that uses radio frequencies for data transmission. Wi-Fi allows wire free fast speed internet connections. It uses the standard IEEE 802.11 consisting of sub classes such as 802.11 a/b/g/n/ac. However, the version n and ac are being used nowadays for high speed data transfer with greater efficiency. Subsequently, "n" was commercialized in 2009 and boosted the market of Wi-Fi. It was embedded with the latest features such as Multiple Input and Multiple Output (MIMO), Orthogonal Frequency Division Multiplexing (OFDM), Space Time Block Coding, cyclic delay diversity etc. These additional capabilities improved the throughput and coverage up to 150 Mbps and 250 m respectively. Also, IEEE 802.11 ac released in 2013 with additional feature of multiuser MIMO.

4.3 Z-Wave

It is an interoperable, low powered Radio Frequency (RF) based wireless communication technology that supports full mesh network. It operates in the sub-1GHz band, thus impervious to interferences from other wireless technologies like Wi-Fi and Bluetooth, ZigBee that operates on 2.4 GHz frequency band. Moreover, it is designed for control and status applications. It supports data rates up to 100 kbps, IPV6 and multichannel operation with backwards compatibility to all predecessor versions.

4.4 Threads

Thread is a wireless mesh network supported protocol based on IPV6 principles. It is designed to support low power IoT devices (IEEE 802.15.4-2006). Moreover, the protocol is independent from other IoT mesh protocols like ZigBee, Z-Wave and BLE. Also, it is simple, secure, reliable and easy to scale.

Table 2. BLE versions comparison (RF wirless world 2018)

Features	Bluetooth 5	Bluetooth 4.2
Speed	Supports up to 2 Mbps	1 Mbps
Range	Outdoor: 200 m with LOS Indoor: 40 m	Outdoor: 50 m Indoor: 10 m
Power Requirement	Low	High
Message Capacity	Large, about 255 bytes	Small, around 31 bytes Actual Data Payload: 17 to 20 bytes
Robustness to operate in congested environment	More	Less
Battery Life	Longer	Smaller
Security Control	Better	Less secure compare to Bluetooth 5.0
Theoretical Data Throughput	2 Mbps. gives about 1.6 Mbps with overhead	1 Mbps
Reliability	High	Low
Digital Life	Better	Less good compare to Bluetooth 5
Support for IoT devices	Yes	No
Bluetooth Beacon	More Speed and Range	Not Popular in this version due to less speed, range and message capacity

4.5   Bluetooth Low Energy (BLE)

BLE is low power consumption light-weight version of classic Bluetooth (Jung et al. 2017). There are quite number of protocols available for mesh networking but what makes BLE so much preferred is its availability in any modern mobile devices. Moreover, BLE architecture follows the same protocol stack as classical Bluetooth BR/EDR consisting of the controller and the host. More so, all applications are developed on top of GAP and GATT layers. Also, Table 2 is showing the difference between BLE version 4.2 and 5. Furthermore, Fig. 1 is depicting the BLE Protocol Stack mainly consisting of physical layer, link layer, L2CAP, GAP and GATT.

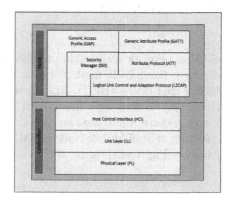

Fig. 1. BLE protocol stack (Leonardi et al. 2018)

Table 3. Mesh based IoT technologies comparison

Characteristics	Zigbee	Sub-GHz	Wi-Fi	Bluetooth	BLE
Physical layer standard	802.15.4	802.15.4 g	802.11	802.15.1	802.15.1
Application focus	Monitoring, control	Monitoring, control	Web	Short range wirless communication	Monitoring, control, low power, proximity control, accurate localization
Speed	Up to 250 kbps	Up to 200 kbps	Up to 72 kbps	2 Mbps	2 Mbps
Battery life (in days)	200–1000+	1000+	0.5–5	1–7	Up to years
Network size	100 s–1000 s	10 s–100 s	32	7	With Mesh Topology can be more than 1000 s
Range (meters)	1–100+	1–7000+	1–30+	1–10+	Long range with mesh topology
Network architecture	Mesh	Point-point, star	Star	Star	Star, mesh
Optimized for	Reliability, low, power, low cost, scalability	Low range, low power, low cost,	Speed	Low cost and convenient	Low cost, very low power, convenient, ble beaconing, reliability

Subsequently, after the detailed literature review and discussion on the technologies available for B5MBHCN, the Table 3 is showing the comparison of all the technologies.

In view of the aforesaid discussion on the IoT technologies and the literature review, the BLE technology is best suited for B5MBHCN due to its easy availability in mobile devices, low power consumption and support for mesh topology. Moreover, talking of the topologies, the mesh ad-hoc network can be either an individual network without the gateway or there can be a network connected to the gateway. However, for this paper, there is no gateway involved in the B5MBHCN.

5   Proposed Network Architecture for B5MBHCN Protocol

The proposed communication network architecture for B5MBHCN is shown in Fig. 2. The network will have fixed BLE mesh network in the hospital comprised of fixed nodes (BLE Fixed Nodes (BFN), BLE Beacon (BB)). Moreover, B5MBHCN will have the ability to deal with the moving nodes as well. Subsequently, in the network architecture, there are two categories of BLE 5 enabled Mobile Node (BMN) consisting of Staff Mobile Node (BSMN) and Guests Mobile Node (BGMN). Furthermore, Fig. 3 is showing the message passing diagram related to the nodes.

Fig. 2. B5MBHCN network architecture

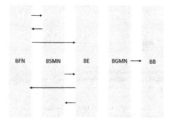

Fig. 3. B5MBHCN message passing diagram

More so, following sub-sections will explain different processes as how the node will join the mesh network, node message transmission process and the procedure for the node to leave the network.

5.1 BLE Node Joins B5MBHCN

BSMN's will be permanently part of B5MBHCN. Initially, as per the protocol all nodes will be considered as BGMN by B5MBHCN. When the node will enter the network, it will be authenticated with the help of BGMN Serial and IMEI number. Moreover, if the node verification will be positive then it will become part of B5MBHCN being BSMN. Also, the protocol will do the topology auto configuration and management. More so, if the system will not authenticate the device then it will be designated as BGMN (not part of B5MBHCN) and can only play with the beacons. Subsequently, the Fig. 4 is showing the process.

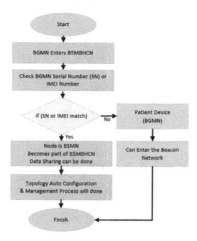

Fig. 4. Node joining B5MBHCN

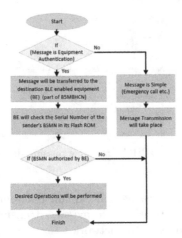

Fig. 5. Node message transmission in B5MBHCN

5.2   BLE Nodes Message Transmission in B5MBHCN

In the proposed protocol, the message transmission is segregated as medical equipment (BLE enabled Equipment (BE)) authentication messages and simple messages like emergency call etc. For instance, when BSMN will send an authentication message to BE, according to the protocol, BE will check the serial number in its flash memory. Moreover, if the sender node is authorized to operate the equipment, the operation will be performed else the task will be finished. Subsequently, simple message transmission will occur except BE authorization messages. The flow chart in Fig. 5 is depicting the scenario.

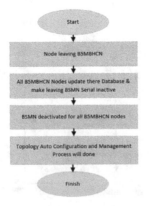

Fig. 6. Node leaving B5MBHCN

5.3 BLE Device Leave B5MBHCN

According to the proposed protocol, the node traceability is only up to BSMN (not for BGMN). If some BSMN will leave the network, its serial number will be deactivated from the nodes databases as shown in Fig. 6.

6 Security (Authentication) in IoT Technology

Talking of authentication, it is a process of matching the credentials entered by the user with the saved one in the relevant device (server) (Ghori and Ghani 2018). Before going into the discussion of the studies associated with authentication protocols for IoT technologies, the following will discuss different attacks to which IoT networks or devices are vulnerable.

6.1 Man in the Middle (MITM) Attacks

MITM is considered to be one of the major attacks for IoT as well as any kind of network. In this attack the attacker intrudes in the communication between the two parties and do the manipulation of the transmitted data in a manner that sender and receiver think they are directly communicating with each other.

6.2 Eavesdropping Attacks

In addition to MITM, Eavesdropping is another threat to the network. eavesdropping is also known as a sniffing or snooping attack. This attack is an invasion where some intruder steal information that any device transmits over a network.

6.3 Replay Attacks

In Replay attack, an attacker may spy (eavesdrop) legitimate messages transmitted during an authentication session. In the later stage, the attacker replays few of these messages to pretend genuine entity for creating a trustworthy session with the target device.

6.4 Impersonation Attacks

In impersonation attack, the malicious user may pretend as a legitimate node or device. These attacks can be in the form of email showing an attacker as a valid user who wants to gain access to the data.

6.5 Works Related to Authentication in IoT

Subsequently, there are some researches done on the authentication protocol for IoT device to device communication to mitigate these security breaches. Fu et al. 2012 developed a group-based authentication protocol for mobile WiMAX networks. Moreover, the protocol is partial capable of mitigating the MITM, Eavesdrop, Replay and Impersonation attacks. Subsequently, Lai et al. (2013) introduced a light weight protocol for authentication in LTE networks for machine type communication capable of mitigating MITM and Replay attack. Also, it can partly cater for Eavesdropping. Moreover, it does not have the capability to cater for the Impersonation attack. Furthermore, Lai et al. (2013), developed another security protocol for LTE network which can cover the MITM and Replay attacks. Lai et al. (2014) proposed secure roaming scheme machine-machine communication that can handle partially the MITM attacks. Also, Lai et al. (2016) developed another secure authentication scheme for machine-machine communication capable of mitigating MITM attack. Chen et al. (2017) proposed a fingerprint-based authentication protocol that can create some sort hindrance against the MITM and Replay attacks. Moreover, Chuang et al. (2018) proposed a lightweight authentication protocol specifically for IoT devices. The protocol has ability to do static as well as continuous and dynamic authentication. Moreover, it can defend against MITM, Impersonation, Eavesdropping and Replay attacks. Subsequently, Moon and Lee (2012) developed an authentication protocol for ad-hoc networks. Moreover, the protocol can authenticate multi-party devices. In summarized form, the authentication will be done based on authentication IDs. Each device in a network will generate and authentication ID and values for broadcasting. The scheme is efficient enough to fight against the MITM, Eavesdropping and Replay attacks.

Moreover, the discussion related to previous researches conclude that the most prominent authentication protocol that can provide higher level security checks for B5MBHCN is the one developed by Chuang et al. (2018) that mitigate all major attacks. In view of the aforesaid, besides the low level built-in BLE security options, the proposed B5MBHCN will be embedded with the authentication protocol for the provision of more secure communication.

7   Security in BLE Networks

In comparison with the predecessor versions of Bluetooth, the version 5 came up with the new advanced features to strengthen the capabilities of IoT based equipment. Due to the enhancement in Bluetooth specifications like more range (up to 200 m) and data rate (2 Mbps) have also increased the security risks. Likewise, with the improved range, the attackers can access the connection even from more distance. Furthermore, with enhanced data transmission speed, the hackers can quickly get the data they require and go offline with in no time. BLE was introduced in the market as low power consumption technology. Due to this feature its security mechanism is quite different from Bluetooth BR/EDR/HS. BLE device pairing results in the generation of Long-Term Key (LTK) instead of the Link Key (LK) as in case of its predecessor versions. For Low Energy versions, the pairing can be done in one of the two ways i.e. Low Energy Legacy Pairing (LLP) and Low Energy Secure Connection (LESC) (introduced in version 4.2).

Also, there are association models for low energy pairing called as Low Energy Pairing Association Models (LEPAM). Like in the classic Bluetooth, the LEPAM is adopted, depending on the input and output capabilities of both devices. The version 4.0 and 4.1 is designed for three methods such as Out of Band (OOB),

Pass Key Entry (PKE), Just Work (JW). Moreover, 4.2 and 5 specification added a device pairing feature i.e. Secure Connection and new method has been introduced named as Numeric Comparison which has proven to be the best for BLE authentication as compared to other methods.

8 B5MBHCN Protocol Security Features

For B5MBHCN, we will utilize Numeric Comparison (as the proposed system requires security) pairing mechanism as it supports LESC. Also, it has some built-in specified security features to cater for against different attacks like eavesdropping. Likewise, the BLE 5 enabled devices utilized in the proposed system will be having displaying as well as typing capability.

Moreover, Bluetooth being the wireless technology is vulnerable to some popular security attacks like MITM, Eavesdropping. In view of the aforesaid, for the proposed protocol design we will embed the authentication protocol developed by Chuang et al. (2018) with the built in BLE authentication features to make it more secure in comparison with the present specifications. Subsequently, it will be more effective against MITM attacks by providing user authentication, ensuring more secure storage of link key and proper handling of the continuous device discovery mode.

9 Conclusion

In this paper, we have done the comparative study related to the BLE mesh networking. According to the literature review, BLE 5 suits best for our proposed system as it requires commonly available Bluetooth enabled wearables and mobile phones. Moreover, the network needs reliability and long range which can be achieved with BLE 5 mesh support. Likewise, we have proposed B5MBHCN protocol and network architecture after a detailed review of wireless mesh technologies. Subsequently, we have discussed the proposed protocol functions like mobile node entering or leaving the network and how the message transmission will occur. Moreover, in next upcoming paper we will show the protocol implementation results along with the detailed discussion of algorithms.

References

Balogh, A., et al.: Service mediation in multi-hop Bluetooth low energy networks based on NDN approach. In: Proceedings of the Twenty Third International Conference on Software, Telecommunications and Computer Networks, Croatia, pp. 285–289 (2015)

Bluetooth Sig, Bluetooth Low Energy. http://www.bluetooth.com/. Accessed 28 Oct 2018

Cabra, J., et al.: An IoT approach for wireless sensor networks applied to e-health environmental monitoring. In: Proceedings of the IEEE International Conference on Internet of Things (iThings), pp. 578–583. (2017)

Celia, G.H., et al.: IoT heterogeneous mesh network deployment for human-in-the-loop challenges towards a social and sustainable industry 4.0. IEEE Access J. **6**, 28417–28437 (2018)

Chen, D., et al.: S2M: a lightweight acoustic fingerprints based wireless device authentication protocol. IEEE IoT J. **4**(1), 88–100 (2017)

Chuang, Y.H., et al.: A lightweight continuous authentication protocol for the Internet of Things. Sens. J. **18**(4), 1–26 (2018)

Darroudi, S.M., Gomez, C.: Bluetooth low energy mesh networks: a survey. Sensors **17**(7), 1467 (2017)

Dubey, S., et al.: IoT application for the design of digital drug administration interface. In: Proceedings of the International Conference on Information, Communication, Instrumentation and Control (ICICIC), pp. 1–5 (2017)

Fu, A., et al.: A novel group-based handover authentication scheme with privacy preservation for mobile WiMAX networks. IEEE Commun. Lett. **16**(11), 1744–1747 (2012)

Ghori, M.R., et al.: Hybrid communication network architecture for palm oil supply chain traceability (POSCT) system. Sindh Univ. Res. J. **50**(3D), 227–232 (2018)

Ghori, M.R., Ghani, A.: Review of access control mechanisms in cloud computing. J. Physic.: Conf. Ser. **1049**, 012092 (2018)

Gogic, A., et al.: Performance analysis of bluetooth low energy mesh routing algorithm in case of disaster prediction. Int. J. Comput. Electr. Autom. Control Inf. Eng. **10**(6), 1075–1081 (2016)

Guo, Z., et al.: An on-demand scatter-net formation and multi-hop routing protocol for BLE-based wireless sensor networks. In: Proceedings of the IEEE Wireless Communication and Networking Conference, New Orleans, LA, USA, pp. 1590–1595 (2015)

Hussain, S.R., et al.: Secure seamless bluetooth low energy connection migration for unmodified IoT devices. IEEE Trans. Mob. Comput. **17**(4), 927–944 (2018)

Iqbal, U., et al.: Intelligent hospital based on IoT. In: Proceedings of the Fourth International Conference on Advances in Electrical, Electronics, Information, Communication and Bio-Informatics (AEEICB), pp. 1–3 (2018)

Jung, C., et al.: Topology configuration and multi-hop routing protocol for Bluetooth low energy networks. IEEE Access J. **5**, 9587–9598 (2017)

Kassem, A.: MedBed: smart medical bed. In: Proceedings of the Fourth International Conference on Advances in Biomedical Engineering (ICABME), pp. 1–4 (2017)

Kim, H. et al.: BLE Mesh: a wireless mesh network protocol for Bluetooth low energy devices. In: Proceedings of the Third International Conference on Future Internet of Things and Cloud, Rome, Italy, pp. 558–563 (2015)

Lai, C., et al.: GLARM: group-based lightweight authentication scheme for resource constrained machine to machine communications. Comput. Netw. **99**, 66–81 (2016)

Lai, C., et al.: SEGR: a secure and efficient group roaming scheme for machine to machine communications between 3GPP and WiMAX networks. In: Proceedings of the 2014 1st IEEE International Conference on Communications, pp. 1011–1016 (2014)

Lai, C., et al.: SE-AKA: a secure and efficient group authentication and key agreement protocol for LTE networks. Comput. Netw. **57**(17), 3492–3510 (2013)

Lai, C., et al.: LGTH: a light weight group authentication protocol for machine-type communication in LTE networks. In: Proceeding of the IEEE Global Communications Conference (GLOBECOM 2013), pp. 832–837 (2013)

Leonardi, L., Gaetano, P., Bello, L.L.: Multi-hop real-time communications over BLE industrial wireless mesh network. IEEE Access J. **6**, 26505–26519 (2018)

Lindemann, A., et al.: Indoor positioning: a comparison of WiFi and Bluetooth low energy for region monitoring. In: Proceedings of the Ninth International Joint Conference on Bio-Medical Engineering Systems and Technologies, Rome, Italy, pp. 314–321 (2016)

Mikhaylov, K., Tervonan, J.: Multi-hop data transfer service for Bluetooth low energy. In: Proceedings of the Thirteenth International Conference on ITS Telecommunications, Tampere, Finland, pp. 319–324 (2013)

Moon, J.S., Lee, I.Y.: Authentication protocol using an identifier in an ad-hoc network environment. Math. Comput. Model. 55(1–2), 134–141 (2012)

Naik, A., et al.: IoT medical attendee. In: Proceedings of the ICACCT, pp. 384–387 (2018)

RF Wireless World, Home of RF and Wireless Vendors and Resources. http://www.rfwireless-world.com. Accessed 20 Nov 2018

Sirur, S., et al.: A mesh network for mobile devices using Bluetooth low energy. In: Proceedings of the 2015 IEEE Sensors, Busan, South Korea, pp. 1–4 (2015)

Thangaraj, M., et al.: Internet of Things (IoT) enabled smart autonomous hospital management system - a real world health care use case with the technology drivers. In: Proceedings of the IEEE ICCIC, pp. 1–8 (2015)

Udawant, O., et al.: Smart ambulance system using IoT. In: Proceedings of the International Conference on Big Data, IoT and Data Science (BID), pp. 171–176 (2017)

Yattinahalli, S. and Savithramma, R.M.: A personal healthcare IoT system model using raspberry Pi 3. In: Proceedings of the Second International Conference on Inventive Communication and Computational Technologies (ICICCT), pp. 569–573 (2018)

Zhang, H., et al.: Connecting intelligent things in smart hospitals using NB-IoT. IEEE Internet Things J. 5(3), 1550–1560 (2018)

Zilani, K.A., et al.: R3HMS, an IoT based approach for patient health monitoring. In: Proceedings of the IC4ME2, pp. 1–4 (2018)

Wireless Sensor Network for Temperature and Humidity Monitoring Systems Based on NodeMCU ESP8266

Wong G. Shun, W. Mariam W. Muda⑩, W. Hafiza W. Hassan⑩, and A. Z. Annuar$^{(\boxtimes)}$⑩

Faculty of Ocean Engineering Technology and Informatics,
Universiti Malaysia Terengganu, 21030 Kuala Nerus, Terengganu, Malaysia
{w.mariam,whafiza,zannuar}@umt.edu.my

Abstract. The paper describes the development of a Wireless Sensor Network for Temperature and Humidity Monitoring System. The prototype is based on NodeMCU ESP8266 module that automatically record the current parameters and allowing the user to interact with the monitoring system wirelessly. A total of three wireless microcontrollers are used as sensor nodes and actuator node to form a wireless sensor network. Each node is connecting to online cloud storage that helps to receive, process and send the information to and from the desired nodes. The data communication from the wireless sensor nodes to the cloud database is done via MATLAB ThingSpeak. Within the monitoring system facility, the access network is based on ESP8266 Wi-Fi network, which are enabling the concept of Internet of Things. The monitoring system is deployed to the room exhaust ventilation system (REVS) which include 3G technology in it allowed the stand-alone REVS system monitoring remotely via web or mobile application at low cost. Experimental results show that the system is capable to use a unified approach to recording, displaying and controlling the temperature and humidity parameters through several IoT platforms: MATLAB ThingSpeak, ThingView App and REVS mobile application developed using MIT App inventor.

Keywords: Wireless sensor network · Remote monitoring · Ventilation system · Internet of Things · Cloud database · MATLAB ThingSpeak

1 Introduction

Wireless sensor network (WSN) is referring to a group of spatially distributed and dedicated sensors that are connected in the same wireless network, where the collected data can be transfer wirelessly. WSN is actually built with several nodes, and a gateway or central node by connecting each other wirelessly at a different location. Each node is consisting of the wireless transceiver, antenna, a microcontroller, electric circuit with the sensors and energy source. The combination of sensors of the node is depending on the user's requirement and condition of the environment. The function of the WSN system is to monitoring and recording the physical conditions of the environment, and

M. Anbar et al. (Eds.): ACeS 2019, CCIS 1132, pp. 262–273, 2020.
https://doi.org/10.1007/978-981-15-2693-0_19

send the collected data to the central location, such as online cloud storage and wait for further investigation or analysis to perform an autonomous task [1].

One of the primary needs for people is a place to stay thus it must be intelligently built to provide healthy, pleasant and secure to keep place in comfort. The domain of intelligent building are listed in [2–6] including indoor environment monitoring, lighting, power management, buildings security, cooling, heating, ventilation, natural day lighting, fire safety and early fire detection system, and building health management. Among all the listed domains, this study focused on the ventilation system.

The exhaust ventilation system is one of the cheapest and most energy-efficient way to improve indoor air quality (IAQ). IAQ has direct implication on occupant's health and well-being [7]. The parameters of air quality such as carbon dioxide, oxygen, carbon monoxide, methanol and volatile organic compounds influence the human health and are responsible for diseases like eye and throat infection, coronary artery disease, asthma, pneumonia, and chronic pulmonary disease [8, 9]. Hence, ventilation system is important in order to sustain occupant's health standard.

The room exhaust ventilation system (REVS) is one of the cheapest and most energy-efficient ways to improve indoor air quality. The REVS is such a method working by depressurizing the room by reducing the air pressure inside the room and let the outdoor air infiltrates through leaks or windows of the room [10]. Generally, the outdoor air is fresher and clean, as the fresh air is moving through the room; it helps to remove pollutants such as odors, gases, particles, moisture and so on. Another best thing about this system is the indoor temperature will stay equilibrium as the outdoor temperature due to the air replacement.

Numerous works have been carried out to propose various techniques of ventilation system including model-based air balancing method for ventilation system [11], an experimental study of energy saving potential in mixing and displacement ventilation with wireless sensor network [12], an energy efficient heat exchanger for ventilation systems [13], and also energy savings and manifold supply ventilation systems [14]. The work in [15] proposed ventilation system that provided the automatic self-sensor-based aeration control that measures the fine pressure decrease in the room using the aeration fan itself without user interference. In contrast, a mathematical approach is employed in [16] to develop the mathematical model of multi-area network ventilation based on the actual content of a multi-area network and uses this as a basis for a computing system. Further, a multi-area network ventilation software is developed to realize input integration, simplify parameter definition, and model typification. Recently, the work in [17] integrated automatic control system of ventilation and air conditioning systems based on the organization of energy-saving air treatment modes in order to improve the economic efficiency of the equipment. Interestingly, the study on ventilation potential strategies in warm winter climate zones are carried out in [18] and [19] for buildings in China and Dubai respectively. Both studies aim to utilize the natural cooling sources in climatic ventilation as a mean to reduce the energy consumption of air conditioning in buildings.

Motivated from these approaches and considering the weather pattern in Terengganu, Malaysia, which is very hot during daytime, and cold at the night, this paper proposed a proper, low cost and efficient ventilation system with the WSN monitoring system. The proposed REVS system is located at specific location in university building and the device will record data of both temperature and humidity of room environment and room ambient. The collected data later will be analyzed by the microcontroller NodeMCU and it will trigger the actuator node to maintaining the people comfort. The main objective of data collection is to study the difference between indoor and outdoor climate condition and evaluate its situation before finding a way to conduct necessary actions.

The proposed system consists of humidity and temperature sensors DHT11, microcontrollers NodeMCU, Wi - Fi router, and exhaust fan. Sensors and actuator fan forming microcontroller nodes that are connected wirelessly and located separately. Thus, each node is actually the fusion of microcontroller with the sensor or actuator, a wireless transceiver module, and power supply. The function of these nodes is to share the information retrieved from a data acquisition through wireless networking. In this case, the sensing parameters are the indoor and outdoor temperature and humidity, whereas the exhaust fan is the actuator. The components and nodes are shown in Fig. 1.

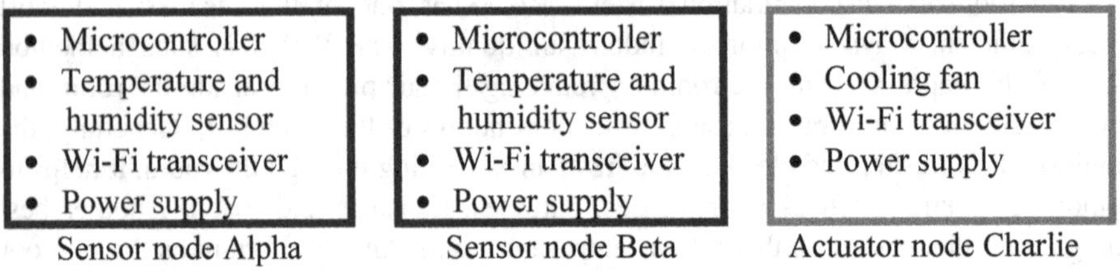

Sensor node Alpha	Sensor node Beta	Actuator node Charlie
• Microcontroller • Temperature and humidity sensor • Wi-Fi transceiver • Power supply	• Microcontroller • Temperature and humidity sensor • Wi-Fi transceiver • Power supply	• Microcontroller • Cooling fan • Wi-Fi transceiver • Power supply

Fig. 1. Components and nodes in this system

Besides that, the data collected from the sensor nodes are storing in online cloud storage. The information will be processed and ready to be received and executed by the actuator node. A mobile application will be created for this system to manipulate, view and control the whole system. Hence, it is able to connect to the wireless network, sharing the information between nodes, and interacting with the user by the mobile application.

2 Methodology

2.1 General Description

The block diagram of the proposed room exhaust ventilation based WSN system is shown in Fig. 2. The system consists of two sensing nodes connected to NodeMCU ESP8266, MATLAB ThingSpeak for visualization from cloud storage, ventilation fan as an actuator and mobile phone to display the monitoring parameters through mobile app, either developed from MIT App inventor or downloaded from Google play store, ThingView.

This system uses two sensor nodes and one actuator node for measuring the parameters and executing the program. The collected data is sent to ThingSpeak (cloud platform) via a wireless network connection from a router. After that, the data is retrieved by the actuator node for the exhaust fan activation, as well as displaying on the mobile app. The mobile app also allows the user to control the fan in three modes: ON, OFF, and AUTO.

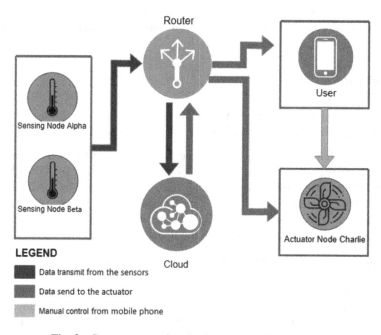

Fig. 2. Components and nodes in smart ventilation system

2.2   Hardware

NodeMCU Microcontroller. NodeMCU is popular in the light weighted electrical project with the main purpose of controlling the operation of the system, especially for the Internet of Things (IoT) system. It provides open-source, programmable and Wi-Fi enabled environment for the developer. As compared to other microcontrollers, such as Arduino, NodeMCU is more precise in size, lower cost and less energy consumption due to the IoT project [20]. These features cause it very suitable for this project.

Temperature and Humidity Sensor (DHT11). DHT 11 is a cheap common sensor used to detect the surrounding environment's temperature and humidity information.

DHT 11 comes with a dedicated Negative Temperature Coefficient (NTC) to measure and output the values of the temperature and humidity as serial data. This sensor can measure temperature form 0 °C to 50 °C and humidity with range 20% to 90% with accuracy ± 1 °C and ±1%. Due to DHT 11 offers perfect quality, fast response, anti-interference on measurement, and low cost [21].

Exhaust Fan. A common exhaust fan that is connected to the actuator node Charlie to depressurize the structure, and hence enhances the air circulation in a structure. Due to the difficulty on the real exhaust ventilation system, the exhaust fan is replacing to exhaust fan in the constructed model. The exhaust fan has a dimension approximately of 20 cm × 20 cm × 4 cm, which can support maximum direct current (DC) of 240 V and 1.52 ± 10% A of rated current with a rated speed of 4500 ± 10% rpm.

Li-ion Rechargeable Battery. Act as the DC power supply to the system. Each node required two units of 18650 batteries in order to supply a nominal voltage of 7.4 V to the microcontroller.

2.3   Software

Arduino IDE. Arduino IDE is used as the programming software for the NodeMCU due to it is using the hardware that is similar to microcontroller Arduino.

ThingSpeak. ThingSpeak is an open source online cloud platform that enables the user to upload and download the data to it as online memory storage. ThingSpeak is integrated with many other open source features such as MATLAB Analysis, MATLAB Visualizations, ThingTweet, TimeControl and etc. Those features are providing benefit on processing the uploaded data. In this paper, MATLAB Analysis and TimeControl feature are used to compute the uploaded data automatically.

MIT App Inventor 2. An open source website-based software that is developed by the Massachusetts Institute of Technology (MIT). This software is using for developing a mobile application. It supports many features on the mobile phone. For instance, the Graphical User Interface (GUI) design, mobile phone sensor accessibility, storage accessibility, connectivity on Bluetooth or Wi-Fi and etc. MIT App Inventor 2 is requiring and recommended to develop a mobile application by using the computer and test the developed app in real-time with a mobile phone. Furthermore, MIT App Inventor 2 is currently supported in developing an Android-based Operating System (OS)'s mobile application only, and it is programmable in Blocks Editor with autosave ability.

2.4   Development of Nodes

In this paper, the Alpha sensor node is acted as the indoor sensor node, whereas the Beta sensor node is acted as the outdoor sensor node. Temperature and humidity sensor DHT 11 is attached to Alpha and Beta node, for collecting the indoor and outdoor temperature and humidity parameters. Then, the sensor nodes are programmed as the flow chart shown in Fig. 3 using Arduino IDE.

According to Fig. 3, the sensor nodes, Alpha and Beta are powered on, then, the sensor nodes are started collecting data. The data is sent and stored at the cloud data logger using ThingSpeak channels. Then, Charlie node retrieved the information from ThingSpeak, and the value of the error is checked as a positive or negative value. If one of the errors is a positive value, then the exhaust fan is activated. Then, the instruction is looped back to the retrieving data of the actuator node, and the retrieved data are checked again and only stop functioning when the power is switched to off. Error is computed using the following equations:

$$\text{Humidity error} = \text{Alpha Humidity} - \text{Beta Humidity} \tag{1}$$

$$\text{Temperature error} = \text{Alpha Temperature} - \text{Beta Temperature} \tag{2}$$

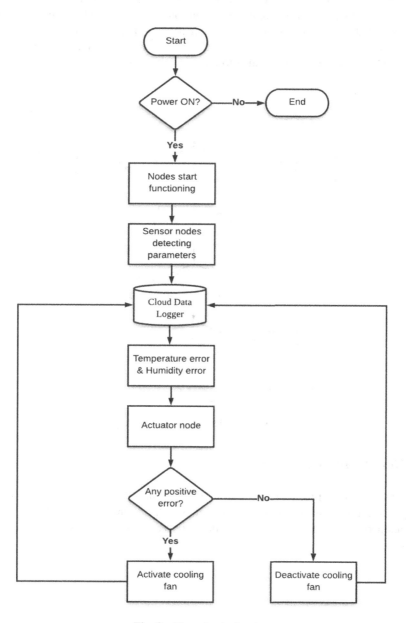

Fig. 3. Flow chart of nodes

2.5   Development of the Mobile App

After the three nodes are programmed and functioned, a mobile app is developed using MIT App Inventor 2. The overall flow for the mobile app for this smart system is shown in Fig. 4. This mobile application is functioned while the application on the mobile phone is opened and the data from ThingSpeak is displayed on the mobile application to the user. Besides that, the smart system is chosen to run in auto mode and manual mode by communicating to the actuator node, and it is ordered to be activated or deactivated the fan in manual mode. After that, the latest information recorded in ThinSpeak is displayed to the user again after few minutes. The mobile application is exited only when the user is decided to quit.

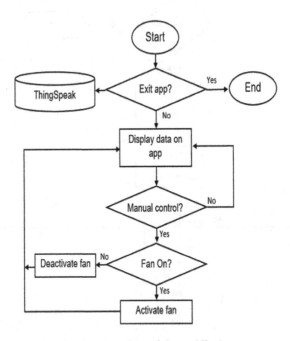

Fig. 4. Flow chart of the mobile App

3   Results and Discussion

This system is tested for four hours, from 4:44 pm until 9:08 pm because the outdoor temperature drops and humidity increases drastically during this hour. The humidity and temperature parameters during the time are recorded in ThingSpeak channels as shown in Figs. 5, 6 and 7.

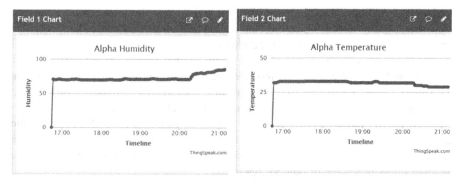

Fig. 5. Visualization of parameters recorded in ThingSpeak channels for Alpha

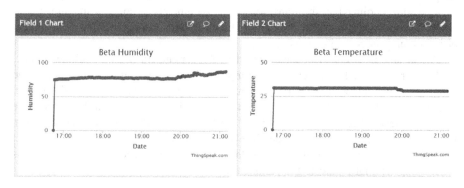

Fig. 6. Visualization of parameters recorded in ThingSpeak channels for Beta

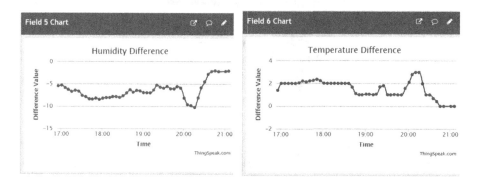

Fig. 7. Visualization of parameters recorded in ThingSpeak channels for humidity and temperature difference

Refer to Figs. 5, 6 and 7 for humidity parameter, the indoor humidity is consistent at the evening, and raised dramatically after 8:00 p.m. However, the outdoor humidity is fluctuated during evening, and raised during the night. The indoor humidity is manipulated with the outdoor humidity due to the activation of cooling fan. Hence, the humidity difference value was getting smaller as shown in Fig. 7. The increasing value of humidity percentage of both nodes is because of the humidity level is increasing at the night. In addition, there is a sudden drop in Fig. 7 at the time around 8:00p.m., while dramatically increasing of the outdoor humidity level has caused the large difference value compare to the indoor humidity value.

The same phenomena was happened again at the temperature reading of both nodes. From Figs. 5, 6 and 7, the temperature has a steady flow at the beginning of the experiment. Then, the temperature reading in Alpha node is dipped slightly due to exchanging the air from the outdoor started around 7:45 p.m. After that, the temperature reading of both nodes dropped significantly around 8:00 p.m. This is due to the sun has set at that time, and causing the temperature surrounding is decreasing. The difference of temperature reading is plotted in Fig. 7, with having a sudden rose due to the large difference value of outdoor parameter.

Besides that, the system took approximately four hours to reduce the humidity and temperature differences nearly to zero. Since the exhaust fan used in this system is a small scaling cooling fan, the transition of the parameters is not in a maximize condition. Therefore, the system required more time to achieve an equilibrium environment of indoor and outdoor situations.

Alpha and Beta channels have recorded the parameters in every single minute, while Charlie channel is retrieved and computed the average and the difference of the data from Alpha and Beta in every five minutes. The processed data in Charlie channel is then retrieved by Charlie actuator node to perform its autonomous task. At the same time, the latest collected data is displayed on the developed mobile app as shown in Fig. 8. The fan stays in AUTO mode if the user is not switching it to ON or OFF mode. The ON and OFF mode of the fan is isolated from the parameters, which means it is functioning without regard to the parameter.

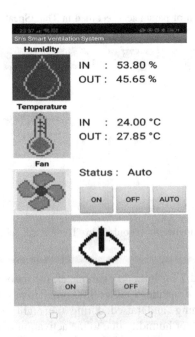

Fig. 8. Mobile app for the system

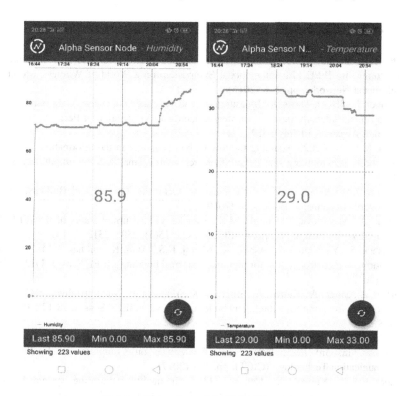

Fig. 9. Alpha channel in ThingView app

In addition, the developed mobile app shown in Fig. 8 only can display the latest data recorded in ThingSpeak. However, the complete visualization through mobile phone can be monitored using ThingView App from Google Store as can be seen in Fig. 9, where it shows the humidity and temperature of Alpha channel.

4 Conclusion

In this study, three NodeMCUs are built as the WSN nodes in this system, which are able to collect temperature and humidity parameters for indoor and outdoor, send the collected parameters to the cloud via ThingSpeak and retrieve the error values from ThingSpeak to activate/deactivate the cooling fan. The proposed system successfully allows the sensor nodes to communicate and interact with the actuator nodes through the ThingSpeak platform. At the same time, the developed mobile app is enabled to interrupt the system for controlling the whole system power, and the fan activation as auto, on and off mode. With the combination of the sensor and actuator nodes and mobile app, this project is becoming a smart portable system that is performed automatically by obtaining the required parameters from the surrounding.

References

1. Rita, T.T., Yubin, X.: A portable Wireless Sensor Network for real-time environmental monitoring. In: IEEE 17th International Symposium on a World of Wireless, Mobile and Multimedia Networks, pp. 1–6 (2016)
2. Kummer, J., Nix, O., Dress, K.: Measurement and verification of energy savings. http://www.buildup.eu/sites/default/files/content/Measurement-and-Verification-of-Eergy-Savings-Issue-Brief.pdf. Accessed 14 July 2019
3. Webb, M.: Smart 2020: enabling the low carbon economy in the information age. https://www.theclimategroup.org/sites/default/files/archive/files/Smart2020Report.pdf. Accessed 14 July 2019
4. Sinopoli, J.M.: Smart Buildings Systems for Architects, Owners and Builders, 1st edn. Butterworth-Heinemann, Burlington (2010)
5. Kumar, A., Srivastava, V., Singh, M.K., Hancke, G.P.: Current status of the IEEE 1451 standard-based sensor applications. IEEE Sens. J. **15**(5), 2505–2513 (2014)
6. Abhishek, S., Yadvendra, P., Ashok, K., Manoj, K.S., Anuj, K., Subhas, C.M.: Ventilation monitoring and control system for high rise historical buildings. IEEE Sens. J. **17**(22), 7533–7541 (2017)
7. Kumar, A., Singh, A., Kumar, A., Singh, M.K., Mahanta, P., Mukhopadhyay, S.C.: Sensing technologies for monitoring intelligent buildings: a review. IEEE Sens. J. **18**(12), 4847–4860 (2018)
8. Kumar, A., Kumar, A., Singh, A.: Energy efficient and low cost air quality sensor for smart buildings. In: 3rd IEEE International Conference on Computational Intelligence & Communication Technology (CICT), pp. 1–4 (2017)
9. Phala, K.S.E., Kumar, A., Hancke, G.P.: Air quality monitoring system based on ISO/IEC/IEEE 21451 standards. IEEE Sens. J. **16**(12), 5037–5045 (2016)
10. Yean, D.K., Chun, C.L., Jing, Y.C.: Multifunctional energy-efficient building with automatic temperature rise prevention mechanism. In: International Conference on System Science and Engineering, pp. 1–4 (2016)
11. Jing, G., Wenjian, C., Deqing, Z., Shuai, L., Can, C.S.: A model – based air balancing method of a ventilation system. Energy Build. J. **174**, 506–512 (2018)
12. Pei, Z., Gongsheng, H.: Experimental study of energy saving potential in mixing and displacement ventilation with wireless sensor network. Procedia Eng. **121**, 1497–1504 (2015)
13. Knissel, J., Peubner, D.: Energy efficient heat exchanger for ventilation systems. Energy Build. J. **159**, 246–253 (2018)
14. Gunner, A., Afshari, A., Bergsøe, N.C., Vorre, A., Hultmark, G.: Energy savings and manifold supply ventilation systems. J. Build. Eng. **7**, 71–77 (2016)
15. Kurihara, Y., Kaburagi, T., Watanabe, K.: Room ventilation control by a self-sensing fan. IEEE Sens. J. **16**(7), 2094–2099 (2015)
16. Tian, Z., Xu, Y., Qian, W.: Research on ventilation computing system for multi-area network model. In: 17th IEEE International Symposium on Distributed Computing and Applications for Business Engineering and Science (DCABES), pp. 48–51(2018)
17. Pudikov, V.V., Litvinova, N.B., Grushkovsky, P.A.: Automatic control system of ventilation and air conditioning systems based on the organization of energy-saving air treatment modes. In: IEEE International Multi-Conference on Industrial Engineering and Modern Technologies (FarEastCon), pp. 1–3 (2018)

18. Zhang, Y., Cheng, R., Long, E., Wang, X.: Climatic cooling potential evaluation and ventilation strategies optimization for city buildings in China. In: 16th IEEE International Bhurban Conference on Applied Sciences and Technology (IBCAST), pp. 692–696 (2019)
19. Alhamad, I.M., AlSaleem, M.H., Taleb, H.: Natural ventilation potential strategies in warm winter climate zones - a case study of Dubai. In: IEEE Advances in Science and Engineering Technology International Conferences (ASET), pp. 1–4 (2018)
20. Handsontec. http://www.handsontec.com/pdf_learn/esp8266-V10.pdf. Accessed 21 May 2019
21. Mouser Electronics. https://www.mouser.com/ds/2/758/DHT11. Accessed 20 May 2019 (26)

Automatic Attendance Taking:
A Proof of Concept on Privacy Concerns
in 802.11 MAC Address Probing

Yichiet Aun$^{(\boxtimes)}$ ⓘ, Ming-Lee Gan ⓘ,
and Yen-Min Jasmina Khaw$^{(\boxtimes)}$ ⓘ

Faculty of Information and Communication Technology,
Universiti Tunku Abdul Rahman, 31900 Kampar, Malaysia
{aunyc,ganml,khawym}@utar.edu.my

Abstract. Modern data communication paradigm involves many unsolicited data transmissions that poses privacy issues given the proliferation of big data and artificial intelligence (A.I.). In 802.x protocol which dominate wireless communication; Wi-Fi enabled devices voluntarily embed devices MAC address during SSID discovery when connecting to access point (AP). Such vulnerability has been massively exploited for unauthorized devices tracking without user consents. This paper proposed an opportunistic attendance taking system (OATA) using MAC address probing as a proof of concepts to demonstrate the significance of this exploit. The intuition is that student's attendance can be implied based on the MAC address of their mobile devices when approaching lecture hall installed with AP(s). The body of this work focuses on comparing the OATA to some prominent attendance taking methods in pervasiveness and accuracy. For the operational hypothesis, a non-synthetic dataset is used for experimental evaluation to simulate realness and to minimize hawthorn effect. OATA is designed to circumvent MAC address randomization that is used on modern IOS and Android OS for accurate tracking. The experimental results showed that OATA is highly accurate at capturing device's presence; achieving true positive rate (TPr) of 0.938 and false positive rate (FPr) of 0.063 with fast convergence time. The significance of this study highlight the concerns that big data coupled with increasingly intelligent A.I. can divulge more information than originally intended. Consequently, user's privacy is compromised as their personal communication devices are demonstrated to be potentially exploited for unsolicited location tracking.

Keywords: 802.11 SSID probes · Unsolicited tracking · Big data · Data privacy · Attendance taker

1 Introduction

The proliferations of Big Data, Data Science and Data Analytics in various domains such as advertisement, e-commerce, the Internet of Things (IoT), cloud computing and virtualization have raised serious concerns of a digital user's privacy [1, 2]. Data on a user's online preferences, interests, frequently visited sites, shopping platforms,

© Springer Nature Singapore Pte Ltd. 2020
M. Anbar et al. (Eds.): ACeS 2019, CCIS 1132, pp. 274–288, 2020.
https://doi.org/10.1007/978-981-15-2693-0_20

financial portals, physical location, etc. are valuable information to various organizations ranging from business or political to security in nature. As such, data privacy is an important aspect to prevent users from being exploited or influenced by the type of information that is targeted on them.

The use of mobile devices for online communication and transactions has now become an integral part of society. In major cities such as China, South Korea and Japan, the use of mobile e-wallets for purchases at retail shops is preferred over the traditional cash or credit card payments [3, 4]. Mobile devices are already essential in communication be it through voice calls, instant messaging, social network or the Internet. It is estimated that 36 percent of the world's population owns at least a smartphone in 2018 and this figure is projected to increase annually [5].

As more and more applications require the use of smartphones for example navigation, e-payments, communication, e-banking, authentication and Internet search, users should be concern about the information and data that is relayed from their smartphone over the telecommunication network [6, 7]. Other related issues are concerning the metadata and geotag generated by smartphones which could reveal sensitive information of a user's current location, usual routes and home address.

Smartphone is one of the most common mobile devices that are carried by the user almost everywhere. It is the primary medium of communication, be it through instant messaging, social network or voice calls. Therefore, the location/whereabouts of a person could generally be determined through the user's smartphone. Telecommunication providers employ big data companies to harness these location data by tracking users over the provider's cellular network. The information of location and data usage of cellular users gathered by these big data companies are filtered sorted and analyzed before being reverted to the telecommunication providers. These data are proprietary to the respective telecommunication network providers because the information is derived from the provider's own cellular network.

However, a similar form of tracking by smartphones could be achieved using passive MAC address probing. The proposed system is based on an opportunistic algorithm to detect the presence of smartphone users with their corresponding mobile phone's MAC address within the confined coverage area of a Wi-Fi access point. This is sourced from the information extracted in the 802.11 management frames. A smartphone would broadcast the Probe Request packets to obtain the SSID information of wireless access points in the vicinity. The Probe Request contains the MAC address of the smartphone which can be associated to a specific user.

As such, the characteristics of MAC address probing together with location-aware Wi-Fi access points, could potentially be exploited for unsolicited tracking of mobile users. This study features a real-time example utilizing an attendance taking system within a designated campus area, to demonstrate the impact of unsolicited mobile user tracking. The implication of this result can be further expanded into industrial applications such as indoor location tracking, user location-preference analysis, location-aware personalized advertisement and location-aware recommendation system.

The remainder of this paper is organized as follows. Section 2 discusses the existing methods of mobile usage and location tracking. Section 3 defines some nomenclature and intuition for this paper. Section 4 introduces a robust method for sniffing MAC address even for randomized MAC using passive MAC address probing (OATA). For contexts, we demonstrate the proposed technique as an attendance taking system. Section 5 presents the experimental results of the proposed method. In Sect. 6, the experimental finding and implications are discussed.

2   Literature Review

Existing smartphone tracking methods are basically categorized into network based, handset based or wifi based. Network based tracking utilizes the telecommunication infrastructure of the service provider together with the subscriber identity module (SIM) that comes together with the user's line subscription. In [8–10], location tracking is conducted by measuring the field strength data of surrounding base stations that is readily available in global system for mobile communication (GSM) networks. Additionally, in [10], the study also looks into predicting future mobility behaviors which are useful in optimizing network resource allocation and enabling fast handoff from one cell station to another. However as indicated earlier, such form of tracking requires access to service provider's telecommunication network.

Handset based tracking [11–15] requires the mobile device to be installed with a location positioning application. The client application would probe the surrounding elements such as cell identification, signal strength, neighboring cells and GPS in order to determine the tracking location of the mobile device. The main disadvantage of handset-based tracking is the need to install location positioning application in the user's communication device. This may lead to security and privacy concerns by the users which may inevitable block/switch off such tracking services on their mobile handset.

One common drawback of network based, and handset-based tracking is the reliance of the existing GSM network infrastructure. The coverage of the GSM network is limited mainly at outdoors. However, GSM coverage is weak or mostly unavailable indoors such as at airports, shopping malls, basement level and office buildings. As such, WiFi based tracking [16–18] have been proposed for indoor positioning. [16] incorporates the use of access points, WiFi tags and data server. The WiFi tags collects the signal strength of information of neighboring access point and sends this to the data server to triangulate the position of the WiFi tag. This approach however requires the use of an additional device (WiFi tags) which have to be carried by the user.

3   Active Fingerprinting vs Passive Fingerprinting

For brevity, the notion of active fingerprinting in this paper refers to method that requires user interaction for taking attendance. Attendance taker can be reduced into a fingerprinting problem. In our domain, the students are the constant while attendance represents their states; or a variable. These systems are designed to detect the presence of an entity within an enclosed proximity during a given period. Attendance taking methods are diverse; which is observable from the implementations, accuracy, robustness and elasticity. We argue that passive fingerprinting can be used to safeguard against attendance taking circumvent technique; that leads to the operational hypothesis of this work. The intuition is that an effective attendance system should be transparent as any form of user awareness of being monitored leads to hawthorn effect and urge to beat the system. We formally define and compare two distinct approaches here:

Active fingerprinting – users are required to interact with the input module of the system to be tracked or recorded. The amount of interaction differentiates the system; with least interaction being the better options. In some contexts, the interaction stage introduces a focal point of circumvention attacks. User need to and are made aware of the attendance taking requirements; and in most cases these awareness leads to hawthorn effect. For example, user need to scan their barcode in RFID scanner, or an app is needed to scan in-class QR code.

Passive fingerprinting – users' attendance is recorded pervasively. Most of these techniques leverage of the proliferation of A.I. especially in the domain of facial recognition. For them to work, these systems are normally bounded with the sensors combined perimeters, and user presence within the monitored zone are identified. Passive fingerprinting is more compute intensive and requires modern infrastructural supports such as IoT on 5G network and edge computing. The main advantage is improved accuracy, reduced user interactions and expanded elasticity depending on the implementations. For example, facial recognition system in lecture halls can pervasively recognize students for automated attendance taking (a prior trained face recognition model is required).

3.1   Intuition

In 802.11x protocols, the discovery of access points (AP) are performed through SSID broadcasts. Assuming AP don't hide their SSID, AP will advertise their network name to neighboring hosts (sometimes with security configurations) for visibility. Compatible client devices in the vicinity constantly intercepts and read these packets rapidly if they are not hooked to any fixed networks; and the discovery will scale down once connected or unless triggered. The SSID broadcasts, when transmitted through the air, are subjected to interception for monitoring use. In a typical SSID broadcast packet, the AP will embed the network name in the payload and preceded by a standard IP header that will include AP's MAC address. On the receiver, the client will send a response to this broadcast (more like a scan technically) that also contain the client's MAC address. These exchanges happen voluntarily regardless of security intentions. Figure 1 illustrates SSID discovery behaviors. This paper presents an opportunistic technique based on these SSID discovery exchanges to recognize users through a MAC address to user identity bindings.

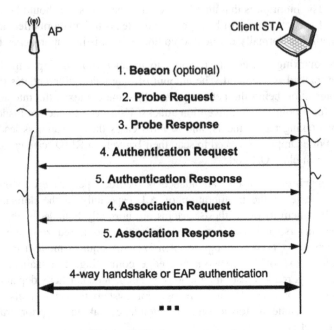

Fig. 1. SSID discovery behaviors

4   Opportunistic Attendance Taking Algorithm (OATA)

This paper proposed using an attendance taking system based on MAC address probing. The intuition is each student now own a smartphone, and when these devices constantly communicates in the background without supervision. The proposed method leverages on the pre-handshake behaviors of 802.11a/b/g/b/AC protocols for user identification. The opportunistic here refers to the pervasiveness, such that student's attendance are taken when they move close to AP (collectors' node) proximity with the smartphone with them; without needing any overt actions like scanning QR codes or tapping the phone on NFC reader. Figure 2 visualize the components of OATA.

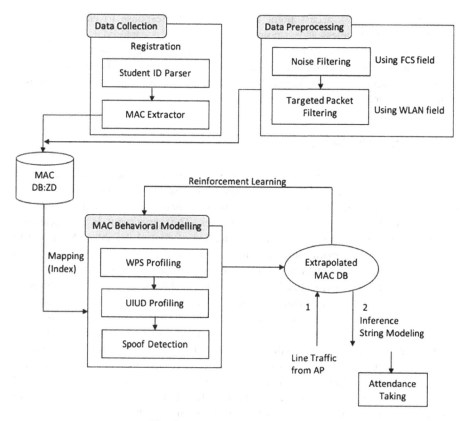

Fig. 2. The components of OATA

OATA is consists of three components; starting with (1) data preprocessing stage for student registrations, (2) MAC address detection stage and (3) robustness enhancement stage using machine learning to compensate for trivial issues. In (1) a database of student-to-MAC address mapping is developed to maintain operational correlations of monitored entities.

In (2) a sensor network is developed for the collection of SSID traffic and a string-matching algorithm is designed for rapid MAC addresses extraction for student recognition. Prior to MAC identification, packets are preprocess using Wireshark filters to clean traffic noise such as AP from another monitoring zone, bad packets, and background traffic from control protocols. Filtering are repeated for both request and response to compensate traffic directionality. *"wlan.fc.type_subtype eq 0x04"* specified the type of packets to be filter. 0x04 is the *Probe Request*. *"wlan.fcs.status == good"* is to check Frame Check Sequence and filter out the malformed packets. *"wlan.fc.-type_subtype eq 0x05"* specified the type of packets to be filter. 0x05 is the *Probe Response*. *"wlan.fcs.status == good"* is to check Frame Check Sequence and filter out the malformed packets. The *"wlan.addr == <wireless access point MAC address>"* is to specify the wireless access point that sent out the response to ensure only the response from the wireless access point in the classroom is captured.

In (3) some co-dependent modules are designed for enhanced robustness. Firstly, a MAC spoofing detection engine is designed to prevent rogue hosts tricking the recognition. Secondly, a host keepalive detection method is designed to continuously monitor hosts presence through periodic probing.

5 Experimental Setup

A smart space is built based on the schematic shown in Fig. 3. Each monitoring corner is assembled with several AP(s) to minimize blind spots; as annotated with red * symbol in the Fig. 3. The lecture hall is the designated space to demonstrate the attendance taking, as indicated with red border. The experiment is conducted on synthetic environment to simplify the manipulation of control variables. A set of 100 students represent the main entity for the system; where 80 of them is selected to 'attend' the class and the remaining 20 are passerby in the walkways. The goal here is to simulate a real ambient to test if the system is capable to pickup the signatures of only the 80 target of interests and recognize the 20 as noise; all while the attendances (of the 80) are being taken without supervision. Sensors (access points) are deployed 25 meters from each other; based on theoretical signal distance for optimized coverage. Note that these AP(s) are not coordinated; all AP(s) talk to a centralized storage hosted to aggregate and collect SSID transactions for next MAC address recognition. SSID are configured to be unique, to prevent overlapping. AP are configured to transmit at maximum power to improve signal strength so that students sitting in the middle are covered. Each participant is assigned to carry only one smartphone with Wi-Fi 4 and above support; each node has Wi-Fi turned on and put in discovering mode; while not connected to any known network nearby. This accounts to 80 unique MAC(s) in the lecture hall and 20 MAC(s) outside the hall. Prior to this, a student ID to MAC address mapping is populated using a *HTML* trick (not discussed in this paper). In iOS devices, the random MAC address functions are turned off to prevent unknown MAC during MAC to student ID matching.

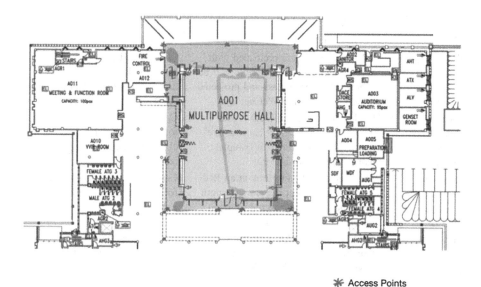

¥ Access Points

Fig. 3. A smart space is built based on the schematic (Color figure online)

Attendance is taken in the interval of 10 min, to ensure students stayed in the class throughout the lecture. Each AP dumps their packets (only SSID due to bandwidth constraints) to the collector node every 10 min through a modified kernel. The collector node receives an average of 3000 SSID broadcast packets in each interval for analytics. The monitoring is conducted for continuous 2 h long. All 80 students are admitted during the time onset, their seating positions are randomized (no seating protocol is designed) and are encouraged to move around but stay within the perimeter. Meanwhile, the other 20 students are positioned outside the hall but within the reach of AP(s) coverage in the lecture hall. The packets collected from these nodes after the sessions are decoded for MAC address for student recognition. Next section evaluates the pervasiveness and accuracy of the proposed system.

5.1   Convergence Time

Rapid convergence is important for real-time attendance taking. The convergence time is measured as the period (in seconds) needed for a student to be recognized from the point of entry. Short convergence is an indicator of effective attendance taking system. For brevity, we do not consider implementation specifics delay, instead we measure convergence based on the delta time, d_t = elapse (detected time − start time), this can be defined formally as C_t = (time$_{attendance\_taken}$ − time$_{enteredthevenue}$). For example, we measure convergence time as the total time needed for student to open WeChat app, navigate to QR scan, and point the camera to the projected QR code on screen. Meanwhile, any inherited processing from these systems such as querying WeChat user database and network delay incurred are not considered. Table 1 summarize the attributes of a set of attendance taking system to be compared.

Table 1. The attributes of a set of attendance taking system to be compared.

Methods	Configurations	Convergence time, C_t
WeChat QR [Active]	All smartphones are preloaded with WeChat app. A new QR code will be generated for each class and projected to be scanned using WeChat app	C_t = elapsed (Start time + seating delay + phone retrieval time + time for student to start scan)
Face Recognition (YOLO) [Passive]	Implemented using YOLO object detection system. Eight cameras are installed beside AP(s) for complete hall coverage for face ID	C_t = elapsed (Start time + time for camera to pick up person as object + time for face recognition)
Iris Scanner [Active]	Students are asked to look at an IRIS scanner installed at the entrance until the indicator turn from red to green. 2 scanners are installed	C_t = elapsed (Start time + time for IRIS reader to turn from red to green)
Fingerprint Scanner [Active]	Students are asked to scan their thumbprint using a thumb reader until a beep is audible. 2 scanners are installed	C_t = elapsed (Start time + time for fingerprint reader to beep)
Student ID Barcode (RFID) [Active]	Students are asked to scan their student card at a RFID reader until 3 beeps are audible. 2 scanners are installed	C_t = elapsed (Start time + time for fingerprint reader to beep 3 times)
Active MAC address system [Active]	Students are asked to connect to designated Wi-Fi network based on the projected SSID name (non-password protected)	C_t = elapsed (Start time + time for student to scan for SSID + time for student to input login credentials + AP authentication time)

We hypothesize that pervasive system has shorter convergence time to demonstrate the unsupervised nature of these comparable. In this section, we evaluate the convergence as a measure of pervasiveness; where lower C_t indicates less interaction that translates to better pervasiveness. The experimental shows result the number of attendances recorded in the interval of 10 s as visualized in Fig. 4. For WeChat QR, YOLO Face Recognition and Active MAC; the convergence time is derived from a timer script to calculate elapse time from onset (student entry time) to offset (user is recognized). For others, the completion time is timed manually using a timer. For better fairness, students enter the hall in a coordinated way (one entrée per queue, next adjacent student on standby, step into scanner when previous entrée is cleared at a time; timer is restarted on the onset of scanning operations). Students are asked to step out from the venue entirely before continuing the experiment with different capture methods.

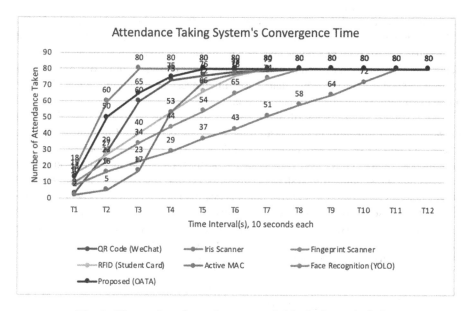

Fig. 4. The number of attendances recorded in the interval of 10 s

Experimental results indicate that passive fingerprinting achieved fastest convergence; we imply that the rapid detection is due to the independence of user interactions. Meanwhile, in active attendance taking; user interactions like user response time and user to reader interaction time contributes to recognition delay. In RFID, fingerprint and iris scanner methods; there are deterministic patterns of attendance count across intervals. One ramification is that in a coordinated environment (student A scan immediately after student A − 1), the convergence time is determined by the speed of readers and how many readers are deployed in parallel. Generally, the complexity of the features used by scanning method will dictate the identification rate; which can be observed as IRIS scanner performed comparably slower than both fingerprint and barcode methods. We deduce that sensor capability is the bottleneck for such attendance system; where each entity is 'served' individually by one sensor at a time. The scenario become more notable in the case of WeChat and Active MAC address system; they recorded considerably fast convergence time despite needing human interactions. The rationale is that when multiple users are attempting to login to the AP for attendance, multiple 802.11x authentications can happen simultaneously on the AP(s); thence, this removed the single node bottleneck issues. Despite this, it is not surprising that the proposed OATA and YOLO still triumph over active methods; achieving full convergence (80 attendances) at 2 intervals earlier. We argue that the marginal differences are due to a small set of users not 'attempting to take attendance'; for example, they are seated but only start to scan QR code several minutes later. The human factor is always a wildcard, and although most attendance system is not time sensitive; this observation further highlight the importance of passive attendance taking methods. On OATA's slower converge compared to YOLO, we deduce that missing SSID broadcast can contributes to some random delays depending on the interference levels in a highly dense space; in addition to commodity hardware buffer capacity limitations to deal with large packets influx. We argue that these differences are negligible since they are ambient-specific rather than human-specific.

We compare the accuracy of these systems to measure the percentage of *correct attendance/total attendance*. For YOLO, the accuracy is measured using-true positive rate (TPr) and false positive rate (FPr). TPr is given by the number of correctly identified students (x), as x/80. FPr is given by the number of incorrectly identified students that are spoofing the system (y), as y/80. For the rest of the systems; recorded attendances are compared to the real attendances manually. The experiment is recon-figured to expose the weakness of each systems. We select 20 students (among the 80) to simulate a 'skip class' scenario; while trying to trick the system by trying to get an attendance outside the hall. Table 2 describes the circumvention method. Meanwhile, Fig. 5 shows the attained attendance accuracy respectively.

Table 2. The circumvention method

Methods	Configurations	Ground truth
WeChat QR [Active]	20 students are asked to get the QR code from their 60 peers sitting in the room	QR code can be shared easily and QR scanner do not distinguished their originality
Face Recognition (YOLO) [Passive]	Photos of the 20 students who skipped class are carried into the class; positioned facing the cameras	Face recognition is easily tricked by a photo unless a whole body scan is used
Iris Scanner [Active]	Photos of IRIS belonging to the 20 who skipped class students are scanned using IRIS scanner	IRIS scanner does not distinguish a real IRIS or a pictured IRIS
Fingerprint Scanner [Active]	20 students (from the hallway) are asked to scan their fingerprint using the fingerprint scanner to masquerade as the 20 students who skipped class	Fingerprint scanner will reject students not recorded in database
Student ID Barcode (RFID) [Active]	20 students (from the hallway are asked to scan the student card of the 20 students who skipped class at the RFID counter	Barcode scanner will decline entrance for students not in database
Active MAC address system [Active]	20 students (who skipped class) are asked to connect to nearby Wi-Fi that are discoverable	Attendance will be credited to anyone within the Wi-FI coverage area time)

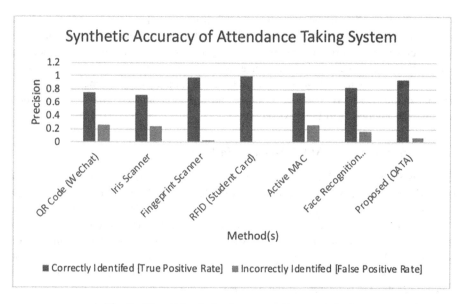

Fig. 5. The attained attendance accuracy respectively

We hypothesize that a robust attendance system must be accurate in detecting the correct attendances from forged attendances. The accuracy scores imply that there is no clear advantage distinction between passive or active methods; and the vulnerabilities that are exploited for fake attendance are implementations specific. RFID achieved TPr of 1.00 having correctly identified 60 instances as legit and 20 are spoofed; which is not surprising as barcode is running on a simple string-matching algorithm. This is followed closely by fingerprint that can sometime be hit-and-miss if there are injuries to the thumb. IRIS scanner and YOLO both achieve TPr above 0.8, but also come with significant FPr. There are two ramifications, (1) these methods use machine learning (ML) for image recognition; and in the case of 60 legit students there are some chances of false recognition (FPr) due to number of samples in training set, classifier's effectiveness, dataset quality and the lighting conditions during on the spot recognition. In addition, (2) the high FPr is due to YOLO recognizing 19 out of 20 students who skipped class as attended based on their pictures. Picture spoofing is a common image circumvention technique. We argue there are better image recognition technique such as using dot projector to map multiple dot to facial features using infrared sensor for forgery detection. In WeChat QR, the FPr is comparably higher despite having short converge time. The reasoning is QR is only not location aware; as a QR code that is assumed to uniquely represent a class (by projecting to the audience in a confined space) is sharable across perimeters. In our experiment, the high FPr is a result of all 20 students (legit students who skipped class) scan the WeChat QR shared by peers inside the class. As for OATA, we achieved 0.938 TPr and 0.063 FPr despite active forgery attempts. The *valid MAC address check* component validates each MAC discovered and compare to a database of registered MAC (that represent the 80 students) to filter out fake MAC; that explains the performance improvement over existing *Active MAC* method. Since OATA operates on valid MAC, it is somewhat prone to MAC address making that explains the difficulty of hitting 1.00 TPr. The ramification of these experiments is that short converge time and improve recognition is plausible when we remove human factor from the attendance taking process. We identified that currently there are three known techniques that mess with OATA accuracy; this include (1) MAC randomization, (2) MAC address spoofing and (2) unrecognized MAC. These shortcomings are addressed in the next section.

5.2   Compensating for MAC Address Masking

OATA is highly pervasive given its rapid convergence time after removing human factor during the attendance taking operation. As OATA leverage on 802.11x SSID discovery for detection, it is vulnerable to protocol exploits. OATA can detect a legit MAC accurately if it is known; but not unknown MAC that is legit but obscured. We reason that although rare, the accuracy of OATA is bottlenecked by the amount of coordinated MAC address manipulations. There are two possible scenarios for unknown MAC: (1) the MAC address of the device does not belong to a student in the class or (2) the MAC address of the device is spoofed or masked. For the former, we argue this as a safeguard mechanism to prevent outsiders from taking attendance. Meanwhile, in MAC address randomization, the true MAC address of Network Interface Card on a protected host is hidden and replaced with some random 8 bytes values. In this case, a properly registered MAC (despite no bad intentions) is not visible to OATA resulting in erroneous attendance taking leading to high false negative. Similarly, an unknown MAC that is rewrote into a legit MAC through address spoofing is capable to circumvent OATA leading to high false positive. The implication is the correctness of discovered MAC might become the point of weakness of the system. In this paper, we leverage on the Wi-Fi Protected Setup (WPS) and Universally-Unique Identifier Enrollee (UUID) exploits to reverse engineer randomized MAC(s) when detected. This technique however assumes that mobile devices strictly enforce these services as IEEE recommended; the limitations are beyond the scope of this paper.

6   Implications and Conclusion

This paper proposed a pervasive attendance taking system to demonstrate the involuntarily tracking of mobile devices. 802.x SSID discovery has been widely exploited; but fixes are limited due to protocol restrictions. Most client sided masking such as MAC randomization is easily reversible using WPS and UIUD hacks to reveal the original MAC. Although MAC recovery methods are case specific; they have been proven effective to prevent obstrufication when used collectively. OATA detect student's attendance based on nearby MAC detection without needing any human interaction or logging into AP(s). In general purpose use, user location become visible when they move into AP proximity in setting crowded with AP(s) provided these AP(s) are synchronized. Common workaround to protect location privacy is detrimental to mobile phone experiences; such as turning off Wi-Fi to prevent SSID discovery would require manual connection to hotspot when needed. Selectively enabling sensors usage permission to applications is a tedious but viable workaround; however, they are becoming less effective since A.I. now leverages on correlation analysis among multiple sensors entities with high level reasoning. For example, OATA can still look at correlated device and user behaviors to profile a mobile device if MAC address is completely obstruficated. Thence, we deduce that sensor ridden phones enabled the A. I. that empower the phones and multiple ambient aware services; but come at the cost of user privacy. The state-of-the-art privacy mechanism like data encryption are less effective especially when A.I. is powerful enough to brute-decrypt using virtually unlimited cloud resources or instead using deep neural network to figure out data correlations effortlessly. At this rate, it is safe to deduce that user privacy is at risk more than ever as A.I. is becoming more intelligent and predicting more high-level insights every day.

References

1. Gruschka, N., Mavroeidis, V., Vishi, K., Jensen, M.: Privacy issues and data protection in big data: a case study analysis under GDPR. In: 2018 IEEE International Conference on Big Data (Big Data), Seattle, WA, USA, pp. 5027–5033 (2018)
2. Dev Mishra, A., Beer Singh, Y.: Big data analytics for security and privacy challenges. In: 2016 International Conference on Computing, Communication and Automation (ICCCA), Noida, pp. 50–53 (2016)
3. Chinw's e-wallet success is an example for Southeast Asia players. https://www.techinasia.com/ewallets-china-southeast-asia-learn. Accessed 15 June 2019
4. Miao, M., Jayakar, K.: Mobile payments in Japan, South Korea and China: cross-border convergence or divergence of business models? Telecommun. Policy 40(2–3), 182–196 (2016)
5. Number of smartphone users worldwide from 2014 to 2020 (in billions). https://www.statista.com/statistics/330695/number-of-smartphone-users-worldwide/. Accessed 15 June 2019
6. Khatoon, A., Corcoran, P.: Privacy concerns on Android devices. In: IEEE International Conference on Consumer Electronics (ICCE), Las Vegas, NV, pp. 149–152 (2017)
7. Sahnoune, Z., Aïmeur, E., Haddad, G.E., Sokoudjou, R.: Watch Your Mobile Payment: An Empirical Study of Privacy Disclosure, IEEE Trustcom/BigDataSE/ISPA, Helsinki, pp. 934–941 (2015)
8. Hellebrandt, M., Mathar, R.: Location tracking of mobiles in cellular radio networks. IEEE Trans. Veh. Technol. 48(5), 1558–1562 (1999)
9. Mihaylova, L., Angelova, D., Honary, S., Bull, D.R., Canagarajah, C.N., Ristic, B.: Mobility tracking in cellular networks using particle filtering. IEEE Trans. Wirel. Commun. 6(10), 3589–3599 (2007)
10. Zaidi, Z.R., Mark, B.L.: Real-time mobility tracking algorithms for cellular networks based on Kalman filtering. IEEE Trans. Mob. Comput. 4(2), 195–208 (2005)
11. Schilit, B., Hong, J., Gruteser, M.: Wireless location privacy protection. Computer 36(12), 135–137 (2003)
12. Smith, M., Szongott, C., Henne, B., von Voigt, G.: Big data privacy issues in public social media. In: 6th IEEE International Conference on Digital Ecosystems and Technologies (DEST), Campione d'Italia, pp. 1–6 (2012)

13. Li, M., Zhu, H., Gao, Z., Chen, S., Yu, L., Hu, S., Ren, K.: All your location are belong to us: breaking mobile social networks for automated user location tracking. In: Proceedings of the 15th ACM International Symposium on Mobile Ad Hoc Networking and Computing, Philadelphia, Pennsylvania, USA, pp. 43–52 (2014)

14. Yun, H., Han, D., Lee, C.C.: Understanding the use of location-based service applications: do privacy concerns matter? J. Electr. Commer. Res. **14**(3), 215–230 (2013)

15. 24 Best GPS Tracking Apps for Android. https://www.redbytes.in/top-10-best-gps-tracking-apps-for-android/. Accessed 15 June 2019

16. Chen, Y., Luo, R.: Design and implementation of a WiFi-based local locating system. In: IEEE International Conference on Portable Information Devices, Orlando, FL, pp. 1–5 (2007)

17. Sakib, M.N., Halim, J.B., Huang, C.: Determining location and movement pattern using anonymized WiFi access point BSSID. In: 7th International Conference on Security Technology, Haikou, pp. 11–14 (2014)

18. Alshamaa, D., Mourad-Chehade, F., Honeine, P.: Mobility-based tracking using WiFi RSS in indoor wireless sensor networks. In: 9th IFIP International Conference on New Technologies, Mobility and Security (NTMS), Paris, pp. 1–5 (2018)

An Efficient Encryption Algorithm for Perfect Forward Secrecy in Satellite Communication

Abid Murtaza[1(✉)], Syed Jahanzeb Hussain Pirzada[2],
Muhammad Noman Hasan[3], Tongge Xu[2], and Liu Jianwei[2]

[1] School of Electronics and Information Engineering, Beihang University,
Beijing, China
abid_murtaza47@hotmail.com
[2] School of Cyber Science and Technology, Beihang University, Beijing, China
xutg@buaa.edu.cn
[3] School of Automation Science and Electrical Engineering, Beijing, China

Abstract. Satellite communication is among those applications where data confidentiality is required, but at the same time, computational resources are limited as well as the delay is critical. For these types of applications, symmetric key encryption algorithms are preferred over asymmetric key algorithms, due to lower computational cost and faster speed of operation. Furthermore, due to various critical aspects of information security, using Perfect Forward Secrecy (PFS) in many communication applications is advantageous. There are two ways to achieve PFS; either a mechanism for new key generation is required, or some protocols are used for sharing new session keys before communication. Both of these ways, at minimum, append additional computational load and delay in communication, which are critical in satellite communication. This is probably the most significant barrier that satellites do not use PFS for every communication. This paper presents a novel encryption algorithm where a message key is generated such that later only Exclusive OR (XOR) operation can be used to produce the ciphertext. Hence, the proposed algorithm eliminates the need for two separate algorithms for message key generation and encryption for PFS. Security analysis and experimental results show that proposed encryption algorithm is not only secure but also faster and cheaper than the widely used AES-CTR encryption algorithm. Therefore it is suitable to be used in satellite communication for PFS.

Keywords: Satellite communication · Encryption · Forward secrecy · Algorithm · Exclusive OR · One-time pad

1 Introduction

Satellites are providing many useful services to the world from decades. The benefits and applications of the satellite are growing with the time & therefore satellites became an integral part of the modern world communication system. Satellite communication is among those applications where communication security is critical, and compromise in security could have serious consequences. Satellite missions have been classified as requiring either high, moderate, or minimal levels of security according to the Consultative Committee for Space Data Systems (CCSDS). Even minimum level security mission may have the following security requirements according to CCSDS [1]:

© Springer Nature Singapore Pte Ltd. 2020
M. Anbar et al. (Eds.): ACeS 2019, CCIS 1132, pp. 289–302, 2020.
https://doi.org/10.1007/978-981-15-2693-0_21

1. Protection of all telecommand data
2. Protection of some telemetry data:
3. Protection of some data in the ground data system

While moderate and high-security space missions require more than these. For the protection of data, mostly, data encryption, data integrity, and authentication services are used. An encryption algorithm is a fundamental security tool which is used primarily to provide data confidentiality but is also used in authentication protocols and data authentication & integrity algorithms. Asymmetric and symmetric key encryption algorithms, both are in use depending upon the application requirements. Generally, applications with limited computational resources or where the computational delay & cost is critical, symmetric key encryption algorithms are preferred over asymmetric encryption algorithms due to its faster speed and lower computational cost. This is why symmetric key encryption algorithms are widely used in modern world applications. Satellite communication is also among those applications where computational resources are considered limited as well as the delay is critical, hence symmetric key encryption algorithms are preferred and also recommended by CCSDS [2].

However, generally, it is not recommended to use the same symmetric key for a longer duration, as there are attacks which exploit the use of the same key for a longer period to fetch the useful information about the key. Therefore, in information security, there is a concept of using a new key for every session or every message, known as Forward Secrecy or Perfect Forward Secrecy (PFS). The significance of PFS is continuously increasing due to several vital aspects. For example, with PFS, in case of a compromise of one key for any reason, only one session or one message is compromised (for which the compromised key was used), while rest of communication (of past and future) remains secure. This is important because we know that data processing capacity & speed of operations is continuously increasing; on the other hand, new attacks and techniques for cryptanalysis are being developed regularly. Therefore, secure encryption algorithms of today if claimed to be broken tomorrow, then the key being used will not remain secret, which means all the communication is also at stake. Secondly, despite the presence of many security algorithms, we have witnessed several information security breaches such as many incidents of hacking and confidential data leakage (e.g., WikiLeaks). This is mostly because of insufficient security at the application level. In this background, PFS could provide vital strength to information security and hence used in many modern-day applications such as Web browsers, messenger application (e.g., WhatsApp), etc.

There are two approaches to achieve PFS in communication applications; the first approach is that the sender and receiver exchange the session key to be used in session every time at the beginning of session through key sharing protocols (e.g., TLS/SSL, SHL, etc. [3]). The alternate option is that both sender and receiver automatically derive a session/message key from the pre-shared key through the same mechanism (e.g., the technique used in WhatsApp messenger application [4]). The problem with both of these approaches of PFS is that they require additional computations as well as delay before the actual encryption process. Such a delay and additional computations are critical in applications such as satellite communications. In this background, this paper presents a novel algorithm which is not only faster than other techniques but is also secure & computationally cheaper, because it uses mainly Exclusive OR

(XOR) operations for encryption and decryption. In the proposed encryption algorithm, a simple message key generation mechanism is proposed such that, after the generation of message key, the ciphertext can be obtained by only XOR operations. So, there is no need for separate key generation & encryption algorithms, and hence computationally it is more efficient than other existing algorithms. Similarly, unlike other existing algorithms decryption process in the proposed algorithm is also based on only simple XOR operation, hence cheaper and faster than others. Finally, despite being efficient, the proposed algorithm is also secure as security analysis shows. Mathematical examination and experimental results validate these claims.

The remaining of this paper is arranged as follow; in section two, we briefly reviewed related work. In Sect. 3, we have proposed our algorithms. In Sect. 4, we have analyzed the security of the proposed algorithm. Section 5 provides implementation results. Section 6 concludes the paper.

2 Related Work

There are several symmetric key encryption algorithms proposed by researchers, and a large number of studies are there to evaluate the performance & comparison of famous algorithms [5–9]. But Advanced Encryption Standard (AES [10]) proposed by Rijndael, is the widely used algorithm because of its stronger security and faster operation than its competitors. The CCSDS also recommends the use of AES for encryption service, AES-GCM (Galois Counter Mode) for AE (Authenticated Encryption) service, and AES-CMAC (Cipher Message Authentication Code) for cipher based authentication service in satellite missions [2, 11]. Many researchers have proposed modifications [12] as well as optimized implementations of AES on software and hardware to further increase its efficiency, including for satellite application [13]. The AES algorithm has different modes of operations [14]; among these, the Counter (CTR) mode supports high-speed operations due to parallel architecture and having no feedback or chaining mechanism. Therefore AES CTR mode is widely used in many applications, including satellite communication.

On the other hand, protocols are also used in many applications to share secret session keys. Such as SSL, SSH, IPsec (IKE) etc. [15]. Several authentication & key exchange protocols are proposed by the researchers for different satellite applications [16–21]. Majority of these protocols use at least three or more messages exchange, while they also use encryption algorithms for secure key establishment. So, we can see that several messages are encrypted with an encryption algorithm using a pre-shared master key, and after that, messages in the session can be encrypted with the session key. Therefore, most protocols are inefficient to be used for PFS in applications where the new session key is used for every new message such as messenger applications. For these applications, a pre-shared key is used to derive new session key [4]. Here still key generation work is required to be executed at both ends in addition to encryption/decryption, which not only consumes computational resources but adds delay as well. Recently authors in [22] have proposed an efficient key-sharing protocol for PFS in satellite application.

Also, some application uses an encrypted message to share the encryption key to be used before sharing the encrypted message. This technique is used in WhatsApp for attachment encryption [4]. This is again an inefficient approach to be used in satellites because; firstly two messages are sent instead of one message. Secondly, the encryption algorithm has to run twice on both sides.

3 The Proposed Algorithm

There are three parts of our proposed algorithm; first is the message key generation, second is the encryption process and finally key sharing method. Before the description of these three parts, we first present the security concept behind the proposed algorithm.

The basic idea of the proposed scheme is derived from the one-time pad (OTP) operation, which is considered as provably secure. The concept of OTP is that if a message of length n bits is XORed with a key of the same size that is not only a secret but also never used again, then for an attacker, it is impossible to correctly and confidently recover the plaintext. This is because the same ciphertext can be produced by 2^n possible combinations of plaintext and key while the attacker has no other information to be sure about what values of plaintext and keys are used to produce ciphertext.

Extending this basic idea, if three numbers of n bits are XORed with each other, then there exist P possible unique permutations of three numbers (as shown in the equation below) that can produce the same ciphertext.

$$p = 2^{2n}$$

So, if the length of all three numbers (say A, B, and D) is two bits each, then there exist $(2^{2*2} = 2^4)16$ possible combinations of A, B, and D that can produce the same ciphertext C as shown in Table 1 below.

Table 1. Simple XOR of three 2 bit numbers

S.No	A	B	B	$C = A \oplus B \oplus D$
1	00	00	00	00
2	00	01	01	00
3	00	10	10	00
4	00	11	11	00
5	00	00	00	00
6	01	01	00	00
7	01	10	11	00
8	01	11	10	00
9	10	00	10	00
10	10	01	11	00
11	10	10	00	00
12	10	11	01	00
13	11	00	11	00
14	11	01	10	00
15	11	10	01	00
16	11	11	00	00

Similarly, for three numbers of 3 bits each, there exist 64 unique permutations producing the same ciphertext. If the three numbers are 128 bit long each, then there will be

$$p = 2^{2*128} = 2^{256}$$

possible permutations that can produce the same output, while, the attacker has no further information, it cannot reach the correct three numbers confidently from resultant number by anyway.

3.1 Pre-requirements

There is a requirement for our scheme to work correctly.

The sender and receiver already have shared two secret numbers of 128 bit each called shared key Ks and initialization vector IV.

Once the key Ks is shared, both communicating parties can expand the number of keys from K1 to Kn through Ks using any same key expansion algorithm such as used for AES, IDEA, or any other. So, both the sender and receiver will have a pre-calculated key pool [K1, Kn] before the encryption process.

3.2 Message Key Generation

In the message key generation mechanism, plaintext blocks of message are placed in the first row of a matrix of size M * N, where M is the number of rows and N is the number of plaintext blocks as shown in Fig. 1. (If N is less than 3, then some padding can be done to make N = 3 at least).

	P1	P2	P3	......	PN
2					
3					
.					
M					

Fig. 1. Key generation matrix

Then plaintext blocks are iteratively XORed to converge to one column in M^{th} row as shown in Fig. 2. During this iterative XOR process, if the number of columns in any row is odd, then the last block will be written as it as to the end of next row as can be seen in Fig. 2 (3rd block of row 2 is written as it as to 3rd row).

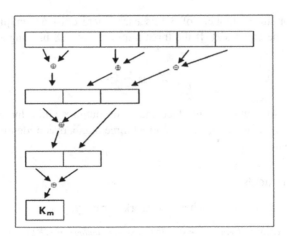

Fig. 2. Iterative XOR process

Here the generated Km is the message key. Mathematically we can see that Km will be

$$Km = P1 \oplus P2 \oplus P3 \oplus P4\ldots \oplus Pn \qquad (1)$$

To find the number of rows M required to converge matrix columns from N to 1 as shown in Fig. 2, we can see that the number of column in the second row is almost half of that in the first row (to be precise "ceil (N/2)"). Similarly, for every next row, the number of columns will be approx half (Ceil (N/2)) of the previous row. So mathematically we can find number of rows M require to converge N columns in our algorithm as shown in Eq. 2

$$M = \text{ceil}\,(\log2\,(N)) + 1 \qquad (2)$$

As the function in the above equation is a log function so we can see that for an increasing number of plaintext blocks N, the number of rows M will increase slowly (as shown in Fig. 3). Therefore, from Fig. 3 we can see that if the message has up to 250 blocks (128 bit each), then the required number of rows for the message key generation will be less than 10.

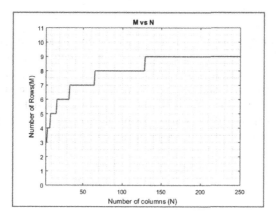

Fig. 3. Number of rows vs. number of columns

3.3   Encryption Process

After the key Km is generated through the above Key generation process, then the encryption process can be as simple as XOR of plaintext with keys, as shown below

$$Ci = Pi \oplus Km \oplus Ki$$

Where 'i' is block number, C is ciphertext, P is plaintext. So, we will have ciphertext blocks as

$$\left. \begin{array}{l} C1 = P1 \oplus Km \oplus K1 \\ C2 = P2 \oplus Km \oplus K2 \\ Cn = Pn \oplus Km \oplus Kn \end{array} \right\} \tag{3}$$

Here K1, K2, and Kn are keys generated from Ks through Key expansion algorithm.

3.4   Decryption Process

Unlike the existing encryption algorithms like AES, the decryption process of our algorithm is very simple and consists of XORing the ciphertext with message key Km and Ki, as shown below.

$$\left. \begin{array}{l} P1 = C1 \oplus Km \oplus K1 \\ P2 = C2 \oplus Km \oplus K2 \\ Pn = Cn \oplus Km \oplus Kn \end{array} \right\} \tag{4}$$

The intended receiver, when gets the message key Km, can easily get the plaintext blocks P1, P2 up to Pn using Eq. 4 very quickly.

3.5   Key Sharing

The proposed algorithm can be used in any application which uses key sharing algorithm or protocols, where Km_i (i.e., Km) can be securely communicated before or with the message (such as protocol in [22]). Because the encryption process of our algorithm is straightforward and fast, so the overall computational cost and time of both (Key sharing and encryption) will be significantly less compared to traditional use of PFS with protocols. However, it is also possible to send the message key Km with the encrypted message as an attached tag generated by Eq. 5 below.

$$Tag\_1 = IV \oplus Km\_1$$
$$Tag\_2 = IV\_1 \oplus Km\_2$$

Or in general

$$Tag\_i = IV\_(i-1) \oplus Km\_i \tag{5}$$

Where IV_1 is right-shift and increment operation on IV as proposed by Bader et al. in [23] for AES-CTR algorithm. i.e.

$$IV\_i = [RS(IV\_(i-1)) + 1] \tag{6}$$

Alternately if our algorithm is used with any protocol for sharing message key, then this IV_i can be used in the encryption process to increase the encryption complexity for attackers as shown in Eq. 7.

$$\left. \begin{array}{l} C1 = P1 \oplus Km \oplus K1 \oplus IV\_1 \\ C2 = P2 \oplus Km \oplus K2 \oplus IV\_2 \\ Cn = Pn \oplus Km \oplus Kn \oplus IV\_3 \end{array} \right\} \tag{7}$$

4   Security Analysis

4.1   Mathematical Analysis

To understand the security of the proposed scheme mathematically, take the following example of encryption of a plaintext consisting of 3 blocks (minimum length requirement of iterative XOR operation of our algorithm) as shown in Fig. 4.

P1	P2	P3
P1 $\oplus$ P2	P3	
P1 $\oplus$ P2 $\oplus$ P3		

Fig. 4.   Key generation example

From Fig. 4 we can see that the generated key according to Eq. 1 will be

$$Km = P1 \oplus P2 \oplus P3$$

The ciphertext will be produced according to Eq. 3 as below:

$$C1 = P1 \oplus (P1 \oplus P2 \oplus P3) \oplus K1 = P2 \oplus P3 \oplus K1$$
$$C2 = P2 \oplus (P1 \oplus P2 \oplus P3) \oplus K2 = P1 \oplus P3 \oplus K2$$
$$C3 = P3 \oplus (P1 \oplus P2 \oplus P3) \oplus K3 = P1 \oplus P2 \oplus K3$$

As the attacker does not have any information about plaintext P1, P2, P3 or Kn (K1, K2, etc.), he cannot get any plain text from the ciphertext C1, C2, and C3 directly. This is because, for C1 in the above equation, there exist 2128 * 2 possible combinations of K1, P2, and P3, which can produce the same C1. And as the attacker has no further information, so it is nearly impossible for the attacker to know that the guessed combination is right or wrong same as OTP. This same is true for C2, C3, and every Cn. Furthermore, we can see that if the number of blocks in a message is n, then according to Eq (1) Km will have the impact of all those n blocks. Therefore there will be 2128 * (n − 1) possible combinations producing the same ciphertext block, so impossible for the attacker to get into original plaintext. Here we can also see that the complexity of our algorithm from the attacker's viewpoint increases directly with the number of message blocks (or message length).

Now suppose the attacker attempts to guess key Ks. So, from the key expansion algorithm, he will get the corresponding Ki (i.e., K1, K2, K3, etc.) according to the guessed key Ks. But this is not enough work for the attacker. Because, from Eq. 3, we know that the ciphertext involves Km, Ki, and Pn. So, knowing Ki alone will not serve the attacker. Therefore the attacker needs to guess the correct Km together with Ki otherwise it is not possible to reach plaintext. This is a similar situation to that we have discussed in Sect. 3. As there is no further information available for attacker except ciphertext so he can never be sure about which correct combination of Ks and Km are used to produce ciphertext among a massive number of possible combinations.

4.2   Depth Analysis

From the depth analysis, we can see that if an attacker attempts to XOR ciphertexts together in the above example to fetch some useful information, then he will get the following results,

$$C1 \oplus C2 = (P2 \oplus P3 \oplus K1) \oplus (P1 \oplus P3 \oplus K2)$$
$$= P1 \oplus P2 \oplus K1 \oplus K2$$

From this equation, we can see that XORing C1 and C2 does not benefit attacker; instead, the resultant has increased one more variable to guess for the attacker.

However, if the attacker continues to combine ciphertext, he may reach a useful equation as shown below

$$C1 \oplus C2 \oplus C3 = (P1 \oplus P2 \oplus K1 \oplus K2) \oplus P1 \oplus P2 \oplus K3$$
$$= K1 \oplus K2 \oplus K3$$

This is again useless for the attacker, as he needs to guess three keys K1, K2, and K3 from the ciphertext C1⊕C2⊕C3, which is as difficult as discussed in Sect. 3. Or in other words, for any wrong guess of Ks, the attacker will get false values of K1, K2 and K3 which can still produce the same result as correct values of K1, K2, and K3 provides. Hence the attacker can never be sure about the correct value of Ks from the above equation.

4.3 Protection Against Compromised Shared Key (Ks)

In the worst case, assume the attacker can identify correct Ks which will produce K1 K2 and K3. Even then, the attacker may not get plain text from the ciphertext because he does not know plain text and Km, as shown in Eq. 3. Where again any wrong guess on Pi and corresponding wrong value of Km will provide the same ciphertext, Ci and the attacker can never be sure about his guess Km & plaintext is right or wrong as in case of OTP. Furthermore, if Eq. 7 is used for the encryption process, this will make encryption further secure because even lost of Ks will not reveal anything to the attacker.

4.4 Chosen Plaintext Attack

Although satellites systems are not supposed to be vulnerable against chosen-plaintext attack, however, let's assume the worst-case scenario where an attacker can get the ciphertext against his plaintext of choice, this may help an attacker to get Ks using Eq. 3. However, if the attacker tries decrypting ciphertext of another user (plaintext unknown to him), he won't be able to get plaintext, because not knowing the plaintext and corresponding Km will put attacker again in a situation of OTP as discussed above.

4.5 Security of Key Sharing Method

Lastly, to analyze the security of key sharing technique proposed, we can see from Eq. 6 that the IV_i is right-shift of IV_(i − 1) which rotates the value and creates randomness in the IV_i. In addition to it, the IV is incremented with one, which further randomizes IV_i compared to IV_(i − 1). So, for every value of i, IV_i is largely different as compared to IV_(i − 1) as every bit is being shifted and then its last byte is incremented by one.

So, from Eq. 6, we can see that not knowing IV, and Km_i, the attacker will not be able to recover the key Km_i correctly, and this is as secure as OTP. Furthermore, for depth, we can see that XORing Tag_1 with Tag_2, the attacker will get the following result.

$$\text{Tag\_1} \oplus \text{Tag\_2} = \text{IV\_1} \oplus \text{IV\_2} \oplus \text{Km\_1} \oplus \text{Km\_2}$$

This situation is even much more difficult than OTP because the attacker does not know anyone of the 4 components in the above equation. Hence we can see that the proposed key sharing scheme is secure mathematically.

From all these analyses, we can see that the algorithm is secure because the attacker cannot get any meaningful information from the generated ciphertext. We analyzed that the proposed algorithm is secure against chosen-plaintext attack, which means it will also be secure against known ciphertext attack, known-plaintext attack, etc. Hence we can claim that the proposed algorithm is secure.

5 Experimental Results

The proposed algorithm has been implemented in software MATLAB (R2015a) using Intel processor with 4 GB RAM. The results of time for encryption and decryption process of the proposed algorithm and its comparison with AES-CTR algorithm up to 8 message blocks are shown in Table 2.

Table 2. Experimental results

No of Blocks	Proposed algorithm		AES-CTR	
	Encryption time (Sec)	Decryption time (Sec)	Encryption time (Sec)	Decryption time (Sec)
1	2.96e−05	3.00e−05	0.180	0.237
2	3.59e−05	3.32e−05	0.241	0.260
3	3.78e−05	3.39e−05	0.344	0.494
4	3.91e−05	3.90e−05	0.462	0.543
5	5.79e−05	5.30e−05	0.561	0.684
6	6.03e−05	6.55e−05	0.867	0.741
7	6.37e−05	8.05e−05	0.942	0.920
8	1.80e−03	3.01e−04	0.982	1.039

From the above table, we can see that the performance of the proposed algorithm is much better than the AES-CTR algorithm. Furthermore, we can also note a trend from the above table, wherein our AES implementation, 0.1 s increases on average in encryption time with an increase in one block, while in our proposed algorithm, encryption time increases in fractions of seconds (i.e., 0.0002 s) with an increase in one message block. So, for every message length and any block number, the performance of the proposed algorithm will always ahead of AES-CTR in Matlab software.

On the hardware with parallel processing capability such as FPGA, all the plaintext blocks can by simultaneously XORed with each other as per Eq. 1 to generate Km in just one clock cycle. Similarly, for Eq. 3, all the components can be XORed with each other to produce the ciphertext in just one block cycle. The proposed algorithm has been implemented on FPGA, and the result confirms that only one clock cycle is required to XOR (Ki, Pi, and Km) for the generation of Ci. The simulation performed using Modelsim simulation software on Xilinx Spartan 3E FPGA is shown in Fig. 5.

If the available memory cores are less than the number of message blocks, then iterative XOR process can be pipelined to increase the efficiency of the implementation of the proposed algorithm.

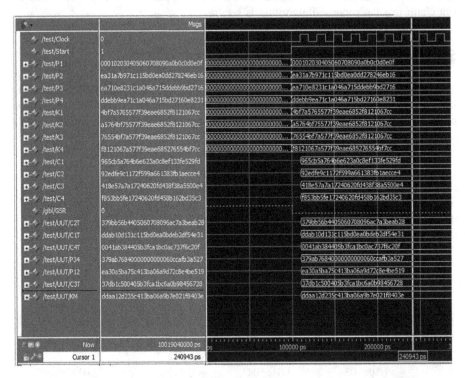

Fig. 5. Simulation results of FPGA implementation of proposed algorithm

6 Conclusion

This paper presents a new and simple algorithm for providing perfect forward secrecy in the satellite communication application. The proposed approach is based on a simple XOR operation; hence, it is lightweight and fast. Security analysis shows that the algorithm is secure. Experimental results show that the speed of the proposed algorithm is better than the famous AES algorithm even though the additional time required for new key generation for PFS using AES has not been considered. Hence the proposed algorithm is suitable to be used in future satellite communication applications.

References

1. CCSDS: The Application of Security to CCSDS Protocols. Informational report (Green Book), CCSDS 350, March 2019
2. CCSDS: CCSDS Cryptographic Algorithms. CCSDS 352.0-B-1, no. November 2012
3. M. Stamp, Information Security : Principles and Practice, 2nd Edition (2011)
4. WhatsApp Inc.: WhatsApp Encryption Overview (2017)
5. Koko, S.O.F.M., Babiker, M.A.: Comparison of various encryption algorithms and techniques for improving secured data communication. Int. J. Comput. Eng. **17**(1), 62–69 (2015)
6. Sharma, S., Bisht, J.S.: Performance analysis of data encryption algorithms. Int. J. Sci. Res. Netw. Secur. Commun. **3**(1), 1–5 (2015)
7. Abd Elminaam, D.S., Kader, H.M.A., Hadhoud, M.M.: Evaluating the performance of symmetric encryption algorithms. Int. J. Netw. Secur. **10**(3), 213–219 (2010)
8. Mushtaq, M.F., Jamel, S., Hassan Disina, A., Pindar, Z.A., Shakir, N.S.A., Mat Deris, M.: A survey on the cryptographic encryption algorithms. Int. J. Adv. Comput. Sci. Appl. **8**(11), 333–344 (2017)
9. Murtaza, A., Jahanzeb, S., Pirzada, H., Jianwei, L.: A new symmetric key encryption algorithm with higher performance. In: IEEE International Conference on Computing, Mathematics and Engineering Technologies – iCoMET, pp. 1–7 (2019)
10. NIST: Advanced Encryption Standard (AES). Fed. Inf. Process. Stand. Spec. Publ. 197 (2001)
11. Weiss, H.: CCSDS standardization of security algorithms for civil space missions. In: SpaceOps 2012 Conference, pp. 1–11 (2012)
12. Forhad, M.S.A., Riaz, S., Sabir Hossain, M., Das, M.: An improvement of advanced encryption standard. IJCSNS Int. J. Comput. Sci. Netw. Secur. **18**(11) (2018)
13. Jahanzeb, S., Murtaza, A., Jianwei, L.: The AES implementation for avoiding single event effects for satellite application. In: IEEE ICEIEC 2019 (2019). In press
14. NIST: Recommendation for Block Cipher Modes of Operation: Methods and Techniques, Spec. Publ. 800-38A
15. Prakash, A., Kumar, U.: Authentication protocols and techniques : a survey. Int. J. Comput. Sci. Eng. **6**(June), 1014–1020 (2018)
16. Zhang, C., Wang, X.: A novel self-certified security access authentication protocol in the space network. In: 14th IEEE ICCT, pp. 1014–1020 (2012)
17. Xue, K., Meng, W., Li, S., Wei, D.S.L., Zhou, H., Yu, N.: A secure and efficient access and handover authentication protocol for Internet of Things in space information networks. In: IEEE Internet Things J. (2019, in press)
18. Yantao, Z., Jianfeng, M.: A highly secure identity-based authenticated key-exchange protocol for satellite communication. J. Commun. Netw. **12**(6), 592–599 (2010)
19. Fereidooni, H., Taheri, H., Mahramian, M.: E2E KEEP : end to end key exchange and encryption protocol for accelerated satellite networks. Int. J. Commun. Netw. Syst. Sci. **2012** (April), 228–237 (2012)
20. Murtaza, A., Jianwei, L.: A simple, secure and efficient authentication protocol for real-time earth observation through satellite. In: IEEE Proceedings of 15th International Bhurban Conference on Applied Sciences and Technology, Islamabad, pp. 822–830 (2018)

21. Lee, Y.: Improvement of key exchange protocol to prevent man-in-the-middle attack in the satellite environment. In: 2016 Eighth International Conference on Ubiquitous Future Networks, pp. 408–413 (2016)
22. Murtaza, A., Xu, T., Jahanzeb, S., Pirzada, H., Jianwei, L.: A lightweight authentication and key sharing protocol for satellite communication. Int. J. Comput. Commun. Control (2019, in press)
23. Bader, A.S., Sagheer, A.M.: Modification on AES-GCM to increment ciphertext randomness. Trans. Int. J. Math. Sci. Comput. 4(Nov), 34–40 (2018)

Social Media, Mobile and Web, Data Policy, and Privacy and Fake News

Iraqi's Organizations Awareness to Prompt Open Source Cloud Computing (OSCC) in Their Service: A Study

Hala A. Albaroodi[1($\boxtimes$)], Mohammed Abomaali[2],
and Selvakumar Manickam[3]

[1] Gifted Education Authority, Ministry of Education, Baghdad, Iraq
hala.albaroodi5@gmail.com
[2] Department of Computer Technology Engineering,
Alsafwa University College, Karbala, Iraq
abomaali@alsafwa.edu.iq
[3] National Advanced IPv6 Centre (NAV6) Universiti Sains Malaysia,
USM, 11800 Gelugor, Penang, Malaysia
selva@nav6.usm.my

Abstract. Guided by Technology Acceptance Model (TAM) and the lack of research on Open Source Cloud Computing (OSCC) in the Iraqi's setting, the current endeavor posits and tests a model. The model encapsulates a number of perception-based, an attitudinal and intentional variable. Though, the afore-mentioned model is argued to correspond to a number of questions, which in turn, portray a gap in the literature. Particularly, the paper investigates the role of perception of the ease of use, usefulness and risk influences on attitude toward and the intention to adopt OSCC in the Iraqi's settings. In addition, it concep-tualized and tested the mediating role of user's attitude. To that effect, a ques-tionnaire was designed and deployed to examine the factors influencing intention to use the new technology of open source cloud computing. The obtained data were subjected to a number of statistical analyses. Particularly, the goodness of measure was assessed through conducting internal consistency test and factor analysis. The former test uncovered that the utilized constructs are reliable. The later analysis suggested the presence of only three variables. Moreover, the interrelationships between the resulted constructs of the frame-work were tested using multiple and heretical regression. Findings of these analyses suggest that consumers' perception of OSCC has a weak effect on their intention to use it. Consumers' attitudes were found to maintain more potent impact on their intention to utilize the new technology. Moreover, consumers' attitude was unveiled to mediate the relationship between perception of OSCC and the intention to use OSCC. The study was concluded with a brief summary, its implications, and suggestion for future researcher.

Keywords: Open Source Cloud Computing (OSCC) · Cronbach's alpha · Information communication technology (ICT) · Software as a Service (SaaS) · Platform as a Service (PaaS) · Infrastructure as a Service (IaaS)

© Springer Nature Singapore Pte Ltd. 2020
M. Anbar et al. (Eds.): ACeS 2019, CCIS 1132, pp. 305–319, 2020.
https://doi.org/10.1007/978-981-15-2693-0_22

1 Introduction and Background

Please Several efforts were made to disconnect users from the hardware requirements of computer usage. Starting with 'time-sharing' uses, which were envisioned in the 1960s, and kept evolving with the manifestations of network computers during the 1990s. The series of advancements; notably extended to financial grid systems in recent years and more recent developments across various industries. The aforementioned statements are justified are resulted from the move toward cloud computing of many academic institutions and businesses. Cloud computing is a new Information System (IS) architecture, that is posited to be the future of computing and an efficient driving force, making its harshest spectators reconsider its benefits in terms of operating systems, client/server architectures, and browsing. Cloud computing demonstrates strong nexus with the reduction of hardware requirements and the minimization of the overall usage complexity, and thus, it is associated with the ease of use.

That said, it is central for developing the premises of the current endeavor to outline the service models associated with cloud computing. Firstly, cloud Software as a Service (SaaS) [1]. That is to say, cloud services can be arranged into several service models. Each model addresses a set of clients' requirements. Three service models catch multiple groups of clients. A group of clients may only require supplied applications by the cloud provider. The mail service provided by Google is an example of such an application. Secondly, cloud Platform as a Service (PaaS) [1]. This type of model may require more capabilities and control over the provisioned resources. Clients can utilize their own applications, using tools and depository libraries that are made available by a cloud provider. Last but not the least, cloud Infrastructure as a Service (IaaS). Under the veil of this service model, customers attain most of the access to the fundamental layers and resources. In other words, the client can choose a particular operating system and install any application on it [1].

The applications of cloud computing are reachable through differing devices, giving the client's employed interface (e.g., web-based e-mail). It is noteworthy that consumers do not have control or managing ability of the cloud underlying infrastructure, - which contains the network, storage, servers, operating systems, and individual applications' abilities -, which in turns limits user's application configuration settings. Instigated by the aforementioned statement, four deployment models emerged namely private cloud, community cloud as well as hybrid and public cloud models.

However, notwithstanding the growing popularity of these models, security concerns are increasingly an obstacle in the face of cloud computing. For that reason, the efficiency and powerfulness of the conventional protection mechanisms are reconsidered given its distinctiveness from the new architecture. Security issues those are associated with the utilization of cloud computing includes, but not limited to, the following:

- Data losses/leakage.
- The assessment of service quality.
- Weakness of authentication mechanisms.

Moreover, cloud computing is considered one of the major encouraging technologies in computing today. Moreover, the emergence of Open Source Cloud Computing (OSCC) as an established method is instigated by the rapid technological development. OSCC is thought to facilitate the attainment of customizable infrastructure through the utilization of this trend for any type of application domain. It is noted that for a developing country, like Iraq, competing in the global market is becoming more challenging. Attaining competitive edges might prove fruitful through wide deployment of OSCC. OSCC is thought to benefit various business activities and arguably vital to ensuring national welfare. It is observed that the Iraqi's government is pressured to increase OSCC investment. Hence, its deployment might increase the chance of maximizing benefits of optimum technological utilization. The modern usage of OSCC suggests the importance of technological resources utilization wherein various capability results in an OSCC that is "plugged" into the global market. Under the veil of network industry (e.g., E-government, E-education, and E-telecommunication), OSCC combined with Network as Services (NaaS) is evidential across different levels of the market place including, but not limited to, vendors, developers of the platforms and applications, and customers.

Under the Iraqi's settings, there is a dearth of literature on the utilization of OSCC. Specificaly, the obtained endeavors are mainly devoted to the study of IT utilization rather than OSCC [e.g., 6, 7]. Moreover, scholarly effort under the Iraqi's context encompasses the scrutiny of the effect of perceived usefulness and ease of use on information systems for small and medium firms [7]. [2, 3] focused on the intention to purchase via the Internet and compared two theoretical models, namely, Technology Acceptance Model (TAM) and Theory of Planned Behavior (TPB) Model. Furthermore, the influences of consumers' demographics and consumers' purchase preferences on attitudes toward using online shopping and online shopping decisions [4] are investigated. Davis tested the effect of perceived usefulness and ease of use on attitudes toward using technology and on intentional behavior ("TAM theory") [5]. In addition, [6] examined the impact of cost of using Internet technology on attitudes and behaviors toward online shopping [7]. Explored the influence of perceived financial cost on the use mobile banking. That said, additional contribution, particularly in the field of OSCC, remains necessary in studying the Iraqi's settings. However, notwithstanding that several researchers adopted TAM theory, the literature lacks on conceptual and empirical endeavors that utilize the theory in positing and testing the effect of trust and shared values on attitude toward and intention to use OSCC for products and services in Iraqi's organizations.

As such, the researcher explores the determinants of OSCC adoption on the bases of Technology Acceptance Model (TAM) [8]. Additionally, in reconciliation with TAM, the authors review the transforming ability in order to explain and estimate users' acceptance of OSCC technology empirically. Extrapolating on TAM, the influence of intention to use and the usage behaviors are posited to be of critical theoretical and empirical value. Figure 1 shows the basic concepts that underlie user acceptance models [9]. To end, an answer to central questions is investigated. That is to say:

- Does perceived usefulness influences attitude toward OSCC?
- Does perceived usefulness elicits intention to use OSCC?
- Does perceived risk influences attitude toward OSCC?
- Does perceived risk elicits intention to use OSCC?

Therefore, findings of the current study are believed to portray a theoretical and industrial significance. That is to say, it is expected to provide cloud providers with better insight on Iraqi's users and forces that demotivate their intention to utilize OSCC. For that reason, the appropriate point of departure is provided by outlining TAM prior to conceptualizing the guiding framework.

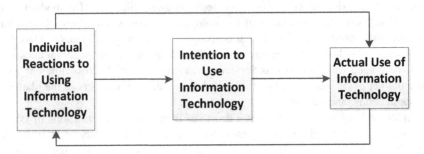

Fig. 1. Basic concepts that underlie user acceptance models [9].

2 Technology Acceptance Model (TAM)

The technology acceptance model (TAM) is posited by Davis et al. [8]. It reflects an instrument to predict the likelihood of the utilisation of a new technology. According to the theory of reasoned action, TAM is, by far, the most widely discussed model among as regards to new technology adoption [10]. Figure 2 illustrates the core concepts and structure of TAM. The Model posit that the use of new technology is guided by two beliefs: perceived usefulness (i.e., the prospective user's subjective thought that using a specific application enhances her/his job performance, within an organisational context) and perceived ease of use (i.e., the degree to which the prospective user expects a target system to respectively reduces the effort required to perform a specific task) [11].

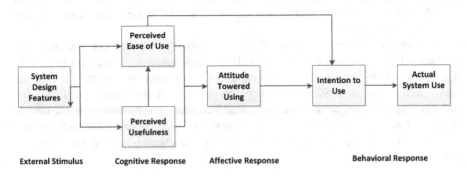

Fig. 2. Technology acceptance model [8]

TAM postulates that actual technology usage is determined by the intention to use, which in turns is resulted from user's attitude toward using a specific technology combined with its perceived usefulness [10]. It theorises that the effects of independent variables (involved system characteristics, processes, and training) on the intention to use a new technology are mediated by perceived usefulness and ease of use. In reconciliation with TAM, perceived usefulness is also influenced by perceived ease of use because when other forces are controlled, a system that is easier to use is posited to be associated with more usefulness.

To that end, it is noteworthy that TAM gained a distinct reputation for its explanatory power in dissecting differences in user behaviour [11]. Polancic et al. performed a Meta analyses of 389 active framework adopting TAM. Their findings support the premises of post-adoption version of TAM. Moreover, they added support to critical relationship between continuous use and successful use of a specific system [12]. With this brief review, the researcher turn to positing the model of the current endeavour and the set of relationships that guides the interaction between the encompassed constructs.

3   Research Framework

In the pursuit of OSCC acceptance, TAM is adopted, giving the invaluable insights it provides. That is to say, the ways users make decisions regarding the acceptance and use of information technologies in organisational settings. In reconciliation with TAM, a framework is posited (see, Fig. 3). Accordingly, a critical weight is given to the determinants of managers decisions regarding a number interventions that elicit a greater acceptance and effective utilisation of IT [5]. Limited by the scope of this endeavour, ICT project managers, it argued that ICT quality managers and ICT senior developers make the decisions as regard to the use of OSCC.

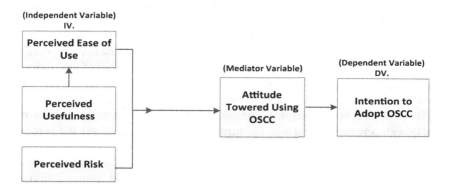

Fig. 3. Modified TAM – A model for OSCC that was adapted from [5] with the perceived Risk [13], attitude toward using OSCC, and intention to use OSCC [9]

The current model suggests that intention to use OSCC acts as a dependent variable. It is defined in terms of the "likelihood that an individual will use the OSCC in the future" [9]. The current paper argues that the aforementioned construct refers to whether the consumer intends to use the OSCC for products or services in the future [9]. To measure the intention to adopt OSCC, a set of measures [4] are adapted and modified [9]. Moreover, attitude toward the use of OSCC is proposed to play a mediating role. It is defined as "the individual's feeling or emotion about using OSCC" [9]. In this context, it is understood based on the sets of positive and negative feelings a consumer associates with the performance of OSCC [9, 14–16]. In measuring this construct and in reconciliation with previous research [9, 14–16], a set of items are adopted and modified to fit the current settings. Additionally, perceived usefulness is posited to function as an independent variable. It is exemplified in terms of "person's perception that using a particular system would enhance his or her job performance" [8]. Though, under this paper's settings, usefulness refers to consumers' perceptions that implies using OSCC enhances the outcome of the organisation to which they are affiliated [17]. To investigate perceived usefulness, a set of items were modified prior to their deployment [5]. Perceived ease of use is proposed to be another independent force. the construct is defined as " person's perception that using a particular system would be free of effort" [8]. In this context, this clarification posit a perceived minimisation of effortful tasks when OSCC is utilised to perform that task [18]. This construct is measured To obtain the perceived ease of use section, we adapt and modify the questions from [8].

Furthermore, perceived risk act the role of independent variable. It means consumers' levels of uncertainty regarding the outcome of a purchase decision; particularly, in the case of a high-priced item or a new technology. Consumers are believed to seek the reduction of resulted anxiety, associated with such decisions, through collecting more information and seeking the recommendations of peers or an entities (private individuals or consumers' advocacy group), that is considered to attain expertise on the subject of matter [13–15, 19–21]. This endeavour argues that "risk" becomes more potent when consumers perceive less informed judgements as regard to purchasing OSCC services or deploying it at the organisational level [22]. Perceived risk is operationalize through a modified scale of measure [13–15, 19–21]. To that effect, it is noteworthy that the hypotheses of the guide the interactions between the encompassed constructs are designated to correspond to the questions of this study, and thereby, fulfil its objectives. That said, the current study extrapolates on TAM in testing the direct and indirect influences of a number of forces as regards to the users for OSCC. As such, it is believed that a perceived ease of use maintains a positive relationship with perceived usefulness. Furthermore, perceived ease of use and perceived usefulness are posited to elicit, positively, attitude toward OSCC. Though, motivated by arguments made in previous conceptual endeavours [8, 13, 23–26] and in reconciliation with TAM, a number of hypotheses (H1–H6) are posited. Figure 4 illustrates the hypotheses.

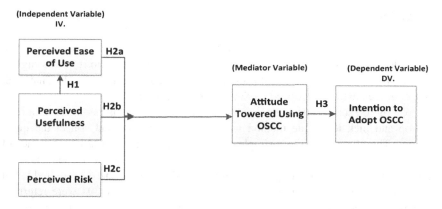

Fig. 4. A model of OSCC and the relationship representation.

4   Method

The questionnaire was piloted prior to its finalisation and distribution. Respondents from a large questionnaire public university were survived. The entire respondent confirmed that they are users of OSCC prior to responding to the questionnaire. Cronbach's alpha was employed to assess internal consistency for each construct [27]. This test is required to determine goodness of a measure [28]. Items with a high reliability measurement are those with a Cronbach's alpha value above .7. To that effect, the reliability of each individual variable was examined. The result indicates high Cronbach's alpha for all constructs in in the current study. Particularly, the results unveiled that perceived ease of use, usefulness, and risk, and attitude toward and intention to adopt OSCC are, respectively, .87, .92, .84, .93, and .86. Therefore, the results support the utilisation of the same set of items encompassed in the questionnaire.

This study attempt to investigate the premises of the conceptual model. Thus, a goodness of measure is employed prior to hypothesis testing. Correlation analysis is used to investigate the posited hypothesis. To that effect, this study employs data that were collected during the period of March 2018–August 2018. As such, it reflects a cross-sectional effort, given that the data were collected in a single attempt for various variables. Moreover, this paper unit of analysis is individual OSCC users in Iraq. This specific selection is resulted from the fact that even among organisations utilising OSCC, not every employee is a user. It is worthwhile to mention that the current endeavour population encompasses OSCC users in Iraq. Giving the absence of a source of users listing, the researchers sought to use Simple Random Sampling (Unrestricted Random Sampling). To accomplish that goal, all potential educational and organisational respondents were targeted to collect the required data. However, this study is devoted to capturing data only from OSCC users. Thus, non-users were instructed to submit uncompleted forms, and the researcher subsequently eliminated all uncompleted forms. The target sample size was 385 OSCC users. A brief introduction on OSCC was clearly stated on the first page of the questionnaire.

5 Results

The Statistical Package for the Social Science (SPSS) [29] is used to analyze the obtained data. Though, non-OSCC user's records were removed prior to assessing the statistical procedures required to fulfil the premises of the current research. That said, the data were entered, categorized, coded, prior to further analyses.

A total of 500 sets of questionnaires were distributed to the users of OSCC in Iraq. The drop and pick technique method were used to distribute and collect the questionnaires. Therefore, by using a simple random sampling method, a list of names of OSCC users was not required giving the random selection of the respondents. As mentioned above, five hundred questionnaires were distributed, and the required target number of questionnaires (sample size) was 385. However, only 204 were returned, 296 questionnaires were not returned, and 31 were rejected as they were largely not useful and incomplete. As such, the 173 complete sets were used to assess the premises of this study. It is noteworthy that the response rate was at 40.8%. Based on existing research [30], a sample size of 100 is required to sufficiently conduct the required analyses. Specifically, this paper analyses section encompasses factor and reliability analyses (goodness of measurement) and a correlation analyses is followed to investigate the relationships between constructs of the hypothesized model.

Moreover, factor analysis is used to assess the underlying structure of variables of the hypothetical model [30]. In addition, when factors' reduction is concluded, the important information in a set of observed variables is held by a new, smaller set of variables that expresses the common trends among the original variables and the substantive for further interpretation (which concerns the identification of the factors or measures that underlie the variables). According to [28], one important step in any data analysis is to understand the dimensionality of the variables of a given model [31]. Factor analysis was conducted in the pursuit of goodness of measure assessment. To that effect, principal component method is applied. According to [32], factor loading is achieved when the value is equal to or greater than 0.50; whereas cross loading is of no concern when its value is equal to or lesser than 0.35. The results of of factor analysis of are presented in Table 2. Kaiser-Mayer-Olkin (KMO) and Bartlett's test, which has a loading of at least 0.90, was used to examine whether the data are valid for performing this method. According to Hair, KMO sampling adequacy is interpreted as follows: marvellous is 90 or above 80, meritorious is 70 or above, middling is 60 or above, mediocre is 50 or above, and finally, miserable is 50 and below. The results indicate that Kaiser-Meyer-Olkin measure of sampling is 0.975, which is considered marvellous, and the Bartlett's test of sphericity is significant at P < 0.01 as illustrated in Table 2 [32].

Principle-axis factor analysis with variety rotation was conducted to assess the underlying structure for the forty items constructing the variables of the hypothesized model. After performing the rotation, three variables were determined, that reflect perception of, attitude toward and intention to use OSCC. The first variable accounted for 75.417% of the variance, the second for 3.066%, and the third for 2.458%. Table 2 clarifies the items and the factor loading for the rotated factors. Though, the occupation and the number of employee constituents were dropped because they had very low loadings.

The first variable is designated to reflect attitude toward; the second is believed to be perception of OSCC (Perceived Usefulness, Perceived Ease of Use, and Perceived Risks); and the third reflect intention to use OSCC. To that end, the variables' reliability was checked to conclude the goodness of measures prior to regressing their respective score. All variables attained a satisfactory Cronbach's alpha. Therefore, the measurements are deemed appropriate for further analyses. As such, the model is redesign. In that sense, perception of OSCC is posited to maintain in influence on attitude toward and the use of OSCC. Attitude toward OSCC, as specified earlier, elicit the use of OSCC. As such, it is positioned, in line with TAM, to mediate the relationship between perception and the use of OSCC.

The work presented is based in part on a published word in Iraq along with the validation. What we have done is to apply the questionnaires on different population and gather different results (Table 1).

Table 1. Factor Analysis

Items	Factor loading			Communality
	1	2	3	
User knowledge towards the usefulness and importance of OSCC				
Occupation				0.166
The number of employees in your organization				0.036
OSCC is mature in Iraq	0.600			0.336
Cloud services are good even without open source systems	0.558			0.703
Open source community and cloud service providers work together	0.701			0.785
Open source is a perfect vehicle to improve cloud computing penetration into organizations	0.742			0.867
Cloud IaaS/PaaS reduces infrastructure costs	0.718			0.816
Have knowledge on cloud computing technology		−.525		
Confident towards using open source software		0.733		0.706
Level of satisfaction with using open source platforms		0.804		0.842
The most preferred of open source software		0.458		0.370
Awareness of the uses and benefits of OSCC		0.703		0.706
Responsible for making decisions on OSCC		0.575		0.336
Attitude towards OSCC				
Using OSCC services would be a good idea	0.780			0.926
Using OSCC services would be more integrating than traditional services (computing, storage, networking)	0.760			0.891

(continued)

Table 1. (*continued*)

Items	Factor loading			Communality
	1	2	3	
Using OSCC services is beneficial to be integrated in the existing system	0.772			0.894
Availability of OSCC services is a concern	0.704			0.834
Perceived Usefulness				
Using OSCC services would enable me to accomplish my requirements more quickly		0.775		0.901
Using OSCC services would be effective for the organization		0.775		0.885
It would be easier to use OSCC services compared to using traditional services (computing, storage, networking)		0.763		0.903
I think OSCC services is beneficial for the organization		0.766		0.910
Perceived Ease of Use				
Learning to use OSCC would be easy for me		0.722		0.842
I find it easy to use OSCC to gain a better software development within the organization		0.556		0.863
I find it easy for me to become skillful in using the OSCC		0.590		0.856
Perceived Risks				
I believe there is a risk of using OSCC services		0.549		0.829
There is a high probability of losing control over data when using OSCC services		0.575		0.806
There is a great Neutrality associated with performance issues when using OSCC services		0.621		0.849
There is a great Neutrality associated with IT governance issues when using OSCC services		0.660		0.869
Overall, I would label OSCC services as an option of negative consequences		0.603		0.672

Table 2. Count. Factor Analysis for the Rotated Factor the Hypothesis Results

Items	Factor Loading			Communality
	1	2	3	
Intention to use OSCC				
I intent to use OSCC services in the future			0.777	0.902
I expect that I would use OSCC services in the future			0.785	0.933
I plan to use OSCC services in the future		0.420	0.760	0.889
KMO	0.975			
Cronbach's Alpha		0.972	0.886	0.931

On the bases of factor analysis findings, a modification of the research's framework is required. To that effect, the researcher restates the hypotheses that guide the model of this thesis. The hypotheses are as follows:

Hypothesis 1: Perception of OSCC is positively associated attitude toward OSCC.
Hypothesis 2: Perception of OSCC is positively associated the intention to adopt OSCC.
Hypothesis 3: Users' attitude toward OSCC is positively associated with the intention to adopt OSCC.
Hypothesis 4: Attitude toward OSCC mediates the relationship between perception of OSCC and intention to adopt OSCC.

Guided by the hypotheses of the current model, the researchers employee multiple and heretical regressions. Though, given that the two forms of regression are extension of leaner regression, a number of assumptions are required to be satisfied prior to these analyses [32]. A test to determine wither any outlier exist was conducted using SPSS 22. The findings unveiled an outlier for attitude toward OSCC. That case was deleted. Additionally, the scattered plots of the three variables uncovered normally distributed values. A regression analyses were ran to detect whether homoscedasticity is violated. This assumption was met. Normality is assessed on the relax role of skewness and kurtosis [33]. That is to say, normal distribution suffers for items that present a kurtosis that fall beyond the range of -2.2 to 2.2 and a skewness of a value between -1 to 1. The test for the three variables indicates normally distributed values. Hence, the skewness and the kurtosis values for the three variables are found to fall within the acceptable threshold. Since the guiding model of this endeavor presents only an independent variable, multicollinearity test is rather fruitless. For that reason, the multicollinearity test (through regression analysis via SPSS 22) indicates that all VIF values for the collinearity statistic fall below two. Given that no value exceeded 3, this assumption is also satisfied. Therefore, in the following sections, the researcher embarks on testing the direct and mediated relationships.

Multiple regressions are utilized to test the direct relationships between the independent and dependent variables. The findings of the analysis assess all direct relations between constructs of the hypothesized model. Specifically, there are three hypotheses positing direct positive relationships.

As mention earlier hypothesis 1 posits that Perception of OSCC is positively associated with attitude toward OSCC. As reported in Table 4, perception OSCC explains only 0.95 per cent of the variance of users' attitude. Though, perception of OSCC was found to be positively predictive of users' attitude ($\beta = 0.309$, P $< .01$). Therefore, the results support hypothesis 1.

Moreover, hypothesis 2 suggests perception of OSCC is positively associated the intention to adopt OSCC. As showed in Table 3. Perception of OSCC explains 11.3 per cent of the variance of the intention to adopt OSCC. As such, perception of OSCC was found to be positively predictive of intention to adopt OSCC ($\beta = 0.336$, P $< .01$). For that reason, the findings support hypothesis 2.

Additionally, hypothesis 3 proposes that users' attitude toward OSCC is positively associated with the intention to adopt OSCC. As demonstrated in Table 5, users' attitude explains 17.9 per cent of the variance of the intention to adopt OSCC. Though, users' attitude was found to be positively predictive of intention to adopt OSCC (β = 0.432, P < .01), making it the strongest predictor. Therefore, the results support hypothesis 3.

Table 3. The relationship perception of OSCC and the intention to adopt OSCC

Independent variables	Dependent variable (intention to adopt OSCC)
Perception of OSCC	0.336**
R Square	0.113
Adjusted R Square	0.11
F Change	0.946

Note: P < 0.01 = **; P < 0.05 = *

Table 4. The relationship perception of OSCC and attitude toward OSCC

Independent variables	Dependent variable (attitude toward OSCC)
Perception of OSCC	0.309
R Square	0.095
Adjusted R Square	0.091
F Change	24.251

Note: P < 0.01 = **; P < 0.05 = *

Table 5. The relationship users' attitude and intention to adopt OSCC

Independent variables	Dependent variable (intention to adopt OSCC)
Users' attitude	0.423**
R square	0.179
Adjusted R square	0.176
F change	50.264

Note: P < 0.01 = **; P < 0.05 = *

Furthermore, Baron and Kenny [34] method of mediation is utilised. The researchers set forth the following steps to determine mediated effect:

The independent variable has to have a significant relationship with the dependent variable.

The independent variable has to maintain a significant influence on the mediating variable.

The mediating variable has to maintain a significant relationship with the dependent variable.

When the mediator is introduced the effect of the independent variable on the outcome variable has to drop significantly (Partial mediation) or present no significant effect (full mediation).

That said, hypothesis 4 posit that attitude toward OSCC mediates the relationship between perception of OSCC and intention to adopt OSCC. As reported in Table 6, the standardized β without introducing the mediator (β = 0.321, P < 0.1) is higher than when the mediator was included (β = 0.181, P < 0.5). Notwithstanding the drop in the independent variable effect on the outcome variable, the relationship between is still significant. Therefore, the findings support partial mediation. As such, hypothesis 4 is partially supported.

Table 6. The Mediated effect

Independent variables	Standardized β1	Standardized β2
Perception of OSCC	0.321**	0.181*
Mediator: users' attitude		0.363
R Square	0.103	0.141
Adjusted R Square	0.097	0.125
F Change	19.946	63.838

Dependent variable: intention to use OSCC

6 Conclusion

The paper has investigated the role of perception of the ease of use, usefulness and risk influences on attitude toward and the intention to adopt OSCC in the Iraqi's settings. In addition, it conceptualized and tested the mediating role of user's attitude. Though, the data were generated from 173 respondents, who contributed to a response rate of 40.8%. These data were analyzed using different tests to assess the goodness of measurement and test the hypotheses. Nevertheless, prior to the full deployment of the final questionnaire, it was piloted to test face validity. Factor analysis unveiled three variables, namely, perception of OSCC, attitude toward OSCC and intention to adopt OSCC. Findings of that analysis and the reliability test suggested the appropriateness of the measurement. Therefore, a restatement of the hypotheses was followed prior to carrying out the tests.

Moreover, findings of the current endeavor uncovered a different structure of regarding the deployment of measurement from developed countries. That is to say, in the Iraqi's context the measurement varied from the one utilized elsewhere. Furthermore, it added to the understanding of users' intention to use OSCC, as a new technological trend, based on the premises of TAM. In reconciliation with that model, the current study suggests a number of factors influencing the utilization of OSCC in Iraq. That is to say, consumers' perception of OSCC has a weak effect on their intention to use it. Consumers' attitude was found to maintain more potent impact on their intention to utilize the new technology. Moreover, consumers' attitude was unveiled to mediate, however weak, the relationship between perception of OSCC and the intention to use OSCC. As such, findings of this paper suggest that, for concern authorities and businesses, users' attitude is central in fostering the adoption OSCC technology. Additionally, it adds to our understanding of the applicability of TAM to the Iraqi's settings.

That said, a shortcoming of this study lies in determining forces that elicit such attitude. Through an enlarged framework might uncover other variables that maintain more potent influence over the intention to use OSCC. For instance, future research might posit forceful effects of other independent variables.

References

1. Buyya, R., Ranjan, R., Calheiros, R.N.: Modeling and simulation of scalable Cloud computing environments and the CloudSim toolkit: challenges and opportunities. In: International Conference on High Performance Computing & Simulation, HPCS 2009, pp. 1–11. IEEE (2009)
2. Breivold, H.P., Crnkovic, I.: Cloud computing education strategies. In: 2014 IEEE 27th Conference, Software Engineering Education and Training (CSEE&T), pp. 29–38. IEEE (2014)
3. Ma'ruf, J.J., Mohamad, O., Ramayah, T.: Intention to purchase via the Internet: a comparison of two theoretical models. Asian Acad. Manag. J. **10**, 79–95 (2005)
4. Wu, S.I.: The relationship between consumer characteristics and attitude toward online shopping. Market. Intell. Plan. **21**(1), 37–44 (2003)
5. Davis, F.D., Bagozzi, R.P., Warshaw, P.R.: User acceptance of computer technology: a comparison of two theoretical models. Manag. Sci. **35**(8), 982–1003 (1989)
6. Shih, H.P.: An empirical study on predicting user acceptance of e-shopping on the Web. Inf. Manag. **41**(3), 351–368 (2004)
7. Luarn, P., Lin, H.H.: Toward an understanding of the behavioral intention to use mobile banking. Comput. Hum. Behav. **21**(6), 873–891 (2005)
8. Davis, F.D.: Perceived usefulness, perceived ease of use, and user acceptance of information technology. MIS Quart. **13**, 319–340 (1989)
9. Venkatesh, V., Morris, M.G., Davis, G.B., Davis, F.D.: User acceptance of information technology: toward a unified view. MIS Quart. **27**, 425–478 (2003)
10. Zhang, N., Guo, X., Chen, G.: Extended information technology initial acceptance model and its empirical test. Syst. Eng. Theory Pract. **27**(9), 123–130 (2007)
11. Venkatesh, V., Davis, F.D.: A theoretical extension of the technology acceptance model: four longitudinal field studies. Manag. Sci. **46**(2), 186–204 (2000)
12. Polančič, G., Heričko, M., Rozman, I.: An empirical examination of application frameworks success based on technology acceptance model. J. Syst. Softw. **83**(4), 574–584 (2010)
13. Teo, T.S.H., Liu, J.: Consumer trust in e-commerce in the United States, Singapore and China. Omega **35**(1), 22–38 (2007)
14. Jensen, M., Schwenk, J., Gruschka, N., Iacono, L.L.: On technical security issues in cloud computing. In: IEEE International Conference on Cloud Computing, CLOUD 2009, pp. 109–116. IEEE (2009)
15. Tsai, C.L., Lin, U., Chang, A., Chen, C.J.: Information security issue of enterprises adopting the application of cloud computing. In: 2010 Sixth International Conference on Networked Computing and Advanced Information Management (NCM), pp. 645–649. IEEE (2010)
16. Jansen, W., Grance, T.: Guidelines on security and privacy in public cloud computing, NIST special publication 800-144. National Institute of Standards and Technology, Washington, DC (2011)
17. Armbrust, M., et al.: Above the clouds: a Berkeley view of cloud computing, Technical report no. UCB/EECS-2009-28. University of California at Berkeley, Berkeley, CA (2009)

18. Britto, M.: An overview of Cloud computing in higher education. In: World Conference on E-Learning in Corporate, Government, Healthcare, and Higher Education, pp. 1062–1071. AACE (2011)
19. Pearson, S.: Taking account of privacy when designing cloud computing services. In: ICSE Workshop on Software Engineering Challenges of Cloud Computing, 2009, CLOUD 2009, pp. 44–52. IEEE (2009)
20. Zhao, G., Rong, C., Li, J., Zhang, F., Tang, Y.: Trusted sata sharing over untrusted cloud storage providers. In: 2010 IEEE Second International Conference on Cloud Computing Technology and Science (CloudCom), pp. 97–103. IEEE (2010)
21. Yang, J., Chen, Z.: Cloud computing research and security issues. In: International Conference on Computational Intelligence and Software Engineering (CiSE), pp. 1–3. IEEE (2010)
22. Foster, I., Zhao, Y., Raicu, I., Lu, S.: Cloud computing and grid computing 360-degree compared. In: Grid Computing Environments Workshop, GCE 2008, pp. 1–10. IEEE (2008)
23. Mukherjee, A., Nath, P.: A model of trust in online relationship banking. Int. J. Bank Market. 21(1), 5–15 (2003)
24. Chiou, J.S.: The antecedents of consumers' loyalty toward Internet service providers. Inf. Manag. 41(6), 685–695 (2004)
25. Liu, R.: A restful architecture for service-oriented business process execution. In: 2008 IEEE International Conference on e-Business Engineering, pp. 197–204. IEEE (2008)
26. Zhang, Q., Cheng, L., Boutaba, R.: Cloud computing: state-of-the-art and research challenges. J. Internet Serv. Appl. 1(1), 7–18 (2010)
27. Cronbach, L.J.: Coefficient alpha and the internal structure of tests. Psychometrika 16(3), 297–334 (1951)
28. Sekaran, U.: Research Methods for Business: A Skill Building Approach, 4th edn. Wiley, New York (2003)
29. Leech, N.L., Barrett, K.C., Morgan, G.A.: SPSS for Intermediate Statistics: Use and Interpretation. Lawrence Erlbaum Associates, Mahwah (2005)
30. Hair, J.F., Bush, R.P., Ortinau, D.J.: Marketing Research within a Changing Information Environment. McGraw-Hill/Irwin, New York (2006)
31. Hair, J., Anderson, R., Tatham, R., Black, W.: Multivariate Data Analysis, 6th edn. Prentice Hall, Upper Saddle River (2006)
32. Hair, J.F., Anderson, R.E., Tatham, R.L., Black, W.C.: Multivariate Data Analysis. Prentice Hall, Upper Saddle River (1998)
33. Sposito, A.V., Hand, M.L., Skarpness, B.: On the efficiency of using the sample kurtosis in selecting optimal lpestimators. Commun. Stat.-Simul. Comput. 12(3), 265–272 (1983)
34. Baron, R.M., Kenny, D.A.: The moderator–mediator variable distinction in social psychological research: conceptual, strategic, and statistical considerations. J. Pers. Soc. Psychol. 51(6), 1173–1182 (1986). https://doi.org/10.1037/0022-3514.51.6.1173

Appraisal on User's Comprehension in Security Warning Dialogs: Browsers Usability Perspective

Christine Lim Xin Yi, Zarul Fitri Zaaba[✉],
and Mohamad Amar Irsyad Mohd Aminuddin

School of Computer Sciences, Universiti Sains Malaysia,
11800 Minden, Pulau Pinang, Malaysia
zarulfitri@usm.my

Abstract. End-user encounters security warnings on a daily basis in different web browsers. Effective security warning is critical to provide a secure environment to end-users to against attack. However, users always encounter problems and challenges when they encounter security warnings due to the poor warning dialogue interface. Element used in the warning interface is important to support users to make an effective decision. A poor warning design will lead a user to become a fraud victim. Hence, there is a need to design an effective warning dialogue by providing useful security features. Although the efficacy of security warning is depending on the interface of security feature, but also highly dependent on the user's perception and understanding. This paper determine to investigates further from the end-user's experience whilst encountering security warnings (i.e. Chrome browser context). An exploratory interview study with 65 participants was conducted to pursue in-depth information about the perceptiveness of users towards current security warnings in three different scenarios. The results show that elements such as icon, colour, wording used in the warning can impact the efficacy of the warning. All the user feedback indicated that there is still room for improvement on the current security warning.

Keywords: Security warning · Browser security · Warning dialogue · Usability · Usable security

1 Introduction

A web browser is an essential tool to access the Internet for accessing and retrieving information resources on the World Wide Web. Today, browsing has become a regular activity for Internet users to access valuable information through millions of sites. For most people, the browser has become the most needed computer program in their daily basic. As Internet users increases, the web browser is one of the widely used applications in the world. Hence, competition among browsers is becoming more intense in the form of updates and version releases as each browser try to compete for user loyalty to dominate in the usage share of web browsers. While web browsers are continually evolving, security threats also increase and diversify. Based on the statistic, the

© Springer Nature Singapore Pte Ltd. 2020
M. Anbar et al. (Eds.): ACeS 2019, CCIS 1132, pp. 320–334, 2020.
https://doi.org/10.1007/978-981-15-2693-0_23

vulnerabilities of the browsers can create many security-related issues in the personal computer system [1]. Consequently, a user may involve the risk of losing valuable assets such as financial information or personal data. As security threats are constantly evolving, security warning can be used to protect users. In a browser environment, a security warning is a crucial strategy used to shield users from the invasion of privacy, malware, or network attack. Security warning act as a mail tool in the browser to inform users of a security risk, enabling them to make security-critical decision to avoid a hazard.

Generally, a warning must be able to capture the user's attention by providing information for users to make inform decisions [2]. Comprehensive security features such as icons, colours, options available and help functions are essential in security warning to accomplish an effective security warning. Different security features may play different roles in the communication process. As a risk communication, end-users must be able to receive enough guidance from the security warning. The effectiveness of security warning usually involves a complex set of consideration which mainly comes from end-users. Hence, it is essential to understand user perceptions when they encounter a security warning in a different situation when they are using browsers.

This paper is organized as follows. Section 2 discusses the related work. Section 3 describes the methodology carried out in this study. Section 3 summarizes and presents all the outcomes from the interview study. Section 4 discusses and highlights the significant findings of this study. Finally, Sect. 5 concludes the paper with a summary of the results.

1.1   Concept of Warning

A warning can be defined as anything that can capture attention to a potentially dangerous situation by prompting people to pay attention to it. When facing difficulties, warnings can influence people to act accordingly [3]. On the other hand, warnings can be described as a communication used to notify the end-users regarding the potential threats and direct them to make a safer decision [4]. Commonly, a warning can be described as something that can make people understand the possible danger or problems that might happen in the future [5]. Therefore, a warning can be viewed as a specific kind of risk communication to convey information on the potentially dangerous hazard that enables advance action from people to avoid potential risk. Fundamentally, warnings can be concluded for three different purposes in different perspectives as shown in Table 1.

Table 1. Purposes of warning [2]

Purposes	Explanation
Provide information	The warning is used to deliver useful information for people so that the information can help them to understand the hazard situation
Influence behaviour	The warning is to influence user behaviour to engage in better and safer decision making
Reminder	The warning is to remind users on the existence of the potential risk

Based on the three purposes, a warning was widely used on physical as well as the digital world that suited its purpose [3]. For instance, warnings can be applied in non-computer and computer context as shown in Fig. 1. All the warnings used in both contexts are meant to make the people more aware and pay attention to the specific or immediate threat.

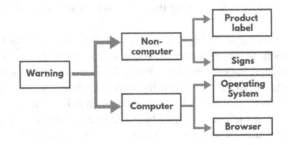

Fig. 1. Application of warning in a different context

1.2 Warning in Non-computer Context

Warnings are critical to creating a safer world for people. It plays a vital role when people are confronting themselves in an unsafe or hazard situation. Warnings are especially important and required to use on roads and construction site. Suitable and relevant safety signs are important warnings that can promote awareness of safety and develop a safe environment at construction sites [6]. Beside road signs and safety signs, many products on the market involve potential risks. Therefore, warnings play a key role in notifying and protecting consumers when using a product. For example, health warnings on cigarette packages are common health risk communication of smoking [7]. In brief, different warnings are used for safety reasons on a daily basis to decrease the likelihood of accidents, health problems, or damage to an individual.

1.3 Warning in a Computer Context

Viewing warnings from a computer perspective, it is an essential medium to protect computer system and users from possible security threats. In the computer context, security warnings can represent as a warning that distracted user's attention to prevent them from unsafe action [8]. As warning can inform users about hazards, it has been widely used and implemented in operating systems and browsers to forewarn them about security threats [9]. Whereas in the browser environment, end users might be alerted with a warning in different scenarios such as download files from the Internet, phishing warning, and browser update. A warning is an effective risk communication that notifies, warns, and advice end-users whenever security threats have been detected in the browser to avoid any possible threats [10]. Usually, the web browser uses warnings to warn people about malware, SSL certificate and social engineering attacks [11]. According to [8], security warnings in the web browser is one of the common ways of alerting and notifying users to possible security threats and preventing a dangerous emerging hazard. While the warning is essential in browser to protect user's computer, modern web browser rely on security indicator and warning dialogue to convey an important message to the end users.

1.4   Problems and Challenges of Security Warnings

A web browser is one of the important applications that end-users always use to perform most of the internet-based activities such as online banking, online shopping and receive emails. For every Internet user, the web browser is the depiction of access key to their private data. As a result, cybercriminals concentrate their strikes on web browsers [12]. As the number of cyber security attack is increasing, designer and web developers have added multiple security parameters to make a browser secure. Security warnings thus used by all web browser developers to strengthen and enhance the browser's security against misconfiguration risks. However, most of the users still disregard the warning due to several issues. Table 2 summarizes all the identified problems and challenges highlighted by different researchers.

Table 2. Problems and challenges of security warning

Problems and challenges	Authors
Lack of understanding of technical wordings	[13–15] and [16]
Inattention towards warnings	[17–20] and [21]
Lack of understanding of warnings	[22, 23] and [24]
Low evaluation of risk from warnings	[25, 26] and [27]
Poor mental model	[28, 29] and [30]
Unmotivated heeding warnings	[18, 31–33] and [34]
Low assessment of the implication of warnings	[11, 14] and [15]
Habituation to the security warning	[35–37, 50] and [38]
Immersion in the primary task	[17, 39] and [40]

From the summarization of Table 2, while most of the research study is focus on the problems independently, this study discovers that inattention towards warning and low evaluation of risk from warnings are strongly related to one another. Based on the security framework proposed by [41], communication delivery is the first step of information-processing. Risk communication is considered to fail unless users notice the communication (attention switch) and aware of the message. Furthermore, the communication should be able to make end-users pay adequate attention to the communication to process the warning. In other words, the security warning should be first able to attract the attention of end-users. Then, comprehension and knowledge acquisition as communication processing is the next step of information-processing. Comprehension refers to the ability of the user in understanding the warning whereas knowledge acquisition refers to the user's ability in learning what to respond for a safer decision after comprehending the warning. Based on the two information-processing steps, the two focus problems in this study are highly correlated with each other. Thus, all these problems are taken into account to improve the current security warning in a browser context. Depending on this, understand the behaviour of end-user regarding these problems can contribute to designing a more effective security warning. The more effective a security warning, the more secure for end-users' valuable assets. To be successful, warnings can achieve its intended purpose by grabbing and sustaining user's attention [43]. Also, a security warning should be able to help users aware of the potential risk for their response.

2 Methodology

An interview study was designed to collect a richer source of information from respondents on the current implementation of the security warning. The interview is an effective approach to collect people opinion for exploring the problem [44]. Hence it is very useful .to establish a foundation to gain insights into how users perceive and respond to a security warning dialogue. The interview was conducted based on one-to-one session in the form of open-ended to discover the problems of low evaluation of risk from warnings, lack of understanding towards warning, and inattention towards warning among users towards the current security warning dialogue. Previous research by [14, 16, 42] chose interview study to examine respondent's understanding and misconception towards the warning interface and its elements.

The research questions in this study were:

- What are the factors that influenced in user's evaluation of risk and attention towards warning in the current implementation of security warning?
- What are the improvements can be made to the current implementation of warning dialogue?

The study was conducted for about one month between 20 December 2018 until 18 January 2019. Similar study conducted by [10, 16, 49] targeted on university students. In this study, majority of the participants were recruited from the Universiti Sains Malaysia, Penang, Malaysia. The interview was conducted in a closed/private room with a quiet background in order to have better communication between the participants. The requirement for participation was that all the participants must age 18 years old and above. This interview was targeting people from a technical and non-technical background. A technical background means that the ones who had studied or had experience work with the computer field whereas non-technical background means that the ones who do not have experience towards the computer field.

Upon arrival, the participant was required to read through and sign a consent form. Then, the interview was carried out with a prototype. The prototype was developed using Microsoft Visual Studio and C# language. The database that was used in this study was MySQL Workbench. The prototype used in this interview because users can experience the current security warning. In the prototype, participants were presented current security warnings for three different scenarios. They needed to imagine that they were performing the task (role play) and accomplished the task. After they completed the task, then the interview was conducted in three different scenarios. Participants will be asked about their opinion towards the current warning. Table 3 shows all the interview questions for all three scenarios. All the interview questions were designed based on the previous study done by [14, 16, 45].

Table 3. Interview questions

No.	Questions
1.	Is the risk identified? What do you think the risk or consequences if you ignore the warning?
2.	What do you understand about the icon?
3.	Do you think the icon is necessary? Why?
4.	Do you think this warning can attract your attention? Why?
5.	How can the warning be improved?

3 Results

In this study, there is a total of 60 Chrome users were recruited in this interview session as [46] suggested that the sample size of the interview study should not less than 60. From the 60 participants, there were 46.67% of male and 53.33% of female. Majority of the participants who involve in this interview were aged from 18 to 25 ($\mu = 21.65$, $\sigma = 1.1618$). It can be noted that most of the participants are familiar with computer technology as more than 90% of participants claimed that they have more than five years of computing experience. Table 4 shows the demographics of the participants.

Table 4. Demographics of participants

Characteristic (N = 60)	Frequency distribution	Percentage distribution (%)
Gender		
Male	28	46.67
Female	32	53.33
Age		
18–25	59	98.33
26–35	1	1.67
36–45	0	0
46–55	0	0
>56	0	0
Educational level		
Postgraduate	4	6.67
Undergraduate	56	93.33
Pre-U	0	0
High School	0	0
Skill		
Technical	20	33.33
Non-technical	40	66.67

In order to examine the problems when users encounter current warnings, the participant had experienced three security warning dialogues as shown in Fig. 2. These warning dialogues were chosen because they show the usability issues which will contribute to the problems as classified in Table 1. Therefore, this interview study attempts to examine user perception towards the security warning that affects the efficacy of security warning.

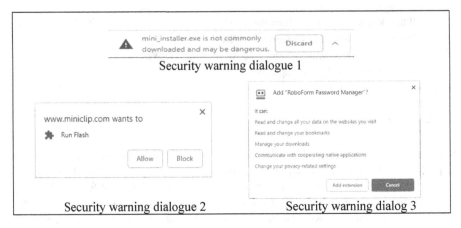

Fig. 2. Security warning dialogues presented in the interview study

3.1   Scenario 1

The result revealed that 41.67% of participants could identify the potential risk from warning. This is due to the warning message that contains some specific words such as dangerous and exe. On the contrary, there are quite several participants who unable to identify the risk from the warning. This indicates that the users have a low evaluation of risk, users cannot identify the actual risk from the warning thus may lead to poor decision making when they encounter the security warning. Then, this study concerned with the question about how participants associate the warning with potential risk. Each participant had to name the risk or consequences if they ignored the warning. Then, the risk was grouped to simplify the evaluation. Excluding five participants who stated that there is no risk associated with the warning and another five participants who are not sure about the risk, the most often named risk was "Virus infection, malware or trojan horse".

Next, the participants were asked about their understanding of the icons used in the warning. According to [48], a warning icon used in scenario one can be known as a universal icon used to represent a hazard situation. Hence, it is crucial to review the user's comprehension of the icon. All the user's opinion from this question were analyzed using NVivo to classifying all the data as shown in Table 5. Based on the results, it can be noted that the most common terms used to describe the warning icon are a warning, danger, sign, attention, caution. Based on the analyze data, it indicates that participants understood the icon as a warning representation. Participants claimed that the icon is a good warning sign that conveys the information of danger, hence people will be more aware and alert of the warning message. Then, the results were used to create a word cloud to reflect the important key point of the user towards the warning icon as depicted in Fig. 3 [47].

Table 5. Word frequency of understanding towards warning icon

Word	Count	Percentage (%)	Word	Count	Percentage (%)
Warning	38	23.9	Means	9	5.66
Danger	29	18.24	Attention	4	2.52
Icon	20	12.58	Caution	4	2.52
Sign	12	7.55	Might	4	2.52

On the other hand, the results from this interview study show that more than 95% of the participants agree with the icon is necessary to be included in the security warning. Only two technical participants disagree with the statement, one of the participants declared that the word is more important than the icon in the presentation of warning. The results revealed that warning icon is an effective visual element used for attention-grabbing. Besides, it can be concluded that the icon can be used for risk communication.

Other than that, the participants also were asked whether the security warning in general can attract their attention. Out of 60 participants, four participants responded negatively. The reason given by the participants are due to the habituation effect, size of the warning message, position of the warning message, and impatient attitude. Contrarily, most of the participants claimed that the security warning could attract their attention due to several factors. It can be noted that the warning icon in red colour can clearly present the existence of potential threats. It is an effective visual stimulus to make people pay more attention to the warning more easily and rapidly.

Lastly, this part of the interview study consists of the question that is related to the improvements needed question. This question aimed to gather opinions from the users to enhance the usability of the security warning. Based on their feedback, improvement in terms of the colour, icon, position, size, and information provided are the top five suggestions given by users.

3.2 Scenario 2

Users always depend on their assessment of risk in making a decision when confronted with a warning. Hence, the way users perceive security threats will influence their responses. The overall result clearly shows that most of the participants cannot identify the risk from the warning. Indeed, even technical users also claimed that they could not identify the potential risk from the warning. The notable discovery for the reasons why participants cannot identify the risk was mainly due to the design of security warning. As P10 noted: "The warning seems very friendly now." This reflects that design will give the wrong impression to the users in evaluating the risk. The perception of security risk in the scenario study will be analyzed in more details in the next question.

328   C. L. X. Yi et al.

Fig. 3. Word cloud of participant's understanding towards icon

Participants were asked about how they think of risk or consequences if they ignore the warning. The result clearly revealed that the majority of participants could not comprehend the underlying potential risk from the warning. The main reason may due to the warning dialogue does not explain the risk or consequences.

In terms of the icon used in this security warning, there are 13 participants who understand the icon correctly as a plugin or extension icon. One interesting finding in this study is that 30% of the participants recognize the icon as the puzzle icon. One immediate observation is that the icon used in this warning cannot help most of the participants to understand the hazardous situation. Presenting an inappropriate icon might be able to influence the user's interpretation of the hazard situation.

Figure 4 shows the reasons for the necessity of the icon to be used in the warning. The results of this interview study show that 61.67% of participants claimed that the icon is not necessarily used in the warning. The main reason was that the icon contains no meaning, participants cannot understand about the icon. Thus, it does not mean anything to them. Besides, the participants also highlighted that they could not get any useful information from the icon. On the other hand, 38.33% of the participants claimed that the icon is necessary to be used in the warning. The main reasons for that are because the icon can be used to symbolize the Flash and attract their attention.

Then, this study investigates whether or not paying attention is due to the elements being used in the warning. Therefore, the participants were asked about whether the security warning can attract their attention. The results show that 34 out of 60 participants agree that the security warning can attract their attention whereas 26 out of 60 participants claimed that the security warning could not attract their attention. It can be noted that the main reason for security warning can attract participant's attention is due to the warning stops them from doing what they want. Most of the participants claimed that they could not proceed with the game without clicking the "Allow" button. Hence, the warning dialogue indirectly can attract their attention. This revealed that security goals always conflict with a user's primary goals due to the distraction of the warning. Besides, respondents also claimed that security warning that using the popup method can attract their attention. This indicates active warning used in the web browser is more effective to attract user's attention as compared to the passive warning.

Participant	Negative Feedback	Participant	Positive Feedback
P1	The icon cannot give some sense of danger because it is black.	P6	The icon can attract my attention.
P3	The dangerous icon should be included in the warning instead of using this icon.	P7	The icon can be used to indicate whether it is a serious warning.
P9	I do not think the icon is important enough.	P18	The icon tells me whether this is an extension or cookies.
P27	The icon does not indicate any warning, or it does not help with the explanation of the warning.	P39	This is the common icon used in the extension for the browser.
P40	The icon is not attention-grabbing.	P46	This icon can be used to symbolize the extension I downloaded is Flash.

- Does not indicate danger
- Does not help in explanation
- Not important
- Not attention-grabbing

- Attract attention
- Indication of the severity of warning
- Symbolization of Flash
- Common icon

Fig. 4. Reasons for the necessity of icon

The last part of this section highlights insights into the future discovery direction of security improvement. Some of the improvements suggested by the participants are summarized. This result revealed that the signal icon and signal words are essential in the security warning. Participants pointed out that the warning dialogue should add "WARNING" to indicate it is a warning.

3.3   Scenario 3

While the current security warning in this study scenario has presented more information regarding the permission, it is important to determine how well the security warning communicate the risk to the users. Therefore, participants were asked whether they can identify the risk from the warning. The result revealed that 78.33% of the participants have a high evaluation of risk in this scenario. Next, participants were asked about how they think of risk or consequences if they ignore the warning. The result shows that most of the participants mentioned that their private data would be stolen if they ignore the warning. This result indicates that participants are very concern about their personal data.

In terms of the icon used in the warning, 26.67% of the participants can identify the icon as the icon used for the Roboform Password Manager application. The interesting finding here is that 3.33% of the participants feel that the icon looks like a pig nose and identified the icon as a robot. Some of them also claimed that the icon looks very cute. This result revealed that adding this icon to the warning cannot perceive the hazard of a warning. Thus this result showed that there was no substantial effect of the icon to a warning.

Based on the findings, 55% of the participants feel that the icon is necessary to identify the extension. The icon can help them make sure they added the correct extension. Although most of the participants agree that the icon is necessary to be used in the warning, however, none of the participants mentioned about this icon represents danger. This means the icon for conveying an important risk is not quite convincing.

Effective warnings must get the users attention to help them avoid or mitigate a hazard. In terms of attention towards warning, the results of this study show that only 6 out of 60 participants responded negatively. To understand why the security warning cannot attract their attention, participants were asked to explain their reasoning. The main reasons are due to lack of warning sign or information, lengthy words with only plain colours and habituation effect. P15 stated that "I see all in black colour and then too many words. Hence I feel like I do not want to read.". Another participant (P27) also said that "The colour of the words is not attractive, maybe it should be in red.". "If I did not read it, I would not know what would happen. A warning should add some significant sign to attract my attention, maybe like a red warning sign.". All the comments from participants revealed that the features provided in the warning have a high impact on the user. In contrast, the main reason that the security warning can attract a participant's attention is due to the detailed information provided in the warning.

To make security warning more useful and effective, participants were asked about what are the required improvements for the security warning. The results revealed that 25 out of 60 participants have no input in this question and satisfied with the current design of the warning. On the contrary, the results revealed that most of the participants suggested to include a signal icon and signal word in the security warning. Interestingly, 15 participants mentioned that the warning could highlight important words like privacy-related settings with colour.

4 Discussion

Interview study gains deeper insights about the two specific problems for the security warning. Based on Fig. 5, it can be noted that there are many factors leading to the usability issues for the security warning. Most of the participants claimed that they have difficulties in perceiving the risk level. Besides, they also claimed that the security warning only could attract their attraction to some extent, this means that users tend to disregard or ignore the warning. This research discovers that the key contributor to the arisen of the two main problems is the element used in the warning. This study also discovers that the used of icon, colour, and wording in the warnings are essential in order to aid users in understanding warning, attract user's attention and improve risk communication. Apparently, a research study by [23] indicated that the comprehension on the level of severity is highly affected by the choices of icon and words. Previous research by [49] and [50] claimed that the combination of a signal icon (exclamation mark) and signal words (WARNING) could aid users in comprehend the hazardous level of the warning. Besides that, [49] also claimed that the interaction of signal word and signal icon could increase the noticeability of security warning, thus attract the user's attention. On the other hand, other users who are lacking in the proficiency of the English language might face the challenges in understanding the technical terminologies in the warning. Consequently, users may have misunderstood towards the warning. Thus, one way to communicate the warning message for those users is to use specific words or icons that individuals with lower-level language also able to interpret and comprehend the warning. Appropriate and concise information should be provided in security warning to give useful support to end-users for making decisions [51]. Overall, this research provides preliminary insights on how different users may have different perception towards security warning. According to [52], an overview of the problems encountered by users is important to reduce usability issue in the warnings. Therefore, all the findings in this study are very useful as evidence regarding creating better risk communication.

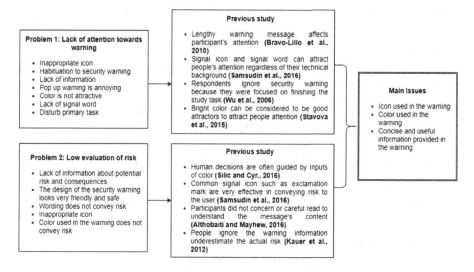

Fig. 5. Derivation of main issues from interview study

5 Conclusion

In conclusion, current security warning implemented in Chrome browser needs some improvements to improve the warning efficiency. The results and findings via the interview session indicated that most of the users have difficulties towards the current security warning. The problems and challenges faced by users when encounter security warning need to be addressed to aid them to make informed decisions. Based on the findings, it can be summarized that the main problems are a low evaluation of risk and inattention towards security warning. By analyzing all the results, it can be noted that the factors in influencing user's evaluation of risk and attention towards warning are mainly due to the icon, colour, information provided in the warning. It can also be concluded that different people may have different perception towards security warning based on their knowledge, demographic or experience. Current findings suggest that security warning should contain comprehensive elements such as signal icon, signal word, understandable word and explanation of risk statement to improve the current security warnings.

References

1. Statista. https://www.statista.com/chart/7451/chrome-most-vulnerable-browser/. Accessed 21 Dec 2018
2. Laughery, K.R., Wogalter, M.S.: Designing effective warnings. Rev. Hum. Factors Ergon. **2**(1), 241–271 (2006)
3. Zaaba, Z.F., Furnell, S.M., Dowland, P.S.: A study on improving security warnings. In: The 5th International Conference on Information and Communication Technology for The Muslim World (ICT4 M), pp. 1–5 (2014)
4. Borger, W., Iacono, L.L.: User perception and response to computer security warnings. In: Workshop on Usable Security and Privacy, Mensch and Computer, pp. 621–646 (2015)
5. Cambridge Dictionary. https://dictionary.cambridge.org/dictionary/english/standardization. Accessed 08 Dec 2018
6. Ng, A.W., Chan, A.H.: Common design elements and strategies in participatory safety sign redesign among construction workers. In: Proceedings of the International Multi Conference of Engineers and Computer Scientists, Hong Kong (2015)
7. Al-Hamdani, M., Smith, S.: Alcohol warning label perceptions: emerging evidence for alcohol policy. Can. J. Public Health **6**, 395–400 (2015)
8. Krol, K., Moroz, M., Sasse, M.A.: Don't work. Can't work? Why it's time to rethink security warnings. In: 7th International Conference 2012 Risk and Security of Internet and Systems (CRiSIS), pp. 1–8 (2012)
9. Bravo-Lillo, C., Cranor, L., Komanduri, S., Schechter, S., Sleeper, M.: Harder to ignore. Revisiting pop-up fatigue and approaches to prevent it, USENIX Association, pp. 105–111 (2014)
10. Amran, A., Zaaba, Z., Mahinderjit Singh, M.: Habituation effects in computer security warning. Inf. Secur. J. Glob. Perspect. **27**(2), 119–131 (2018)
11. Reeder, R.W., Felt, A.P., Consolvo, S., Malkin, N., Thompson, C., Egelman, S: An experience sampling study of user reactions to browser warnings in the field. In: Proceedings of the 2018 CHI Conference on Human Factors in Computing Systems, p. 512 (2018)
12. Zammouri, A., Moussa, A.A.: Safebrowse: a new tool for strengthening and monitoring the security configuration of web browsers. In: 2016 International Conference on Information Technology for Organizations Development (IT4OD), pp. 1–5 (2016)
13. Biddle, R., Van Oorschot, P.C., Patrick, A.S., Sobey, J., Whalen, T.: Browser interfaces and extended validation SSL certificates: an empirical study. In: Proceedings of the 2009 ACM Workshop on Cloud Computing Security, pp. 19–30 (2009)
14. Raja, F., Hawkey, K., Hsu, S., Wang, K.L.C., Beznosov, K.: A brick wall, a locked door, and a bandit: a physical security metaphor for firewall warnings. In: Proceedings of the Seventh Symposium on Usable Privacy and Security, p. 1 (2011)

15. Harbach, M., Fahl, S., Yakovleva, P., Smith, M.: Sorry, i don't get it: an analysis of warning message texts. In: Adams, A.A., Brenner, M., Smith, M. (eds.) FC 2013. LNCS, vol. 7862, pp. 94–111. Springer, Heidelberg (2013). https://doi.org/10.1007/978-3-642-41320-9_7

16. Zaaba, Z.F., Boon, T.K.: Examination on usability issues of security warning dialogs. J. Multi. Eng. Sci. Technol. 2(6), 1337–1345 (2015)

17. Wu, M., Miller, R.C., Garfinkel, S.L.: Do security toolbars actually prevent phishing attacks? In: Proceedings of the SIGCHI Conference on Human Factors in Computing Systems, pp. 601–610 (2006)

18. Whalen, T., Inkpen, K.M.: Gathering evidence: use of visual security cues in web browsers. In: Proceedings of Graphics Interface, pp. 137–144 (2005)

19. Seifert, C., Welch, I., Komisarczuk, P.: Effectiveness of security by admonition: a case study of security warnings in a web browser setting. Secure Mag. 9, 1–9 (2006)

20. Sobey, J., Biddle, R., van Oorschot, P.C., Patrick, A.S.: Exploring user reactions to new browser cues for extended validation certificates. In: Jajodia, S., Lopez, J. (eds.) ESORICS 2008. LNCS, vol. 5283, pp. 411–427. Springer, Heidelberg (2008). https://doi.org/10.1007/978-3-540-88313-5_27

21. Anderson, B.B., Vance, A., Kirwan, C.B., Eargle, D., Jenkins, J.L.: How users perceive and respond to security messages: a NeuroIS research agenda and empirical study. Eur. J. Inf. Syst. 25(4), 364–390 (2016)

22. Downs, J.S., Holbrook, M.B., Cranor, L.F.: Decision strategies and susceptibility to phishing. In: Proceedings of the Second Symposium on Usable Privacy and Security, pp. 79–90 (2006)

23. Egelman, S., Cranor, L.F., Hong, J.I.: You've been warned: an empirical study of the effectiveness of web browser phishing warnings. In: Proceedings of the SIGCHI Conference on Human Factors in Computing Systems, pp. 1065–1074 (2008)

24. Sunshine, J., Egelman, S., Almuhimedi, H., Atri, N., Cranor, LF.: Crying wolf: an empirical study of SSL warning effectiveness, pp. 399–416 (2009)

25. Egelman, S., Schechter, S.: The importance of being earnest [In Security Warnings]. In: Sadeghi, A.-R. (ed.) FC 2013. LNCS, vol. 7859, pp. 52–59. Springer, Heidelberg (2013). https://doi.org/10.1007/978-3-642-39884-1_5

26. Althobaiti, M.M., Mayhew, P.: Users' awareness of visible security design flaws. Int. J. Innov. Manag. Technol. 7(3), 96 (2016)

27. Kauer, M., Pfeiffer, T., Volkamer, M., Theuerling, H., Bruder, R.: It is not about the design-it is about the content! Making warnings more efficient by communicating risks appropriately (2012)

28. Asgharpour, F., Liu, D., Camp, L.J.: Mental models of security risks. In: Dietrich, S., Dhamija, R. (eds.) FC 2007. LNCS, vol. 4886, pp. 367–377. Springer, Heidelberg (2007). https://doi.org/10.1007/978-3-540-77366-5_34

29. Wash, R., Rader, E.: Influencing mental models of security: a research agenda. In: Proceedings of the 2011 New Security Paradigms Workshop, pp. 57–66 (2011)

30. Bravo-Lillo, C., Cranor, L., Downs, J., Komanduri, S.: Poster: what is still wrong with security warnings: a mental models approach. In: SOUPS'10: Proceedings of the 6th Symposium on Usable Privacy and Security (2010)

31. West, R.: The psychology of security'. Commun. ACM 51(4), 34–40 (2008)

32. Herley, C.: So long, and no thanks for the externalities: the rational rejection of security advice by users. In: Proceedings of the 2009 Workshop on New Security Paradigms Workshop, pp. 133–144 (2009)

33. Shi, P., Xu, H., Zhang, X.L.: Informing security indicator design in web browsers. In: Proceedings of the 2011 iConference, pp. 569–575 (2011)

34. Mesbah, S.: Internet science-creating better browser warnings. Seminar Future Internet WS1415, Network Architecture and Services (2015)

35. Brustoloni, J.C., Villamarín-Salomón, R.: Improving security decisions with polymorphic and audited dialogs. In: Proceedings of the 3rd Symposium on Usable Privacy and Security, pp. 76–85 (2007)

36. Akhawe, D., Felt, A.P.: Alice in Warningland: a large-scale field study of browser security warning effectiveness. In: USENIX Security Symposium, pp. 257–272 (2013)

37. Bravo-Lillo, C., et al.: Your attention please: designing security-decision UIs to make genuine risks harder to ignore. In: Proceedings of the Ninth Symposium on Usable Privacy and Security, p. 6 (2013)

38. Anderson, B.B., Kirwan, C.B., Jenkins, J.L., Eargle, D., Howard, S., Vance, A.: How polymorphic warnings reduce habituation in the brain: insights from an fMRI study. In: Proceedings of the 33rd Annual ACM Conference on Human Factors in Computing Systems, pp. 2883–2892 (2015a)

39. Sharek, D., Swofford, C., Wogalter, M.: Failure to recognize fake internet popup warning messages. Proc. Hum. Factors Ergon. Soc. Annu. Meet. 52(6), 557–560 (2008)

40. Sasse, M.A., Brostoff, S., Weirich, D.: Transforming the 'weakest link'—a human/computer interaction approach to usable and effective security. BT Technol. J. 19(3), 122–131 (2001)

41. Cranor, L.F.: A framework for reasoning about the human in the loop. In: UPSEC'08 Proceedings of the 1st Conference on Usability, Psychology, and Security, pp. 1–15 (2008)

42. Bravo-Lillo, C., Cranor, L., Downs, J., Komanduri, S., Sleeper, M.: Improving computer security dialogs. In: 13th International Conference on Human-Computer Interaction (INTERACT), pp. 18–35 (2011)

43. Anderson, B.B., Vance, T., Kirwan, B., Eargle, D., Howard, S.: Users aren't (necessarily) lazy: using NeuroIS to explain habituation to security warnings (2014)

44. Alshenqeeti, H.: Intervewing as a data collection method: a critical review. Engl. Linguist. Res. 3(1), 39–45 (2014)

45. Krol, K., Moroz, M., Sasse, M.A.: Don't work. Can't work? Why it's time to rethink security warnings. In: 2012 7th International Conference Risk and Security of Internet and Systems (CRiSIS), pp. 1–8 (2012)

46. Baker, S.E., Edwards, R., Doidge, M.: How many qualitative interviews is enough? Expert voices and early career reflections on sampling and cases in qualitative research (2012)

47. Williams, W., Parkes, E.L., Davies, P.: Wordle: a method for analysing MBA student induction experience. Int. J. Manag. Educ. 11(1), 44–53 (2013)

48. Silic, M., Cyr, D.: Colour arousal effect on users' decision-making processes in the warning message context. In: Nah, F.F.-H.F.-H., Tan, C.-H. (eds.) HCIBGO 2016. LNCS, vol. 9752, pp. 99–109. Springer, Cham (2016). https://doi.org/10.1007/978-3-319-39399-5_10

49. Samsudin, N.F., Zaaba, Z.F., Singh, M.M., Samsudin, A.: Symbolism in computer security warnings: Signal icons and signal words. Int. J. Adv. Comput. Sci. Appl. (IJACSA) 7(10), 148–153 (2016)

50. Amer, T.S., Maris, J.M.B.: Signal words and signal icons in application control and information technology exception messages—Hazard matching and habituation effects. J. Inf. Syst. 21(2), 1–25 (2007)

51. Zaaba, Z.F., Furnell, S., Dowland, P.: End-user perception and usability of information security. In: HAISA, pp. 97–107 (2011)

52. Zaaba, Z.F., Furnell, S.M., Dowland, P.S.: Literature studies on security warnings development. Int. J. Perceptive Cogn. Comput. (IIUM) 2(1), 8–18 (2016). https://doi.org/10.31436/ijpcc.v2i1.22

Empirical Investigations on Usability of Security Warning Dialogs: End Users Experience

Farah Nor Aliah Ahmad, Zarul Fitri Zaaba[(✉)],
Mohamad Amar Irsyad Mohd Aminuddin, and Nasuha Lee Abdullah

School of Computer Sciences, Universiti Sains Malaysia,
11800 Gelugor, Penang, Malaysia
zarulfitri@usm.my

Abstract. The dependencies of the computer and the Internet keep increasing among the users. Thus, it poses to the increasing number of attacks as a result of using various application and tools. Security warning conveys an alert on the potential harm users might expose such as malware and any kind of attacks on their computer. In practice, most of the end users tend to ignore the security warning as it shows the messages repeatedly, although they have been exposed to many risks. A security warning dialogue is supposed to catch the user's attention and comprehension however, because of users' past experiences such habituation makes them became less focus. One-to-one interview session with 60 participants was conducted in order to gain further comprehension among the end users experiencing security warning and to investigate the usability issues of current security warning implementation. It is deemed of necessity to discover these usability issues in the current context of security warning presentations. The result revealed that the problems and challenges continue to persist such as difficulties to make a decision, difficulties to comprehend technical jargons, lack of attractiveness of current security warning and issues of habituation or repeated exposures of warnings.

Keywords: Usability · Security warning · Usable security · Security · Human-computer interaction

1 Introduction

The Internet can be considered as a necessity to make our life easier. It becomes very crucial for users as part of their daily needs. Regardless of any ages, the people are relying on the Internet a lot to gain information, keep in touch with others and entertainment. By 2018, almost 3.6 billion people are using the Internet regardless of any platform either using computers, smartphones or table device [1]. With such technologies, people are not aware of possible menaces. The threats become very contagious and spreadable cross the world. According to [2], there are many types of attacks which pose threats to the user if they are not aware of the security warning such as malware, account hijacking, vulnerabilities and etc. Therefore, to prevent the threats occurred to the minimum level, the security warning plays a role as the line of defence

© Springer Nature Singapore Pte Ltd. 2020
M. Anbar et al. (Eds.): ACeS 2019, CCIS 1132, pp. 335–349, 2020.
https://doi.org/10.1007/978-981-15-2693-0_24

to tell users that they are potentially exposed to harm. According to [3], a security warning is a warning system to remind computer users from the security breaches. In fact, [4] claimed that warning is meant to designed to prevent the people from harm. The security warning is crucial to the user because it gives a message to alert of any security threats recognized and protect the threats damage the computer system.

Although the security warning conveyed an alert to the users regarding the potential harm that might expose to them, the users tend to disregard the security warning because of some reasons. [5–7] claimed that users tend to disregard neither read nor understand the security warnings and fail to attract their attention. Also, most users believe that decision that they made when they encountered security warning is a false positive or their computer is safe against any attack because they think that antivirus is enough to protect their computer [6]. [7] stated that the users interpret a warning message with an optimistic way after encountering a dialogue repeatedly. On the other hand, [8] and [9] revealed that the usage of technical terms in security warning is also one of the reasons the users disregard the security warning. Thus, it can be noted that previous works revealed various issues on how end users perceive security warnings. This paper determines to reaffirm the issues by interview session in order to gauge deeper comprehension. This paper is structured as follows: Sect. 2 presents an overview of warning in a computer environment and summaries the problem and challenges in security warning; Sect. 3 describes the methodology utilising the interview session; Sect. 4 presents the result and findings; Sect. 5 highlights the discussion; finally ends with the conclusion in Sect. 6.

2 Related Work

2.1 Warning in Computer Environment

A computer security warning is to serve as a reminder to computer users from the security breaches [3]. According to [10], a security warning is a common method of alerting users from any harms and avoiding them from dangerous acts. A security warning is used in various application to inform the user of a security risk and it encourages users to take secure action to prevent becoming a victim of malware infection or information leakage [7]. However, the users tend to ignore security warning even though security warning conveys messages that tell users that the computer is exposing to various threats. According to [11], the users find that the security warning as an annoyance although it defends the system from harm.

Security warning can be encountered while installing application, open emails' attachment and restarting the computer [12]. Nevertheless, security warnings in a computer can be displayed while the battery is low, the caps lock is on and opening a file. Apparently, security warning can be categorized into the balloon, in-place warning, notification, dialogue box and a banner [13]. Figure 1 presents some of the examples of security warning that available on the computer. Then again, Table 1 describes the usage of each type of security warning message based on the given example.

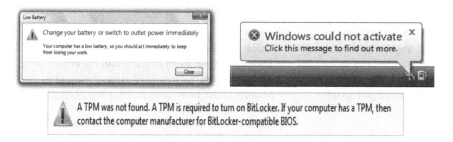

Fig. 1. Examples of security warning interface [13]

Table 1. The description for the type of security warning interface [13]

Types	Example
Banner	Used to give information that prevents a problem upon the users completing the task
Dialogue box	Focusing on critical warning usage that involves information and users must respond to warning promptly
In-place	Focusing on delivering information that might prevent a problem upon users are making choices to the warning system
Notifications	To give important events or status that can be ignored by the user or at least for a temporary
Balloon	As a control in a situation that affects input. This state is mostly not meant, and the user might not conscious the input affected

The focal point of this study is on the dialogue box context. One of the rationales choosing this context is because the implication of making the wrong decision on warning in dialogue box is more severe comparing the other context of warnings. In addition to that, most of the findings also utilizing the dialogue box in their studies [8, 9, 11, 12]. Therefore it is important to have an appropriate guideline in designing the warning from the usability perspective. A guideline is designed to produce a proper security warning interface based on the type of security warning [13]. It explains the design concept that needs to put, capitalization, concision of sentence, icons and terminology. This guideline provides a complete example to distinguish correct and incorrect warning message. However, with the current implementation, security warnings are designed in various way depending on developer's viewpoint. The next section discusses regarding the problem and challenges of the current security warning encountered by the users.

2.2 Problem and Challenges

There are many approaches to improve the usability of the existing security warning. In most cases, the users had difficulty to understand the usability correctly and not able to utilize it. The users do not know the way to interact with the security tools and technologies which later might lead them in making the wrong decision.

Table 2. The problems and challenges

Problems and challenges	Description
Unheeding towards security warning	• People pay less attention if the context is similar [7] • User ignores the warning because of the effects of habituations [20]
Unable to interpret security warning	• Security advice from a non-expert is less likely to overlap with the experts [21] • Users tend to misconstrue of security warning dialogue context as other dialogues [7]
Unable to comprehend the usage of technical jargons	• Users unable to comprehend the technical terms usage in the warnings [9] • The ActiveX control, scripts and active content definition is barely comprehending by the users [14, 15, 22]
Misappraise of Risk from Warning	• Most of the users responded to security warning without fretting or mindful reading to understand the warning's content [23]
User unable to comprehend the implication of warning	• User did not understand the security warnings' element [16] • User cannot comprehend requisite details and did not find the text easy to resolve and understand the security warning [24]
User demotivated towards the attention of warning	• Users think that their capability or might think that they have nothing worse happened and less affected toward security warning [25]
Habituation effects	• Users ignore warning upon experience towards dual-task interference (DTI) which failing to pay attention to the warning [26] • Normality bias which is users experiencing warning repeatedly and dismiss different dialogues and underestimate it over time [7] • High habituation effects in static warning compared to polymorphic warning [36]
The poor mental model of computer security warning	• There are eight "folk models" that can be used [27] • The mental model will become weaker if a warning is withheld for a day [28]

Table 2 presents the eight classifications of problems and challenges towards the security warning implementation. According to [7], the users pay less attention to the warning upon encountered with various dialogue in certain frequency as the dialogue looks similar to them. Apart from that, [15] evaluated the respondents' comprehension of technical terminology during the interview and online survey and the outcomes show that advanced user is generally able to understand the technical terminology while most beginner respondents unable are not. It shows that these problems can be considered severe because in reality the vast majority of users are from the beginner background. This work determines to reaffirm the problems experienced by the users as presented from the literature works.

3 Methodology

The interview was conducted on a one-to-one basis to discover the trends of user's comprehension and perception and to analyze in-depth understanding of issues among the users towards security warning.

Previous research by [16, 17] chose an interview session to carry out the experiments and to gain more details about the security warning. This interview was targeting the participant from a technical and non-technical background. A person from the technical background means a person who has studied or involved in computer related field while the non-technical background means who have a slight knowledge of computer related field. Apart from that, [29] categories non-technical group from non-computer related college majors and technical participants had computer-related college majors. In this research, the technical background was identified as the one who has or currently majoring in courses such as computer science and engineering while the non-technical background is the one who majoring in courses not related to computer science and engineerings such as art, management, biology, education, accounting and communication.

The interview was well promoted via social networks such as Facebook, Twitter and WhatApps and word of mouth. Most of the participants were from the Universiti Sains Malaysia, Pulau Pinang main campus. The interview was held in a closed room in order to have better communication and comfortable surroundings. A previous study by [3, 10, 11, 13, 15] were also recruiting the students to be their participants for their interview session.

A simulation of warning was used as a prototype in the interview session. The prototype was developed using Microsoft Visual Studio 2017 with C# language and. Net framework. The database used in this experiment was Microsoft SQL Server Management Studio 2017. The prototype was used in this interview because it is able to gather basic information faster and to present the scenario and context of warning in a presentable manner. A prototype gives optional information such as user's profile data, able to highlight the information the data site is given and rate the percentages of the information entered. This work was supported by [10, 30] where they conducted a semi-structured interview using the prototype to test their experiment. On the other hand, [7] also interviewed to investigate experimental design matter, user's reaction matter and usability matter in their studies. On the contrary, [17] was interviewed to investigate the comprehension and attention of the participants toward symbolism which is a signal icon and signal words in security warning.

In the prototype, the participants were presented with three tasks that they have to perform. They needed to imagine that they were performing the task in each scenario and accomplished the task as they have done before. The interview was conducted 20 to 30 min.

Before the interview session started, the participants were given some brief instruction by the principal investigator regarding the experiment. The interview was aimed to gain a participant's comprehension and response based on the script prepared [9]. The time for the participants made the decision and the conversation of the experiment was recorded for analysis (i.e. automatically via interaction between user and prototype). The actions (i.e. users' decision, time accomplish one task etc.) were recorded in the database. In addition, audio conversations were also recorded with the consent from the participants. The audio interviewed were then coded, transcribe and analyzed. The coded were done by another researcher to avoid any biases.

4 Results and Findings

The interview gained a total of 60 responses where all the participants have been briefly instructed on how the flow of the interview and given their consent for the data and the recording to be used in this research. Previous research by [17] also recruited 60 participants while [35] recruited 30 participants. This can be concluded that the 60 participants in the research can be considered a sufficient sample size. The responses were treated as confidential as possible where no real information about the participants were revealed. The vast majority of the participants were from the Universiti Sains Malaysia, Pulau Pinang as this work had been well promoted and conducted in the university. Table 3 illustrates the result for the demographics section of the participants.

Table 3. Demographics

Characteristic (n = 60)	Frequency distribution	Percentage (%)	Mean	Std. deviation
Gender				
Male	8	86.7	0.13	3.43
Female	52	13.3		
Age				
18–25	59	98.3	0.02	0.129
26–35	1	1.7		
36–45	0	0		
46–55	0	0		
>56	0	0		
Major				
Technical	34	56.7	0.43	0.500
Non-technical	26	43.3		
Education level				
High school	0	0	0.02	0.129
Pre-U	0	0		
Undergraduate	59	98.3		
Postgraduate	1	1.7		

4.1 Practical Tasks and Interviews

In this part, participants were required to undergo three scenarios of security warnings. For each task, the participants need to imagine that they were performing the task and accomplished the task as they have done it before. The participants need to decide for each task. After that, they need to answer interview questions based on the security warning dialogue presented to them. In the previous study, five of security warning dialogues were presented to the participants in order to gain a clear understanding of the user's knowledge in security warning [9]. On the other hand, [3, 15] also used three scenarios in their interview study with similar aims like the current work. Series of questions were asked in order to find out their understanding about the signal icons, to understand consequences of actions, the difficulties that they encountered upon receiving the warning and to probe more details about the attractiveness of current version. These questions were set based on previous research by [17] that also conducted an interview session to gain more details perception and comprehension among the participants. Table 4 illustrates the questions asked in each scenario.

Table 4. Question for interview session

No	Questions
1	What do you think if you clicked 'RUN'/'OPEN'/'INSTALL'? Is it bad?
2	What do you understand about the icon A? Do you think it is necessary?
3	What do you understand about the icon B? Do you think it is necessary?
4	What are the difficulties that you faced when you received this warning?
5	Do you think this warning attract your attention? Please explain

4.1.1 Scenario 1

In Scenario 1, the participants need to imagine that they have downloaded the file and trying to open a file named SyncBackSetupDE.exe in their computer. The file located at D:\Incoming in their computer. When the participants open the file, the security warning dialogue pops up in their computer.

Security warning in Scenario 1 prompted the participant to make a decision. The participants need to make a decision either to 'RUN' or 'CLOSE'. The decision time for all the participants was recorded. Upon completing all the tasks, the participants need to answer an interview question based on a security warning in Scenario 1.

First, the participants were asked on their first action upon they received this warning. It can be noted that the majority of the participant would read the message first and make their decision to 'RUN' the file which was 47% of them. Some of the reasons from the participants were:

i. "I read first and decided to 'RUN' because of trusted publisher" (P13)
ii. "I am making sure to read to ensure that the file is not harmful" (P31).

However, there were some of the participants who decided to run straight away (30%) because they always see the warning and they feel no worry to open the file. This indicates that some of the participants have no attention towards the warning and tends to habituate with the situations [6, 18]. The next question is to know the comprehension of the signal icon in the yellow shield. The question was also asked either the icon is necessary or not. Majority of the participants understands that the icon is a warning icon and the icon is necessary to be placed because it alerts the user to read the message. Figure 2 shows the security warning that encountered by the participants in the interview session.

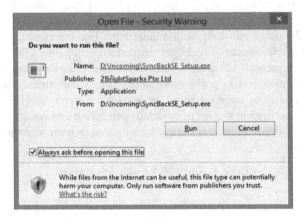

Fig. 2. Security warning 2

The next question is to know the comprehension of the file icon. According to [15], the icon means the application/file exe icon. The majority (56%) of the participants understand well that the icon is application/file exe icon in security warning. Also, the majority of the participants think that it is necessary to put the icon in the warning.

Next, the question was asked to the participants to identify the difficulties they had when they received this warning. Most of the participants have difficulties in understanding technical term such as.exe, type, publishers you trust. When we probe further, the participants claimed that terminology was too technical for them and they did not understand why it needed to be there. In general, and on balances, participants were able to decide due to the previous exposures to the warnings.

4.1.2   Scenario 2

Scenario 2 was depicted in Fig. 3. The participants need to imagine that they have downloaded the document file from Microsoft Outlook named test.docx in their computer desktop. When they are trying to open the document, the security warning pops up.

Security warning in Scenario 2 prompted the participant to make a decision. The decision time for all the participants was recorded. Upon completing all the tasks, the participants need to answer an interview question based on a security warning in Scenario 2. The first question asked in this section was the first action upon receiving this warning. It can be noted that most of the participants would decide to open the file which 70.3% of them because it does not look dangerous for them. Also, only a

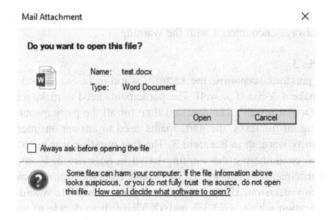

Fig. 3. Security warning 2

minority of them would decide to cancel. However, some of them would read the message carefully before deciding either to open or cancel.

These are amongst the reasons the participants decide to open the file:

i. "The icon does not look dangerous" (P8)
ii. "The software is trusted because it is from Microsoft" (P48)
iii. "It is just a document" (P60).

It can be noted that most of the participants feel that the colour of the icon affects the level of dangerous in the security warning. Hence, it is important to use a suitable colour to convey the message is dangerous or not. However, one of the reasons they decide to open the file which is "it is just documented". It can be noted that in this situation, the participants underestimate the risk in the security warning. This behaviour can lead to a problem such as being hacked, loss of potential assets and privacy [13].

Next, the question was asked regarding the word icon and either the icon is necessary or not. The icon means Microsoft Word icon [13]. It is one of the Microsoft office products. Majority of the participants answered it correctly even though the majority of them were from a non-technical background and they answered that the icon is necessary to put in the warning message.

The other question was asked to the participant about the blue icon and either it is necessary or not. The blue icon means question mark icon which indicates help [13]. Majority of the participants answered that the icon means question mark icon and it has confused them to decide as it looks safe. Thus, it posed conflict from what users' perceive and the real meaning of the question mark icon.

After that, the next question was to probe the difficulties that the participants faced when encountered with this warning. Again, most of the participants (62%) do not understand the technical term as well as some of the icons. Also, they do not understand the function of checkbox in the warning. One claimed that it should be automated from the warning to decide on behalf of the users. The last question was asked to the participants either the warning attract their attention or not. Majority of the participants which 55% of them claimed that the warning message attracts their attention because they were not always encountered with the warning.

4.1.3   Scenario 3

Similar to the previous scenarios, the security warning in Scenario 3 prompted the participant to make a decision as well. The participants need to make a decision either to 'Install' or 'Do not install'. The decision time for all the participants was recorded. Upon completing all the tasks, the participants need to answer an interview question based on a security warning in Scenario 3. The first question was asked regarding the first action upon encountering the warning based in Scenario 3. It can be noted that most of the participants which are 53.3% would read the warning carefully before proceeding to any decision. However, some of the participants would decide not to install the application which is 23.3% and 18.3% of them decide to install the application. These were the feedback on the reason's participants read the message carefully:

i. "The red icon looks dangerous" (P3)
ii. "I am afraid if something bad happened to my computer" (P40)
iii. "It stated that the publisher is unknown in bold font" (P51) (Fig. 4).

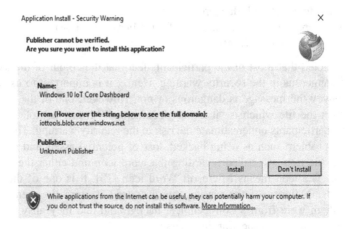

Fig. 4. Security warning 3

Also, the comprehension towards the signal icon was asked in this warning. The question was asked about the globe icon and either it is necessary or not. It can be noted that the majority of the participants (83%) do not understand the icon because they have not seen the icon before. The next question was asked regarding the red icon and either it is necessary or not. The red icon means the error icon which indicates something wrong and high possibility of unsafe [15]. Most of the participants misinterpret the icon as a warning icon (71%). Only a minority of them answered as error icon.

On the other hand, the question was asked regarding the difficulties that the participants faced when they encountered this warning. Again, most of the participants have difficulties in understanding the technical term, signal icon and hard to make a decision. However, a minority of them had no difficulties at all. Lastly, the question was asked the attractiveness of the message to the participants. It can be noted that the majority of the participants claimed that this message attracts their attention. Some of the reasons are stated as follows:

i. "The red icon looks dangerous" (P8)
ii. "The publisher is unknown" (P13).

4.1.4   General Questions

In this section, the interview study presents questions related to the improvement needed and another opinion regarding the current implementation of the security warning. The questions were aimed to gather more opinion from the user. Table 5 indicates the questions that had been asked. It can be noted that most of the participants claimed that the term is easier to understand mostly by those who were from the technical background users compared to non-technical background users. They also claimed that the technical terms sometimes tend to make things more complicated. It should be clear to the reader to ease their burden in deciding. The next question was asked about the presentation of current security warning implementation. 92% of the participants claimed that the security warning should be further improved. These were the reasons that express by the users:

i. "People do not like many words" (P1)
ii. "The words should be bold if it dangerous" (P4)
iii. "Use layman term so the most user would understand the message" (P7)
iv. "The colour is dull" (P52).

Table 5. General Questions

No	Questions
1	What do you think of the usage of a technical term in current security warning? Why it is used?
2	What do you think of the presentation of the current security warning? Do you think it should be improved? Why?

5   Discussion

Based on the results and findings discuss in the previous section, it can be noted that there is a corresponding need to improve the current implementation of security warning regarding the usability. In this study, 92% of the participants suggested that the current implementation of security warning can be further improved. The most notable difficulties face by the users were the difficulties in comprehending the technical terminologies used in this warning. It tends to make the interface of the security warning plain, dull and less user-friendly. In all the three scenarios, users prefer to use the layman term or less technical term so that both backgrounds either technical or non-technical users could understand the message very well. Our work confirmed with the previous findings where it had been revealed by [9, 14] that users experienced significant problems with technical terms. Our results also suggested that users experienced significant issues with the usage of signal icons and words use as a claim in [17]. Besides that, according to [5, 19], most of the participants did not pay attention when the security warning popped up. Our work revealed that even though the details of information in security warning is short, the users still have difficulties in understanding the warning and making a decision. They tend just to ignore it and proceed with an action without reading it where the consequences may be severed. The resulted behaviour such as ignoring the warning is correlated with the user's attention [6]. On the other hand, it is not surprising that some of the participants claimed that they had no difficulties at all with the current context of warning as they can clearly explain the meaning of the terminology used in the security warning as well as signal icon. The colours and the presentation of warnings may affect users' understanding and attention towards it. Apart from that, the similar security warning appears repeatedly which leads to habituation effects. Previous experiment conducted by [36] proved that the static security warning obtained high habituation among the participants. Thus, it is crucial to improve the security warning especially from the usability context so that users can pay more attention towards the security warning to prevent them from any harmful threats. The summary of the work is presented in Fig. 5.

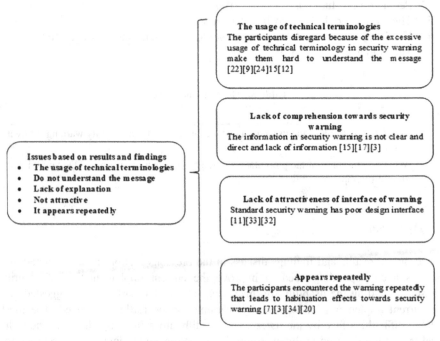

Fig. 5. Summary of discussion

6 Conclusion

In conclusion, there are corresponding needs to improve the security warnings based on the continuous studies on usability issues in the warnings. It is crucial to discover the problems that arise in the computer security field for safety purposed in term of a personal asset, identity and also financial data. Our work has reaffirmed the previous studies and our work mapping the problems in further details as depicted in Fig. 5. The usage of technical terminologies, lack of explanation and the warning were not attractive were amongst the most highlighted findings in this study. Therefore, security warnings should be designed to map with the problems above and challenges experienced by the users.

On the other hand, there are some limitations to this work. This work is more focusing on dialogue box because most of the users encounter it in our daily life while using a computer and not the other contexts such as notification, balloon, in-place and banner. Apart from that, this research gained insights from mainly student's perspective where the majority of them were from the Universiti Sains Malaysia.

For future works, the enhancement to improve the current version of security warning is needed to tackle the severe issues such as excessive usage of technical jargons, lack of attractiveness and hard to make a decision. It is expected that with the new design of security warnings, it will be able to increase attractiveness that leads the user to heed the security warning and increase the comprehension of the message context of the warnings to the users.

References

1. Mahajan, A.: 3.6 billion active internet users worldwide by 2018 with nearly 50% penetration. https://dazeinfo.com/2014/11/26/india-overtake-us-second-largest-internet-user-base-2015-half-world-internet-access-2018-emarketer/. Accessed 31 Sept 2018
2. Passeri, P.: Cyber attacks statistics. https://www.hackmageddon.com/2018/02/22/january-2018-cyber-attacks-statistics/. Accessed 31 Sept 2018
3. Amran, A., Zaaba, Z., Mahinderjit Singh, M.: Usable security: revealing end-users comprehensions on security warnings. In:4th Information Systems International Conference, ISICO 2017, pp. 635–631, Elsevier B.V., Penang (2017)
4. Wogalter, M.: Purposes and scope of warnings. Hum. Factors Ergonom. 3–9 (2006)
5. Schechter, S., Dhamija, R., Ozment, A., Fischer, I.: The emperor's new security indicators. In: The 2007 IEEE Symposium on Security and Privacy, p. 15. IEEE, Oakland (2007)
6. Akhawe, D., Felt, A.: Alice in warningland: a large-scale field study of browser security warning effectiveness. In: Proceedings of the 22th USENIX Security Symposium (2013)
7. Minakawa, R., Takada, T.: Exploring alternative security warning dialog for attracting user attention: evaluation of "Kawaii" effect and its additional stimulus combination. In: IIWAS 2017: The 19th International Conference on Information Integration and Web-based Applications and Services. Association for Computing Machinery, Salzburg (2017)
8. Bravo-Lillo, C, Cranor, L.F., Downs, J.S., Komanduri, S.: POSTER: what is still wrong with security warnings: a mental models approach. In: Proceedings of the Sixth Symposium on Usable Privacy and Security, Redmond, WA (2010)

9. Bravo-Lillo, C., Cranor, L.F., Down, J.S., Komanduri, S.: Bridging the gap in computer security warning. A Mental Model Approach, pp. 18–26 (2011)

10. Krol, K., Moroz, M., Sasse, M. A.: Don't work. Can't work? Why it's time to rethink security warnings. In: 2012 7th International Conference on Risks and Security of Internet and System (CRiSIS) (2012)

11. Samsudin, N., Zaaba, Z.: Security warning life cycle: challenges and panacea. J. Telecommun. Electron. Comput. Eng. 9(2–5), 53–57 (2017)

12. Amran, A., Zaaba, Z., Mahinderjit Singh, M.: Habituation effects in computer security warning. Inform. Secur. J.: Glob. Perspect. 27(2), 119–131 (2018)

13. Microsoft. https://docs.microsoft.com/en-us/windows/desktop/uxguide/mess-warn. Accessed 31 Sept 2018

14. Zaaba, Z., Furnell, S., Dowland, P.: A study on improving security warning (2014)

15. Zaaba, Z., Teo, K.: Examination on usability issues of security warning dialogs. J. Multidisc. Eng. Sci. Technol. (JMEST) 2(6), 1337–1345 (2015)

16. Raja, F., Hawkey, K., Hsu, S., Wang, K.LC., Beznosov, K.: A brick wall, a lock door and a bandit: a physical metaphor for firewall warnings. In: Proceedings of the Seventh Symposium on Usable Privacy and Security, Pittsburgh, USA, pp. 1–20 (2011)

17. Samsudin, N.F., Zaaba, Z.F., Sing, M.M., Samsudin, A.: Symbolism in computer security warnings: signal icons and signal word. Int. J. Adv. Comput. Sci. Appl. (IJACSA) 7(10), 148–153 (2016)

18. Wu, M., Miller, R., Garfinkel, S.: Do security toolbars actually prevent phishing attacks? In: CHI 2006, pp. 601–610. ACM, Québec (2010)

19. Motiee, S., Hawkey, K., Beznosov, K.: Do windows users follow the principle of least privilege?: investigating user account control practices. In: Symposium on Usable Privacy and Security (SOUPS), p. 13. ACM, Washington (2010)

20. Anderson, B.B., Kirwan, C.B., Jenkins, J.L., Eargle, D., Howard, S., Vance, A.: How polymorphic warnings reduce habituation I the brain: insights from fMRI study. In: Proceeding of the 33rd Annual ACM Conference on Human Factors in Computing Systems, pp. 2883–2892 (2015)

21. Ion, I., Reeder, R., Consolvo S.: "…no one can hack my mind": comparing expert and non-expert security practices. In: Symposium on Usable Privacy and Security (SOUPS). USENIX (2015)

22. Furnell, S.M., Jusoh, A., Katsabas, A.: The challenge of understanding and using security: a survey of end-users. In: Computer and Security, The International Source of Innovation for the Innovation Security and IT Audit Professional (2006)

23. Althobaiti M.M., Mayhew, P.: User's awareness of visible security design flaws. Int. J. Innov. Manag. Technol. 3(7) (2016)

24. Harbach, M., Fahl, S., Yakovleva, P., Smith, M.: Sorry, I don't get it: an analysis of warning message texts. In: Adams, A.A., Brenner, M., Smith, M. (eds.) FC 2013. LNCS, vol. 7862, pp. 94–111. Springer, Heidelberg (2013). https://doi.org/10.1007/978-3-642-41320-9_7

25. Mesbah, S.: Internet science-creating better browser warnings. Seminar Future Internet WS1415 (2015)

26. Jenkins, J.L., Anderson, B.B., Vance, A.: More harm than good? How messages that interrupt can make us vulnerable. Inform. Syst. Res. 27, 1–17 (2016)

27. Wash, R.: Folks models of home computer security. In: Symposium on Usable Privacy and Security (SOUPS) (2010)

28. Vance, A., Kirwan, B., Bjorm, D., Jenkins, J., Anderson, B.B.: What do we really know about how habituation to warnings occurs over time? A longitudinal fMRI study of habituation and polymorphic warning. In: Computer Human Interaction (CHI 2017), Denver, CO, USA (2017)

29. Kang, R., Dabbish, L., Fruchter, N., Kiesler, S.: My data just goes everywhere: user mental models of the internet and implications for privacy and security. In: Symposium on Usable Privacy and Security (SOUPS), pp. 39–50 (2015)
30. Shepherd, L.A., Archibald, J., Ferguson R.: Reducing risky security behaviours: utilising affective feedback to educate users. In: Proceedings of Cyberforensics (2014)
31. Redmiles, E., Malone, A., Mazurek, M.: I think they're trying to tell me something: advice sources and selection for digital security. In: IEEE Symposium on Security and Privacy, pp. 272–288. IEEE (2016)
32. Das, A., Khan, H.: Security behaviors of smartphone users. Inform. Comput. Secur. 1(24), 116–134 (2016)
33. Anderson, B.B., Vance, A., Kirwan, B., Eargle, D.: User aren't (necesserily) lazy: using NeuroIS to explain habituation to security warnings. In: Thirty Fifth International Conference on Information System, Auckland (2014)
34. Bravo-Lillo, C.A.: Improving computer security dialogs: an exploration of attention and habituation. PhD thesis, Carnegie Mellon University (2014)
35. Zaaba, Z., Furnell, S., Dowland, P.: Literature studies on security warnings development. Int. J. Percept. Cogn. Comput. (IJPCC. 2, 8–13 (2016)
36. Anderson, B., Vance, A., Kirwan, C., Jenkins, J., Eargle, D.: From warning to wallpaper: why the brain habituates to security warnings and what can be done about it. J. Manag. Inform. Syst. 33, 713–743 (2016)

Vulnerabilities in Online Food Ordering Website

Ji-Jian Chin[✉], Yvonne Hwei-Syn Kam, and Vik Tor Goh

Faculty of Engineering, Multimedia University, Cyberjaya, Malaysia
{jjchin,hskam,vtgoh}@mmu.edu.my

Abstract. In this paper, we show several vulnerabilities in the ordering mechanism of one of Malaysia's online food ordering services company (which we will call "Company X") website. In particular, we show that the system is open to several kinds of abuse, demonstrating two proof-of-concept attacks we carried out, as well as discuss more potentially disruptive theoretical attacks. We also suggest several countermeasures to rectify the issues, that are not only applicable to Company X website, but also to other similar online ordering systems.

Keywords: E-commerce · Vulnerabilities · Online portal · Attacks

1 Introduction

As e-commerce continues to grow in Malaysia, more and more organisations rely on websites and mobile apps to conduct businesses. The Department of Statistics Malaysia in a recent survey provided a figure that RM447.8 billion worth of revenue from online transactions occurred in 2017, of which RM152.6 billion comes from the services industry [1].

This is the reason why many traditional retailers operating from brick-and mortar stores also offer their services and products through their respective online portals. Typically for stores that sell physical goods, they will showcase their products online and allow shoppers to directly purchase them. Once the transaction is complete, the store ships the orders or the shopper does in-store pickups. Ultimately, these online portals facilitate business-to-consumer transactions, thus increasing profitability for businesses while offering greater convenience and value for consumers.

However, implementing a secure online portal is not a trivial undertaking. According to [3], any existing security vulnerability will almost always be uncovered and exploited. In recent history, as e-commerce websites continue to grow without proper security audits and regulations, more and more such vulnerabilities have been uncovered [4, 5, 7, 8].

© Springer Nature Singapore Pte Ltd. 2020
M. Anbar et al. (Eds.): ACeS 2019, CCIS 1132, pp. 350–357, 2020.
https://doi.org/10.1007/978-981-15-2693-0_25

Unfortunately, such is also the case with Company X's online web portal. In our effort to satiate our hunger, we discovered some security-related shortcomings with Company X's online ordering mechanism. Despite the convenience that the online portal afforded, some design choices could potentially result in losses to both Company X and its customers.

Proof of concept attacks are important as they are conducted to verify that a vulnerability exists and that indeed it is possible to attack a system via that vulnerability. One such example showcasing the weaknesses of Norwegian Bank systems was done by Espelid et al. in [2].

In this paper, we explain our observations and corresponding proof-of-concept (PoC) attacks that exploit the shortcomings of Company X's online portal. The rest of the paper is organised as follows; in Sect. 2, we describe the ordering procedure using Company X's online web portal, followed by a description of the proof-of-concept (PoC) attacks against the online web portal in Sect. 3. In Sect. 4, we discuss two further theoretical attacks that are potentially more disruptive and costly. We discuss some potential countermeasures that can be deployed to thwart these attacks in Sect. 5 and finally, we give some concluding remarks and disclaimers in Sect. 6.

2   Ordering from Company X's Website

In this section, we describe how a user can place orders to Company X via their online web portal. First, the user navigates to the URL and selects between delivery and collection. For the uninitiated, the delivery method allows a rider to deliver the order to a user's specified location within 30 min, whereas collection requires the user to physically go to the specified shop to retrieve their order.

Either way, once the method to receive the order is confirmed, the user is then brought to the main menu where the user can select from a variety of promotions and à la carte items offered by Company X. Placed orders will be stored in a basket as displayed on the right column. Once the order is completed, the checkout button at the bottom right has to be clicked to bring the user to the checkout menu.

At the checkout menu, the user is required to key in their personal details to enable collection. Only 3 fields are required, namely the user's name, phone number, and email address. Additionally for delivery, the user's address for the order to be sent to is required as well. Figure 1 exhibits the checkout menu. Once the order is placed, a confirmation screen will be shown and the order confirmation will also be sent to the user's email as entered.

Unfortunately this simple procedure makes the online portal susceptible to various abuse, as demonstrated in the next section.

Fig. 1. Checkout menu and required fields.

3 Proof-of-Concept (PoC) Attacks

In this section, we demonstrate two simple PoC attacks carried out in May 2019 via the online web portal ordering system. The two conceptual attacks are the **impersonation order** and the **fake order**.

3.1 Impersonation Order

The first is an impersonation attack, whereby the first author placed an order on the second author's behalf. In this case, the order was placed with the second author's knowledge and consent. However we would like to emphasise that the contrary could very well have happened.

We will refer to the entity placing the order as the attacker while the entity whose identity is being taken advantage of as the victim for this attack, e.g. the first author is the attacker placing the order on the second author, the victim's behalf.

Since the online ordering system does not require any user authentication, the attacker simply has to navigate to the website URL and place the order. Our experiment was conducted using the collection method, whereby an order was placed using the victim's credentials as in Fig. 2a.

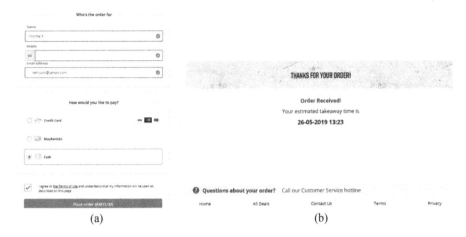

Fig. 2. (a) Victim's credentials used in (b) Confirmation of order. Impersonation order.

As Fig. 2b displays, the order was confirmed and placed under the victim's email that was keyed in.

Upon querying the store cashier regarding collection procedures, the cashier mentions that if the victim does not show up to pick up the order, protocol dictates that the store calls the victim to provide reminders. Finally, if the victim still does not collect the order, the prepared order is discarded at Company X's loss, while the victim may at best face potential harassment from the store calling regarding an order the victim did not place, or at worst face potential reputation loss and discredited, either being blacklisted as a customer or denied service in the future.

3.2   Fake Order

In this second attack, the authors attempted to place an order using bogus credentials. As a proof of concept, a fictitious entity named Vivian Han was generated with a random structure-preserving phone number 012-5532123 and a temporary disposable mail generated using https://temp-mail.org under vihihan@mailhub.top.

We placed another order with the fictitious account as referenced in Fig. 3a, to which we received confirmation as referenced in Fig. 3b. The order confirmation was also received in the temporary mail inbox, as referenced in Fig. 4.

Fig. 3. (a) Fake entity credentials used (b) Confirmation of order for fake entity in making a fake order.

The attack should already incur losses up to this stage if the attacker does not collect from the store. Even worse is if the fake order was done by delivery, as the rider will deliver the order to the wrong address, and if the address in inhabited, will certainly cause conflict with the inhabitants of the address who are oblivious to the order.

Fig. 4. Order confirmation arrived through disposable email.

4 Theoretical Attacks

In this section we discuss two additional attacks in theory. The attacks were not carried out conceptually as it may incur financial losses on behalf of Company X. The two theoretical attacks discussed are the preemptive collection attack, as well as the denial of service attack.

4.1 Preemptive Collection

A preemptive collection attack occurs when the victim places a legitimate order under the knowledge of the attacker. Since by conducting both previous conceptual attacks that the store does not require any credentials from the person collecting the order, the attacker may be informed of the victim's order beforehand and preempts the user in collection, thereby denying the victim proper service. The situation is made worse if the victim prepaid for the order using either bank transfer or credit card, therefore forfeiting both order and payment.

4.2 Denial of Service

A more skilled hacker with access to a botnet swarm may be able to flood the system with fake orders. Since the system requires no prior registration of users before placing orders, the hacker can program the botnet swarm to randomly select delivery addresses, select random combination of menu items and checkout the orders using randomly generated fictitious accounts.

If the attack occurs simultaneously, Company X's online portal will be brought down for maintenance, thus denying them opportunity profits from potential orders.

A more damaging scenario occurs if these fake orders are interspersed masquerading as honest orders, to which the orders are not collected. Since the phone numbers provided will not be in actual service (or worse, if they are and belong to innocent parties oblivious to what is happening), the orders will generally be wasted, incurring financial losses on Company X.

5 Remedial Countermeasures

The main reason the attacks in the previous section are viable is because the ordering procedure lacks any entity authentication prior to engaging in the ordering confirmation. These attacks can be easily circumvented by deploying a login mechanism prior to placing the order, for example, as practised by a food and beverage (F&B) provider in Malaysia. The F&B provider's online portal requires users to register, verify emails and phone numbers before creating an account that allows users to place future orders. Clicking on Start Order brings user to the login screen as referenced in Fig. 5, which requires the user to authenticate themselves before continuing with the ordering procedures. Hackers wanting to place fake orders would have to go through the hassle of registration with temporary emails in order to obtain account confirmation links prior to placing these orders. Furthermore, the login mechanism can prevent impersonation orders as the hackers will now require the honest user's credentials prior to gaining ordering capability on behalf of that user.

Fig. 5. Website requires user to login to a registered account prior to placing orders.

A second layer of authentication to circumvent fake orders would require the user to click on a confirmation link generated using a hash function on the order details, sent by either SMS or email to the respective phone or email that is registered to the user making the order before proceeding to confirm the order and start the food preparation. This will help to prevent fake orders or erroneous orders that may cause financial loss if the user does not collect after ordering, as the user with the proper registered phone or email is required to confirm the order prior to it being prepared.

A last remedial countermeasure would require a policy change in terms of staff handling the delivery of these orders. Staff should be trained to collect some authentication token from the user, confirming that the order does indeed belong to the collecting person. This will help circumvent orders being given to the wrong collecting entity.

As usual, security comes at the cost of convenience. However, in the case of Company X, this convenience comes with a high risk of abuse. Therefore, it is advisable for Company X's management to reconsider the balance between user convenience and security trade-offs in light of these vulnerabilities we just revealed.

6   Conclusion and Disclaimer

In this paper, we demonstrated two conceptual attacks carried out against Company X's online ordering web portal. We discussed two other more potentially damaging attacks that may occur. Lastly we proposed three remedial actions which may help deter such attacks from occurring.

Since the attacks were proof of concept only, the authors honoured both orders placed while conducting the conceptual attacks and made good on payments during collection, thus not incurring any loss on the part of Company X.

Lastly, Table 1 summarises the attacks, the potential victims facing losses, as well as whether the proof of concept attack was conducted as part of the experiment. The authors re-emphasise that no actual financial loss was incurred on any parties when conducting this work.

Table 1. This table summarises the vulnerabilities of the Company X web portal ordering system and on honest users.

Attack	Parties facing potential losses	Experiment conducted?
Impersonation orders	Honest users, Company X	Yes
Fake orders	Company X	Yes
Preemptive collection	Honest users, Company X	No
Denial of service	Company X	No

At the point of publication, the authors have made multiple attempts to contact Company X's management to facilitate controls to circumvent the attacks described, but the management have yet to respond to our requests for discussions. Additionally a MyCERT report was lodged with Cybersecurity Malaysia [6], who have confirmed the vulnerabilities and have made their own attempts to reach out to Company X's management as well. Based on our correspondence with MyCERT up at the point of writing, no responses from Company X have been obtained by Cybersecurity Malaysia either.

References

1. E-commerce transactions enjoying healthy growth. The Star Online, May 2019. https://www.thestar.com.my/news/nation/2019/05/14/ecommerce-transactions-enjoying-healthy-growth/
2. Espelid, Y., Netland, L., Klingsheim, A.N., Hole, K.J.: A proof of concept attack against Norwegian internet banking systems. In: Tsudik, G. (ed.) FC 2008. LNCS, vol. 5143, pp. 197–201. Springer, Heidelberg (2008). https://doi.org/10.1007/978-3-540-85230-8_18
3. Fonseca, J., Vieira, M., Madeira, H.: Testing and comparing web vulnerability scanning tools for SQL injection and XSS attacks. In: 13th Pacific Rim International Symposium on Dependable Computing (PRDC 2007). pp. 365–372. IEEE (2007)
4. Khrais, L.T.: Highlighting the vulnerabilities of online banking system. J. Internet Bank. Commer. **20**(3) (2015)
5. Marchany, R.C., Tront, J.G.: E-commerce security issues. In: Proceedings of the 35th Annual Hawaii International Conference on System Sciences, pp. 2500–2508, January 2002. https://doi.org/10.1109/HICSS.2002.994190
6. MyCERT: Malaysia computer emergency response team. https://www.mycert.org.my/. Accessed 18 July 2019
7. Sun, F., Xu, L., Su, Z.: Detecting logic vulnerabilities in e-commerce applications (2014)
8. Yao, Y., Ruohomaa, S., Xu, F.: Addressing common vulnerabilities of reputation systems for electronic commerce. J. Theoret. Appl. Electron. Commer. Res. **7**, 1–20 (2012). https://scielo.conicyt.cl/scielo.php?script=sci_arttext&pid=S0718-18762012000100002&nrm=iso

Threats Against Information Privacy and Security in Social Networks: A Review

Ahmed Al-Charchafchi$^{(\boxtimes)}$ ⓘ, Selvakumar Manickam,
and Zakaria N. M. Alqattan

National Advanced IPv6 Centre (NAv6), Universiti Sains Malaysia (USM),
Penang, Malaysia
ahmed.h.mustafa@gmail.com,
{selva,zakaria.alqattan}@usm.my

Abstract. This review paper is an attempt to cover the arising threats against information privacy and security in the attractive Social Network environment that represents a rich mine of user personal data. First, the paper discusses the information privacy, while many researches have been found in the relevant literature with respect to privacy in Social Networks, more efforts are needed especially on data leakages that happen to each entity including Social Network users, service providers, third and external parties, and how data linkages can produce useful information to these parties. Second, the paper discusses the information security focusing on the social engineering threats, while many efforts have been found in the relevant literature with respect to social engineering in the Internet in general, only few attempts cover the topic in the Social Network environment. In this paper, threats of fake accounts, identity theft, and spear phishing are discussed specifically in the Social Networks. Furthermore, the paper presents the roles of Social Network users and service providers to protect information privacy and prevent threats against information security. This review paper is an attempt to become a guideline to current information privacy and security threats in Social Network environment, and to pave the way for the researchers to investigate more solutions for these threats in future works.

Keywords: Social Network · Social Media · Privacy · Security · Data leakage · Data linkage · Social engineering · Fake account · Identity theft · Spear phishing

1 Introduction

Within last two decades, a rapid growth of using Social Networks (SN)s around the world can be observed. The SN services can be produced as websites or smartphone applications with user generated contents. According to the last Hootsuite global digital report [1], the number of Social Media users has significantly risen within last six years from 1.857 billion users in 2014 to 3.484 billion users until January 2019, the latter represent around 45% of the total world population as shown in Fig. 1(a). On the other hand, the average spent time by users has risen from 1 h and 37 min per day in 2014 to 2 h and 16 min per day in January 2019 as shown in Fig. 1(b). SN services such as

© Springer Nature Singapore Pte Ltd. 2020
M. Anbar et al. (Eds.): ACeS 2019, CCIS 1132, pp. 358–372, 2020.
https://doi.org/10.1007/978-981-15-2693-0_26

Facebook and LinkedIn have a significant role in people daily life for social and business communication.

(a)   **(b)**

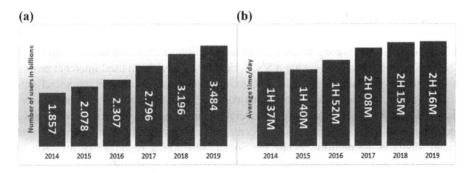

Fig. 1. (a) Number of Social Media users (in billions) within six years (adapted from [1]) (b) Average spent time per day for Social Media users within six years (adapted from [1])

One of the main objectives of the SN existence is information sharing; therefore, people who want to make benefit from SN services cannot avoid sharing different types of information including their personal data. Noteworthy, collecting these data is considered a legitimate work if it happens based on the user knowledge and consent [2]. SN environment represents a great attraction to many attackers that exploit any small vulnerability available in the SN platform or any lack of user awareness. The attackers intent can be one of the following two intents or both: the first is to leverage the huge amount of user data that are available within the SN which represent threats against privacy, and the second is to initiate different malicious activities which represent threats against security [3].

There are many security threats that exploit any small vulnerability in the attractive SN environment. Such technical vulnerabilities can be fixed, and the security of the SN platform can be strengthened using many technical solutions. The problem is that technical solutions have no recognized effect when the attackers exploit the lack of user knowledge and awareness in a social engineering attack [4]. For this reason, this paper aims at investigating the state-of-the-art researches regarding to information privacy and security threats in SNs. This paper is an attempt to: (a) cover the threats against information privacy including data leakages and linkages to each entity within the SN environment; (b) discuss the most common social engineering attacks against information security including fake accounts, identity theft, and spear phishing attacks. Furthermore, the countermeasures against privacy and security threats have been discussed briefly within each subsection.

Noteworthy, traditional security threats that are available in the Internet in general such as spams, malwares, and DDoS attacks are out of the scope of this review paper. Next, Sect. 2 will define SN and present a general background. Section 3 will present the previous works and discuss the methodology of this review paper. While Sect. 4 will discuss privacy threats in SNs including data leakages and linkages, Sect. 5 will explore the social engineering threats including three types of attacks. Finally, Sect. 6 will discuss the solutions and conclude this review paper.

2 Social Network Background and Definition

Before going on to investigate the current information privacy and security threats in SNs, it is important to define what a SN is. Few terms have been used interchangeably in the literature to investigate SNs. The most common terms are "online social network", "social network site", "social networking site", and "social networking services" [5]. On the other hand, the term "social media" is used to cover a broad range of emerging web-based applications in recent years. Some researchers mentioned that Social Media is the platform, while the Social Networking is the act of a person to communicate and interact with his/her online community (p. 17) [6].

SN sites were defined by Boyd and Ellison as *"web-based services that allow individuals to (1) construct a public or semi-public profile within a bounded system, (2) articulate a list of other users with whom they share a connection, and (3) view and traverse their list of connections and those made by others within the system"* [7]. According to this definition, a website that was launched in 1997 called (SixDegrees.com) represents the first SN that allowed creating profiles and adding friends in a list, by combining many features of earlier blog, chat, and community websites. At early stages, SNs had a limited purpose of representing the real life as a virtual online world. SNs help to maintain and solidify existing offline connections between persons having a family relationship, or they are school or work colleagues, or they are living in the same town or city, or any common offline relation in the real life [7, 8]. In few years later, SNs popularity rapidly grew and more services were added such as photo and video sharing with the ability of friends tagging. The purposes of using SNs have been widely varied and become not only for social interaction but also for general news sharing and business interaction. Furthermore, the rising popularity of smartphones with their easy and fast features paved the way to the SN service providers (SP)s to develop their services as mobile applications and leads to much more SN users [8]. At this point, SNs can be classified into multiple categories depending on the main purpose of usage [9, 10], the most common categories are general SNs (such as Facebook, Instagram, Pinterest, and Qzone), business SNs (such as LinkedIn and XING), academic SNs (such as ResearchGate and Academia), microblogging and news update (such as Twitter and Tumblr), and media sharing SNs which include video sharing (such as YouTube and TikTok) and photo sharing (such as Flickr) as shown in Fig. 2.

Despite of big differences among the above mentioned SNs, a SN include four main entities: SP, user, third parties who develop applications and launch them on the SN platform, and other external parties who can be any stakeholders such as advertisers or academic researchers. The flow of user data happens among these four entities, while services are provided as an exchange for user data [11], as shown in Fig. 3. Threats against information privacy and security in SN environment can arise from any of these entities which will be discussed in the next section.

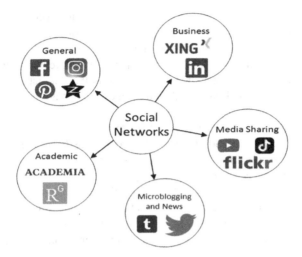

Fig. 2. Social Networks categories

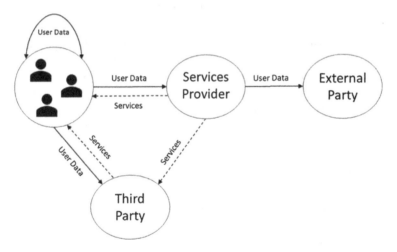

Fig. 3. Flow of user data among Social Network entities (adapted from [10])

3 Previous Works and Review Methodology

Since a wide range of information privacy and security threats exists in the SN environment, this review paper covers study areas regarding to information privacy including data leakages that happen to each entity including SPs, users, third parties, as well as data linkages by external parties. On the other hand, this paper discusses the information security focusing on the social engineering threats including fake accounts, identity theft, and spear phishing. According to relevant literature, many efforts have been found with respect to threats, issues, challenges, and attacks that arise in terms of information privacy, information security, or both privacy and security in a SN environment. Different categories of information privacy and security threats are presented and discussed in this paper, part of these categories is available in different surveys as shown in Table 1, while collecting and formulating those categories in a single research is the significance of this review paper. Most previous efforts have been covered traditional security threats that are available in the Internet in general such as spams, malwares, and DDoS attacks; therefore, those topics are not presented in this review paper.

The search criteria of this review paper are to retrieve relevant articles written in English and published from 2009 to 2019. The search has been performed within the main academic databases and search engines including ACM Digital Library, Google Scholar, IEEE Xplore, ScienceDirect, and SpringerLink. The search has been performed using the shown terms in Table 2. The titles, keywords, and abstracts of the articles have been examined, and after eliminating the duplicates and invalid content, the remaining were 40 articles. Those articles are included in this review paper in addition to two books, two PhD theses, and few digital and statistical reports about SN platforms usage.

Table 1. Previous works

Research Work	Year	Data leakages\linkages to\by:				Social engineering threats		
		Other users	SP	Third parties	External parties	Fake accounts	Identity theft	Spear phishing
[11]	2012	✓	✓	✓	✓	✗	✗	✗
[12]	2014	P	✗	✗	✓	✓	P	P
[13]	2015	✗	✗	✗	P	✓	P	P
[9]	2016	✗	✗	✗	✗	✓	P	P
[3]	2017	✓	✓	✓	✓	P	P	✗
[14]	2017	✓	✓	✗	✓	✗	✗	✗
[15]	2017	✓	✗	P	✗	✓	P	P
[16]	2018	✓	✓	✗	✗	✓	P	P
[2]	2019	✓	P	P	✓	✗	P	✗
[17]	2019	✗	✗	✗	✗	✓	P	✓

Note: "P" means partially covered.

Table 2. Used terms in the search process

Category	Terms	No. of selected articles
SN information privacy	"Social Network" and: "information privacy" or "privacy threats" or "privacy issues" or "privacy concerns" or "data leakage" or "data linkage"	24
SN information security	"Social Network" and: "social engineering" or "social engineering threats" or "social engineering attacks" or "fake accounts" or "identity theft" or "spear phishing"	16

4 Information Privacy Threats in Social Networks

Privacy is not a simple and single notion; rather it has many dimensions including physical privacy, social privacy, and information privacy, only the latter is within the scope of this review paper. When a researcher attempts to dive in the topic of information privacy, the term "Personally Identifiable Information (PII)" is commonly used. PII was defined in [18] as *"information which can be used to distinguish or trace an individual's identity either alone or when combined with other public information that is linkable to a specific individual"*. There are few categories of data leakages and linkages that leads to undesired PII disclosure and represents a real threat against information privacy in the SN environment [3, 11], those categories can be described as follows:

4.1 Data Leakages to Other Users

While talking about Internet services, a user can be any individual who take advantage of these services. In a SN environment, the user is any individual who join the SN to communicate with other users of the SN. They may be directly connected users by having a link between them in the social graph (in Facebook it means that they are friends). Or they may be indirectly connected users with two or more hops away from each other in the social graph (in Facebook it means that they are friends of friends). All other SN users who are not directly or indirectly connected users represent the general public [11]. The data that a user chooses to post on his/her own page are called "Disclosed Data" [19], those may include their status updates, personal news and opinions, photos, videos, current location, and so on. When a user decides to share something on a SN platform, he/she needs to know how to control the shared information and whom to be allowed to access this information. The role of SPs is to allow their users to fully control sharing of their data as their personal privacy requirements, this control can be achieved by using the privacy settings provided by the SP to limit access to some data, while disclose other data with a selected individuals or in a SN group. In case that a user has failed to choose the appropriate control on his/her privacy settings, those data can be disclosed to users other than the desired [20]. An example is when you share a photo on Facebook in which some of your friends appeared, you can use the tagging feature to tag your friends, and all the friends of your friends can also see that photo unless you limit the privacy settings to only your tagged friends.

While the SPs are responsible for information privacy and should ensure the feasibility of their privacy settings, users' role is to develop themselves to leverage all the required privacy settings. Incautious and careless user behavior is strongly considered as one of the most significant vulnerabilities in modern and large-scale ICT systems [21]. A fast search in the literature, a researcher can find thousands of security and privacy solutions that have been widely proposed in last decade, whereas the development of user training and awareness toward protecting their personal information is still need more efforts. The efforts should be duplicated for using the SN platforms as a result to the continuous updating of the SN services as well as their security and privacy settings.

4.2   Data Leakages to the Service Provider

After discussing information control and access in the previous subsection, the role of collecting and storing the user data lies on the SP. There are some compulsory data that a user needs to upload as a requirement to join a SN, those data are called "Service Data" and often include legal name, age, gender, email, phone numbers. Another type of user data is "Behavioral Data", those are data that can be collected depending on user behavior, what user does, where, when, and with whom, and so on [19]. Previous study investigated the privacy concerns of SN users, it was found that these concerns arise as a result of the inappropriate and extensive collection and storage of users' personal information [20].

After user releases his/her personal data, the responsibility of data protection becomes on the burden of the SPs. The SPs often claim transparency in dealing with user data, SPs present all details related to user personal data in their Privacy Policies and Terms of Service agreement documents [3]. In fact, using SNs in "accept all or leave" concept means that a user does not have a real choice if he/she does not agree with these policies and terms while still needing services of a certain SN. Another issue is that agreement documents can be modified and updated at any time; therefore, the user need to read them repeatedly. The readability of these policies and terms agreement documents is a questionable issue. Recent studies found that users often ignore reading those agreement documents when enrolling in SNs [22]. In other words, SPs need to follow the principle of transparency in dealing with their users, and the principle of accountability in dealing with users' personal information in order to ensure that there is no data leakage to them as a SP or to any other party as what will be discussed in the next two subsections.

4.3   Data Leakages to Third Parties

Users can make use of many available social applications to enjoy more services or play games on the SN platforms. SNs provide special Application Programming Interfaces (API)s with complete documentation to motivate the developers to build their applications and games on the SN platform. For example, Facebook games are so attractive to users because they allow to play with user's friends and too many other Facebook users at the same time. The APIs that are provided for the third-party application developers, give them permissions to access user data. The privacy threat arises when these permissions allow to access all user personal information and more than the actual needed data to let the application works properly [23].

In the literature, there are some attempts to design new permission systems for applications on the SN platforms, one of those is designing schemes that allow least-privilege data access in Facebook, the proposed solution asks for user agreement about unexpected data access, and proved to use only the least amount of needed information without affecting the main functionality of the developed application (p. 51) [24]. As developers represent a third-party entity in the SN environment, it is a critical point for the SPs to ensure that there is no data leakage to the developers by limiting the permissions given to them and by notifying the SN users of what data will be disclosed in case of using these applications.

4.4   Data Leakages and Linkages by Other External Parties

The massive amounts of SNs data that are continuously uploaded and updated by SN users, cause a high motivation for different external parties to gather those data and take advantage of them either for declared legitimate purposes or for hidden and malicious purposes. Valuable contents and relationships can be collected about the SN users and those data can cause the success of many business stakeholders. As SNs popularity highly increased within last two decades, SN represents one of the best environments that allows advertisers to target their customers nowadays (p. 131) [25]. While using most of the SN services for free, the arising question is who can fund the huge human and technical infrastructure of SNs? The answer according to Statista global report confirms that the majority of SNs revenues are generated through advertising, for example Facebook advertising revenue in 2018 came to about 55 billion US dollars, whereas other revenues were only 825 million US dollars [26].

On the other hand, SNs user data have a big role in researches that depend on people demographic factors in many fields such as recruiting participants for health researches (Epidemiology), researches that analyze people views and behavior in social science (Sociology), or researches that explain variance in offline crime and disorder patterns (Criminology) [27–29]. Even employing the user data in the academic researches may not represent a leakage, but it is a secondary use that is not clearly declared to the users and represent a threat against information privacy.

Data leakages can be happened from a single SN or from multiple data sources. Data linkages can be achieved by collecting data from different SNs and often leverages machine learning techniques and correlation approaches which will lead to more accurate profiling of individuals [30, 31]. According to Pew Research Center report, 73% of Americans uses more than one Social Media platform in 2018 [32]. The Facebook–Cambridge Analytica represents the most famous privacy violation scandal; in this event, personal data of 230 million US adults were collected from different sources (Facebook, Internet browsers, e-commerce websites, voting results, and so on) and employed for the benefit of political election campaign of the current US president [33, 34]. In fact, when SNs shares users' data with any external parties, they often use many anonymization techniques by adding pseudo random data instead of the personal identifiable data. The issue here that SP should guarantee preserving user privacy by choosing a strong and effective anonymization technique against any de-anonymization technique that may be used by any stakeholder [35].

At the end of this section, it can be concluded from the above-mentioned leakages and linkages, the size of privacy threats that you may face by using the SN platforms. Reading Privacy Policy and trying to understand what inside, and learning privacy settings of your SN, can help to mitigate some of your data leakages to other users, but cannot play any role to mitigate the discussed leakages to the SP or any third or external parties. Therefore, the duty of protecting information privacy needs a collaborative work among all the SN entities and stakeholders.

5 Social Engineering Threats in Social Networks

While different types of attacks represent real threats to the SN environment security, employing social engineering by the attackers has the most significant role for threatening the information security. Social engineering attacks target individuals by influence and persuasion to disclose personal information or even implement malicious activities [4]. The complexity of social engineering attacks is higher than other security threats because of the ability to use a combination of social and technical strategies together to achieve a malicious task. SNs represent a high value mine of user information that can be leveraged by social engineering attackers as a source of victims' information and as a channel to implement the attacks (p. 161) [36]. Based on previous studies, it is concluded that information security is not just a problem of technology, but it is a strongly related problem of human behavior that depends on their security awareness [37, 38]. The strategy is often implemented by trying to create a close relationship with the victims in order to collect more information about them, their friends and relatives, the groups they are part of, the organizations they are work for, and so on. The threats of social engineering are not limited to cybercrimes, but the risk rises more significantly when talking about disclosing the current location of the victim and trying to implement a physical crime [11], as shown in Fig. 4. While traditional social engineering threats include phishing, vishing, baiting, shoulder surfing, dumpster diving, and watering hole [4]; the most common social engineering threats in SN environment can be described as follows:

5.1 Fake Accounts

A fake account is a SN profile with a hidden identity. As easiness of joining a SN platform, attracts attackers to enroll in these SNs, without the need to disclose their real identities and with free cost as compared to other online services. On the other hand, SNs often recommend those new enrolled fake profiles to other legitimate users to add them as friends; unfortunately, many of users do not care to add those recommended fake profiles in order to appear as popular persons with too many friends, despite that such behavior allows disclosing of their personal data to unknown friends [38, 39]. The attackers in this environment like any other online community, may be humans or social bots depending on the attack strategy. Malicious activities which are implemented by using a large number of fake accounts on the SN are also known as Sybil attack, these accounts can quickly distribute spams, malwares, spreading rumors, or corrupting online voting [40].

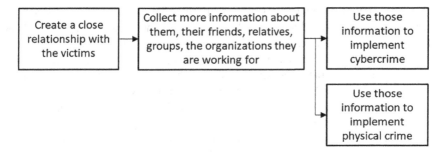

Fig. 4. Social engineering strategy

When Facebook published its first "Enforcement Number Report" in 2018, the number of fake accounts that had been disabled was 583 million in only three months, which represented more than quarter of Facebook active users at that time [41]. This expresses how the fake profiles represent a real challenge against the security of SNs.

There are many current solutions that SPs produce to prevent this type of attacks, these include the adoption of more trusted authentication mechanisms such as demanding the social or passport number from any new user. Another solution is to link every new user identity to a phone number and demanding a verification code that has been sent to that phone number in order to verify his/her real identity [42]. Regarding to the non-human attacker (social bot), a response test such as crypto puzzles can verify if the new user is a real human [43]. In addition, many SNs allow users to report suspicious profiles that violates their policies and terms agreement, while accepting user feedback to improve SN services against any security and privacy breach. As SPs present their solutions regarding to fake accounts, the main role to recognize such profiles still lies on users' burden. In Facebook for example, if those fake accounts still without any friend in their list and have been reported by other users and blocked by groups admins, Facebook can easily disable those accounts; otherwise, it is more difficult to limit these threats.

5.2 Identity Theft

After discussing fake accounts in the previous subsection, it is important to recognize a riskier fraud technique, it is known as identity theft. This is implemented using the identity of a real person, this can be happened either by cloning or compromising the account of the victim. Cloning an already available account is implemented by creating a new profile with same name and photo of the victim on the same SN, the attacker leverages the publicly shared information of a user and try to persuade the same persons in the friend list of the victim, claiming that current profile is a new profile for the same person (the victim). A cross-site cloning is also can be implemented by using the publicly shared information of a user on another SN, and creating a new profile on a specific SN that the victim has not yet registered in [43]. Building relationships with people who know the victim, allows the disclosure of more personal data about the victim and his/her friends as well.

A Compromised account is a legitimate profile that was created by his/her real owner before being hijacked by an attacker. In this case, no need to clone an available profile or add friends, all personal data of the victim and his/her friends will become visible to the attacker in the moment that he can compromise the real profile. In other words, the attacker leverages the network of trust that the victim has built in the past. Profiles can be hijacked by stealing user login information via phishing or exploiting website vulnerabilities [44]. In other words, compromising an account means that your friend on the SN platform may not be the real persons who you know, but an attacker who uses their accounts. An arising question is why the discussion of identity theft coming within social engineering threats while many other researches classifies it within technical threats [3, 12, 15]; in fact, attackers need social engineering knowledge to choose their victims in order to cloning or compromising their profiles. Furthermore, attackers need to well impersonate the original persons in order to persuade their friends and enlarging the network of victims.

Because recognizing an identity thieve is not easy for the SN user. Many solutions can be found in the side of a SP. Cloned account attacks can be detected based on their malicious behavior from the very beginning of their creation. While the detection of compromised account attacks is more difficult because of the past trust that has built between the real profile owner and the SP. As a solution for compromised accounts detection, a number of social behavioral features are defined to detect behavioral deviation between the real profile owner and the attacker such as top activity, top webpage, top transmission between two pages, and average action latency [45].

5.3 Spear Phishing

While traditional phishing targets as more people as possible, spear phishing targets specific group of individuals such as employees of an organization. In a SN environment, spear-phishing targets a specific group of SN users, whom have been selected depending on their personal specifications [8]. An example is using SNs as a data source of an organization staff then targeting them by messages on the SN platform or separate emails, asking them to open a URL which leads them to a fake website of that organization, in this website the victims may provide more sensitive data such as their login credentials. In this case, the information security of the person will be breached; as well as the information security of that organization.

Either the attacker uses the SN platform to send messages or just uses the SN as a source of the victim personal information, using any technical solution such as firewalls and advanced authentication mechanism is not a feasible solution in case of a person falls for a phish [46]. A case study by security professionals at their organization founds that it is necessary to categorize the organization employees into distinct groups to understand their needs and specifications in order to predict their behavior. This mechanism helps the organization to develop more focused awareness and training programs to prevent spear phishing [47].

At the end of this section, you can conclude from the above-mentioned social engineering attacks, the risk that you and your organization may face by using the SN platforms in an incautious or careless behavior. While network devices need to be protected using technical solutions, user awareness needs to be improved for social engineering threats because the success of these attacks mainly depends on defrauding the persons.

6 Discussion and Conclusion

As SNs becomes an important part of people daily life, this review paper has tried to cover the arising threats against information privacy and security in this attractive and rich environment of user personal data. The role of SPs is to allow their users to fully control sharing of their data as their personal privacy requirements by using the provided privacy settings, as a result to the continuous updating of the SN services as well as their security and privacy settings, much more effective training programs are needed for the development of user awareness toward protecting their personal information and to leverage all the required privacy settings. By following the principles of responsibility, transparency, and accountability, SPs need to present clear and easy to understand Privacy Policies agreement documents and obtain their users trust and satisfaction. As reading Privacy Policy and learning privacy settings of the SN platforms can help to mitigate some of data leakages to other users, this cannot play any role to mitigate data leakages to the SP, third or external parties; therefore, the duty of protecting information privacy needs a collaborative work among all the SN entities. It is a critical point for the SPs to ensure that there is no data leakage to third parties (applications developers) by limiting the given permissions and by notifying their users of what data will be disclosed in case of using those applications. SPs should guarantee preserving user privacy by choosing a strong and effective anonymization technique against any de-anonymization technique that may be used by the external parties.

The complexity of social engineering attacks is higher than other security threats because of the ability to use a combination of social and technical strategies together to achieve a malicious task. To prevent fake account creation, it is important for every SP to adopt more trusted authentication mechanisms such as demanding passport number and linking every new user identity to a phone number in order to verify the real identity. Regarding to social bots, a response test such as crypto puzzles can verify if the new user is a real human. SN users need to report suspicious profiles that violates policies and send feedback to improve SN services against any security and privacy breach. Because recognizing an identity thieve is not easy for the SN user. Many solutions can be found in the side of a SP. Cloned account attacks can be detected based on their malicious behavior from the very beginning of their creation. While compromised account attacks can be detected based on behavioral deviation between the real profile owner and the attacker. Using technical solutions such as firewalls and advanced authentication mechanism is not a feasible solution in case of spear phishing because the success of these attacks mainly depends on defrauding the persons. While network devices need to be protected using technical solutions, much more effective training programs are needed for the development of user awareness to prevent social engineering threats. Finally, authors of this review paper hope to use this research as a guideline to current information privacy and security threats in SNs, and to pave the way for the researchers to investigate more solutions for these threats in future works.

References

1. Hootsuite: We Are Social - Digital report. https://wearesocial.com/es/digital-2019-espana
2. Kizza, J.M.: Ethical and Secure Computing, pp. 229–257 (2019). https://doi.org/10.1007/978-3-030-03937-0
3. Kayes, I., Iamnitchi, A.: Privacy and security in online social networks: a survey. Online Soc. Netw. Med. **3–4**, 1–21 (2017). https://doi.org/10.1016/j.osnem.2017.09.001
4. Krombholz, K., Hobel, H., Huber, M., Weippl, E.: Advanced social engineering attacks. J. Inf. Secur. Appl. **22**, 113–122 (2015). https://doi.org/10.1016/j.jisa.2014.09.005
5. Heidemann, J., Klier, M., Probst, F.: Online social networks: a survey of a global phenomenon. Comput. Netw. **56**, 3866–3878 (2012). https://doi.org/10.1016/j.comnet.2012.08.009
6. Heravi, A.: Privacy attitudes and behaviours in online social networking (2017). https://trove.nla.gov.au/version/253863687
7. Boyd, D.M., Ellison, N.B.: Social network sites: definition, history, and scholarship. J. Comput.-Mediated Commun. **13**, 210–230 (2008). https://doi.org/10.1111/j.1083-6101.2007.00393.x
8. Salehan, M., Negahban, A.: Computers in human behavior social networking on smartphones: when mobile phones become addictive. Comput. Hum. Behav. **29**, 2632–2639 (2013)
9. Adewole, K.S., Anuar, N.B., Kamsin, A., Varathan, K.D., Razak, S.A.: Malicious accounts: dark of the social networks. J. Netw. Comput. Appl. **79**, 41–67 (2017). https://doi.org/10.1016/j.jnca.2016.11.030
10. Kumari, P.: Requirements analysis for privacy in social networks. In: 8th International Workshop for Technical, Economic and Legal Aspects of Business Models for Virtual Goods (2010)
11. Novak, E., Li, Q.: A survey of security and privacy in online social networks. College of William and Mary Computer Science Technical report, vol. X, pp. 1–32 (2012)
12. Fire, M., Goldschmidt, R., Elovici, Y.: Online social networks: threats and solutions. IEEE Commun. Surv. Tutorials **16**, 2019–2036 (2014). https://doi.org/10.1109/COMST.2014.2321628
13. Deliri, S., Albanese, M.: Data Management in Pervasive Systems, pp. 195–209. Springer, Heidelberg (2015). https://doi.org/10.1007/978-3-319-20062-0
14. Pham, V.V.H., Yu, S., Sood, K., Cui, L.: Privacy issues in social networks and analysis: a comprehensive survey. IET Netw. **7**, 74–84 (2017). https://doi.org/10.1049/iet-net.2017.0137
15. Rathore, S., Sharma, P.K., Loia, V., Jeong, Y.S., Park, J.H.: Social network security: issues, challenges, threats, and solutions. Inf. Sci. **421**, 43–69 (2017). https://doi.org/10.1016/j.ins.2017.08.063
16. Ali, S., Islam, N., Rauf, A., Din, I.U., Guizani, M., Rodrigues, J.J.P.C.: Privacy and security issues in online social networks. Future Internet **10**, 114 (2018). https://doi.org/10.3390/fi10120114
17. Sahoo, S.R., Gupta, B.B.: Classification of various attacks and their defence mechanism in online social networks: a survey. Enterp. Inf. Syst. **00**, 1–33 (2019). https://doi.org/10.1080/17517575.2019.1605542
18. Krishnamurthy, B., Wills, C.E.: On the leakage of personally identifiable information via online social networks. In: ACM SIGCOMM Computer Communication Review, p. 112. ACM (2012)

19. Schneier, B.: A taxonomy of social networking data. IEEE Secur. Priv. **8**, 88 (2010). https://doi.org/10.1109/MSP.2010.118
20. Islam, M.B., Watson, J., Iannella, R., Geva, S.: A greater understanding of social networks privacy requirements: the user perspective. J. Inf. Secur. Appl. **33**, 30–44 (2017). https://doi.org/10.1016/j.jisa.2017.01.004
21. Öğütçü, G., Testik, Ö.M., Chouseinoglou, O.: Analysis of personal information security behavior and awareness (2016). https://doi.org/10.1016/j.cose.2015.10.002
22. Obar, J.A., Oeldorf-Hirsch, A.: The biggest lie on the Internet: ignoring the privacy policies and terms of service policies of social networking services. Inf. Commun. Soc. 1–20 (2018). https://doi.org/10.1080/1369118x.2018.1486870
23. Kavianpour, S., Ismail, Z., Shanmugam, B.: Classification of third-party applications on Facebook to mitigate users' information leakage. Adv. Intell. Syst. Comput. **569**, 144–154 (2017). https://doi.org/10.1007/978-3-319-56535-4_15
24. Tian, Y.: Privacy Preserving Information Sharing in Modern and Emerging Platforms (2018). https://doi.org/10.1184/R1/6721127.v1
25. Lipschultz, J.H.: Social Media Communication: Concepts, Practices, Data, Law and Ethics. Routledge, Abingdon (2017)
26. Statista: Facebook: annual revenue 2018| Statistic. https://www.statista.com/statistics/268604/annual-revenue-of-facebook/
27. Whitaker, C., Stevelink, S., Fear, N.: The use of Facebook in recruiting participants for health research purposes: a systematic review. J. Med. Internet Res. **19** (2017). https://doi.org/10.2196/jmir.7071
28. Williams, M.L., Burnap, P., Sloan, L.: Crime sensing with big data: the affordances and limitations of using open-source communications to estimate crime patterns. Br. J. Criminol. **57**, 320–340 (2017). https://doi.org/10.1093/bjc/azw031
29. Williams, M.L., Burnap, P., Sloan, L.: Towards an ethical framework for publishing Twitter data in social research: taking into account users' views. Online Context Algorithmic Estimation Sociol. **51**, 1149–1168 (2017). https://doi.org/10.1177/0038038517708140
30. Goga, O., Perito, D., Lei, H., Teixeira, R., Sommer, R., Tr-13-002, Ly: Large-scale Correlation of Accounts Across Social Networks. (2013)
31. Shu, K., Wang, S., Tang, J., Zafarani, R., Liu, H.: User identity linkage across online social networks. ACM SIGKDD Explor. Newsl. **18**, 5–17 (2017). https://doi.org/10.1145/3068777.3068781
32. Pew Research Center: Social Media Use 2018: Demographics and Statistics. https://www.pewinternet.org/2018/03/01/social-media-use-in-2018/
33. Beilinson, J.: Facebook Data May Have Been Illicitly Used for Politics, and It Started With a Quiz - Consumer Reports. https://www.consumerreports.org/privacy/facebook-data-illicitly-collected-for-politics-and-what-it-means-for-privacy/
34. Isaak, J., Hanna, M.J.: User data privacy: Facebook, Cambridge analytica, and privacy protection. Computer **51**, 56–59 (2018). https://doi.org/10.1109/MC.2018.3191268
35. Abawajy, J.H., Ninggal, M.I.H., Herawan, T.: Privacy preserving social network data publication. IEEE Commun. Surv. Tutorials **18**, 1974–1997 (2016). https://doi.org/10.1109/COMST.2016.2533668
36. Cross, M.: Social Media Security. Syngress (2014)
37. Albladi, S.M., Weir, G.R.S.: User characteristics that influence judgment of social engineering attacks in social networks. Hum.-Centric Comput. Inf. Sci. **8**, 5 (2018). https://doi.org/10.1186/s13673-018-0128-7
38. Al-Qurishi, M., Al-Rakhami, M., Alamri, A., AlRubaian, M., Rahman, S.M.M., Hossain, M.S.: Sybil defense techniques in online social networks: a survey. IEEE Access **5**, 1200–1219 (2017). https://doi.org/10.1109/ACCESS.2017.2656635

39. Apte, M., Palshikar, G.K., Baskaran, S.: Frauds in Online Social Networks: A Review, pp. 1–18 (2018). https://doi.org/10.1007/978-3-319-78256-0_1

40. Ferrara, E., Varol, O., Davis, C., Menczer, F., Flammini, A.: The rise of social bots. Commun. ACM. **59**, 96–104 (2014). https://doi.org/10.1145/2818717

41. Rosen, G.: Facebook Publishes Enforcement Numbers for the First Time. https://newsroom.fb.com/news/2018/05/enforcement-numbers/

42. Li, F., Mittal, P., Caesar, M., Borisov, N.: SybilControl, vol. 67 (2012). https://doi.org/10.1145/2382536.2382548

43. Bilge, L., Strufe, T., Balzarotti, D., Kirda, E.: All your contacts are belong to us, vol. 551 (2009). https://doi.org/10.1145/1526709.1526784

44. Egele, M., Stringhini, G., Kruegel, C., Vigna, G.: Towards detecting compromised accounts on social networks. IEEE Trans. Dependable Secur. Comput. **14**, 447–460 (2017). https://doi.org/10.1109/TDSC.2015.2479616

45. Ruan, X., Wu, Z., Wang, H., Jajodia, S.: Profiling online social behaviors for compromised account detection. IEEE Trans. Inf. Forensics Secur. **11**, 176–187 (2016). https://doi.org/10.1109/TIFS.2015.2482465

46. Hong, J.: The state of phishing attacks. Commun. ACM **55**, 74 (2012). https://doi.org/10.1145/2063176.2063197

47. Thomas, J.E.: Individual cyber security: empowering employees to resist spear phishing to prevent identity theft and ransomware attacks. Int. J. Bus. Manag. **13**, 1 (2018). https://doi.org/10.5539/ijbm.v13n6p1

Author Index

Printed in the United States
By Bookmasters